A GUIDE TO MANUSCRIPTS
AND DOCUMENTS
IN THE BRITISH ISLES
RELATING TO
THE FAR EAST

A GUIDE TO MANUSCRIPTS
AND DOCUMENTS
IN THE BRITISH ISLES
RELATING TO
THE FAR EAST

COMPILED BY

NOEL MATTHEWS

AND

M. DOREEN WAINWRIGHT

EDITED BY

J. D. PEARSON

Professor of Bibliography
with reference to Asia and Africa
School of Oriental and African Studies
University of London

OXFORD UNIVERSITY PRESS

1977

Oxford University Press, Walton Street, Oxford OX2 6DP

OXFORD LONDON GLASGOW NEW YORK
TORONTO MELBOURNE WELLINGTON CAPE TOWN
IBADAN NAIROBI DAR ES SALAAM LUSAKA ADDIS ABABA
KUALA LUMPUR SINGAPORE JAKARTA HONG KONG TOKYO
DELHI BOMBAY CALCUTTA MADRAS KARACHI

ISBN 0 19 713591 9

British Library Cataloguing in Publication Data

Matthews, Noel
    A Guide to manuscripts and documents in the British Isles relating to the Far East.
    Index.
    ISBN 0 19 713591 9
    1. Title 2. Wainwright, Mary Doreen 3. Pearson, James Douglas 4. University of London. School of Oriental and African Studies.
    016.95   z3001
    Archival resources on East (Far East) – Great Britain
    Library resources on East (Far East) – Great Britain

*Printed in Great Britain
at the University Press, Oxford
by Vivian Ridler
Printer to the University*

PREFACE

THIS volume continues the series of guides to manuscripts in European languages in the British Isles prepared by the School of Oriental and African Studies. The first, containing material on South and South-East Asia,[1] was published in 1965, the second, on Africa,[2] in 1971. It is the intention to complete the series with a volume for the Near and Middle East which is under preparation.

The Far East, or East Asia, which furnishes the scope for the present work, is taken as consisting of the vast land mass of China and the adjacent territories of Japan, Korea, and the uttermost eastern parts of the Soviet Union. Tibet was included in the South and South-East Asia volume.

The bulk of the material was collected by Dr. Wainwright and Dr. Matthews in the three years ending in 1965 in the course of a programme of visits to all likely repositories in England, Scotland, Wales, Northern Ireland, and Eire. After writing up notes on the appropriate collections or items found, these were submitted for comments to those in charge of the library or archives depository. Many of these custodians were good enough to correct the entries for their institutions and to suggest for inclusion additional material, overlooked at the time of the first search.

In addition to the information collected by Wainwright and Matthews and the calendars, catalogues, and lists compiled and published by the several libraries, archives, and museums, a number of works of a general character has been drawn on:

Leslie R. Marchant, *A Guide to Archives and Records of Protestant Christian Missions from the British Isles to China, 1796–1914* (University of Western Australia Press, 1966).

Rosemary Keen, *A Survey of Archives of Selected Missionary Societies* (Church Missionary Society, London, 1968).

A few items relating to ships have been taken from:

Shipping; A Survey of Historical Records edited by P. Mathias and A. W. H. Pearsall (Newton Abbot, 1971).

The undersigned has attempted to bring up to date the material collected by Doctors Wainwright and Matthews. Although not possessed of the resources and time to repeat their visits or to circularize all likely repositories, he has been able to add much new material brought to notice through the examination of many catalogues and surveys published since 1965. It has also proved profitable to work through the geographical indexes to the reports on collections made by the National Register of Archives, its annual *List of accessions to repositories* (continued since 1972 as *Accessions to repositories and reports added to the National Register of Archives*), and those reports, as yet unindexed, which seemed likely to embody relevant material.

---

[1] *A Guide to Western Manuscripts and Documents in the British Isles relating to South and South East Asia*, London, O.U.P., 1965.

[2] *A Guide to Manuscripts and Documents in the British Isles relating to Africa*, London, O.U.P., 1971.

It must again be emphasized that the mention of any document, or class of documents, does not necessarily imply that it is available for study. Material less than thirty years old may not normally be consulted in the public repositories—in others the closed period may still be fifty years.

As before, it is a pleasure to acknowledge the unstinting assistance provided by the numerous librarians, archivists, and curators of museums to the compilers. While these are far too many for their names to be listed individually, special thanks must go to the staff of the National Register of Archives who have always shown themselves willing, and indeed eager, to give every possible help. Much useful advice was also obtained from the deliberations of a special seminar under the chairmanship of Professor W. G. Beasley held in the History Department of the School of Oriental and African Studies.

The volume has been published with the assistance of a financial grant from the Publications Committee of the School. It may be regarded as part of the United Kingdom's contribution to the Sources for the history of the nations: Asia and North Africa, projected by the International Council on Archives.

J. D. PEARSON

March 1975

CONTENTS

ENGLAND

LONDON (*continued*)

REST OF ENGLAND

REPUBLIC OF IRELAND

PAPERS IN PRIVATE CUSTODY

ENGLAND

LONDON

ARMY MUSEUMS OGILBY TRUST

85 Whitehall, London, S.W.1

SPENSER WILKINSON PAPERS

Letter written by General Sir Ian Hamilton in Tokyo about the Russo-Japanese War. 30 March 1904. (In 23.)

BANK OF ENGLAND

Archive Section, Bank of England, Threadneedle Street, London, EC2R 8AH

The principal records of the Bank of England are described by Sir John Clapham in *The Bank of England*, 2 vols. (Cambridge, 1944). Records relating to the areas covered by this *Guide* are mainly those of stocks for which the Bank has acted as Registrar within the last hundred years. While permission to inspect early records may be granted to bona fide scholars known to the Bank or sponsored by a person or organization of standing, access to records of less than one hundred years old is not allowed, though consideration is given to specific inquiries falling within the period. Application should be made in writing to the Secretary of the Bank.

THE BAPTIST MISSIONARY SOCIETY

93-7 Gloucester Place, London, W1H 4AA

The Baptist Missionary Society, which was founded in 1792, set up its first mission station in China in 1860 and was active in North China and Shanghai until about 1951. Work was started in Hong Kong in 1953. Some of the society's records were destroyed when its premises were bombed in 1940, but a good collection has survived and these have been newly sorted and inventoried. The records of the last fifty years are not open to students. (Marchant, pp. 27-9; Keen, BMS/1-13; Mary M. Evans, *Baptist Missionary Society. Papers relating to China 1860-1914*; catalogued 1965.) (NRA 10412.)

I. MINUTE BOOKS

General Committee. 1815-1914. 49 vols., continuing.
Bible Translation Society. 1839-1914. 4 vols., continuing.
Candidate Board Committee. 1860-1914. 3 vols.
China, Ceylon, and France Subcommittee. 1861-7. 1 vol.
Finance Subcommittee. 1865-1914. 29 vols., continuing.
Zenana Mission Committee (later became Women's Subcommittee). 1867-1914. 14 vols., continuing.
China Subcommittee. 1884-1914. 7 vols., continuing.
Medical Mission Auxiliary. 1902-40. 12 vols., continuing.
Medical Mission Professional Subcommittee. 1907-37. 2 vols., continuing.

II. MISSIONARIES' CORRESPONDENCE AND PAPERS, consisting mainly of letters and papers from, but also to and concerning, individual missionaries. A detailed calendar is available. (The reference number following each entry indicates the box in which the papers are stored.)

Dixon, Herbert: 5 letters from Tai Yuan Fu. 1887-8. (CH/1.)

Edwards, George: 1 letter from Peking. 1916. (CH/1.)

Farthing, George B.: 85 letters and papers from Tai Yuan Fu, Tientsin, Chou-P'ing, Shanghai, &c. 1887-1901. (CH/8.)

James, Francis H.: 6 letters from Peking and England. 1884-8. (CH/1.)

Jenkins, Herbert S.: 8 letters from England and Wales. 1903-4. (CH/1.)

Jones, Alfred G.: 332 letters and telegrams from Chefoo, Ch'ing-Chou-Fu, Tsing Chen Fu, Tientsin, &c. 1868-1905. (CH/5-8.)

Kingdon, E. F.: letter from Shanghai. 1867. (CH/1.)
Laughton, R. F.: letter from Chefoo. 1868. (CH/1.)

Richard, Timothy: 247 letters and papers from Tai Yuan Fu, Tsing Chou Fu, Shansi, Peking, &c. 1877-1905. (CH/2-4.)

Hong Kong: correspondence and papers. 1949-50. 1952.

III. HOME SECTION CORRESPONDENCE

1. Home Secretaries' correspondence and papers about mission finances, legal and property matters, &c. The correspondence is largely with British and foreign, including Chinese, Government officials, and deals with such questions as indemnification for loss in the Boxer rising. See, especially:

A. H. Baynes: correspondence. 1880–1904. (H/21–22.)

Secretariat correspondence. 1928–49.

Medical letters. 1924–49.

2. Bound volumes of letters, dating from 1736, collected by various Home Secretaries. These volumes often contain personal letters to and from missionaries, and letters to other Baptist ministers in the United Kingdom.

IV. CANDIDATES' APPLICATION PAPERS

Application forms and references for nearly all the missionary candidates who were accepted after 1881.

V. REPORTS. Printed for private circulation to Committee members:

China Christian Universities Association. 1940–57.

United Board Christian colleges. 1940–54.

Shantung University: Shantung Christian Board of Governors. 1928–30.

Cheloo University. 1940–8.

Inter-Provincial Council and Committees. 1943–6, 1948–9.

Annual reports (hospitals, &c.). 1938–47.

China hospitals. 1938–47.

VI. MISCELLANEOUS

Clara R. Southwell: diary of a tour in Canada and Japan. 1910.
Manuscripts in Chinese and miscellaneous papers.

BEAVERBROOK LIBRARY

33 St. Bride Street, London, EC4A 4AY

Two letters from Gonnoske Komai to Ralph Blumenfeld, in one of which he explains a reference in one of his verses to kissing. 1928. (KO 1–2.)

BIBLE CHURCHMEN'S MISSIONARY SOCIETY

157 Waterloo Road, London, S.E. 1

The Society operated in South China 1924–51 and in West China 1923–51. (Keen, BCMS/1.)

Minutes 1923– .

BRITISH AND FOREIGN BIBLE SOCIETY

146 Queen Victoria Street, London, EC4V 4BX

The activities of the Society (founded in 1804) cover all parts of the world, including the Far East. Its records are complete and there are no restrictions on access, but until the papers have been sorted and arranged, they cannot be opened to independent research workers. Inquiries should be made to the Librarian who will, where possible, make arrangements for the production of the records required. Advance notice is essential and some form of sponsorship is required. (Marshall, pp. 32–3; Keen, B&FBS/1–6.)

Oriental Committee: minutes, including copies of correspondence. 1804–9. 1 vol.

Special subcommittees (largely China): minutes. 1882–1905. 7 vols.

China subcommittee (including Japan, Korea): minutes. 1905–38. 4 vols., numbered 8–11.

Reports of China agency (printed). c. 1889–1941.

BRITISH LIBRARY OF POLITICAL AND ECONOMIC SCIENCE

London School of Economics, Houghton Street, Aldwych, London, WC2A 2AE

WELBY COLLECTION on banking and currency. Papers of Reginald Earle Welby, 1st Baron Welby (1832–1915).

Vol. I

8. Reports on Japanese currency, 1862–3, by G. Arbuthnot (of the Treasury). [1868.] 66 pp.

Vol. III

8–11. Reports on Japanese currency by G. Arbuthnot (of the Treasury). [4 parts. 1862–3.] ff. 101–32.

12. Copy of correspondence between the Duke of Newcastle, Secretary of State for the Colonies, and Sir H. Robinson, Governor of Hong Kong, on the currency of the Colony. 1863. With manuscript notes by Welby. ff. 134–46.

13. [Treasury?] correspondence respecting the Hong Kong currency. 1874. ff. 147–61.

Vol. V

44. Letter of S. E. Spring Rice to Welby about Hong Kong currency and the export of Mexican dollars. 26 July 1893. ff. 233–5.

90. Correspondence addressed to the Bengal Chamber of Commerce, on the future of China trade. 11 October–16 November 1892. ff. 587–8.

100. Report of G. Jamieson to the Earl of Rosebery on the balance of trade between China and foreign countries, &c. 1893. ff. 626–38.

108. Memorandum by George W. Johnson for the consideration of the Colonial Currency Committee: proposed legalization of the Japanese yen at Hong Kong. 7 December 1893. Typescript. ff. 743–5.

Vol. VI

26. The money of the Far East. Typescript with manuscript corrections. ff. 175–88.

Vol. IX

17. Minute by George Arbuthnot on Hong Kong currency, with notes by Welby. ff. 84–5.

74–6. Correspondence between Welby and R. M[eade] about the striking of a British dollar for Singapore and Hong Kong. 7–11 July 1894. ff. 205–11.

Two letters to Sir R. Giffen about the Russo-Japanese War, the first from Spencer Wilkinson, 23 March 1904, the second from John Sterling, 18 March 1905. (Giffen correspondence, vol. ii, f. 124, ff. 134–5.)

Census, Weihaiwei, 1921. General report and tables. 1921. Typescript. (Misc. 170.)

'Entwicklung vom Volkseinkommen in Japan, 1903–1919', and 'Über Indexziffern in Japan', by Saburo Shiomi. 1923. Typescript. (Misc. 165.)

'Chinese mass education movement' by Yang-chu James Yen, with a summary statement and a covering letter to Professor Tawney. 1934. Typescript. 127 ff. (Misc. 561.)

BRITISH LIBRARY, REFERENCE DIVISION

Great Russell Street, London, WC1B 3DG

The following list of manuscripts in the British Museum has been compiled from the various catalogues, which are described in detail in *The Catalogues of the Manuscript Collections in the British Museum*, by T. C. Skeat (2nd edn., 1962). The printed catalogues cover accessions received up to 1945, and the Gladstone Papers which are described in a separate catalogue published in 1953. It was impossible to examine all later accessions for relevant material, and we have had to rely on the short descriptions and lists available in the Manuscript Room. Two of these have been published in facsimile by the *List and Index Society*. It is probable, therefore, that some items have been missed, but it is unlikely that any major collections have been omitted. Some large collections, not yet indexed, but certain to contain relevant material, have been noted briefly.

An Italian version of the travels to Cathay, &c.,

c. 1318–1330 of the Franciscan Odoric of Pordenone, or Friuli, transcribed by the Cavaliere Alessandro di Mortara from an ancient copy in his possession: entitled 'Memoriale del Viaggio di frate Oderigo di Friuli'. Early 19th century. 27 ff. (Add. 33756. Grenville Library, li.)

'Le liure de missire marc paul, natif de venise, des condicions et costumes des principales Regions de Orient': the travels of Marco Polo, divided into three books, with table of chapters and prologue. The text is apparently a translation from the Latin version of Frà Francesco Pipino of Bologna. Mid 15th century. (Eg. 2176. See Arundel MS. 13.)

A transcript from the rare edition in German of the Travels of Marco Polo printed at Nuremberg in 1477, taken from a copy in the Imperial Library at Vienna and certified as exact, 29 August 1817, entitled 'Hie hebt sich an das fuch des edeln Ritters vñ landtfarers Marcho Polo'. 59 ff. (Add. 33755. Grenville Library, lii.)

Explanation of Chinese words. 15th–16th centuries. (Sloane 1524, ff. 1b–7.)

131 coloured maps of Europe, Asia, and Africa, with brief remarks in Latin; in an Italian hand of about 1500. (Add. 23925.)

Portolano containing thirteen coast maps, including, the world (f. 1b), and South-East Asia including a rough indication of the China coast northwards, c. 1508. The volume appears to be a copy of one of the early portolani of Visconti Maggiola of Genoa. 12 ff. (Eg. 2803.)

Sir Hugh Willoughby's voyage for the discovery of Cathay in 1553. (Cotton Otho E. VIII, 6, f. 10.)

Portolano made about 1562 with the names in Spanish, including a map of the East Indies from the Persian Gulf to Cauo de Cauayro [? in Korea] and Timor (ff. 10b, 11). (Eg. 2860.)

'Relaciones de Viajes (1563–9)', including 'descrubimiento y principio del Estrecho de Magallanes, quien lo descubrió, y en que año fué, y por que causa: . . . y otras relaciones de los descrubimientos de las yslas de Pomiente, Nueva Guinea, China é Filipinas'; 'Roteiro para sacar por figura y navegar desde la Costa de la Nueva-España de la mar del Sur hasta las islas de Pomiente, y de alli para la China, &c. (Add. 9944.)

Portolano entitled 'Universalis et integra totius orbis Hidrografia ad verissimam Luzitanorum traditionem descripcio Ferdinãdo $\frac{W}{M}$ Este livro fes Fernão Vãz Dourado'; containing seventeen maps. [1573.] 42 ff. *Portuguese*. (Add. 31317. See W. de G. Birch, *Commentaries of A. Dalboquerque*, Hakl. Soc. vol. ii, 1878, p. cxviii.)

Account by Michael Locke of Sir Martin Frobisher's

voyage for discovery of a passage to Cathay. 1574. (Cotton Otho E. VIII, 8, f. 41.)

Instructions for an expedition to Cathay by the North Seas, in the vessels the *Aide*, the *Gabriele* and the *Michael*: signed Martin Furbisher. 1578. (Cotton Otho E. VIII, 33, f. 107.)

Collection of geographical charts by Juan Martinez de Messina, including China and Japan. 1578. (Harl. 3450.)

Instructions and chart supplied to merchants for a voyage to China. 1580. (Lansdowne 122/5.)

'Carta que escrivio el rey Francisco de Bungo en Japon para su Sanctidad' Gregory XIII: the alleged offer of one of the princes of the Japanese island of Ximo to embrace Christianity, 11 January 1582; followed by a note of the presents sent to him by the Pope. (Add. 20915, f. 64. No. 10 in a collection of miscellaneous papers in Spanish and Latin.)

Account by Richard Madox, of an expedition to discover a southerly route to China; the account is continued only to the arrival on the coast of Guinea. 1582. (Sloane 2496, ff. 70–83.)

Journal of Captain Edward Fenton's voyage in 1582 to the Moluccas and China by way of the Cape of Good Hope. (Cotton Titus B. VIII, 22, f. 171.)

Annual letters to the Jesuit Order from Padre Luis Fröes, Jesuit missionary in Japan. 1591, 1592. (Sloane 3456.)

Annual reports relating to the state of the Jesuit missionaries in Japan. 1593–1686. *Spanish* and *Portuguese*. (Add. 9859.)

Report on the state of the Jesuit missions in Japan: the crucifixion of Japanese Christians and of missionaries: disputes between Jesuits and Franciscans and a defence of the acts of the missionaries in China and Japan. 1597. *Portuguese*. (Add. 9858.)

Papers relating to the Portuguese colonies in Asia and Africa.

1. Letters and papers relating to the East Indies and other Portuguese colonies, 1599–1640, including information from Dom Francisco da Gama, Count of Vidigueyra, as Viceroy of India, respecting the exclusion of all clergy, except Jesuits, from Japan (f. 19. *Spanish*). (Add. 28432.)

2. Ordinances, &c., for the Portuguese colonies in Asia and Africa, consisting of copies of orders, grants, appointments, &c., in Portuguese, and including orders of Dom Duarte de Menezes and Dom Francisco Mascarenhas, Governors of the Portuguese Indies, to the captains of the forts and cities in nearly all the settlements (ff. 19, 166, 171). (Add. 28433.)

Instructions to Edward Fenton, sent on a voyage to China; signed W. Burghley, R. Leycester and Fr.

Walsingham (the first part wanting). 16th century. (Cotton Otho E. VIII, 42, f. 127.)

Discussion concerning the possibility of a North-West passage to Cathay. 16th century. (Lansdowne 100/4.)

Account of the establishment of the Christian faith in Japan. 1601. *Spanish*. (Add. 9857.)

Extracts from the journal of Captain John Saris describing his voyage to the Red Sea, Java, the Moluccas and Japan, 1611–12. The beginning is in the hand of Alexander Dalrymple, hydrographer to the East India Company, and later to the Admiralty. 18th century. (Add. 19300.)

Correspondence of factors in the East Indies, merchants, and sea captains, with Sir Thomas Smith and Sir Maurice Abbott, Governors, and the Board of the East India Company and others, with bills of lading and other papers, originals and copies, 1611–44, including letters from Richard Cock at Firando, Japan, 16 July and 11 October 1620 (ff. 60, 63). (Eg. 2086.)

Journals of voyages to the East Indies, including 'A treue Relation of my voyadge intended by God grace for Succadanie, Potane and Jappan, in the good shipp caulled the Hosiander', 11 April–2 September 1615, continued by 'my voyadge now bound for Ossica, Meaco, and Surungona', 11 September 1615–13 March 1616 (ff. 13–80). (Eg. 2121.)

Diary of Richard Cocks, head of the English factory at Firando, or Hirado, in Japan. Vol. I, 1 June 1615–5 July 1617: Vol. II, 6 July 1617–17 January 1619 and 5 December 1620–24 March 1622. 210 ff. and 239 ff. (Add. 31300 and 31301.)

Various sailing directions chiefly for Malaysia and the Chinese Sea. 1617, 1621. *Dutch*. (Eg. 1851, ff. 60, 113b.)

Relation, with drawings, of the voyage, shipwreck, and captivity of Padre Adriano de Las Cortes, at Chanceo, in China. 1621–6. *Spanish*. (Sloane 1005.)

'A true discourse of our Voyage bound for the North West Passage and so by Japan', &c., in the ship *Charles* from London, by Captain Luke Fox. May–October 1631. 18th-century copy. (Add. 19302.)

Arte de lengua Japona. [Rome, 1632.] (Sloane 3459.)

'Annuall Letters written out of Japonia in the yeare of our Lorde 1625, 1626, 1627, to … Mutio Vitelleschi, Generall of the Society of Jesus', with a dedicatory letter from the translator Thomas Somerset, fifth son of Henry Somerset, Earl of Worcester, addressed to his father. The translation is probably made from an Italian edition, *Lettere Annue*, &c., Rome, 1632. The letters are written by John Baptista Bonelli, Macao, 15 March 1626 (f. 2b); Peter Moreion,

Macao, 31 March 1627 (f. 52b); John Roiz Giran, Macao, 31 March 1627 (f. 91); Christopher Ferreria, Japan, 14 September 1627 (f. 123b); and with a postscript entitled 'of the death of Leonard Massudadenzo, who was beheaded for the Catholicke Faith in the cittie of Ximabara' on 13 December 1627, dated 'Japonia', 25 January 1628 (f. 163). c. 1632–42. 165 ff. (Add. 33761. Grenville Library, vii.)

Nineteenth-century copy of 'Journal of a voyage of a fleet of four ships and two pinnaces, set forth by Sir William Courteene, Knt. The design for India, China, Japan, &c., on a new discovery of Traffic in those parts', by Peter Mundy. 1636 and 1637. (Add. 19281.)

Abstract of the travels in India, China, &c. of G. A. Mandelslo, by J. LeFanu. 1638–9. *French.* (Stowe 988/6, ff. 58–98b.)

Observations on the Tartars of China and their language. 1650. *French.* (Sloane 2872.)

'Journael van Batavia naer Japan', a journal of a voyage in the ship *Dolphin* from Batavia to Japan, and then by Malacca to Ceylon, Surat and back to Ceylon. 16 July 1662–16 May 1663. (Eg. 1852, f. 3.)

Letters of French missionaries in the East. 1647–76. (Add. 19303.) Including:

f. 5. Autograph letter of Jacques le Faure in China. 21 November 1660.

f. 31. Extracts from letters of missionaries in Persia, Tonkin and Siam. 1665–9.

f. 65. Copies of letters from Cape Verde, Cape of Good Hope, China, Siam, and Isfahan. 1670–6.

Various papers concerning the Grand Duchy of Tuscany, including (ff. 277–331): 'Ragguaglio d'un discorso havuto con un Padre della Compagnia di Giesù [John Grueber of Vienna] venuto della China, à di 31 Genaro, 1665, in Firenze' relating to the institutions, religion, manners, &c. of China. (Add. 16506.)

Collection of original papers, most of them communicated to Sir Hans Sloane and forming part of the Philosophical Transactions of the Royal Society, 1665–1701, including (ff. 81–9) meteorological observations made at Emüy in China by James Cunningham, F.R.S., physician to the East India factory at Chusan in China. (Sloane 4025.)

Description of a Chinese almanack by Siem de St. Pierre. 1671. (Add. 4394, no. 3.)

Journal kept by William Gifford and Thomas James, factors of the English East India Company, during the establishment of a factory at Tonqueen [Tonkin]. 1672–7. (Sloane 998.)

A collection of charts and views of headlands, drawn about 1680, and including: Macao; Ladrone Islands; chart of Europe, Asia, and Africa. (Add. 15737.)

Journal of a voyage to the kingdom of Tonquin [Tongking] bordering upon China, by Captain Robert Knox. A fragment only. 1681. (Lansdowne 1197, ff. 12–13.)

Papers relating to [the colony of Sacramento and the Southern boundaries of Portuguese America], and to subjects connected with the Jesuits of Portugal, their mission in China, &c. 1681–1726. *Spanish, Portuguese, Latin.* (Add. 21003.)

Account of the voyages of William Dampier through the South Seas. 1681–91. (Sloane 3236, ff. 1–13, 29–233.)

Journal of the voyage of William Ambrose Cowley, mariner, from Cape Virginia to the Cape de Verde Isles, to China, Java, Cape of Good Hope, and Holland. 1683–6. 2 copies. (Sloane 54 and 1050.)

Collection of papers on various Chinese subjects: Chinese Christianity; grammar; geography, &c. by Michaelis Xin Fò Cum. 1687. *Latin.* (Sloane 853.)

List of papers given by Hendrick van Buijtenheim, President of the Dutch factory in Japan, to his successors. 1688. *Dutch.* (Sloane 2910, ff. 292, 295.)

Miscellaneous autographs, 1507–1808, including that of Saint-Martin, missionary in China, dated Louvo, 9 December 1687 (f. 13). (Add. 27548.)

Chart of the coast of China, by Captain John Kempthorne, June 1688. (Sloane 3665, f. 65.)

Journal of a voyage through the Straits of Magellan to the South Seas, by Richard Simson. 1689. 2 copies. (Sloane 86 and 672.)

Diary of a journey from Java to Siam and Japan, by Engelbert Kaempfer. 1690. *German.* (Sloane 2921.)

Drawings and descriptions of Japanese plants, by Engelbert Kaempfer. 1690. (Sloane 2914 and 2915.)

Manuale Botanicum plantarum Japonicarum, by Engelbert Kaempfer. 1691. (Sloane 74.)

Notes on Chinese customs; catalogue of plants in China; and index of Chinese words. 1697–9. (Sloane 2376, ff. 76–111.)

Copies of documents relating to controversies between the Jesuit and other missionaries in China with regard to certain religious observances among the Chinese converts. 1697–c. 1700. (Eg. 2212.)

G. G. FORTESCUE. FORTESCUE (GRENVILLE) MSS. (Sometimes known as the Dropmore MSS.) H.M.C. 30: Fortescue I (13th R. III), Fortescue II (14th R. V), Fortescue III–X.

Papers of William Wyndham Grenville, Baron Grenville (1759–1834), Secretary of State for Home and the

Colonies, 1789–91, President of the Board of Control, 1790–3, Secretary of State for Foreign Affairs, 1791–1801, Prime Minister and First Lord of the Treasury, 1806–7, &c. The collection includes a few letters of Robert Pitt, son of Thomas Pitt, Governor of Madras, from Amoy and Canton where he was engaged in trade, 1699–1701; some of Thomas Pitt's letters from Fort St. George refer to trade with China, and there are scattered references to such trade throughout the collection. *c.* 1698–1820. (The calendar compiled by the Historical Manuscripts Commission is very adequately indexed.)

Various papers relating to the Jesuit missionaries in China. (Add. 16913.)

f. 2. 'Memoire instructif, en forme de Journal, sur ce qui c'est passé au sujet des Missions de la Chine, depuis l'arrivée en cet Empire de Monseigneur de Tournon, Patriarche d'Antioche, aujourdhuy Cardinal, jusqu'au départ de Monseigneur Maigrot, Vicaire Apostolique, Evesque de Conon.' 1704. Imperfect.

f. 32. 'Relation des affaires de la Chine, touchant la Religion, 23 Dec. 1708' in a letter from one of the missionaries in China. At the end is a Latin translation of an Imperial edict for the expulsion of missionaries not having an Imperial diploma, dated 24 July 1708; and a copy of a letter from Charles, Bishop of Conon, to Père Gorbillon, Superior of the French Jesuits at Peking, dated Canton, 11 February 1707. *French.*

f. 42. Copy of an attestation by Père Claude Visdelou and Père Antoine Beauvolier, of an act of recognition of Chinese idolatry by Charles Maigrot, Bishop of Conon, in 1699. *Latin.*

f. 44. 'Relatio sepulturae magno Orientis Apostolo S. Francisco Xaverio erectae in Insula Sanciano, anno saeculari MDCC', by Père Gaspard Castner.

f. 60. 'Epistola R. P. Joannis Francisci Gerbillon, Soc. Jesui, Missionariorum Gallorum apud Sinas Superioris Generalis, ad Patrem Michaelem Angelum Tamburinum, Soc. Jesu Vicarium Generalem', dated Peking, 13 November 1705.

f. 65. Copy of a letter from Père Dominique Turpin to Père Du Halde, dated Pondicherry, 6 February 1716. *French.*

f. 67. 'Del estat présent de la mission de la Chine' consisting principally of a dissertation on the meaning of the words 'Tien' and 'Xam Ti' to show that the Chinese religion is not opposed to the worship of the true God. Imperfect.

f. 91. 'Acta inter Majestatem suam Tartaro-Sinicam, Legatum Apostolicum et Mandarinos, a 26 Nov. 1720, usque ad discessium, ejusdem Legati Pechino, tertia Martii 1721.'

f. 116. 'Mémoires sur le Royaume de Mien [Pegu], de

Monseigneur Claude Visdelou, Evêque de [Claudiopolis], traduction du Chinois', dated Pondicherry 27 January 1722; accompanied by extracts from several printed works.

f. 131. Tract in defence of the Jesuit missionaries in China, in their controversy with the 'Missions Etrangères'. Imperfect. *French.*

f. 154. 'Copie sur l'original de la Lettre des Mess. Fiberge et Triffacier, Supérieurs des Missions Etrangères, pour l'avertir des friponneries des Jésuites de la Chine sur le culte de Confucius', &c. Paris, 25 September 1702.

'A relation of the most famous and renowned states and kingdoms . . . throughout the world' in four books. Book two includes Asia, China, and Japan. 17th century. (Harl. 6249.)

A description of Asia in a book of miscellaneous collections. 17th century. (Harl. 2334. f. 83.)

History and description of China, extracted from Père Martin and others. 17th century. *French.* (Sloane 1019, ff. 206–30.)

Remarks on the Great Wall of China and part of Tartary by Dr. Edward Browne. 17th century. Imperfect. (Sloane 1913, f. 24.)

Account of China. 17th century. (Sloane 1950, f. 5.)

Original manuscript of Engelbert Kaempfer's history of Japan. 17th century. *German.* (Sloane 3060.)

Collections of Engelbert Kaempfer relating to Japan. 17th Century. *German, Dutch, Latin.* (Sloane 3061 and 3062.) They include:

1. Extracts from a Japanese work describing the massacre of Christians at Arima. 1683. (Sloane 3061, ff. 69, 83.)

2. List of the Mikados from earliest times to 1688. (Sloane 3061, ff. 24–43.)

3. Account of various journeys in Japan. 1684–6. *German.* (Sloane 3061, ff. 104–14.)

4. Account of a journey from Nagasaki to Jeddo [Tokyo] by D. Six. 1669. *German.* (Sloane 3061, ff. 90–9.)

5. Notes on the trade of the Dutch East India Company with Japan. 17th century. *German.* (Sloane 3061, ff. 118–27.)

Letters to and from Engelbert Kaempfer together with other papers chiefly relating to the Dutch East India Company, including (f. 50) a list of Japanese books to be procured by Hendrick van Buijtenheim, President of the Dutch factory in Japan, for Herbert de Jager of Batavia. 17th century. *Dutch.* (Sloane 3064.)

Description of the third voyage of the Dutch to Cathay and China in 1596. 17th century. (Sloane 3364.)

Spanish–Chinese vocabulary, by Padre Francisco Varo, of the Order of Preachers in China. 17th century. (Sloane 3419.)

Dutch map of Japan. 17th century. (Add. 5414, no. 9.)

Coloured map on vellum of the east coast of Asia from Sumatra to Japan. First half of 17th century. (Add. 5415.)

'Relacion y noticias de el reino del Japon', &c. 'de Don Rodrigo de Vivero [afterwards Conde de Valle], quien la dedica ala Catholica Real Magestad del Rei Nuestro Señor, de 1609'; with copies of royal commissions to Don Rodrigo de Vivero, and other papers. 17th century. (Add. 18287.)

'Mapa reducido que abraza todo lo descubierto de las costas occidentale de la America y las Orientale de la Asie.' Early 17th century. (Add. 17647C.)

Copies of papers in Spanish and Portuguese relating to Portugal and its dependencies, including 'Breue informacão sobre alguas cousas das Ilhas da China', &c. (f. 3); relations, &c., concerning India, China, &c. 1605, 1626 (f. 158). (Add. 28461.)

'Guerras del Tartaro, y conquista del grande Imperio de la China. Primero Parte', with a short addition respecting the Dutch in China in 1649. 17th century. (Add. 28495.)

Dutch portolano containing forty-nine coloured maps and views, including Tonking (f. 46b); Hainan (f. 48b); coast of China (ff. 50b, 52b); Formosa (ff. 94b, 96b); Japan (f. 98b). 17th century. 101 ff. (Add. 34184.)

'Itinerario Orientale': an Italian translation of the *Itinerario de las Missiones* (in India, China, &c.) of Fr. Sebastian Manrique, a Portuguese Augustinian, which was published at Rome in 1649. The translation, which is a rough copy containing many corrections, is close, but on a revision the translator has marked several passages for excision. 17th century. ii+166 ff. (Add. 38026.)

An English–Chinese dictionary containing only the first portion of the alphabet from A to D. 17th century. (Or. 2284.)

Maps and plans of countries in Asia, including coast map of Asia, from Arabia to Japan, late 17th century. (A. *Dutch*); and map of Whampoa Reach, Canton, with soundings (B). 17th–19th centuries. (Add. 31343 A–X².)

Letters from Frà Bernardino dalla Chiesa, Bishop of Peking, and Frà Basilio di Gemona, Vicar Apostolic of Xen Si, both with the order of Reformed Franciscans, to the College de Propaganda Fide and to Pope Innocent XII, on the condition of the church in China. Peking, 6 and 7 October 1700; Lin Ching Cheo, 22 October 1701. *Italian.* (Add. 31022, F1–3.)

Tracts, copies of correspondence, and other papers relating to the Catholic missions in China, chiefly in connection with the controversy between the Jesuit and other missionaries on questions of Chinese doctrine and ritual; collected apparently by Jean François Fouquet, Jesuit missionary, and afterwards Bishop of Eleutheropolis. *c.* 1700–1740. 3 vols. (Add. 26816–18.)

Vol. I (Add. 22816) contains the following papers:

1. Treatise on the funeral rites of the Chinese, the cult of the dead, etc., written upon the occasion of the burial of Antonio Provana, Jesuit missionary at Canton, in 1723. *Latin.* (f. 5b.)

2. 'Testament de l'impératrice, mère de l'empéreur chinois qui regne aujourd'hui', 25 June 1723, with explanatory notes. (f. 105. A Latin version is at f. 112.)

3. Mode of burial of a Chinese empress, *c.* 23 March 1737; translated from Chinese into Latin by the Franciscan 'Carolus Horatii a Castorano'. (f. 117.)

4. Correspondence of Jean François Fouquet with Pères de Goville, Hervieu, and others, on controversial subjects connected with Chinese religion. 1721 and 1736. *Latin, French, Italian.* (ff. 128–206.)

5. Memorial of Michael Angelo Tamburini, General of the Jesuits, to Pope Benedict XIII, in defence of the Jesuit missionaries in China. [1725.] *Italian,* with marginal remarks in *Latin.* (f. 233.)

6. 'Ragguaglio de' principij e de' progressi che ha avuti la religione christiana in una famiglia Tartara congiunta de sangue colla reale che attualmente regna nella Cina.' (f. 282.)

7. Letter from Sigismondo Maria Calchi, Barnabita, at Canton, to Pope Clement XI. 21 October 1721. *Italian.* (f. 320.)

8. Letter from the Jesuits at Peking to Michael Angelo Tamburini, General of the Order. 17 July 1722. *Latin.* (f. 337.)

9. 'Transumptum Diarii missi ab imperatore Sinarum ad Summum Pontificem [Clement XI] super legationem [Caroli Ambrosii Mezzabarbae] patriarchae Alexandriae' containing accounts of interviews of the legate with the Emperor, etc. 24 December 1720–21 January 1721. (f. 350.)

Vol. II (Add. 26817) contains the following papers:

1. Letters from Pope Innocent XIII to the Emperor of China. 1726. *Latin.* (f. 1b.)

2. Observations by Charles Maigrot, Bishop of Conon, upon the memorial of the General of the Jesuits to the Pope in the preceding volume. *Latin.* (f. 4.)

3. 'Observationes in librum cui titulus Sinensis Imperij libri classici sex . . . e Sinico idiomate in Latinum traducti a patre Francesco Noel' &c. 1711. (f. 56.)

4. 'Observationes [by the Bishop of Conon] in scriptum Jesuitarum [vol. i, f. 350] quo varia Sinarum Imperatoris mandata referuntur.' 1721. (f. 81.)

5. 'Acta causae rituum seu Ceremoniarum Sinensium' with other printed papers. 1693–1715. (ff. 93–133.)

6. 'Responsum episcopi Eleutheropolitani ad questionem hanc gravissimam, an . . . ad sacerdotium promovere nativos Sinensis expediat', 20 July 1726; signed with autograph corrections (f. 144): with other 'riposte' of the same in 1723 concerning the mission of the Patriach of Alexandria to China in 1720. (f. 144.)

7. 'De octo permissionibus quae neophytis Sinensibus concessae sunt brevis sed accurata consideratio, per Joannem Franciscum Nicolai Archiepiscopum Mirensem.' 29 April 1735. Copy certified by the author. (f. 164.)

8. Answers of Giovanni Francesco da Leonessa, Bishop-elect of Berito, and Vicar Apostolic of Hu Quang in China, to questions of the Holy Office concerning the religion of the Chinese. Rome, 11 and 19 July 1699. (ff. 190, 205.)

9. 'Récit fidelle de ce qui regarde le Chinois nommé Jean Hou, que le p. Foucquet Jésuite amena de la Chine en France dans l'année 1722.' (f. 231.)

10. Copies and extracts of letters from missionaries in China. 1717–35. *Latin, French, Italian.* (ff. 280–381.)

11. Controversial correspondence of the Bishop of Eleutheropolis with Pères Bertrand de Linyères and Pierre de Goville. 1723 and 1736. *Italian, French.* (ff. 383–414.)

Vol. III (Add. 26818) contains the following papers:

1. Copies and extracts of controversial correspondence of the Bishop of Eleutheropolis, on matters of Chinese doctrine. 1723–6. *French, Italian.* (ff. 1–65, *passim.*)

2. 'Editto dell' Imperadore della Cina vicino alla sua morte.' 1722. (f. 76.)

3. Rites observed at the burial of a Chinese empress. *Latin.* (f. 80.)

4. 'Eclaircissement sur les quatre lettres Chinoises, Thien, Ty, Tsong, Che': a controversial tract on the interpretation of the meaning of the words used in the will of the Emperor Kan-hy; with an answer in Latin. (ff. 107, 111. An Italian version of the tract appears at f. 9.)

5. Two tracts entitled 'Judicium de quibusdam funebribus honoribus Sinensium' and 'Clausula de ceremoniis Sinensibus' written by the Bishop of Eleutheropolis on two letters concerning the burial of Antonio Provana, Jesuit missionary at Canton, in 1723. (ff. 129, 140. A duplicate of the first tract occurs at f. 98.)

6. 'Propyleum Templi veteris Sapientie seu Aditus ad antiqua monumenta Sinensium. Ostenditur quenam origo sit illorum monumentorum, tum proponitur Problema Theologicum . . . an et qua ratione dici possit . . . per characterem Tao designari Deum Summum, quem nos Christiani colimus.' (f. 146.)

7. Lists of the missionaries in China from 1552 to 1772, and of the Christian churches in the various provinces of China. (f. 159.)

8. 'Controversia Sinica': a list of the various works printed pro and contra the Jesuits in China in their controversy with the Dominicans and Franciscans, 1634–1733; preceded by a list of the bishops' names and titles occurring in the same. (f. 177b.)

9. 'Textus quidam ex libro antiquissimo Tao Ke Kim excerpti quibus probantur Santissimae Trinitatis Mysterium Sinicae genti olim notum fuisse.' (f. 201.)

10. 'Extrait du grand Dictionaire Historique en six tomes', being a compendious account of China and its history to about 1704. (f. 224.)

'Relacion hecha al Summo Pontifice Clemente XI por el P. Fr. Francisco Gonzalez de San Pedro de Predicadores, . . . Misionero Appostolico en la China': an account of the dissensions between the Jesuits and other missionaries in China during the seventeenth century, and of the proceedings of Charles Thomas Maillard, Cardinal de Tournon, Vicar Apostolic in India and China, 1701–10; followed by further advices on the religious disputes in 1712–13, and the condemnation of the Jesuits by Innocent XIII in 1723. In 7 parts. *Spanish.* (Add. 20807, ff. 1–287.)

'Keae shing pin teze tsëen': a Chinese and Spanish lexicon, arranged phonetically, by Antonio Diaz, a Dominican; with an explanation of the tones prefixed. This is apparently the original manuscript, written at Foo-ning-Chou in Fokien, between the years 1702 and 1704. (Add. 19257. Printed by Klaproth in his *Verzeichniss der Chinesischen Bücher und Handschriften.*)

Journals by Dr. Louis Dumeney of the fourth voyage of the *Sidney* to India and China. 1703–4. (Sloane 2296, ff. 2–30.)

Papers relating to China among the correspondence and papers of Cardinal Filippo Antonio Gualterio (d. 1728):

1. 'Catalogue des livres Chinois, apportés de la Chine par le Père [Jean François] Foucquet, Jésuite en l'année 1722', arranged in classes. (Add. 20583A.)

2. Various papers, including (2) 'Des lettres de la Chine, et des degrés de littérature, où ils entrent après des examens reglés par l'Etat', 1707 (f. 4); (3) copy of a letter on the subject of a papal letter referring to disputes between Dominican and Jesuit missionaries in China. *n.d.* (f. 24. *Italian*); (4) frag-

ment of a treatise by the Bishop of Conon on Chinese manners, religion, &c. (f. 35. *Latin*); (5) 'Testament de l'Impératrice mère de l'Empereur Chinois qui regne aujourdhuj [1723]' with remarks by the same (f. 44); (6) 'Edit de l'Empereur de Chine mourant' 'publié la soixante et unième année de Khan Hii, le treizième jour de l'onzième lune' [1722]. (f. 52. See Add. 20396, f. 12.) (Add. 20583B.)

Letters of Don Annibale Albani, including a letter from 'Frà Giovanni da Fano, Capucino, Missionario del Tibet', 2 July 1708. *Italian*. (Add. 20424.)

Collection of original Spanish papers and tracts on the Chinese missions, 1711. (Add. 20807.)

Letter from David Wilkins to Bishop Chandler on the affinity of Chinese with other Oriental languages. 1721. (Add. 6488, no. 8.)

Abstract of Captain Oloff Erickson Willman's 'Voyage to the East Indies with brief account of the Kingdom of Japan in 1648–54' made by Philip Henry Zollman. 1725. (Sloane 4048, ff. 93–4.)

Account of an earthquake in China, by Du Halde. 1732. (Add. 4432, no. 52.)

Specimen Lexici Sinensis, by Gottlieb Siegfrid Bayer, Professor at St. Petersburg. 1734. (Sloane 3960.)

Original book of orders and letters of Commodore George Anson, during his voyage round the world, in the *Centurion*, with the squadron under his command, including (at f. 7) an order from the viceroy of Canton, dated 27 July 1743. July 1740–December 1743. (Add. 15855.)

BENTHAM PAPERS (Add. 33537–64.)
Correspondence and papers of the family of Bentham, consisting of letters to and from Jeremiah Bentham and his two sons, Jeremy, the well-known philanthropist, and Sir Samuel, the naval architect and engineer; with a few letters at the end addressed to George Bentham, son of Sir Samuel; autograph notes, memoranda, and dissertations of Jeremy Bentham for many of his works; travels of Jeremy and Samuel Bentham; topographical memoirs; accounts; &c. The papers were used by Sir John Bowring for his edition of Jeremy Bentham's *Works*, 1838–43, and by Lady Bentham in her *Life of Brigadier General Sir Samuel Bentham*, 1862. 28 vols. Including:

Correspondence, containing many letters that passed between Jeremy and Samuel, while the latter was in Russia. 1744–1847. 10 vols. (Add. 33537–46.)

Miscellaneous papers of Jeremy Bentham, including, 'Chinese Commercial Station to be founded by the Belgian Government'. 18 August 1831. (f. 255.) (Add. 33551.)

Travels of Jeremy and Samuel Bentham, including

an account of the travels of Samuel through Russia to Siberia, 1781–2 (ff. 108–). 292 ff. (Add. 33552.)

Fair copy of letters and papers written by Sir Samuel Bentham during his travels through Russia and Siberia in 1781–3. (Add. 33554, ff. 1–58.)

Letterbook containing copies of letters of introduction of Samuel Bentham on his journey to Russia and of his own letters to his father and brother Jeremy, 13 July 1779–8 April 1780. At the beginning is 'A Copy of propositions of Samuel Bentham which, in January 1783, were delivered by him to Prince Potemki[n], for the perusal of the Empress of Russia upon his return to Petersburg from visiting Siberia and other parts of that empire as far as the borders of China'. 70 ff. (Add. 33555.)

Letter-book, similar to the above, containing copies of letters of Samuel Bentham. 13 July–31 January 1783. 235 ff. (Add. 33556.)

Letter-book, containing copies of correspondence of the Bentham family, chiefly of Samuel's letters, as above. 13 July 1779–26 October 1784. 314 ff. (Add. 33557.)

Letter-book, containing copies of correspondence of the Bentham family, similar to the preceding volume. 1 August 1780–12 May 1791. 498 ff. (Add. 33558.)

'Memoirs of Samuel Bentham, Esq., continued in a series of letters from himself and others during his ten years' absence from England, being the compilation of a friend, 1790.' The letters are those contained in Add. 33555–8, and there are maps of the countries travelled through in vol. i, f. 61 and vol. iii, ff. 179, 180. 3 vols. (Add. 33560–2.)

Original letters of French ecclesiastics and others, including letters from Michel François Savary, missionary, Macao, 26 September 1754 (f. 55); Francisco Sanchez Abad, minorite missionary, *n.d.*, 1745 (f. 56); Franciscus a Concepcione, missionary, 11 June 1745 (f. 58); Onufruis Villiani, Jesuit missionary, Macao, 4 January 1755 (f. 59). (Add. 24208.)

Papers relating to East India Company ships bound for Canton. (Add. 18019.)

f. 1. Diary of John Misenor and others, supercargoes of the East India Company ships *St. George* and *Stafford*, bound for Canton; with lists of shipping, prices current, &c. January 1747–January 1748.

f. 52. Similar diary and papers of Henry Palmer and others, for the ships *Grantham* and *York*. 1749–50.

f. 93. Similar diary and papers of Edward Phipps and others, for the ships *Clinton* and *Suffolk*. 1753.

Copies of letters from Francisco Marques de Tavora, Viceroy of Portuguese India, to various Indian princes and Portuguese officials in India and China, including, in vol. ii (ff. 3–46), letters for Macao. 1750–4. 2 vols. *Portuguese*. (Add. 20911 and 20912.)

Letter from Father Gaubil in Peking to M. de l'Isle. 1752. (Add. 4107/166. Birch papers.)

'Octroy accordé par S.M. le Roy de Prusse, pour faire commerce à Bengale, et aux côtes voisines. Du consentement de la Royal Compagnie de la Chine établie à Embden. 1753. Printed. (Eg. 1756, f. 275.)

Letters to Joseph de Guignes, member of the Académie des Inscriptions, &c., upon the supposed connection between the modern Chinese and the ancient Egyptian hieroglyphic characters and inscriptions. 1759–67. (Add. 21416. See *Phil. Trans.*, xii, p. 685.)

Collections relating to the Jews, by Emanuel Mendes da Costa, including copy of a letter from the Jews of London to the Jews in China, 1760 (f. 2. *Hebrew*), with copy of a letter relating to the preceding letter (f. 4). (Add. 29868.)

Miscellaneous papers relating to the Spanish navy, 1740–82, including (4) extracts from dispatches relating to Ceuta and to the Spanish-Chinese squadron, 1765 (f. 21). (Add. 20926.)

Papers relating to Horatio, Viscount Nelson and his wife, including at the end (f. 11) a paper in Chinese entitled 'Hien pi che man chuen pin' or government answer to the petition of the Che-man [? German] ship, respecting port regulations at Canton, endorsed 'Hoppo's [Superintendent of Customs] answer to my petition at Canton in yᵉ year 1770, I. Thomas'. (Add. 28333.)

Papers of Isaac Titsingh, head of the Dutch factory at Nagasaki from 1778 to 1784, ambassador to Peking 1794 to 1795, &c. (Add. 18098–102.)

1. List of places in the islands of Japan. 18th century. (Add. 18098.)

2. Papers on the history of Japan. 2 vols. *Dutch*. (Add. 18099 and 18100.)

Vol. I: Account of the principal landed proprietors of Japan, their incomes, &c. (f. 1); list of the state officials, their salaries, &c. (f. 29); list of successive emperors of Japan from the beginning of the seventeenth century to the beginning of the eighteenth century (f. 61); further lists of landed proprietors, and of temples (f. 62); names of the streets of Nagasaki (f. 83).

Vol. II: Copies of Japanese inscriptions, from seals, cylinders, &c. (f. 1b): 'Inlyding tot de beschryving van het naalde steeken en moxa branden, in verscheide ziektens' (f. 6); 'Aanteekeningen omtrend de Dayries of opper vorsten, en de sjogoons of kroons bevelhebberen; beneevens het jaarlyks ceremonieel in het Paleis te Jedo; de vyf groote Feest of compliment daagen, en het Feest der Lantaarns' (f. 7).

3. Copies of letters written by Izaac Titsingh while Governor of the Dutch settlement at Chinsura in Bengal, Councillor at Batavia, and ambassador at Peking, and while in England; addressed to his relatives and others. 16 January 1790–28 April 1797. *Dutch* and *English*. (Add. 18101.)

4. 'Journal d'un voyage à Peking' translated from the Dutch autograph of Isaac Titsingh, containing the diary of his journey from Canton to Peking as head of the Dutch embassy, &c. 22 November 1794–11 May 1795. *French*. (Add. 18102.)

Annotations on the Dayris or sovereigns of Japan' by Isaac Titsingh. 1782. (Add. 9396.)

'Vocabularium Sinico-Mantschuico-Ruthenum, juxta ordinem rerum compositum ab Alexei Leontieff, anno 1773, cum interpretatione Germanica Gerhardi Martens . . . 1782.' (Add. 18104.)

Journal of a mission to India and China by an agent of the Austrian government, in connection with the Company trading in the East. The writer left Nantes 6 October 1782, visited several places in Southern India and Macao and Canton, and returned to Falmouth, 20 July 1785. *French*. 73 ff. (Add. 32165.)

Bedenkingen over de Tiedrukening der Chineizen na het gevoelen der Japanners; beneevens eenige Aanmerkingen nopens der Oorsprouk der Japanners; en eene gereegelde Jaartelling van der Opvolging der Chineesche en Japansche Vorsten tot het Jaar 1784, door Isaac Titsingh. (Add. 9394.)

BANKS CORRESPONDENCE (Add. 8098–9, 33977–82, and 35262). See Warren R. Dawson, *The Banks letters* (London, 1958).

1. From Alexander Duncan, Canton, mainly about sending plants and seeds from China. 1788–96. (Dawson, pp. 280–2.)

2. From John Duncan. 1784–7. (Dawson, loc. cit.)

3. With Jan Frederik van Beck Calkoën (1772–1811) on an engine used in China for watering barren and elevated ground. 1801–2. (Add. 8099, f. 395. Dawson, p. 197.)

4. From William Kerr, plant collector, Canton. 1804–10. (Add. 33981. Dawson, pp. 486–7.)

5. With John Reeves, Tea Inspector to the East India Company. 1812–27. (Add. 33982 and 35262. Dawson, pp. 575–7, 695–6.)

6. From Dudley Adams, announcing the completion of a pair of globes to be presented by Lord Macartney to the Emperor of China on behalf of the King. 1792. (Add. 33979. Dawson, p. 5.)

7. With Chrétien Louis Joseph De Guignes, French consul at Canton, and his father, Joseph De Guignes, orientalist. 1791–3. (Add. 8098. Dawson, p. 255.)

Chinese–Latin dictionary by Basile de Glemona, a missionary in China. [1788.] (Add. 25316.)

Plans by Manuel de Agote.

1. 'Plano del Rio por el qual se navega con embarciones menores entre Macao y Canton.' 1792. (Add. 17641A.)

2. 'Plano de la Ciudad de Macao.' 1792. (Add. 17641B.)

Statements concerning the trade between Europe, India, and China in general, and the English East India Company's trade in particular. 1792. (Add. 13818.)

Original drawings made by Sir John Barrow, William Alexander, Samuel Daniell, and Captain Henry William Parish, R.A., on the embassy to China under Lord Macartney in 1792–3. Some were engraved for Sir George Staunton's *Account of an Embassy to China*, London, 1797, some for Sir John Barrow's *Travels in China*, London, 1804, and some for his *Voyage to Cochin China*, London, 1806. 37 ff. (Add. 33931.)

Thirty-seven water-colour drawings, made for the most part in 1792–3 on Lord Macartney's embassy to China, by William Alexander and Samuel Daniell. Many of them have been engraved, either for Sir John Barrow's *Voyage to Cochin China*, 1806, or for his *Travels in China*, 1804. 37 ff. (Add. 35300. Barrow Bequest, vol. i.)

'Translated extract of a letter from a Missionary in Pekin in China' relating to the English Embassy there of Lord Macartney and Sir George Staunton. 1792–4. (Stowe 307/13, f. 256.)

Journals by William Alexander of his voyage to China in the embassy of Lord Macartney. 105 ff. (Add. 35174.)

1. 'Journal of a voyage to Pekin in China, on board the Hindostan E.I.M., which accompanied Lord Macartney on his embassy to the Emperor', kept by William Alexander, draughtsman to the embassy, and later Keeper of Prints and Drawings in the British Museum (1808). The squadron, consisting of the *Lion*, the *Hindostan*, and the *Jackal* sailed on the 21 September 1792 and arrived at the mouth of the Pei-ho on 5 August 1793. The journal continues the description of the voyage in junks up the river to Peking, the reception of the embassy, and their proceedings to 26 November 1793, on which day Alexander re-embarked on board the *Hindostan*. (f. 1.)

2. Another journal of the same voyage in the *Hindostan* by Alexander being a strictly nautical account of the outward voyage, 21 September 1792 to 5 August 1793, and of the homeward voyage, 25 November 1793 to 10 September 1794; preceded by a list of persons belonging to the Chinese embassy on board

the *Lion* and *Hindostan* (f. 41), the 'Quarter Bill' (f. 41b), and a list of officers and men on board the *Hindostan* (f. 42). There are in addition, among other papers, water-colour drawings of Chinese coastlines (ff. 60–75), drawings and codes of signals used in the voyage (f. 76b), and an account of the Alexander family, &c., by Edward Hughes, August 1897. (f. 104.)

'A Journal of his Majesty's ship Lion' kept by Sir Erasmus Gower during his voyage to China, when he conveyed there the British ambassador, Lord Macartney; illustrated with maps and sketches. 1 October–7 September 1804. (Add. 21106.)

Maps, plans, and sketches of places and scenes in China, executed for Lord Macartney on the occasion of his embassy to China, 1792 to 1794, by H. W. Parish of the Royal Artillery. (Add. 19822.)

Log book kept by Griffin Hawkins, midshipman on board the East India Company's ship *Triton* sailing from Deptford to India and China and back, 30 October 1792–30 October 1794. At the end are lists of the ship's crew and passengers (f. 121b), tables of signals (f. 123), a few drawings of landfalls (f. 130b) and one of the ship (f. 134). After these are added an extract from the log of the ship *Exeter* showing the eastern passage to China, 18 November–27 December 1793 (f. 135), and log of the brig *Emmanuel*, London to Copenhagen, 14 November–30 December 1794 (f. 141). 1792–4. 144 ff. (Add. 35348.)

WELLESLEY PAPERS

Correspondence and papers, official, political, and private, of Richard Colley Wellesley (1760–1842), 2nd Earl of Mornington (1781), Baron Wellesley (1797), and Marquis Wellesley (1799), Governor-General of Bengal, 1797–1805, and Foreign Secretary 1809–12. [For a complete list of these papers see our *Guide to Western Manuscripts . . . relating to South and South East Asia*.]

SERIES I. 1352 vols. (Add. 12564–13915.) Including: Drafts of letters from Lord Wellesley, &c., to the Governor of Macao, and others; with other papers relating to Portuguese affairs in the East Indies. (Add. 13703.)

Statements concerning the trade between Europe, India, and China, in general, and the East India Company's trade in particular. 1792. (Add. 13818.)

Papers concerning the opium trade. 1801. (Add. 13822.)

Report of European relations with, and the history of, China, in connection with a proposed embassy to that country. (Add. 13875.)

Journal kept on board the ship *Frederick* in the China Sea. August–October 1803. (Add. 13882.)

Extracts from Churchill's collection of voyages and travels, 1704, relating to printing in China. 18th century. (Sloane 1983, f. 85.)

Japanese books for keeping simples. 18th century. (Sloane 2937.)

Description of Chinese fruits; notes from the account of China, by Domingo Fernandez Navarette; catalogue of a collection relating to the natural history of China. 18th century (Sloane 4019, ff. 23, 145, 146–51.)

A collection of views of headlands, and outlines of coasts, chiefly those seen on voyages from England to India and China; formerly belonging to Alexander Dalrymple, Hydrographer to the Admiralty. 18th century. (Eg. 854.)

'Chinese historie, ofte vertlooning der Keÿsers, en jene keÿserin die tsedert de 1078 jaren naar den anderen in het rÿk van China geregeent hebben, en waar van de ondervolgende schilder pruitjes gemakkt, mitsgaders volgens der Chinesen beschrÿving van tÿt tot tÿt, tot op de regering vanden present tot China regerende keÿser, en Tartar Kong-gÿ [1661–1723] voor waaragtig bevonden zÿn, en gehouden werden', &c. Illustrated with paintings. 18th century. (Add. 11688.)

A vocabulary in Burmese and Chinese, with a few explanatory notes in Russian. 18th century. (Add. 11710.)

Chinese–Portuguese dictionary. 18th century. (Add. 13962.)

Journal of a voyage of the *Argo* from Madras to China and the Cape of Good Hope, with charts of Batavia Road, &c. 18th century. (Add. 15741.)

'Libro de Controversias de China, divido en tres tratados, por el R^do Padre, Fr. Domingo Navarrete, de la Orden de Predicadores, Ministrro antiguo en la China, 1668.' 18th century. (Add. 16933.)

A phonetic Chinese dictionary, arranged from right to left, in columns, between printed lines, with renderings in Portuguese, Latin, and French. 18th century. (Add. 19258.)

Dictionarium Latino-Sinicum. 18th century. 2 vols. (Add. 23620 and 23621.)

'Boca Bulario [Chino-Español] de lengua Sangleya [a Chinese dialect spoken in the Philippine Islands] por las letraz de el A.B.C.', &c. 18th century. (Add. 25317, f. 2. *Or. MSS. & Pr. Bks.*)

'Arte de la lengua Chio Chin', otherwise called Chin-Chen, from a town of that name in the province of Fokien in China. 18th century. (Add. 25317, f. 313b.)

Two papers by Isaac Titsingh, head of the Dutch factory at Nagasaki, &c. 18th century. (Add. 25318. See also Add. 9390–7, 18099, and 18100.)

1. 'Aanteekeningen omtrent de Daijris, of Opper-Vorsten, en de Sjogoens of Kroons Bevelhebberen, benevens het Jaarliks Ceremonieel in het Paleis to Jédo, de vijf groote Feest of Complimentdagen, en het Feest der Lantaarns.' (f. 2.)

2. 'Inleiding tot de Huwlijks plechtigheden' on the marriage ceremonies of the Japanese. (f. 93.)

LEYDEN AND ERSKINE PAPERS (Add. 26555–621.) Papers of Dr. John Leyden (1775–1811), physician, orientalist, and poet, and William Erskine (1773–1852), historian and orientalist.

1. Paper by Dr. Leyden on the study of the Indian and Chinese languages. (Add. 26567.)

2. Miscellaneous notes and translations of oriental literature by Dr. Leyden, including historical notes on China and India (f. 2); history of Kashgar (f. 58). (Add. 26578.)

3. Various papers, including copies and notes of ancient oriental inscriptions (f. 57b). (Add. 26588.)

4. Tracts by Dr. Leyden on the method of investigating oriental languages, &c. (Add. 26600.)

5. Philological collections by William Erskine, including grammar and vocabularies of the Kaffra, Singhalese, Turki, Mongol, and other languages (f. 42). (Add. 26604.)

6. Collections of William Erskine, consisting chiefly of alphabets, vocabularies, &c. of the Marathi, Sindi, Kashmiri, Pushtu, Chinese, Javanese, and other languages; with original letters from Lieutenant F. Irvine and others interspersed. 1796–1810. (Add. 26605.)

Soundings of Galong Bay and Teenpehien, in the Island of Hainan, China. 18th century? (Add. 32451 A².)

Collection of charts and plans of coasts, rivers, islands, &c. drawn for military or sailing purposes, many having reference to the voyages and naval engagements of Admiral Richard, Earl Howe (d. 1799); including China (D. 102–7) and Japan (D. 108). 18th–19th century. (Add. 38076.)

A collection of Chinese phrases of four characters, with French and Latin translation. 18th century. (Or. 831.)

ABERDEEN PAPERS. Correspondence and papers, official and private, of George Gordon, afterwards Hamilton-Gordon, 4th Earl of Aberdeen (1784–1860), Foreign Secretary, 1828–30, 1841–6, Secretary for War and the Colonies, 1834–5, Prime Minister, 1852–5. 321 vols. (Add. 43039–358 and 51043.)

A. Royal correspondence, &c. 1813–60. (Add. 43039–55.)

B. Correspondence with Prime Ministers. 1827–60. (Add. 43056–72.)

C. Correspondence as Ambassador to Austria. 1813–14. (Add. 43073–9.)

D. Correspondence as Foreign Secretary. 1828–30. (Add. 43080–122.)

E. Correspondence as Foreign Secretary. 1841–6. (Add. 43123–87.)

F. Correspondence relating to Home Affairs. 1808–60. (Add. 43188–208.)

G. Private papers of Lord Aberdeen and his family. 1800–59. (Add. 43209–28.)

H. General correspondence. 1801–60. (Add. 43229–56.)

I. Letter-books. 1813–60. (Add. 43257–334.)

J. Diaries. 1802–19, 1828–35. (Add. 43335–41.)

K. Miscellanea. (Add. 43342–54.)

L. Printed Cabinet memoranda. (Add. 43355–8).

Journal kept on board the ship *Frederick* in the Chinese Sea, August–October 1803, &c. (Add. 13882.)

A Japanese and German dictionary by Julius Klaproth, compiled with the help of the Japanese Ssinsson or Yssey in the year 1806, from a Japanese and Chinese lexicon, printed in Jeddo [Tokyo]. It includes a list of names (f. 120), a description of Japan (f. 125b), the streets in Jeddo (f. 131), &c. (Add. 21437.)

'A detail, or memoir, on the powder Dosia, and on Koboe Daysi, who discovered it; by Isaac Titsingh': bound with five letters written by Isaac Titsingh, 1806–11. (Add. 9390.)

Meteorological journal, with notices of remarkable occurrences, kept at Canton and Macao in China, by W. Kerr. 1809. (Add. 8964.)

THE PALMERSTON LETTER-BOOKS. Letter-books of Henry John Temple, 3rd Viscount Palmerston (1784–1865), Secretary at War, 1809–28, Foreign Secretary, 1830–4, 1835–41, 1846–51, Home Secretary, 1852–5, Prime Minister, 1855–8, 1859–65. 1810–65. 173 vols. (Add. 48417–589.)

I. Letter-books as Secretary at War. 1820–8. 4 vols. (Add. 48417–20.)

II. Army estimates. 1810–28. 18 vols. (Add. 48421–38.)

III. Howard de Walden (originals). 1835–40. 5 vols. (Add. 48439–43.)

IV. Foreign Office letter books. 133 vols. (Add. 48444–576.)

V. Loose drafts and papers from Foreign Office letter-books. (Add. 48577.)

VI. Private letter-books. 1853–65. 6 vols. (Add. 48578–83.)

VII. Private accompts. 1806–42. 2 vols. (Add. 48584–5.)

VIII. Private accompts-ledger. 1834–8. (Add. 48586.)

IX. Miscellaneous. 3 vols. (Add. 48587–9.)

BATHURST PAPERS (H.M.C. 76: Bathurst. Loan 57)

Letter from Viscount Melville to Henry, 3rd Earl Bathurst, with enclosure about trade with China. 6 April [1812].

Letter from George Rose to Viscount Melville, mentioning rights of East India Company in China and the fur trade between America and China. 1812.

Papers of Henry Jules Klaproth relating to China.

1. Supplement to the Imperial Geography entitled *Tae tsing yih tung che*, by Henry Jules Klaproth. (Add. 11703.)

2. 'Historischer Atlas von China, in ein und swanzig Karten' by H. J. Klaproth, 1821; the explanatory text only; and geographical nomenclature of the country of the Mongols, Kalkas, &c. by H. J. Klaproth. (Add. 11704.)

3. A collection of maps of China, drawn by H. J. Klaproth, from Chinese authorities, with the names translated by him partly into German and partly into French. (Add. 11705.)

4. Various maps of China, including engraved maps of the provinces of Kiangnan and Tchekiang with manuscript notes by Klaproth; original maps of Cochin China by the Jesuits; engraved maps of Chinese Tartary; maps of the province of Omsk in northern Tartary and of the central north of Mongolia by Klaproth; and a large engraved map of Chinese Tartary, with manuscript notes by Klaproth. (Add. 11706.)

5. 'Notitia linguae Sinicae, auctore P. Premare. Codex in charta Sinica manu ipsius auctoris, ut verisimile est, exaratus.' (Add. 11707.)

6. A recent transcript of the above work, by Stanislaus Julien, containing only the introduction and second part. (Add. 11708.)

7. 'Han Tsu Si Y, Sive Basilii a Glemona Dictionarum Sinico-Latinum juxta clavium ordinum, auctum et emendatum ab H. J. Klaproth, 1813.' (Add. 11709.)

Journal of Captain John Johnson during a voyage to India and China, &c. 1814–17. (Add. 29861.)

Journal of William Fanshawe Martin as 1st Class Volunteer on board H.M.S. *Alceste* during her voyage with Lord Amherst's abortive mission to China. 3 February 1816–17 August 1817. 103 ff. (Add. 41456. Martin Papers, vol. cxi.)

Journal of the East India Company ship *Dorsetshire*, Nat[haniel] Turner commander, kept by Charles William Hales, captain's clerk, on a voyage from London to Whampoa Island, Canton, and back via the Cape of Good Hope, calling at St. Helena and Ascension Island. 15 February 1817–26 April 1818. (Add. 45127.)

Letters from James B. Urmston, at Macao and Canton, to Sir Hudson Lowe, Governor of St. Helena. 4 December 1817–20 November 1821. (Add. 20228, f. 53. Hudson Lowe Papers.)

Letters and papers of John Reeves, the naturalist, relating chiefly to an index made by him to the Chinese Gazetteer of Imperial Officials, known as the Red Book. The index is now Or. 6200. *c.* 1820. (Add. 39255, f. 52.)

Notices of and references to letters received by Major-General Hardwicke from Dr. N. Wallick on a voyage to Penang, Singapore, and China in 1822. (Add. 9870.)

'History of Macao, a Portuguese Settlement in China, comprehending the most remarkable events from its commencement to the introduction of a Constitutional Government in 1822, and Sketches of its foreign relations; with plans and engravings. By Sir Andrew Ljungstedt, Knight of the Royal Swedish Order of Wasa.' 1822. (Add. 27377.)

Letter to M. M. Maher from Père Joaquim Affonso Gonçalvez, missionary in China; from Lintin. 20 February 1824. *Spanish.* (Add. 29960F.)

Collections for a history of the East India Company, by James Pulham; consisting chiefly of extracts from the minutes of the proceedings of the directors, and other official documents. *c.* 1825. (Add. 24934.)

'Tchun-Tsieou, Le Printems et l'automne ou Annales de la Principauté de Lou, depuis 722 jusqu'en 481 avant l'Ere chrétienne, etc. Ecrites par le célèbre Philosophe Confucius, l'an 480 avant Jésus-Christ, après qu'il se fut démis de la charge de Ministre d'Etat qu'il possédoit à la cour de Lou, etc. Et traduites en françois par Le Roux Deshauterayes, 1750. Transcrit sur le MS. original appartenant à la Bibliothèque du Roi.' June 1831. 82 ff. (Add. 30242.)

BROUGHTON PAPERS (Add. 36455–83.)

Correspondence and papers of John Cam Hobhouse, 2nd Bart. (1831), Baron Broughton de Gyfford (1851), Secretary at War 1832–3, and President of the Board of Control 1835–41 and 1846–52. 29 vols. Including:

I. General correspondence, political and private. 1774–1867. 17 vols. (Add. 36456–72.)

II. Correspondence of Sir J. C. Hobhouse as President of the Board of Control with George Eden, Earl of Auckland, Governor-General of India. Lord Auckland's correspondence covers a large part of the First Chinese War. April 1835–May 1841. 2 vols. (Add. 36473 and 36474.)

III. Correspondence of Sir J. C. Hobhouse with the India House. July 1846–January 1852. 2 vols. (Add. 36479 and 36480.)

IV. Engraved plans, viz.: 'Sketch of the operations against Canton, January to March, 1841' published by James Wyld, geographer to the Queen; and 'Plan of Attack on the Heights and Forts near the City of Canton under the command of Major-General Sir Hugh Gough, K.C.B., 25 May, 1841.' (Add. 36483 A and B.)

AUCKLAND PAPERS (Add. 37689–718.)

Letter-books and minute-books of George Eden, 2nd Baron (1814) and 1st Earl (1839) of Auckland, Governor-General of India. 1836–42. 30 vols. Including:

'China Book' consisting of copies of minutes and letters of Lord Auckland, written to British Plenipotentiaries and commanders, &c., in China during the Opium War in 1840–2. The letters are addressed to Captain Charles Elliot and Admiral Sir George Elliot, Naval Commander-in-Chief, acting as joint Plenipotentiaries; Admiral Sir James John Gordon Bremer, Naval Commander-in-Chief before Admiral Elliot; General Sir Hugh Gough, Commander of the Land Forces; Sir Henry Pottinger, who superseded Captain Elliot as Plenipotentiary after the unsuccessful preliminary treaty in January 1841; Admiral Sir William Parker, who succeeded Admiral Elliot in November 1841; and others. 7 April 1840–24 February 1842. 3 vols. (Vol. ii is a duplicate of vol. i.) (Add. 37715–17.)

The Gladstone Papers contain the following items relating to the Far East (taken from the index to *The Catalogue of the Gladstone Papers*, 1953) but it is very likely that, in addition, relevant material can be found among the 750 volumes of correspondence, official papers, and Cabinet minutes.

Memorandum on the Chinese War. 1840. (Add. 44777, ff. 60–2.)

Memoranda on the opium trade. 1841–3. (Add. 44729, ff. 115, 129; 44733, f. 136.)

Memoranda on relations with China. 1859–63. (Add. 44394, f. 262; 44591, ff. 141, 144; 44748, ff. 121, 123; 44752, f. 260.)

Memoranda relating to the colony of Hong Kong. 1843–5. (Add. 44732, f. 194; 44734, f. 13; 44735, f. 2.)

Memorandum relating to the Russo-Chinese treaty. 1860. (Add. 44394, f. 264.)

Coloured plan of the city of Peking by a Chinese artist, with references in English to the Chinese names of the buildings added in 1842. (Add. 19577.)

Letters addressed to General Sir James Hope Grant while on service in India and China; including seven letters from Sir Colin Campbell, Baron Clyde, 20 June 1849–23 January 1860; a letter from Sir Archdale Wilson, 10 October 1857; two letters from Sir William Rose Mansfield, 1st Baron Sandhurst (1871), 23 October 1858 and 28 January 1860; three letters from Sir James Outram, 4 October 1859–11 August 1861; a letter from Sir Edward Lugard, 10 December 1859; and a letter from Nikolai Pavlovich Ignatieff, Russian representative at Peking, 7/19 October 1860. (Add. 41295, ff. 66–120.)

Letters to Colonel John Barrow from officers of all ranks and civilians who took part in the various Arctic expeditions in search of Sir John Franklin. Correspondence with some writers continued long after they had ceased to take an active part in Arctic exploration, especially Sherard Osborn who wrote long and frequent letters from his subsequent stations, during Lord Elgin's embassy to China, &c. 1849–92. 4 vols. (Add. 35306–9. Barrow Bequest, vols. vii–x.)

A Chinese and English vocabulary. [1850?] (Or. 7428.)

A Chinese–English vocabulary, transcribing the sounds of the Chinese words in the Chinese character. c. 1850. (Or. 10886.)

English–Loochooan dictionary with many phrases in the higher style of the literate, and a glossary of derivatives from the Chinese language, by B. J. Bettelheim. 1851. (Or. 40.)

Catalogue of the Chinese manuscripts in the British Museum, by A. Prevost. 1854. (Or. 11623.)

Letters of Major-General Charles George Gordon, to members of his family, written chiefly during military operations in which he was engaged, from the Crimean War to the siege of Khartoum; with sketch-maps. At f. 23 is a letter from Major Gordon to Moh Wang, one of the leaders of the Tai Ping rebels, dated 18 October 1863, with a sketch-map, which were found on the body of Wang when he was murdered; and at f. 42 is a sketch-map of the districts round Soochow, which were held by the rebels and were conquered from them in 1862–4, drawn by General Gordon. 1855–84. 51 ff. (Add. 33222.)

GORDON PAPERS, [MOFFITT COLLECTION]. Letters and papers of Major-General C. G. Gordon (1833–85). 22 vols. (Add. 51291–312.)

I. Letters from General Gordon to his sister, Mary Augusta Gordon, including some written from China. 1855–84. (Add. 51291–8.)

II. Letters mainly to Mary Augusta Gordon from other correspondents. (Add. 51299–301.)

III. Official papers of General Gordon including some (in Add. 51302) relating to China, and press-cuttings on the visit of Li Hung Chang to England. (Add. 51302–4.)

IV. General and family correspondence. 1857–84. (Add. 51305.)

V. Miscellaneous. (Add. 51306–12.)

GORDON PAPERS [BELL COLLECTION]. Letters and papers of Major-General C. G. Gordon (1833–85). 23 vols. (Add. 52386–408.)

I. Correspondence. 1855–84. (Add. 52386–90.)

II. Official Papers. (Add. 52391–7.) Including:

1. General history of the Tai-ping rebellion, with occasional annotations by Gordon. (Add. 52391.)

2. History of the Tai-ping rebellion during 1862–3, with occasional annotations by Gordon. (Add. 52392.)

3. Papers concerning the 'Ever Victorious' army. 1863–71. (Add. 52393–4.)

4. Maps of China and Africa. (Add. 52396.)

III. Correspondence of Sir H. W. Gordon mainly concerning his brother General Gordon. 1864–86. (Add. 52398–403.)

IV. Miscellaneous papers. (Add. 52404–8.)

Letters of General Gordon (a) to his brother Henry, 17 June 1855 and (b) to his aunt, Miss Amy Enderby, 3 August 1877. (Add. 56105D.)

For Gordon's Chinese papers see the article by E. D. Grinstead in British Museum Q. 28 (1964), pp. 83–5.

Diaries by Lieutenant-Colonel Charles Deymer Baillie of service in the Far East, including the Chinese war of 1860. 1857–74. 2 vols. (Add. 50954–5.)

Chinese imperial decrees and memorials by officials, relating to the war with England and France and the flight of the Emperor from Peking, found in Sinho on 12 August 1860 and in Yuang Ming Yuan, the Summer Palace, on 8 October 1860, and translated into English chiefly by Sir Thomas Francis Wade, Chinese Secretary to Lord Elgin. Before 12 August 1860; 26 August–13 September 1860. 55 ff. (Add. 37633.)

Letter-book of General Sir James Hope Grant containing copies of letters written chiefly as commander of British Forces in the second China War. 1860–1. (Add. 52414.)

Fragment of an autobiography of General Sir James Hope Grant; together with Vote of thanks from the House of Lords and House of Commons, 1861. (Add. 52415.)

Seven letters from General Gordon, whilst in command of the 'Ever-victorious Army' against the Taiping rebels, to Lieutenant Arthur Johnson Danyell, about surveys in the neighbourhood of Shanghai. 26 November 1862–5 March 1863 and n.d. With a photograph of Gordon in 1862. (Add. 56105D.)

Autobiography of the Taiping leader, known as Chung Wang, translated by W. Lay in 1863. Copied in 1910 by Mr. J. H. Teesdale. English. (Or. 11179.)

Address from British and other merchants at Shanghai to Lieutenant-Colonel Charles George Gordon, expressing their admiration of his conduct in suppressing the Taiping rebellion; with the signatures of the merchants. 24 November 1864. 2 ff. (Add. 34480.)

Narrative of a voyage round the world undertaken by H. S. Ashbee in 1880. The work was evidently intended for publication, but it does not seem to have been published as a whole, though the two brochures *A Ride to Peking*, London, 1881, and *The Metropolis of the Manchus*, London, 1882, may have formed, or been meant to form, chapters of it. The present manuscript is incomplete, ending with the chapter 'Bombay to Karli Caves Nov. 28 to 29'. (Add. 38808, ff. 87–213.)

Letter from Major-General Charles George Gordon to Major-General H. S. Palmer, A.D.C. to the Governor of Hong Kong. 17 July 1880. (Add. 41996, f. 90.)

Papers relating to a scheme for laying railways in China, mainly letters between A. Constable and John Pender, M.P., with extracts from newspapers, &c. 1883–4. (Or. 7611.)

Letters of Marshal L. H. H. Lyautey on Japanese threats to French Indo-China and Siam. 1896–7. 1904. (Eg. 3292.)

Chronology of the Japanese and Chinese adapted to the European era, by Isaac Titsingh. 19th century. (Add. 9391.)

'Remarks on the chronology of the Chinese, according to the opinions of the Japanese, accompanied with some inquiries respecting the origin of the Japanese and their fabulous chronology, forming the basis of the government of their first Dayri, Zin-moe-ben-O, followed by a regular Epact of the succession of Chinese and Japanese monarchs: by Isaac Titsingh.' 19th century. (Add. 9392.)

Chronology of the Japanese and Chinese, by Isaac Titsingh. 19th century. (Add. 9393.)

Nipon-O-day-itze-ran, or a short detail of the Dayris of Japan, by Isaac Titsingh. 19th century. (Add. 9395.)

Descriptions of the wedding ceremonies among farmers, mechanics, and merchants in Japan; description of the funerals and the festivals in honour of the gods; and two descriptions of the island Jeso, by Isaac Titsingh. 19th century. (Add. 9397.)

Charts of China.

1. Charts of China, partly drawn by European hands. 7 rolls. Early 19th century. (Add. 16363 A–G.)

2. Charts of the coast of Fuhkeën, China, drawn by Europeans. Early 19th century. 17 rolls. (Add. 16364 A–R.)

3. Charts of the coast of China, drawn by European hands. First half of 19th century. 21 rolls. (Add. 16365 A–X.)

Papers and collections, by Julius Heinrich Klaproth, on the Chinese and Tartar languages, with notices and a few drawings of antiquities in the East. 19th century. *German.* (Add. 18105.)

Drawings of Chinese manufactures of tea, china, rice, silk, cotton, and of Chinese boats, by a native artist trained in a European school. 3 vols. 19th century. (Add. 19763–5.)

Papers, memoranda, and notes on Oriental literature and superstitions, with catalogues of, and extracts from, manuscripts, by Nathaniel Bland. 19th century. 2 vols. 215 ff. and 347 ff. (Add. 30378 and 30379.)

Maps and charts of Canton and Macao.

1. Nine maps and views of Canton, the Canton River, and Macao. 19th century. (Add. 31348.)

2. Charts showing the inner passage of the Canton River from Canton to Macao, with the note 'taken from original Spanish chart'. 19th century. (Add. 31349 and 31350.)

'Essays on the philosophy of analysis' by Charles Babbage (1791–1871), mathematician; with, at f. 168, a note in the hand of F. H. A. Humboldt on Chinese numerical symbols. 172 ff. 19th century. (Add. 37202.)

RIPON PAPERS. SECOND SERIES. (Add. 43510–644.)

Correspondence and papers of George Frederic Samuel Robinson, 1st Marquis of Ripon (1827–1909), Secretary of State for War, 1863–6, Secretary of State for India, 1866, Viceroy of India, 1880–4, First Lord of the Admiralty, 1886, Colonial Secretary, 1892–5. 19th century.

A. Royal correspondence. (Add. 43510–11.)

B. Special correspondence. (Add. 43512–64.) Including:

1. Successive Colonial Secretaries and Under-Secretaries. (Add. 43551–8.)

2. Colonial Governors: Hong Kong. (In Add. 43564.)

C. Correspondence chiefly relating to India. (Add. 43565–619.)

D. Family correspondence (Add. 43620.)

E. General correspondence. (Add. 43621–40.)

F. Diaries. (Add. 43641–3.)

G. Miscellanea. (Add. 43644.)

DILKE PAPERS. 168 vols. (Add. 43874–967, 49385–455, and 49610–12.)

Correspondence, literary manuscripts, and other papers of Sir Charles Wentworth Dilke (1843–1911), author and politician. Correspondents include W. E. Gladstone, Robert Arthur Talbot Gascoyne, 3rd

Marquis of Salisbury, Archibald Philip Primrose, 5th Earl of Rosebery, John Wodehouse, 1st Earl of Kimberley, J. A. Balfour, Henry Campbell-Bannerman, &c. 19th–20th century. These papers have been used by Stephen Lucius Gwynn and Gertrude Mary Tuckwell, *The Life of the Rt Hon. Sir Charles W. Dilke, Bart., M.P.* 2 vols. (1917), and by Roy Jenkins, *Sir Charles Dilke: a Victorian tragedy* (1958).

'The Peking Legations: a national uprising and international episode', by Sir Robert Hart, Inspector-General of Chinese Imperial Customs. 1900. An autograph article written in pencil, together with corrected proofs, for publication in the *Fortnightly Review* (1 November 1900). (Add. 46499.)

BALFOUR PAPERS. Papers of Arthur James Balfour, 1st Earl Balfour (1848–1930), Prime Minister, 1902–5, Foreign Secretary, 1916–19, &c. 19th–20th century. 280 vols. (Add. 49683–962.)

A. Royal correspondence. (Add. 49683–7.)

B. Correspondence with Prime Ministers, &c. (Add. 49688–97.)

C. Cabinet, Committee of Imperial Defence, and Foreign Affairs. (Add. 49698–756.)

D. Correspondence chiefly relating to Home Affairs. (Add. 49757–830.)

E. Family correspondence. (Add. 49831–7.)

F. General correspondence. 1872–1929. (Add. 49838–69.)

G. Letter-books. 1885–95. (Add. 49870–91.)

H. Literary MSS. (Add. 49892–962.)

Miscellaneous papers relating to Central Asia, including Kashgar, Yarkand, and East Turkistan, collected by R. B. Shaw (1839–79). 269 ff. (Or. 5336.)

Message on thin paper, damaged in places, from Sir Robert Hart, addressed to the Foreign Consuls at Tientsin or the officer commanding any European troops, requesting immediate relief for the besieged Peking legation. 9 p.m., Saturday, 23 June [1900]. (Add. 40730, f. 91.)

ARNOLD-FORSTER PAPERS. Papers of Hugh Oakeley Arnold-Forster (1855–1909), Parliamentary Secretary to the Admiralty, 1900–3, Secretary of State for War, 1903–6. 83 vols. (Add. 50275–357. These papers were used by M. Arnold-Forster in *The Right Honourable Hugh Oakeley Arnold-Forster; a memoir by his wife*, 1910.)

I. Papers as Parliamentary Secretary to the Admiralty. (Add. 50275–99.) Including (Add. 50294c iv): Chinese ships.

II. Papers as Secretary of State for War. (Add. 50300–35). Including (Add. 50334): Colonel W. H. H.

Waters, *Reports on the campaign in Manchuria in 1904*, 1905; printed.

III. Diaries. 1903–8. (Add. 50336–53.)

IV. Miscellaneous. (Add. 50354–7.)

Russian political documents, including, 'Obzor dokumentov kasayushchikhsya peregovorov s Yaponiei v 1903–1904 g. i khranyashchikhsya v Kantselyrii Osobago Komiteta Dalnyago Vostoka': a list of documents relating to negotiations with Japan in 1903–4, preserved in the Chancery of the Special Committee of the Far East, followed by copies of the documents themselves which are taken from the correspondence between the Russian home authorities and their representatives in the Far East. 11 July 1903–26 January 1904 O.S. (Add. 39325, f. 13.)

Notes and extracts for use in speeches, including Chinese Labour. Before 1908. (Campbell Bannerman papers. Add. 41243A, ff. 166–75.)

Three letters from Dr. Sun Yat Sen, Chinese republican leader, to G. E. Musgrove. The first encloses the translation of a proclamation 'To All Friendly Nations'. New York, 6 December 1909 and 11 January 1910; and San Francisco, 22 March 1910. (Add. 39168, ff. 138–52.)

Index to the Yi ching (Book of changes), by Sir Everard Fraser (1859–1922). Chinese–English. (Or. 11324.)

An English translation of Sun Yat Sen's San Min Chu i ('The Peoples' Three Principles'), by Mrs. Elizabeth G. Chapman (Mrs. B. Burgoyne Chapman.) 1926–7. (Or. 11138.)

Narrative by Ernest Philip Higgs (d. 1956), of the Shanghai Power Company, about his experiences in Shanghai, 1941–5. Typescript copy. (Add. 49380D.)

Letters from Dr. W. M. Stevenson to her cousin Mrs. G. Ewart, written from Peking, where her husband was employed in the Diplomatic Service. 1959–61. *Reserved.* (Add. 57526.)

CECIL OF CHELWOOD PAPERS. Correspondence and papers of Lord Edgar Algernon Robert Cecil, Viscount Cecil of Chelwood (1864–1958), Parliamentary Under-Secretary for Foreign Affairs, 1915–16, Assistant Secretary of State for Foreign Affairs 1918, Lord Privy Seal, 1923–4, Hon. Life President of the League of Nations Union. 134 vols. 20th century. (Add. 51071–204.)

BELL COLLECTION

A collection by Sir Charles Alfred Bell of summaries in English of various Tibetan works, mainly Buddhist. 20th century. (Or. 11813 and 12061. For a detailed list of the contents see our *Guide to . . . South and South East Asia*, p. 79.)

A list of signatories to the reply message for the British literary, artistic, and scientific circles. (Chinese and English texts with signatures of leading Chinese.) Peking. 1954. MS. and typescript. 24 ff. (Or. 12209.)

Undated MSS.

Map of China, &c. down to the island of Sumatra. (Cotton Augustus I, 2, f. 45.)

Note of certain defects in the instructions and preparations for Captain Carlyle's voyage to China, &c. to be supplied. (Cotton Otho E. VIII, 60, f. 150.)

Treatise on Chinese method of fishing with ducks. Much obliterated. (Lansdowne 101/7.)

Clearance papers for cargo of ships bound for China. (Lansdowne 110/47.)

List of subscribers and sums subscribed to the expenses of a voyage to China. (Lansdowne 113/1.)

Short account of the provinces and affairs of China. (Lansdowne 154/16, f. 186.)

Short account of China. (Lansdowne 254/16, f. 186.)

Vocabularies of Chinese words explained in Latin, Spanish, and Italian. Also prayers, catechisms, and creeds in Chinese and Latin. Compiled in China 'by some missionaries'. (Lansdowne 765.)

Chinese–English vocabulary. (Lansdowne 809/1, f. 1.)

Drawings of plants of Japan from the collection of — Witzen of Amsterdam. (Add. 5018.)

View of Peking. (Add. 5024.)

Drawings of Japanese temples, habits, &c. by Japanese artists; also Chinese drawings of birds and flowers. (Add. 5252.)

Drawings of Chinese plants with their names in Chinese. (Add. 5292–4.)

Collection of Chinese drawings including:

1. The process of silk manufacture in China.
2. The process of cultivating rice in China.
3. Fishes.
4. Birds and plants.

(Add. 5303.)

Coloured map of the east coast of Asia, with the adjacent islands from Sumatra to Japan. (Add. 5415, I. 1; *Catalogue of maps*, iii. 297.)

Chinese–French vocabulary. (Add. 6655.)

Chinese–English vocabulary. (Add. 6664.)

View of the porcelain tower at Nanking by Joseph Antony van der Dores. (Add. 9047, no. 8.)

Papers relating to China and the East. (Add. 9265.)

Account by Father Valentin Carvalho of the reasons for the expulsion by the Emperor of Japan of all Christian priests. *Portuguese.* (Add. 9856.)

Coloured map of the island of Chusan, with outlines of the city Ting-nae, &c. by a Chinese artist. (Add. 17327.)

Manuscript maps of military engagements, camps, fortifications, &c. in various parts of the world, including (vol. lxiv, 1–3) the Far East. (RUSI maps. Add. 57699.)

Chinese–Latin dictionary. 2 vols. 907+4 pp., 1079+179 pp. and notes. (Or. 4537 and 4538.)

Dialogues, English–Chinese. (Or. 6883).

Chinese–Latin dictionary. 548 ff. (Or. 7371.)

An English–Chinese vocabulary. (Or. 7593.)

Notes on Chinese Buddhist literature by — Watters. (Or. 7607.)

A dictionary of the Hakka district compiled by Dr. Eitel. Hakka, German, English. 4 vols. (Or. 8209.)

Ninety-three booklets of Moso magical texts in the native pictographic script, with English and Chinese translation of ten, partial English translation of eighteen more, and descriptive labels in English and Chinese on the remainder. Bound in 3 volumes. (Or. 11417–509.)

BRITISH MUSEUM (NATURAL HISTORY) LIBRARY

Cromwell Road, London, SW7 5BD

There are six main libraries in the Natural History Museum: General, Botany, Entomology, Mineralogy, Palaeontology, and Zoology. Apart from the manuscripts listed below—whose location in each case is indicated by the name of the library in which it is housed—the various departments also possess un-catalogued correspondence and lists of specimens relating to the Museum's collections, both of which categories may contain material on the Far East. See *Catalogue of the books, manuscripts, maps and drawings in the British Museum (Natural History)*, 8 vols., London, 1903–40. Later accessions are entered in a card-index in the General Library.

Correspondence of Sir Joseph Banks (1743–1820), naturalist and explorer, with botanists and other scientists all over the world. There are a few correspondents with interests in, or living in, China, including:

Clarke Abel, botanist

Earl Bathurst, diplomat

Thomas Manning, botanical collector

John Reeves, East India Company Inspector of Tea at Canton

Sir George Staunton, orientalist

Sir Alexander Dalrymple, who wrote on the activities of the E.I.C. at Amoy and Canton

(1 vol. of transcripts, the originals of which are in many cases now dispersed, made by Dawson Turner. See Warren R. Dawson, *The Banks letters*, London, 1958. *Botany*.

Descriptions of animals observed on a voyage to Canton, with original water-colour drawings. 2 vols. (*Zoology*. This is the manuscript cited by Broussonet in his *Ichthyologia* (1782) under *Clupea thrissa*.)

'Catalogue of such Chinese and Japanese plants whose Chinese characters are known and are botanically described . . .' by James Lind, addressed to Sir Joseph Banks. 1789. (*Botany*.)

Extract of a letter from F. J. Burge to the Zoological Department concerning fossils from China. 14 May 1883. (*Palaeontology*.)

PAPERS OF CHARLES BOUGHEY RICKETT

1. 'Notes on the Birds of Penang and on other subjects of Chinese natural history', including 'Description of the Min and Yuen Fu Rivers, Fokhien Province, China', 'The Rice-Bird of China [Emberiza aureola]', &c. 1884–1908. (*Zoology*.)

2. 'Notes on the birds of Fokhien Province, S.E. China, 1889–1904', &c., with sketch-map and index. 1908. Two letters written by J. D. D. La Touche about Chinese birds, dated 1919 and [1926], are attached to p. 123. ff. [16], vii, 273. (*Zoology. Bird Room*.)

Notebooks of F. Ludlow containing field notes on birds, mainly in Tibet but including one volume on Chinese Turkestan, 1929–30. 1928–47. 10 vols. (*Zoology*.)

Catalogue of Chinese skin collection made by Alistair Morrison, 1940–1. 3 vols. (*Zoology. Bird Room*.)

THE CHARTERED BANK

38 Bishopsgate, London, E.C.2

The Chartered Bank of India, Australia, and China was founded in 1853 following the abrogation of the monopoly held by the East India Company since 1600, and has branches throughout the Far East. The Bank has an extensive collection of records, and although they are not available for general consultation specific questions might be answered on application to the Secretary of the Bank at the Head Office, address as above. For a history of the bank see Compton Mackenzie, *Realms of Silver: one hundred years of banking in the East*, London, 1954.

CHINA ASSOCIATION

Broad Street House, 54 Old Broad St., London, E.C.2

The China Association was founded in London in 1889 to watch over the interests of British companies trading with China. The only manuscript records which have been retained are: committee minutes from 1889 to date (7 vols.), and committee correspondence since 1926. Access to both these classes is restricted, but requests for specific information from bona fide students will be sympathetically considered. A complete set of (printed) annual reports is also available.

THE CHINA INLAND MISSION

Overseas Missionary Fellowship
Newington Green, London, N. 16

The China Inland Mission was founded in 1865 by James Hudson Taylor (1832–1905), who had worked in China from 1853 to 1857 with the Chinese Evangelization Society. In 1951 the Mission was forced to leave China, and its activities were extended to other countries in East Asia. Very few original records survive, apart from the various publications of the Mission. The following items are the only surviving manuscript records. (Marchant, p. 35.)

I. Original letters addressed to the Chinese Evangelization Society.

1. 'Letters from Missionaries', consisting of original letters addressed to the Society by missionaries in Hong Kong and Shanghai, including the Revd. W. Lobscheid, J. Hudson Taylor, Arthur Taylor, Dr. W. Parker, Mr. Roberts, and others. 3 February 1853–20 May 1855. 1 vol.

2. 'Missionaries' Journals', consisting of long original journal-letters addressed to George Pearse, Honorary Secretary to the Society, by the Revd. W. Lobscheid, Dr. W. Parker, J. Hudson Taylor, and Arthur Taylor, mainly from Hong Kong and Shanghai, but including accounts of visits to other parts of China. 23 February 1853–31 December 1855. 1 vol.

II. Copies of journals and letters written by J. Hudson Taylor in China. 1850–74. Letter-books. 11 vols.

1. Extracts from letters written by Taylor, chiefly to members of his family, before leaving England, with one addressed to George Pearse of the Chinese Evangelization Society (25 April 1851). 1851–3. 176 pp.

2. Copies of letters, &c. 29 July 1850–3 May 1855. 150 pp.

3. Journal of a voyage from Liverpool to Shanghai, in the *Dumfries*, captain Morris, beginning 19

September 1853. Taylor reached Shanghai on 1 March 1854, and the journal continues to 4 October. 170 pp.

4. A continuation of Taylor's journal in China, from 5 October to 30 December 1854 (pp. 171–240); with extracts from Letters, 1850–6 (pp. 1–83). 153 pp. (paginated 171–240 and 1–83.)

5. Copies of letters written by Taylor to his parents, sister, and others; including a journal-letter to his sister, dated 24 August 1854, covering the period of the voyage and early months in China. 1854–5. 162 pp.

6. Copies of letters written by Taylor, mainly to members of his family, some written in journal form. June 1855–March 1856. 206 pp.

7. Extracts from letters written by Taylor. 23 March 1856–18 April 1858. 205 pp.

8. Extracts from letters written by Taylor. 6 July 1858–3 May 1866. 192 pp.

9. Extracts from letters written by Taylor. 19 June 1866–7 October 1868. 199 pp. (Second Series 1.)

10. Extracts from letters written by Taylor. 13 March 1869–15 August 1874. 191 pp. (Second Series 2.)

11. 'Sundry writers': extracts from letters written in China between 1862 and 1869, a number by James Meadows. 92 pp.

III. Material used in the biography of James Hudson Taylor. 2 folders.

1. Numerous papers, including typescript copies of, and extracts from, Taylor's letters; original letters written by Taylor in Ireland and England in 1866; a modern manuscript extract from Taylor's diary, January to May 1866; various original letters and papers relating to Taylor; and drafts for various chapters of the biography. There is also an original letter from G. C. Gordon, dated 28 December 1865. 1865–82.

2. Similar papers to the above, including typescript copies of letters written by Taylor to his parents and others on his third visit to China, November 1872 to August 1874; typescript copies of, and extracts from, Taylor's letters from China written in 1886, 1888–9, 1893, 1898, 1899; copies of other letters, from 1868 onwards; 'Notes of conversations with dear Father on our journey out to China together in 1894'; 'The Principles of the Mission written on the s.s. *Germanic*, Monday March 26, 1894'; 'Developments of Church life in China', a paper read in Melbourne in May 1898 by D. E. Hoste, Taylor's nephew; typescript copies of letters written from China by D. E. Hoste, 1900–4, with some originals dated 1901, and some pressed copies, dated 1901. 1868–1904.

IV. Monographs by early members of the Mission.

CHURCH MISSIONARY SOCIETY

157 Waterloo Road, London, SE1L 8UU

The Church Missionary Society, founded in 1799, established missions in China in 1837 and in Japan in 1869. The manuscript records are almost complete, but the fifty-year rule in general applies to them. There are a number of typescript inventories and a new catalogue is being prepared. There are also many printed records. For the history of the Society see Eugene Stock, *The History of the Church Missionary Society*, vols. i–iii, 1899 and vol. iv, 1914. (Marchant, pp. 38–46; Keen, CMS/1–17.)

GENERAL SECRETARY'S DEPARTMENT

Committee minutes. 1799 to date.

Correspondence with missions &c. China, 1912–1960; Japan, 1878–1960.

MEDICAL DEPARTMENT

Correspondence with missions, &c. China, 1911–60; Japan, 1917–52.

EAST ASIA: GENERAL (G1)

Correspondence (outgoing). 1882–1909. 4 vols. (AC 1.)

Correspondence (incoming). 1914–17. (AC 2.)

Correspondence (incoming and outgoing). 1933. (AC 3.)

Circular books (to mission secretaries). 1916–34. 2 vols. (AZ 1–2.)

East Asia Committee minutes. 1895–1905, 1910–57. 5 vols. (C1.)

Précis book. 1915–34. 1 vol. (P1.)

CHINA MISSION (C/CH)

I. Individual letter-book containing copies of outgoing letters, including letters to Japan, 1882. 1852–83. 1 vol. (C/CH/I1.)

L. Letter-books containing copies of outgoing letters, including letters to Japan for the years 1869 to 1873. 1834–82. 3 vols. (C/CH/L1–3.)

M. Mission books containing copies of incoming correspondence, reports, and papers, including letters from Japan for the years 1868 to 1880. From 1875 the volumes contain separate sections for the Japan Mission. 1834–62, 1868–80. 3 vols. and 5 vols. (C/CH/M1–9.)

O. Original incoming letters, journals and papers. 1834–80. 8 boxes. (C/CH/O.) Among the papers are the following:

Government papers and correspondence. 1839–80.

Minutes. 1852–80.

Miscellaneous reports. 1869–80.

Honorary treasurer's letters to the Home Secretary. 1851–79.

Miscellaneous letters. 1835–74.

Miscellaneous papers, plans, &c. 1851–77.

Medical certificates. 1845–80.

Newspaper cuttings. 1870–80.

Printed pamphlets. 1851–80.

Papers relating to finance. 1849–79.

Letters and papers from Archbishops and Bishops:

   a. Archbishop of Canterbury. 1878.
   b. Bishop Burdon. 1874–80.
   c. Bishop Moule. 1880.
   d. Bishop Russell. 1875–8.
   e. Bishop Smith. 1844–71.
   f. Bishop A. J. Smith. 1852–63.

Letters and papers from individual missionaries:

The Revd. Charles Atkinson: letters. 1866–8.
S. L. Baldwin: letters. 1879.
The Revd. David T. Barry: letters. 1879.
The Revd. James Bates: letters, reports. 1867–80.
Josiah Blakeley: letters. 1876.
The Revd. William Brereton: letters. 1875–9.
The Revd. John S. Burdon: letters, journals. 1853–69.
The Revd. W. H. Collins: letters, journals, reports, documents. 1849–80.
Mrs. Collins: letters. 1880.
The Revd. R. H. Cobbold: letters, journals. 1849–56.
The Revd. A. W. Cribb: letters, journals. 1863–71.
The Revd. Edmund Davys: letters. 1876–80.
The Revd. Dzeng Tsu Sing: letters, papers. 1877–8.
The Revd. Arthur Elwin: letters, journals. 1870–80.
The Revd. William L. Farmer: letters. 1848–9.
Miss Lydia M. Fay (schoolmistress): letters 1865–8.
The Revd. Matthew Fearnley: letters, journal. 1855–60.
Maurice D. Fitzgerald: letters. 1875.
The Revd. Thomas G. Fleming: letters. 1860–2.
Miss Mary A. Foster: letters. 1860.
John Fryer: letters. 1863–5.
Dr. James Gault: letters. 1872–80.
J. R. Gamwell: letters. 1866–9.
The Revd. F. F. Gough: letters. 1851–80.
Mrs. Mary Gough: letters. 1875.
Mrs. Ann M. Gough: letters. 1869–77.
Miss Ellen T. Gough: letters. 1878.
The Revd. H. Gretton: letters. 1867–73.
The Revd. John Grundy: letters. 1878–80.
The Revd. Joseph C. Hoare: letters. 1875–80.
The Revd. John Hobson: letters, reports, papers. 1848–61.
Miss Houston: letters. 1877.

The Revd. Arthur B. Hutchinson: letters. 1871–81.
The Revd. Robert D. Jackson: Letters. 1851–3.
John Jepson: letters, reports. 1877.
Miss M. Jones: letters. 1878–88.
George Lanning: letters. 1876–9.
Miss Matilda Laurence: letters. 1873–9.
The Revd. Llewelyn Lloyd: letters, reports, journals. 1877–80.
Lo Sam Yuen: journal. 1866.
Lui Fong Sing: papers. 1875.
The Revd. Francis McCaw: letters, journals. 1855–7.
The Revd. Thomas McClutchie: letters, journals. 1844–79.
The Revd. John E. Mahood: letters. 1871.
The Revd. E. T. R. Moncrieff: letters, journals, papers. 1850–2.
The Revd. A. E. Moule: letters, journals, papers. 1861–78.
The Revd. (later Bishop) George E. Moule: letters, journals, papers. 1858–79.
C. Nicholson: letters. 1870–4.
The Revd. O. Kwong Liao: letters. 1879.
The Revd. John B. Ost: letters. 1880.
The Revd. Robert N. Palmer: letters. 1870–8.
The Revd. John Piper: letters. 1867–73.
The Revd. Henry Reeve: letters, journals, papers. 1853–7.
The Revd. (later Bishop) W. A. Russell: letters. 1848–72.
Mrs. Mary A. Russell: letters. 1879.
The Revd. James H. Sedgwick: letters, reports. 1875–80.
Archibald D. Shaw: letters, reports. 1877.
The Revd. Sing Eng Teh: letters. 1877–9.
The Revd. George Smith: letters, journals. 1836–9.
Miss Elizabeth Smith: letters. 1860–5.
The Revd. Edward B. Squire: letters. 1836–9.
Mrs. Squire: letters. 1838–9.
The Revd. Robert Stewart: letters. 1876–80.
Mrs. Stewart: letters. 1879.
The Revd. Thomas Stringer: letters, journals. 1862–5.
Birdwood van Somerin Taylor: letters, journals. 1878–80.
The Revd. Jarvis Valentine: letters, journals. 1863–80.
The Revd. Charles F. Warren: letters, journals. 1865–8.
The Revd. William Welton: letters, journals, reports, papers. 1848–55.
The Revd. John R. Wolfe: letters, journals, reports. 1862–79.

CHINA GENERAL (including CHINA MISSION for the years 1880 to 1895) (G1/CH)

I. Individual letter-books, containing copies of outgoing letters. 1883–1914. 4 vols. (G1/CH/I1–4.)

L. Letter-books, containing copies of outgoing letters. 1882–97. 5 vols. (G1/CH/L4–9.)

O. Original incoming letters. 1881–4. 2 boxes. (G1/CH/O.)

P. Précis book containing précis of all incoming papers, and comprising China Mission, 1881–5, South China, 1885–7, Mid China, 1885–7. 1881–8. 1 vol. (G1/CH/P.)

SOUTH CHINA MISSION (G1/CH1)

L. Letter-books, containing copies of outgoing letters. 1897–1934. 5 vols. (G1/CH1/L1–5.)

I. For individual letter-books see G1/CH/I1–4, above.

O. Original incoming letters. 1885–1934. 16 boxes. (G1/CH1/O1–16.)

P. Précis books containing précis of all incoming papers. 1888–1934. 5 vols. (G1/CH1/P1–5.)

MID CHINA MISSION (from September 1912 known as CHEKIANG MISSION) (G1/CH2)

L. Letter-books containing copies of outgoing letters. 1897–1934. 5 vols. (G1/CH2/L1–5.)

O. Original incoming letters. 1885–1934. 16 boxes. (G1/CH2/O1–16.)

P. Précis books, containing précis of all incoming papers. 1888–1934. 5 vols. (G1/CH2/P1–5.)

WEST CHINA MISSION (separated from Mid China Mission in 1887) (G1/CH3)

L. Letter-books, containing copies of outgoing letters. 1897–1934. 4 vols. (G1/CH3/L1–4.)

O. Original incoming letters. 1898–1934. 11 boxes. (G1/CH3/O.)

P. Précis books, containing précis of all incoming papers. 1898–1934. 3 vols. (G1/CH3/P1–3.)

FUKIEN MISSION (separated from South China Mission in 1900) (G1/CH4)

L. Letter-books, containing copies of outgoing letters. 1900–34. 6 vols. (G1/CH4/L1–6.)

O. Original incoming letters. 1900–34. 14 boxes. (G1/CH4/O.)

P. Précis books, containing précis of all incoming papers. 1900–34. 4 vols. (G1/CH4/P1–4.)

KUANGSI-HUNAN MISSION (separated from South China Mission in 1911) (G1/CH5)

L. Letter-books, containing copies of outgoing letters. 1911–34. 2 vols. (G1/CH5/L1–2.)

O. Original incoming letters. 1911–34. 2 boxes. (G1/CH5/O.)

P. Précis book, containing précis of all incoming papers. 1911–34. 1 vol. (G1/CH5/P.)

JAPAN MISSION (C/J and G1/J). See *Papers of the Japan Mission 1868–1934*. Catalogued: Rosemary A. Keen. 1967. (NRA. 12769.)

I. Individual letter-books, containing copies of outgoing letters.

   a. 1882. See China Mission, C/CH/I1, above.

   b. 1888–1914. 2 vols. (G1/J/I1–2.)

L. Letter-books containing copies of outgoing letters.

   a. 1869–73. See China Mission, C/CH/L, above.

   b. 1874–87. 1 vol. (C/J/L1.)

   c. 1887–1934. 9 vols. (G1/J/L2–10.)

M. Mission book, containing copies of incoming correspondence, reports, and papers. See China Mission, C/CH/M, above, which includes letters from Japan, 1868–80, and contains a separate section for Japan from 1875.

O. Original incoming letters.

   a. 1868–74. See China Mission, C/CH/O, above.

   b. 1875–80. 1 box. (C/J/O). Included among the papers are the following:

Minutes of meetings. 1872–8.

Miscellaneous letters. 1874–80.

Plans and printed matters. 1875–80.

Medical certificates. 1875–80.

Lists and indents. 1876–9.

Papers of individual missionaries:

The Revd. Walter Andrews, Nagasaki: letters. 1879.

The Revd. David T. Barry (visitor): letters. 1879.

The Revd. John Batchelor, Hakodate: letters. 1876–9.

The Rt. Revd. Bishop Burdon (Hong Kong): letters. 1878.

The Revd. Henderson Burnside, Nagasaki: letters. 1870–4.

The Revd. Walter Dening, Hakodate: letters, journals. 1873–80.

The Revd. George Ensor, Nagasaki: letters. 1868–71.

The Revd. (later Bishop) Henry Evington, Osaka: letters, journals, papers. 1874–80.

The Revd. (later Bishop) Philip K. Fyson, Niigata: letters, papers. 1874–80.

Mr. (later Revd.) Stephen Koba, Kagoshima: letters. 1880.

The Revd. (later Archdeacon) Herbert Maundrell: letters, journals. 1875–80.

The Revd. John Piper (mission secretary), Yedo (Tokyo): letters, journals, papers. 1869–80.

The Revd. Charles Warren, Osaka: letters. 1873–80.

The Revd. James Williams, Hakodate: letters. 1876–9.

P. Précis books, containing précis of all incoming papers. 1881–1934. 7 vols. (G1/J/P1–7.)

THE SOCIETY FOR PROMOTING FEMALE EDUCATION IN CHINA, INDIA, AND THE EAST (F.E.S.)

The Society was founded on 25 July 1834, and its work was finally merged with the Church of England Zenana Missionary Society in 1899.

1. Minute books. 1834–86 & 1895–9. 6 vols. (F.E.S./AM1–6.)

2. Mission accounts (very little detail). 1863–88. 2 vols. (F.E.S./F1/1–2.)

3. Home accounts. 1874–85. 1 vol. (F.E.S./F2.)

4. Annual reports. 1858–65, 1867–70, 1872–90, 1893–6, 1898–9. Printed. (F.E.S./Z1.)

CHURCH OF ENGLAND ZENANA MISSIONARY SOCIETY (C.E.Z.)

1. Committee minutes:

General Committee. 1880–1953.
Executive Committee. 1898–1938.
Finance Committee. 1881–1957.
Publications Committee.
Candidates Committee.

2. Correspondence with missions, including the Kuangsi-Hunan and Fukien missions. 1921–56.

LOOCHOO NAVAL MISSION

Annual reports, 1846–54.

Journals, correspondence and papers. 1842–57.

UNOFFICIAL DEPOSITED MATERIAL (ACC.)

CHINA

Papers of William Brereton. 1875–96. (Acc. 1.)

Papers of Miss Eleanor Harrison. 1896–1922. (Acc. 19.)

Papers relating to Bishop Christopher Sargent of Fukien. 1938–53. (Acc. 20.)

Letters of Dr. C. F. A. Gutzlaff. 1850. (Acc. 46.)

Hangchow Mission memoranda book. 1864–76.

Finance committee, Shanghai, memoranda book. 1884–96. (Acc. 98.)

Letters of Mrs. Amy I. Wilkinson. 1898–1913. (Acc. 99.)

Pamphlets and readers. (Acc. 105.)

JAPAN

Letters and journals of Katharine Tristram, 1888–1931. (Acc. 104.)

Newspapers (*The Light of the world*). 1905–7. (Acc. 122.)

Bishop J. Mann MSS. (Acc. 180.)

COMPANIES REGISTRATION OFFICE

Department of Trade and Industry, Companies House, 55–71 City Road, London, EC1Y 1BB

The Companies Registration Office, London, keeps records relating to live companies (public and private) registered in England and Wales under the Companies Acts, and for at least twenty years after the removal of their name from the register, in respect of companies which have been dissolved. Thereafter, documents considered worthy of retention are placed in the charge of the Keeper of Public Records at the Public Record Office. The companies include, of course, many relating to the areas covered by this Guide.

The Companies Registration Office, London, also has records of companies incorporated overseas which have established a place of business in England and Wales.

The Registrar of Companies, Edinburgh, maintains similar records in relation to companies incorporated in Scotland and overseas companies having an established place of business in Scotland.

CONFERENCE OF MISSIONARY SOCIETIES IN GREAT BRITAIN AND IRELAND

Edinburgh House, 2 Eaton Gate, London, S.W.1

The Conference was formed following the World Missionary Conference held at Edinburgh in 1910. Keen, CBMS/1–4.)

China Committee: minutes. 1928–37.

Far East Committee: minutes. 1937–53.

Asia Committee: minutes, 1953–62; papers, 1953–6.

China. Literature papers (1 box); papers (44 boxes). 1942–51.

Japan. Papers. 2 boxes.

Shantung Christian University: British Joint Board minutes. 1922–5.

Advisory committee on education in colonies: education reports (including Hong Kong). c. 1940–c. 1950.

CONGREGATIONAL COUNCIL FOR WORLD MISSION

11 Carteret Street, London, S.W.1

Many of the records of the London Missionary Society date back to the foundation of the Society in 1795. They include Board Minutes, 1795 to date, Committee Minutes (incomplete), copies of memorials from the Society to Governments, 1856–1931, reports (incomplete), correspondence official and personal, journals, and miscellanea. Of these the journals, the early correspondence, and some of the minutes and miscellanea are catalogued.

The thirty-year rule applies in principle, but may be lifted in individual cases. (NRA 4110; Marchant, pp. 63–7; Keen, CCWM/1–6.)

In 1966 the Society merged with the Commonwealth Missionary Society (Congregational) to become the Congregational Council for World Mission. In 1973 the archives (to 1940) were transferred to the School of Oriental and African Studies (q.v.) which issued in the same year a guide by C. Stuart Craig, *The archives of the Council for World Mission (incorporating the London Missionary Society): an outline guide.*

CONSERVATIVE OVERSEAS BUREAU

32 Smith Square, London, S.W. 1

There is incidental material relating to the area covered by this *Guide* in the files of the Conservative Party's Overseas Bureau. This might be made available to bona fide research students on application to the Secretary.

DR. WILLIAMS'S LIBRARY

14 Gordon Square, London, WC1H 0AG

Papers of John Jones (1700–70), including, 'Extract of a letter written by a Jesuit who had resided thirty-two years in China; communicated to me by Monseigr Fouquet [viz. Dr. Arthur Smyth, now Bishop of Down, &c. and by him to me, J. J.]'. (12.64.19)

FOREIGN OFFICE LIBRARY

Cornwall House, Stamford Street, London, S.E. 1

In accordance with the provisions of the Public Record Act 1958, the Foreign Office has now transferred to the Public Record Office (q.v.) most of the open-period private papers of the type described in *A guide to Western Manuscripts . . . relating to South and South East Asia* (1965). Confidential papers (F.O. print) are also available at the Public Record Office.

GLEN LINE LTD.

16 St. Helen's Place, London, E.C. 3

Papers relating to voyages by the company's ships to the Far East. (Mathias and Pearsall, pp. 51–4.)

GREATER LONDON RECORD OFFICE
(LONDON RECORDS)

County Hall, London, S.E. 1

Copy of insurance policy. 11 February 1775. (O/140/12.)
1. Captain Richard Parks of the ship *Admiral Pocock* for Rowley Kent, surgeon of the ship *Morse*.
2. Alexander Wych Esq. &c., Madras insurers.
The ship *Morse* from Malacca to Canton to London.

Bond. 19 January 1778. (O/140/13.)
1. Rowley Kent, mariner. Twickenham, Middlesex.
2. Gershon Isaac, merchant. London.
Security on voyage of *Royal George* to Madras and China.

CANON BARNETT MSS.

Notes on the poor in China; ink-drawings of Chinese; notes on conversations on the church with missionaries in China and Japan. [1890.] (535–6. NRA. 12596, p. 31.)

GUILDHALL LIBRARY
Aldermanbury, London, EC2P 2EJ

Foreign registers: China, 1820–38. (Guildhall Library, *Bulletin*, no. 38, A. 1.)

Diary of an agent of a London tea merchant, possibly George Dent, grocer and tea dealer, 55 Blackman Street, Borough, at Macao, and on voyage from Macao to Sydney on the *Lord Amherst*, 1842–3. (*List of accessions to repositories in 1966*, p. 39.)

HOUSE OF LORDS RECORD OFFICE

London, SW1A 0PW

THE RECORDS OF PARLIAMENT

The records of Parliament in the post-medieval period comprise the records of the House of Lords and of the House of Commons respectively. Of these, the former are the most important as they include not only the domestic records of the Upper House but also the records of Parliament as a whole. They have been preserved at Westminster since the sixteenth century and are now kept in the House of Lords Record Office, where they are available to the public. They have been calendared in some detail in the Reports of the Historical Manuscripts Commission for the period 1499 to 1693, and from 1693 to 1714 in a series of volumes published on behalf of the House itself. There are manuscript lists of the titles of documents relating to the period 1714 to the mid nineteenth century in the Lords Record Office, which are gradually being brought up to date.

On the basis of these lists and calendars, the relevant Lords records are noted below for the period to 1858, with two principal exceptions: (1) Acts of Parliament have not been listed. Printed texts of the Public Acts are, however, available in *Statutes of the Realm* (to 1714), and thereafter in the official sessional volumes of Statutes or in *Statutes at Large*. Private Acts are listed in *Statutes of the Realm* and in *Statutes at Large*, but in order to obtain texts of pre-1798 Acts it is frequently necessary to consult the original Act in the House of Lords Record Office. (2) Proceedings in Committee, often containing references to bills which were considered but left no papers behind, are not listed below, but reports made from the Committees are frequently noted, and a further guide both to these proceedings and to all other Lords manuscripts is provided in the printed series of *Journals of the House of Lords* (1510 to date) and their collected indexes. Additional information may be obtained from the Clerk of the Records, to whom it is advisable to give 24 hours' notice of a search, by letter or telephone.

The records of the House of Commons were destroyed by fire in 1834, with the main exceptions of the original Journals (1547–1800) and certain seventeenth-century papers which had been preserved continuously among the Lords, and some of which are included in the list below. The scanty Commons material subsequent to 1834 is not calendared and has not been listed here. It remains under the jurisdiction of the House of Commons but may be consulted in the House of Lords Search Room on application to the Clerk of the Records. Manuscript guides to this material are available in the Lords Record Office Search Room, but only a certain proportion of the material is open to students.

In connection with the papers of both Houses of Parliament, attention should be drawn to the two printed series of *Parliamentary Papers* (1801 to date) in which may be found a great proportion of the Bills, Reports from Committees and Commissions,

and Accounts and Papers laid before the Houses in the nineteenth and twentieth centuries. The Papers have general indexes and are described in P. and G. Ford, *Guide to Parliamentary Papers* (2nd edn., 1959), although the authors do not there explain the relation of the printed papers to the series of originals still preserved at Westminster.

Maurice F. Bond's *Guide to the records of Parliament* was published by H.M.S.O. in 1971.

It must be emphasized that the list below contains in the main only those entries in the House of Lords calendar which refer obviously to China and China trade. There may well be further material relating to China under headings listed as East India returns, accounts, and so on. For the latter see our *Guide to western manuscripts and documents in the British Isles relating to South and South East Asia*, 1965.

Presentation date[1]

1813

19 March	Reports respecting East India and China trade; viz. return and 11 papers. (L.J. XLIX 197.)
25 March	Accounts concerning imports and exports for three years ending 5 January 1813, distinguishing the value of imports from the East Indies and China from all other imports. (L.J. XLIX 219.)
9 April	Motion for reports respecting East India and China trade. (L.J. XLIX 289.)
13 April	Return to order for reports on East India and China trade. (L.J. XLIX 298.)
15 April	Motion for papers respecting China trade. (L.J. XLIX 307.)
28 April	Accounts respecting East India and China trade; viz. list and eight papers. (L.J. XLIX 312.)
3 May	Account of duties on India and China goods for five years. (L.J. XLIX 337.)
4 May	Account of duties on India and China goods for five years. (L.J. XLIX 341.)
19 June	Four papers concerning the East India Company, including one, not listed in the *Lords Journal*, being a return to an order for accounts of the value of goods sold by the Company and of goods imported from China. (L.J. XLIX 512.)

1820

19 May	Accounts of imports and exports from Canton ordered. (L.J. LIII 81.)
25 May	Accounts of imports and exports from Canton. (L.J. LIII 82.)

---

[1] In the House of Lords collection documents are normally calendared on the date on which they were presented to the House of Lords, not the date on which they were written.

7 June   Motion for India and China trade accounts. (L.J. LIII 114.)

28 June   India and China trade accounts. (L.J. LIII 172.)

5 July   Further motions for papers on India and China trade. (L.J. LIII 252.)

10 July   Papers on India and China trade. (L.J. LIII 278.)

1821

16 February   Motion for foreign trade accounts, including East India and China trade. (L.J. LIV 46.)

2 March   India and China trade accounts. (L.J. LIV 77.)

15 March   Accounts concerning trade with Canton; with one annex. (L.J. LIV 100.)

23 March   India and China trade accounts; with two annexes. (L.J. LIV 122.)

2 April   India and China trade accounts. (L.J. LIV 153.)

4 May   Papers respecting India and China trade. (L.J. LIV 385.)

1829

5 June   Papers respecting trade with India and China. (L.J. LXI 553.)

1830

9 February   Papers concerning the finances of the East India Company and the trade with the East Indies and China. (L.J. LXII 13.)

9 February   Select Committee appointed to enquire into the state of the East India Company and the trade between Great Britain and the East Indies and China (L.J. LXII 14.)

18 February   East India, &c. Committee: witnesses to attend. (L.J. LXII 30.)

23 February   East India, &c. Committee: evidence to be printed and witnesses to attend. (L.J. LXII 35.)

25 February   Papers respecting East India and China trade ordered. (L.J. LXII 39–40.)

2 March   East India, &c. Committee: witness to attend. (L.J. LXII 47.)

3 March   East India, &c. Committee: witnesses to attend. (L.J. LXII 49.)

4 March   East India, &c. Committee: ordered leave to report from time to time. (L.J. LXII 53.)

5 March   East India, &c. Committee: witness to attend. (L.J. LXII 60.)

5 March   East India, &c. Committee: message to House of Commons for witness to attend. (L.J. LXII 60.)

12 March   East India, &c. Committee: message from House of Commons with leave for witness to attend. (L.J. LXII 113.)

12 March   East India, &c. Committee: witnesses to attend. (L.J. LXII 114.)

25 March   East India Company's China trade accounts ordered. (L.J. LXII 163.)

29 March   Orders for certain accounts concerning the East India Company's China trade made on 25 March to be discharged and other orders made. (L.J. LXII 169.)

2 April   East India, &c. Committee: witness to attend. (L.J. LXII 191.)

5 April   Petitions for opening India and China trade to all referred to Select Committee. (L.J. LXII 194.)

5 April   Account of money paid for freight, &c. of the East India Company's China trade delivered and referred to Select Committee. (L.J. LXII 195.)

26 April   Accounts of charges on East India Company's shipping at Canton delivered and referred to Select Committee. (L.J. LXII 219.)

29 April   East India, &c. Committee: witnesses to attend. (L.J. LXII 260.)

30 April   Accounts concerning exports to China delivered and referred to Select Committee. (L.J. LXII 280.)

3 May   List of Hong Kong merchants delivered and referred to Select Committee. (L.J. LXII 306.)

6 May   East India, &c. Committee: witnesses to attend. (L.J. LXII 334.)

11 May   Account of foreign trade with China delivered and referred to Select Committee. (L.J. LXII 366.)

13 May   East India, &c. Committee: witness to attend. (L.J. LXII 384.)

21 May   Papers concerning the East India Company's China trade delivered and referred to the Select Committee. (L.J. LXII 478.)

3 June   East India, &c. Committee: witnesses to attend. (L.J. LXII 583.)

8 June   East India, &c. Committee: witness to attend. (L.J. LXII 651.)

10 June   Message to Commons for a witness to attend East India, &c. Committee. (L.J. LXII 697.)

10 June   East India, &c. Committee: witnesses to attend. (L.J. LXII 699.)

11 June   East India, &c. Committee: witnesses to attend. (L.J. LXII 709.)

14 June   Statement ordered of British articles exported in American vessels to China and East Indies. (L.J. LXII 720.)

17 June   East India, &c. Committee: witness to attend. (L.J. LXII 738.)

2 July   Statement of British goods exported in American vessels to China and the

East Indies, 1818–30. (L.J. LXII 792.)

12 July — Correspondence concerning commercial intercourse at Canton. (L.J. LXII 866.)

19 July — Report from the East India, &c. Committee. (L.J. LXII 905. Report printed in Appendix No. I to L.J. LXII.)

21 July — Account of military stores exported to India and amount paid by the East India Company for commercial freight of trade with India and China. (L.J. LXII 914.)

1831

15 February — Papers concerning the trade of India and China. (L.J. LXIII 230.)

25 February — Papers concerning the trade of India and China. (L.J. LXIII 259.)

8 December — Accounts concerning India and China trade ordered. (L.J. LXIV 9.)

13 December — Motion (made and withdrawn) for correspondence between the factory at Canton and the Court of Directors of the East India Company concerning the last differences at Canton. (L.J. LXIV 12.)

1832

23 January — Letters concerning China trade ordered. (L.J. LXIV 26.)

6 February — Accounts concerning India and China trade. (L.J. LXIV 39.)

7 February — Further accounts concerning India and China trade. (L.J. LXIV 40.)

23 March — India and China trade accounts. (L.J. LXIV 116.)

1833

12 February — Papers ordered concerning foreign trade with China and finances of India. (L.J. LXV 24.)

21 February — Papers concerning India and China trade ordered. (L.J. LXV 38.)

15 March — Five papers concerning trade with the East Indies and China. (L.J. LXV 85.)

25 March — India and China trade accounts. (L.J. LXV 109.)

22 April — Accounts concerning finances of India, and India and China trade. (L.J. LXV 181.)

24 April — Further papers concerning finances of India, and India and China trade. (L.J. LXV 191.)

18 June — Statement and accounts concerning India and China trade. (L.J. LXV 436.)

8 July — India and China trade accounts. (L.J. LXV 476.)

24 July — Papers ordered concerning voyage of the ship *Amherst* to North-East Coast of China. (L.J. LXV 519.)

25 July — Paper concerning voyage of the ship *Amherst* (as above) delivered. (L.J. LXV 521.)

16 August — China and India Trade Bill referred to a Select Committee under Standing Order 198. Also amendments to said Bill. (L.J. LXV 588.)

17 August — China and India Trade Bill: report from Select Committee. (L.J. LXV 590.)

1834

17 March — Orders in Council concerning China and India trade. (L.J. LXVI 74.)

1837

3 July — Courts in China Bill. (Parchment Collection.)

1840

14 February — Papers concerning trade with China ordered. (L.J. LXXII 51.)

19 March — Accounts of trade of Canton from 1820. (L.J. LXXII 126.)

27 March — Papers concerning China. (L.J. LXXII 150.)

13 April — Order in Council of 3 April 1840 relating to China. (L.J. LXXII 226.)

14 April — Order in Council of 4 April 1840 relating to China. (L.J. LXXII 234.)

12 May — Motion for Address concerning the Chinese War. (L.J. LXXII 291.)

29 June — Message to Commons for report on China trade. (L.J. LXXII 440.)

2 July — Report of Commons Select Committee on China trade. (L.J. LXXII 456.)

1843

14 February — Thanks of the House to Lt.-Gen. Sir H. Gough and the naval and military forces in China. (L.J. LXXV 28.)

17 March — Address for correspondence concerning China. (L.J. LXXV 96.)

3 August — Act for the better government of Her Majesty's subjects resorting to China. (L.J. LXXV 570.)

24 August — Account showing remittances from China 1841–1843 inclusive. (L.J. LXXV 646.)

1844

8 February — Account of liabilities on account of opium compensation and expenses of the China War. (L.J. LXXVI 19.)

17 May — Papers concerning China. (L.J. LXXVI 247.)

8 July — Statement of the foreign trade with China and account of inland and transit duties of the Chinese Empire. (L.J. LXXVI 486.)

1846

14 August   Ordinance passed in 1845 by the Chief Superintendent of British trade in China. (L.J. LXXVIII 1275.)

1847

9 July   Return of the number of letters sent to and received from India, China, Ceylon and Singapore by private ships during the years 1835 and 1845 respectively. (L.J. LXXIX 682.)

1850

1 August   Ordinances issued in 1849 by the authorities in China. (L.J. LXXXII 415.)

1851

8 April   Address for papers concerning the Chinese War. (L.J. LXXXIII 120.)

1853

12 August   Papers concerning the civil war in China. (L.J. LXXXV 635.)

1854

9 August   Papers ordered concerning expenditure by the Government of India on account of the expedition to China. (L.J. LXXXVI 485.)

1855

23 July   Chinese Passenger Ships Bill. (L.J. LXXXVII 355.)

[*1855*]   House Bills (Box 2): Chinese Passenger Ships.

1857

12 February   Address for papers concerning relations between British residents and natives at Canton. (L.J. LXXXVIII 516.)

20 February   Correspondence concerning operations in the Canton River. (L.J. LXXXVIII 526.)

24 February   Motions for resolutions concerning the war with China. (L.J. LXXXVIII 532.)

9 March   Motion for questions to be put to Judges on the opium trade with China. (L.J. LXXXVIII 547.)

12 March   Address for papers concerning smuggling in China. (L.J. LXXXVIII 551.)

8 May   Address for papers concerning Hong Kong, Chusan, &c. (L.J. LXXXIX 18.)

8 May   Address for papers concerning opium. (L.J. LXXXIX 18.)

20 March   Papers ordered concerning the opium trade (India and China). (L.J. LXXXVIII 567.)

8 May   Address for paper concerning bullion imported into British possessions east of Cape of Good Hope from China each year since 1849. (L.J. LXXXIX 18.)

12 May   Motion for Address concerning Chinese prisoners at Hong Kong. (L.J. LXXXIX 24.)

14 May   Return of the value of British manufactures exported to China in each year since 1833. (L.J. LXXXIX 26.)

14 May   Return of the value of goods and merchandise imported to Great Britain from China in each year since 1849. (L.J. LXXXIX 26.)

14 May   Account of the bullion exported from Great Britain to China in each year since 1849. (L.J. LXXXIX 26.)

15 May   Return of bullion imported into British possessions east of Cape of Good Hope from China in each year since 1849. (L.J. LXXXIX 30.)

4 June   Correspondence between the Foreign Office and the Commercial Association of Manchester concerning China, 1846–8. (L.J. LXXXIX 60.)

9 June   Correspondence, 1829, 1830, 1831, concerning the growth of opium in India and export of opium from India to China. (L.J. LXXXIX 73.)

24 August   Motion for copy of legal opinion taken by the East India Company, dated 5 August 1857, concerning the manufacture and sale of opium. (L.J. LXXXIX 421.)

24 August   Papers concerning opium (as above) delivered. (L.J. LXXXIX 421.)

1858

25 March   Extract from a dispatch from Governor Sir John Bowring to the Secretary of State for the Colonies, dated 31 July 1857, on Chinese prisoners at Hong Kong. (L.J. XC 95.)

21 June   Address for papers concerning emigration from Hong Kong and the Chinese Empire since January 1853. (L.J. XC 282.)

28 June   Chinese Passenger Act (1855): Amendment Bill. (L.J. XC 312.)

1 July   Marriages (Moscow, Tahiti, and Ningpo) Bill. (L.J. XC 331.)

5 July   Amendments to Marriages (Moscow, Tahiti, and Ningpo) Bill. (L.J. XC 356.)

6 July   Motion for return of number of coolies from India or China who have landed in any of the British East or West Indies, 1835–June 1858. (L.J. XC 367.)

SMALL CLASSES, HOUSE OF COMMONS

Deposited papers (library) include papers relating to the trade of Central Asia, 1864; reports on trade at the Treaty Ports in China for 1876. (Bond, op. cit., p. 238.)

SAMUEL PAPERS. Papers of Herbert Louis Samuel, 1st Viscount Samuel (1870–1962), Liberal statesman, including correspondence on Chinese labour in South Africa with Lord Balfour, F. H. P. Creswell, Winston Churchill, J. B. Seely, and others. (Bond, op. cit., p. 283.)

IMPERIAL COLLEGE OF SCIENCE AND TECHNOLOGY

College Archives, College Block, Imperial College, London SW7 2AZ

Letter from A. E. Agassiz to T. H. Huxley on geological observations in Japan. 14 July 1892. (6. 177.)

Letter from Baron Chuzaburo (1873–1934) to William Cawthorne Unwin (1838–1933), Professor of Engineering. 22 July 1910. (Unwin 197.)

Letter from Joji Sakurai (1858–1938) to Henry Edward Armstrong (1848–1937), Professor of Chemistry.

IMPERIAL WAR MUSEUM

Department of Libraries and Archives, Imperial War Museum, Lambeth Road, London, SE1 6HZ

The Imperial War Museum has relics of the First and Second World Wars primarily, and a rapidly growing collection of documents which are not yet completely catalogued. These include a very large collection of aerial propaganda leaflets. The material relevant to this guide relates chiefly to the experiences of prisoners of war (Allied and Japanese) and includes both official and private documents; some of the latter have had a limited circulation in Army periodicals, &c. Among the manuscripts are:

Four letters of Vice-Admiral R. V. Hall describing his involvement as Rear-Admiral Yangtse in the Sino-Japanese War, 1937–8. (Accessions to repositories 1973.)

Diary of Ken Attiwill. 1941–5. 3 vols. (523.11.)

Correspondence relating to service of R. M. Tinkler with 24th Royal Fusiliers 1917–18 and as a detective in the Shanghai Municipal Police. 1919–30. (List of accessions to repositories in 1970, p. 48.)

J. M. Philips: Letters from an employee of the Asiatic Petroleum Company, describing the situation in Canton during the rise of the Kuomintang. 1924–6. Microfilm. (List of accessions to repositories in 1972, pp. 10–11.)

Diary of Sgt. G. Kemsley as a prisoner of war in the Far East. 1941–5. (List of accessions to repositories in 1971, p. 49.)

'The New Order. War edition, published daily. No. 1, 16 February 1942.' Cyclostyled journal issued by the Japanese to British prisoners of war in Singapore.

Memoirs of a prisoner of war in the Far East, by Captain L. J. T. Marsh. 1942–5. Microfilm. (List of accessions to repositories in 1972, p. 10.)

'Within'—the magazine of No. 10 Hut, Kowloon P.O.W. Camp, Hong Kong. 1942–3. 5 vols. (528.191.)

Manuscript diary of J. F. Willin while a P.O.W. in Japanese hands. 18 January 1942–12 September 1945. 4 vols. (528.23.)

Papers of Brigadier L. R. S. MacFarlane on his experiences as a Japanese prisoner of war. 1942–5. (Accessions to repositories 1973.)

Manuscript diary of a Japanese civilian internee—Kurahachi Fukudu, a business man in Singapore arrested in December 1941 and sent to India. He was Internee No. 402 in Singapore. Diary in English and Japanese; was apparently confiscated by the Commandant of the Japanese Internment Camp near Delhi. 1943.

Blue-print of Burma–China railway. 1943.

Account of fighting at Kohima. 1944. Microfilm. (List of accessions to repositories in 1972, p. 11.)

Collection of material concerning pantomimes staged by P.O.W.'s at Ube, Japan. 1944–5. (528.23.)

Camp Standing Order, Motoyama, Japan. 1945. Typescript. Pp. 2. (528.23.)

Copy of letter written by John Edwards describing the arrest of Japanese war criminals in Formosa. 1946. Typescript. Pp. 5. (528.23.)

Presidential Unit Citation; Republic of Korea. 1950. Korean, with typescript translation. (516.314.)

Training notes on methods of jungle warfare by Major-General O. C. Wingate. n.d. Typescript. (K. 44654.)

Papers of Lieutenant-General A. E. Percival relating to the Second World War in the Far East, fall of Malaya, &c. Confidential.

INDIA OFFICE LIBRARY, EUROPEAN MANUSCRIPTS SECTION

Foreign and Commonwealth Office, 197 Blackfriars Road, London, SE1 8NG

MANUSCRIPTS IN EUROPEAN LANGUAGES. These are collections of private papers acquired by the Library since its foundation in 1801. Those acquired before 1937 have been calendared in some detail in the following:

Catalogue of manuscripts in European languages belonging to the Library:

(a) Volume I: *Mackenzie Collections*, Part I. The 1822 Collection and the Private Collection, by C. O. Blagden (1916).

(b) Volume I: *Mackenzie Collections*, Part II. The General Collection, by E. H. Johnston (not published).

(c) Volume II, Part I: *The Orme Collection*, by S. C. Hill (1916).

(d) Volume II, Part II: *Minor Collections and Miscellaneous Manuscripts*: Section I by G. R. Kaye and E. H. Johnston (1937). Section II by E. H. Johnston (not published).

The reference J or K and a number after some of the entries below indicate that the document referred to is included in one or other volume of the Kaye and Johnston calendar.

The unpublished volumes (I, part ii and II, part ii) have been printed and copies are available in the Reading Room, but publication is being deferred pending the compilation and printing of indexes to them.

The papers acquired since 1937 are entered on a card index which was reproduced and published in photo offset by G. K. Hall of Boston in 1964: some of them are described in handlists. Accessions are listed in the annual reports of the Library and Records.

A general introduction to the European manuscripts will be found in S. C. Sutton, *A guide to the India Office Library with a note on the India Office Records* (2nd edn., 1967; reprinted with corrections 1968. pp. 20–31).

WILKS MSS. Copies of and extracts from India Office Records made mainly by Thomas Wilks, who in 1787 was employed to investigate the India Office Records, and his brother William Morton Wilks. (MSS. EUR. D. 35–45. K. 122–32.) Including:

'Collection relative to China by Mr. T. Wilks.' Copies of and extracts from documents concerning China, Japan, &c. 1623–99. iv, 392 pp. (MSS. EUR. D. 41.)

'References relative to the Privileges of the English in China.' This gives the titles of some dozen volumes of records dating from 1726 to 1734, together with the first and last words of each section of each volume. 25 pp. (MSS. EUR. D. 42.)

A collection of extracts headed, 'Vol. V, 1618–1620'. (MSS. EUR. D. 44.) Including:

a. pp. 30–4. 'Letter from the Company's Factors at Nagasaki, in Japan, with account of trade there. 10 March 1619/20. [No. 521.]' The letter is signed Wm. Eaton. (See *Calendars of State Papers: East Indies 1617–1621*, No. 817, pp. 355–60.)

A copy of the Asia portion of the Itinerarium Mundii (printed in vols. II and III of R. C. Temple, *The Travels of Peter Mundy in Europe and Asia 1608–1667*, 1914 and 1919). (MSS. EUR. G. 1. K. 1.) Including:

pp. 201–10. 'Relation 25th. Our departure from Macao . . . 1637.'

pp. 211–34. 'Relation 26th. From the time of our departure Tayfoo until our arrival at Macao again . . . 1637.'

pp. 234–40. 'Relation 27th. Our Departure from Macao . . . 1637.'

MACKENZIE MSS

Description of the island of Formosa, its capture by the Dutch and its recapture in 1661 by the Chinese, included among extracts translated from Henrick van Quellenburgh's *Vindiciae Bataviae ofte Refutatie van het Tractaet van J. B. Tavernier* . . . (Amsterdam 1684.) (Mackenzie 1822, 12. *b*, pp. 70–180.)

'Candid Considerations respecting Netherlands privi-ledged Company to be erected for the Chinese Trade.' 1815. Translated from the Dutch, *Octroij voor een Asiatische en voor den Chinesischen Theehandel geoctroi-jeerde Compagnie.* (Mackenzie 1822, 18 (2), pp. 105–67.)

'Chronology of the Dynasties of China. Translated from De Guignes for Col. Mackenzie.' From M. Deguignes, *Histoire Générale des Huns, des Turcs, des Mogols et des autres Tartares* . . . (Paris, 1756). (Macken-zie, Private, 9 (4), pp. 213–33.)

Translation of '[Rapport van] De Commissie tot de Oost-Indische Zaken, aan het Staats-Bewind der Bataafsche Republiek.' Secret report of the Commission for East India affairs to the Directory of State of the Batavian Republic, 31 August 1803. This includes (p. 96), 'the tea trade with China'; (p. 116), 'the trade with Japan'. (Mackenzie, Private, 15. Rough copy of the same report in Private, 70.)

'North and East Tartary.' A number of extracts translated, apparently from a Dutch printed work. (Mackenzie, Private, 86. I. (9), pp. 123–9, 131–3, 135–44, 146, 148, 149, 153–8.)

'Observations and Orders of the Court of Directors to the China Council on the improper interference of the Kings Officers and the constant residence of Europeans in China without leave.' Incomplete. [Post 1780.] (Mackenzie, General, 67, pp. 357-66.)

ORME MSS. Papers of Robert Orme (1728-1801), historiographer to the East India Company. Including:

'Etat contenant le denombrement des Familles et le Tribut de chaque Province de la Chine sous la Dinastie des Ming, fondée en 1639 et éteinct en 1664, publié par le nommé Leang, au bas d'une parte [carte?] général de cet empire et traduit par l'Evêque d'Ecrinée.' Copy. (Orme O.V. 4 (10), pp. 93-5. Recopied in Orme, India, XVI (5).)

Account of the *Pitt*'s passage from Batavia to Canton and back. 1758-9. (Orme O.V. 67, pp. 71-2. Copied in Orme, India, XVII (20).)

Letter from Abbé Grosier in Paris to—proposing publication of a manuscript descriptive of China. 12 June 1774. (Orme O.V. 72 (20), pp. 167-8.)

'Les grandes annales de la Chine, traduites du Chinois, par le P. de Mailla.' A brief description of the translation by Father de Mailla of the manuscript referred to above. (Orme O.V. 72 (24), pp. 191-4.)

Letter from M. d'Anville in Paris to Orme regarding a memoir on China. 4 May 1776. (Orme O.V. 72 (22), pp. 171-2.)

Letter from [the Abbé] Raynal in Paris concerning memoirs on China. 23 February 1776. (Orme O.V. 72 (22), pp. 175-6.)

'Notes I [Orme] made in reading Duhald's China, Vol. I'. (Orme O.V. 88 (12), pp. 121-38, 139-51.)

Letter from the East India Company's Agent at Bantam to the King of Tywan. 18th century? (MSS. EUR. E. 228.)

Narrative by John Dean of a voyage on board the *Sussex* from Canton towards England. 1738-9. (MSS. EUR. B. 2. K. 11.)

Microfilm of papers of Sir George Leonard Staunton (1737-1801), diplomat, who accompanied Lord Macartney on a mission to China in 1792. The papers include letters to his relatives and friends, 1753-1800. (Reel no. 676.)

Remarks in the Brittania [sic] East Indiaman bound for Madras and China, probably by John McQueen, surgeon of the *Britannia*: journal 1757-9. (MSS. EUR. D. 675.)

Registers for the years 1778, 1781, 1786, 1788, 1789, 1794, 1799, 1801, 1810, of sales of China and Bengal raw silk at the India House, consisting of printed lists of bales, to which manuscript notes have been added.

(MSS. EUR. E. 75-76, D. 101, C. 16-19, B. 17, D. 102, C. 20, A. 7. K. 188.)

Nineteen letters to Sir George Leonard Staunton and his son, Sir George Thomas Staunton. 1780-1804. (Reel no. 676. Microfilmed before export.)

Letters and papers, relating to trade between China and India. 1780-1811. (MSS. EUR. D. 624.)

Account of the loss of the H.C.S. *Halsewell*, 5 January 1786, and gangway and order book of H.C.S. *Hope* for voyage to China and back. December 1812-October 1814. (MSS. EUR. E. 318.)

ELPHINSTONE COLLECTION. Papers, dated 1790-1859, of Mountstuart Elphinstone, Governor of Bombay 1819-27, include letters from John Fullerton-Elphinstone in Canton. (MSS. EUR. F. 88.)

'Embassies to China.' An account of intercourse between Europe and China, with some concluding remarks. [?c. 1797.] iv, 166 pp. (MSS. EUR. E. 55. K. 134.)

Extracts from the Honble. Court's Correspondence with Canton concerning Chinese books, drawings of Chinese plants, and Chinese lanterns. Also lists of books. 1804-18? (MSS. EUR. D. 562/16.)

Lists of contents, in rough chronological order, of twenty-seven volumes of extracts or records, 1608-1762, including references to China and Japan. 'The set of 27 volumes of extracts is not the same set as the 27 volumes of "Miscellaneous Factory Records" now on record at the India Office, but there is a good deal of common matter in the two sets.' [1809 or 1810.] 3 vols. (MSS. EUR. D. 124-6. K. 230.)

Brief index to the three preceding volumes, under headings which include Japan. [c. 1822.] (MSS. EUR. D. 127. K. 231.)

Copies of the official logs of nine voyages to India and China made by Captain Thomas Arnoll Davis (1794-1887). 1810-28. (MSS. EUR. E. 286.)

Four letters of Sir Thomas Stamford Raffles, and reports by Daniel Ainslee and William Wardenaar, on the trade mission from Java to Japan in 1813. (MSS. EUR. F. 33. Raffles Collection X, pp. 39-134. K. 241. See Lady Raffles, *Memoir of the life and public service of Sir Thomas Stamford Raffles . . .* (1830), and D. C. Boulger, *Life of Sir Stamford Raffles* (1897), pp. 177-81.)

Four Chinese and Latin dictionaries, written in the same handwriting. None of the four volumes is dated, but the third bears the entry 'Received from the Chairman's Room, 27 August 1813'.

'Chinese dictionary. Chinese and Latin.' 524, 145 pp. (MSS. EUR. C. 25. K. 253.)

'Chinese–Latin Dictionary MS.' 909 pp. (MSS. EUR. C. 26. K. 254.)

'Dictionary. Latin and Chinese.' 984 pp. (MSS. EUR. C. 27. K. 255.)

'Chinese Dictionary. Latin and Chinese.' 984 pp. (MSS. EUR. C. 28. K. 256. Identical with C. 27 above, but the Chinese appears to be by different scribes.)

'A narrative of Occurrences and Remarks made on board his Majesty's late ship "Alceste" by Captain Murray Maxwell, C.B., when employed in conducting the Embassy to and from China in the years 1816 and 1817.' ii, 271 pp. (MSS. EUR. A. 8. K. 286.)

AMHERST COLLECTION. Correspondence and papers, c. 1789–1835 of William Pitt, 1st Earl Amherst (1773–1857). Including a few papers relating to his Embassy to Peking, 1816–17. (MSS. EUR. F. 140.)

Letter of J. B. Urmston, James Molony, and William Fraser in Canton, dated 29 December 1820, to the Court of Directors. Also letter of J. B. Urmston, dated 14 December 1820, to the Secretary, East India House, enclosing two copies in Chinese of the will of the late Emperor Kia King, and a translation by Dr. Morison. (MSS. EUR. D. 134. K. 365.)

MOORCROFT MSS. Papers of William Moorcroft (1765?–1825), relating mainly to the period 1820–5 when, as Superintendent of the Company's stud in Bengal, he travelled to Bukhara to obtain stallions. He planned to go to Bukhara by way of Yarkand, but after reaching Leh had to abandon that route and go via Peshawar, Kabul, and Bamiyan. He reached Bukhara early in 1825 and died on the return journey. The collection consists of journals, correspondence, &c. and includes some papers of George Trebeck, Moorcroft's general assistant on the expedition. See H. H. Wilson, *Travels in the Himalayan provinces of Hindustan and the Panjab, in Peshawar, Kabul, Kunduz and Bokhara, by Mr William Moorcroft and Mr George Trebeck from 1819 to 1825.* 2 vols. London, 1841. (EUR. A. 20–1, B. 50–1, C. 39–43, D. 236–69, E. 5, E. 113, F. 35–41, G. 27–31. K. 307–64.)

['Bokhara and return from Bokhara.'] Contains notes, two letters, and journal. (MSS. EUR. D. 254.)

Copies, made by Charles Trebeck, of various routes, including, 'Leh to Yarkand'; 'roads by which the commerce of Russia with Toorkistan and the western Provinces of the Chinese Empire is chiefly carried on.' (MSS. EUR. C. 42.)

'Routes obtained at Koondooz'. Copies made by Charles Trebeck in 1834. The routes include, 'From Fuezabad to Yarkund', 'From Bokhara to Astrakan'. (MSS. EUR. C. 43.)

Copy of letter to C. T. Metcalfe, on the way of approach to Chinese Tartary, &c. [1820.] (MSS. EUR. D. 257, pp. 39–41.)

Copy of letter to George Swinton, on the Chinese and Kashgar. 18 April 1821. Incomplete. (MSS. EUR. D. 262, pp. 27–34.)

Continuation of above letter to George Swinton, on the trade from Russia and from China to Ladakh, &c. (MSS. EUR. D. 263, ff. 8–56.)

'8th Fasciculus of a Journal from the 17th August to 16 September [1820] and from Ritanka ke Joth in Koolloo to Toongloong in hither Tartary. William Moorcroft.' 92 pp. (MSS. EUR. D. 243.)

'Detail Book.' This gives daily expenses for the period 1 October 1820–31 December 1821, and contains also some special accounts, including 'Translation of Meer Izzut Ooolah's account of his journey to Yarkund'. (MSS. EUR. 268.)

'Detail Book 1st January 1822 to 29th April 1823.' Daily expenses, and also special accounts, including 'Luteef's expenses to Yarkund and return', and 'Hajee's expenses to Yarkund and return.' (MSS. EUR. D. 269.)

Diaries of Mary Wimberley, 1825–37, including an account of a voyage made in the company of her husband to Java and Macao. (Photo. EUR. 72.)

Letter, dated 19 May 1827, from Benjamin Guy Babington (1794–1866), with an extract from the *Pekin Gazette* concerning destruction of Chinese troops near Kashgar. Also 'A facsimile and translation of a Chinese map of the seat of war in Western Tartary Novr 28, 1828'. 5 ff. Printed. (MSS. EUR. D. 638.)

Catalogue of the drawings made in China by W. Alexander during E. McArtnay's [*sic*] Embassy. 1830. (MSS. EUR. D. 562/13.)

Correspondence dating from 1840–41, relating to the military operations at Canton, main correspondents including Sir Jasper Nicholls, 1778–1849, C.-in-C. Bengal 1839–43, Lord Auckland, 1784–1849, Governor-General from 1836 to 1841 and Sir Hugh Gough, C.-in-C. of British troops in China who captured the Canton forts in 1841. (MSS. EUR. D. 643.)

Extracts from a memorandum by Captain Thomas Townsend Pears (1809–42), commanding engineer in the China War (1840–2), relating to the advance of an expeditionary force up the river Peiho to attack Peking. (MSS. EUR. D. 648.)

Two letters of J. J. Walker at the British Consulate, Fuh chow, to Sir George Staunton, M.P., dated 10 May and 9 July 1847. Also printed questionnaire headed 'Hints for queries to be suggested to the Residents at the five ports open to British commerce, and at the British colony of Hong Kong', with Walker's replies. This was read to the Royal Asiatic Society at meetings on 18 March and 1 April 1848. (MSS. EUR. F. 18/11. J. 832.)

Official file originally in possession of the British Consulate at Canton, concerning disputes over tariff payments to the Chinese, compensation claims by merchants, and the location and construction of a British settlement at Canton. 1851. (MSS. EUR. D. 754.)

HALIFAX COLLECTION. Papers of Sir Charles Wood, 1st Viscount Halifax (1800–5), as President of the Board of Control, 1852–5, and as Secretary of State for India, 1859–66. (MSS. EUR. F. 78.) Including:

India Board Papers. India. No. 39. China Expedition.

Copies of letters written by Franklin Richardson Kendall (1839–1907) of the Peninsular and Oriental Steam Navigation Company to his mother in England, including some which tell of his life and work in Hong Kong and elsewhere. Xerox copy. (Photo. EUR. 60.)

Documents relating to the estate of Thomas Charles Pattle of Canton. c. 1865. (MSS. EUR. F. 117/VI.)

Letter from J. I. Murray at Hong Kong. 1866. (MSS. EUR. D. 580.)

Microfilms of Memoirs of James Molony written in 1871. Molony (b. 1785) was appointed as a writer to China in May 1802; he eventually became second member of the Select Committee in Canton, and retired in 1822. (Reel no. 682. Original in the possession of Lady Longley.)

Catalogue of Chinese books presented to the India Office Library by the Royal Society in 1876, by Professor H. A. Giles. (MSS. EUR. D. 451.)

CURZON PAPERS. Papers of George Nathaniel Curzon, Marquis Curzon of Kedleston (1859–1925). He travelled extensively in the Middle and Far East, U.S.A., &c. mainly between 1887 and 1894; was Under-Secretary India Office, 1891–2, Parliamentary Under-Secretary Foreign Affairs, 1895–8, Governor-General and Viceroy of India, 1899–1905, Lord Privy Seal, 1915, member of the Inner War Cabinet, 1916–18, Foreign Secretary, 1919–23. Author of *Russia in Central Asia in 1889 and the Anglo-Russian question* (1889), *Persia and the Persian Question* (1892), and *Problems of the Far East* (1894) &c. 1882–1925. (MSS. EUR. F. 111.)

Section I. Papers previous to his appointment as Governor-General 1882–98.

1–14. Correspondence.

18. Various essays, including: 'Strange cities in the Far East, (i) Seoul in Korea', and 'Destinies of the Far East'.

20. A paper on British and Russian commercial competition in Central Asia, read by Curzon before the British Association in September 1889, and notes for a lecture on Central Asia delivered by Curzon in the same year.

Papers concerning Curzon's books, including manuscripts and copies of the books.

26. Manuscript of *Russia in Central Asia in 1889 and the Anglo-Russian Question.*

27. Copy of *Russia in Central Asia.*

28. Papers on Central Asia up to 1890, including correspondence about *Russia in Central Asia . . .* c. 1880–90.

34. Manuscript of *Problems of the Far East.* 1894.

35. Manuscript of additions to *Problems of the Far East*, for a new edition published by Constable in 1895. c. 1895.

36. Annotated copy of *Problems of the Far East.* 1894.

37. Notebook and notes used for *Problems of the Far East*, with correspondence about the book. 1893–8.

39. Manuscript of a monograph on the Pamirs published by Stanford for the Royal Geographical Society in 1896. c. 1896.

40. Notes for the final monograph on the Pamirs in 1896. c. 1896.

41–2. Two copies of *The Pamirs and the Source of the Oxus.* 1899.

43. Two notebooks of notes and jottings. c. 1890–9.

44–5. Envelopes containing bibliographical notes. c. 1890–9.

Papers relating to Curzon's travels

72. Correspondence, news-cuttings, and notes about Japan, Japanese customs, and trade. 1895–7.

73. Photographs of Japan and Korea. c. 1900.

74. Correspondence, periodicals, official papers, notes, news-cuttings, &c. relating to Korea. 1894–1904.

75. Printed official correspondence relating to Korea, China, and Japan. 1896–7.

76. Printed official correspondence relating to China and Japan. 1895–8.

77. News-cuttings relating mainly to China. c. 1894–1901.

78–80. Printed official correspondence relating to China. 1882–98.

81. Notes, news-cuttings, printed papers, and correspondence relating mainly to Burma and China. 1882–98.

89. Correspondence concerning Yunnan. 1894–6.

90. Printed official correspondence, news-cuttings, and notes about the Yunnan Railway. 1895–1909.

92. Printed Government reports, papers, and telegrams relating to the Far East. 1892–8.

93. Miscellaneous correspondence and notes on the Far East. 1895–8.

94. Envelope containing news-cuttings entitled 'Problems of the Far East. Yellow Peril'.

95. Maps of the Far East, and notes by Curzon. c. 1898.

96. Envelope containing bibliographical notes on the Far East.

97. Journals and pamphlets containing articles on the Far East. 1887–98.

98. Two pocket books and a bundle of correspondence relating to Curzon's journey to the Pamirs. 1893–4.

99. Notebook containing notes on Curzon's travels on the Indian frontier, the Pamirs, and Afghanistan. 1894.

Papers concerning frontiers

114. Printed official correspondence respecting Central Asia 'made for me in F.O. in 1898'. 1873–88.

115. Printed official correspondence respecting Central Asia 'made for me by F.O. in 1898'. 1871–98.

116. 'Letters on Central Asia and on my book on the Indian frontier.'

125. Scrapbook of news-cuttings and notes relating to Afghanistan, the Indian frontier, Russian policy in Central Asia, and Afghanistan, Persia, and Arabia.

Section II. Papers as Governor-General and Viceroy. 1899–1905

135–217. Demi-official correspondence. MS., typescript, and print.

218–38. Private correspondence while Viceroy.

Foreign and frontier policy

388. Military report on Russian Turkestan or Central Asia. 1905.

392. Three parts of a set of four of a map of Turkestan and the countries between the British and Russian dominions in Asia. c. 1883.

394. News-cuttings about Russia in Central Asia, and a report by a secret agent on his journey in Central Asia. 1905.

395. Foreign Department notes on railway construction in China; printed correspondence about railways in China, with maps; remarks on the navigation of the Upper Yangtse Kiang; and a note on

railway extension from Burma into Yunnan, &c. 1903–17.

396. Foreign Department. Secret E. Proceedings about communications between Burma and China. March 1905.

397. Maps of Manchuria, Burma, Siam, Japan, with notes on archaeological remains and ancient monuments, and other papers. c. 1895–1906.

398. Scrapbook of news-cuttings about the Far East, &c. Vol. ii. 1898–1917.

399. Folder entitled 'Foreign Affairs', containing copies of official papers. 1898–1905.

Section IV. Printed volumes

536–9. Summary of Lord Curzon's Administration: Foreign Department. Vol. v. Burma–Siam, Burma–China, Shan States, Chin-Lushai, and Naga Hills, &c.

688. Russia in Asia, Persia, Turkey in Asia, and North China: summary of principal events during the year 1898. 1898.

689. Russia in Asia, Persia, Turkey in Asia, and North China: summary of principal events during the year 1899. 1899.

696. Summary of principal events in Afghanistan, Chinese Turkestan, the Hindu Kush Border, Russia in Asia, Northern China, Persia, and Turkey in Asia during 1900. 1900.

697. Summary of principal events in Afghanistan, Chinese Turkestan, the Hindu Kush Border, Russia in Asia, Northern China, Persia, and Turkey in Asia during 1901 and 1902.

698. Distribution of the Russian military forces in Asia (correct to 1 June 1902).

699. Russian advances in Asia. No. V. 1882–4.

700. Russian advances in Asia. No. VII. 1890–5.

SIR GEORGE WHITE MSS.

Papers of General Sir George Stuart White (1835–1912), who served in India from c. 1858–98, taking part in the conquest of Burma in 1885 and later in the pacification of Upper Burma. (MSS. EUR. F. 108.) Including:

Letter from Sir Charles Bernard, Chief Commissioner of Upper Burma, to Gen. White, forwarding copy of a memorandum on the convention between India and China (with map of the frontier). 5 November 1886. (ID/1–3.)

Memorandum on the Burmo-Chinese frontier. Unsigned. c. 1886. (ID/4.)

Map of Chinese frontier. c. 1886. (ID/5.)

Copy of speech of Sir Richard Temple in the House of Commons on the opium trade with China. 3 May 1889. (MSS. EUR. F. 86, N. 283. Temple Collection.

ERSKINE PAPERS. Papers of W. E. Erskine (1773–1852), Orientalist. (K. 290–304. J. 814–19.) Including:

Extracts from various works on Armenians, Parsis, Tartars, Turks, &c. (MSS. EUR. C. 10. pp. 441–70.)

One of Erskine's notebooks, containing (p. 47) Tartar letters and writing; (p. 53) Stick-law of China and Tartary; (p. 63) Tartar and Persian offices. (MSS. EUR. B. 4.)

Glossary of Turki words. (MSS. EUR. A. 4.)

'Oriental Chronology and Geography MS., Erskine.' This notebook includes two accounts of Bokhara, notes on Turkestan, and 'Travels of Syed Izzet-Ulla from Attok to Kashmir, to Tibet, to Yarkand, to Kashgar, to the Capital of China, from Kashgar to Quqan, to Samarkand, to Bokhara, to Balkh . . .' 5 August 1812–16 December 1813. (MSS. EUR. D. 28.)

Chinese–Latin dictionary. The signature of Sir William Jones appears at the end of the volume. (MSS. EUR. C. 119.)

Old East India Company Library catalogues, compiled in the nineteenth century. (MSS. EUR. D. 562.) Including:

'Catalogue of the drawings made in China by W. Alexander, during E. McArtnay's Embassy' (1830). (No. 13.)

'Rough lists of the Chinese books sent for the Honble. Company on the *Earl Camden*. Also on the *Royal George*, 2 Sept. 1806.' (No. 14.)

'Chinese Catalogue.' (No. 15.)

papers of Andrew Parke Hume (1904–65), I.C.S. 1927–47, comprising weekly letters home to his parents in Norfolk, diaries, tour diaries and newspaper cuttings, including material on Japan and the Second World War. (MSS. EUR. D. 724.)

Fourteen letters from Sir Mark Aurel Stein to Mr. and Mrs. E. J. H. Mackay. July 1928–November 1937. (MSS. EUR. D. 526.)

Diaries of Sir (Alexander) Frederick Whyte (1883–1970), President of the Legislative Assembly of India 1920–5 and Political Adviser to the National Government of China 1929–32. Two of the five volumes describe a visit to China, Japan, Korea, and Manchuria as an independent political observer, June–October 1934. (MSS. EUR. D. 761.)

Papers of the Royal Institute of International Affairs, Shanghai Study Group. (In the Anderson papers, MSS. EUR. D. 806.)

BELL COLLECTION

Papers of Sir Charles Bell (1878–1945), who worked in the I.C.S. from 1889 to 1918. He was an intimate friend of the Dalai Lama and visited Tibet in 1920 and 1933. He also travelled in Mongolia, Siberia, Manchuria, and China. Part of the collection is official and remains closed until the open period for all the papers is reached. (MSS. EUR. F. 80.)

5a 106. Translation of news from a Chinese newspaper. 1934. (1 f.)

5g 1. Papers regarding Mongolia (43 ff.), including: newspaper cuttings, 1936; correspondence with Mr. Wangyal; 1st and 2nd numbers of the Mongol newspaper 'Batahalog'; note by Capt. R. Scott on Inner Mongolia, March 1937; letter from Owen Lattimore concerning Dr. Wang, 14 May 1937.

5g 2. Papers regarding Manchuria (72 ff.) These include newspaper cuttings and also eight typed and duplicated reports by Charles Bishop Kinney, at the head office of the South Manchuria Railway Company at Dairen, on various aspects of the Manchurian situation, 1935–8.

5g 4. Treaties:
   1. Soviet-Mongolia Treaty. November 1921.
   2. Soviet-Peking Treaty. May 1924.
   3. Soviet-Mukden Treaty. September 1924.
   4. Soviet-Japan Treaty. January 1925.

5i 9. This includes:
   Peking convention, 1906.
   Anglo-Russian agreement, 1907.

5i 17. China notebook, written by Bell.

5i 21. Twenty-nine maps, including Manchuria, Mongolia, the Siberian Railway, &c.

Unpublished introduction by Dr. F. W. Thomas to his *Tibetan literary texts and documents concerning Chinese Turkestan.* (3 vols., publ. Royal Asiatic Society 1935, 1951, 1955.) (MSS. EUR. C. 163.)

Typescript account of the evacuation of Rangoon by the Chartered Bank of India at the end of February 1942, after the invasion of Burma by the Japanese. 6 ff. (MSS. EUR. D. 750.)

Undated MSS.

Outline of a catalogue of Buddhist (Chinese) books, by S. Beal. (MSS. EUR. D. 453.)

Chinese–Latin Dictionary. Also 'Explication des Clefs Chinoises'. (MSS. EUR. D. 494.)

Chinese–Latin Dictionary. (MSS. EUR. C. 118.)

Manchu–Tartar and Latin dictionary. (Royal Society collection.) (MSS. EUR. C. 100.)

'South of the mists', unpublished account of the history of Yunnan by Stanley Wyatt-Smith of the Chinese Consular Service 1907–45. (MSS. EUR. D. 796.)

The following collections may contain relevant material:

ADAM COLLECTION. Papers, dated 1795–1825, of John Adam, Member of the Governor-General's Council 1819–23 and Acting Governor-General 1823. (MSS. EUR. F. 109.)

AMPTHILL COLLECTION. Papers of Arthur Oliver Villiers Russell, 2nd Baron Ampthill (1869–1935), as Governor of Madras, December 1900–April 1904, and December 1904–February 1906, and *ad interim* Viceroy and Governor-General of India, April–December 1904. 36 vols. of files of MSS. and 47 vols. of printed works. (MSS. EUR. E. 233.)

ARGYLL PAPERS. Microfilms of the papers of George Douglas Campbell, 8th Duke of Argyll (1823–1900), Secretary of State for India, 1868–74. *c.* 1866–75. (Reels nos. 311–25. Originals in the possession of the Duke of Argyll.)

BAILEY COLLECTION. Papers, dated 1890–1965, of Lieutenant-Colonel Frederick Marshman Bailey (1882–1967), Indian Army 1900–38, Indian Political Service 1906–38. He accompanied Younghusband on the mission to Lhasa, 1903–4, and mapped large areas of the borderlands between Tibet, China, and India during the years 1905–9. (MSS. EUR. F. 157.)

CLIVE COLLECTION. Papers of Robert, Lord Clive (1725–74), President and Governor of Fort William in Bengal, 1757–60, and 1764–6, and of his son Edward Clive, 1st Baron Powis (1754–1839), Governor of Madras, 1798–1803. 95 boxes and an index. (MSS. EUR. G. 37.)

CROSS COLLECTION. Correspondence of Richard Assheton Cross, 1st Viscount Cross (1823–1914), as Secretary of State for India, 1886–92. 57 vols. (MSS. EUR. E. 243.)

DUFFERIN AND AVA PAPERS. Microfilms of the papers of Federick Temple Hamilton-Temple Blackwood, 1st Marquis of Dufferin and Ava (1826–1902) as Viceroy and Governor General of India, 1884–8. (Reels nos. 490–535. Originals in the possession of the Marchioness of Dufferin and Ava. The rest of the collection is in the Public Record Office of Northern Ireland.)

ELGIN COLLECTION. I. Papers of James Bruce, 8th Earl of Elgin (1811–63), as Viceroy and Governor-General of India, 1862–3. (MSS. EUR. F. 83.) II. Papers of Victor Alexander Bruce, 9th Earl of Elgin (1849–1917) as Viceroy and Governor General of India, 1894–9. (MSS. EUR. F. 84.)

FITZROY COLLECTION. Papers of Yvonne Alice Gertrude FitzRoy (1891–1971) as Private Secretary 1921–5 to Alice, Marchioness of Reading, Vicereine of India. 1921–39.

FOWLER PAPERS. Papers of H. H. Fowler, later Viscount Wolverhampton (1830–1911), as Secretary of State for India, 1894–5. (MSS. EUR. C. 145.)

HAMILTON COLLECTION. Correspondence of Lord George Francis Hamilton (1845–1927), as Secretary of State for India, 1895–1903. MS., typescript, and print. (MSS. EUR. D. 508–10 and C. 125–6.) Including (no. 44): letters to Hamilton with related papers, all concerning China. December 1900–October 1901.

LANSDOWNE PAPERS. Papers of the Marquis of Lansdowne (1845–1927), as Viceroy and Governor-General of India, 1888–94. (MSS. EUR. D. 558.)

LINLITHGOW COLLECTION. Correspondence and papers of Victor Alexander John Hope, 2nd Marquess of Linlithgow (1887–1952), as Governor-General of India 1936–43. (MSS. EUR. F. 125.)

LYTTON PAPERS. Papers of Edward Robert Bullwer Lytton, 1st Earl of Lytton (1831–91), Viceroy and Governor-General of India, 1876–80. *c.* 1876–91. (MSS. EUR. E. 218.)

MORLEY PAPERS. Papers of John, 1st Viscount Morley of Blackburn, as Secretary of State for India, 1905–10, and March to May 1911. (MSS. EUR. D. 573.) Including: 'Thibet & Russia. Ld Curzon's views.' 1906–7. (43c, f. 81.) See Molly C. Poulter, *A catalogue of the Morley collection*, 1965.

NAPIER OF MAGDALA COLLECTION. Correspondence and papers of Robert Cornelis, 1st Baron Napier of Magdalen and Caryngton (1810–90) as Commander-in-Chief of the Bombay Army, 1865–8; as Commander-in-Chief, India, 1870–6; and as Governor of Gibraltar, 1876–82. (MSS. EUR. F. 114.)

NORTHBROOK COLLECTION. Correspondence relating to Indian affairs of Thomas George Baring, 1st Earl of Northbrook (1826–1904) Under-Secretary of State for India, 1859–61 and 1861–4, Viceroy and Governor-General of India, 1872–6. 6 vols. MSS.; 17 vols. printed. (MSS. EUR. C. 144.)

REID PAPERS. Papers of Sir Robert Neil Reid (1883–1964), Member of the Executive Council of Bengal 1934–7, Acting Governor of Bengal 1938–9, and Governor of Assam 1937–42. 1918–63. (MSS. EUR. E. 278.)

WHITE PAPERS. Papers of Sir Herbert Thirkell White (1855–1931), Lieut.-Governor of Burma, 1905–10. *c.* 1886–1910. (MSS. EUR. E. 254.)

INDIA OFFICE RECORDS

Foreign and Commonwealth Office, 197 Blackfriars Road, London, SE1 8NG

The East India Company's first Far Eastern factory was established at Hirado in Japan in 1613. From there factors were sent to Nagasaki, the Ōsaka-Kyōto area, and to Edo, and voyages were made to Tsushima, the Ryūkyū Islands, Vietnam, Cambodia, and Thailand; but the Japanese factory was not successful and it was closed in 1623. The first attempts to trade with China were similarly abortive and it was only towards the end of the seventeenth century that a regular commerce was established. Failing to set up an agency at Chusan, the Company had to be content with Canton, where trade developed at first through the offices of a Chinese official and then, from the 1750s, through a permanent factory. With the Charter Act of 1833 the Company lost its trading monopoly, but an agency was maintained until 1840.

Exploration in Chinese Turkestan and political interest in the area began in the early nineteenth century. In 1893 the Government of India appointed an Agent at Kashgar designated 'Special Assistant for Chinese Affairs to the Resident at Kashmir', while on the North-Eastern Frontier of British India there was a continuing interest in Yunnan affairs. [The Records also contain documents on the Japanese occupation of Burma during the Second World War (India Office Library and Records, *Report . . . 1971*, pp. 72–8).]

The India Office Records comprise the records of (*a*) the East India Company, 1600–1858; (*b*) the Board of Control, 1784–1858; (*c*) the India Office, 1858–1947; and (*d*) [not used for this Guide] the Burma Office, 1937–48. A 'Summary of archive categories' is given as an Appendix to *India Office Records, Report for the years 1947–1967*. Accruals since then are shown in a joint annual report with the Library.

A useful introduction to the Records will be found in the following: William Foster, *A guide to the India Office Records 1600–1858* (1919);[1] Joan C. Lancaster, *A guide to lists and catalogues of the India Office Records* (1966). The following press lists were printed: *List of General Records 1599—1879* (1902); *List of Marine Records* (1896); *List of Factory Records* (1897); *List of Proceedings, Consultations, etc., Bengal 1704–1858* (1899); *List of Proceedings, etc., Bengal 1859–1897* (1899); *List of Proceedings, etc., Bombay 1702–1900* (1902); *List of Proceedings, etc., Madras 1702–1900* (1904); *List of Proceedings, etc., North-Western Provinces and other Minor Administrations 1834–1899* (1902); *List of Proceedings, etc., India 1834–1858* (1900); *List of Proceedings, etc., India 1859–1898* (1900); *Chronological list of Parliamentary Papers relating to the East Indies 1801–1907* (1909); *List of Parliamentary Collections* (1913); mimeographed lists of other series were prepared. It should, however, be noted that most of the printed and mimeographed lists are being superseded, as an over-all archival referencing scheme for the Records proceeds. They will be replaced by a general guide

to the whole archive and detailed guides to each archival category. These, now in active preparation, include the following: S. J. McNally, A guide to the records of the Accountant General's Department; M. I. Moir, A guide to the records of the Political and Secret Department; A. J. Farrington, A guide to the records of the Military Department. There is also a detailed *Catalogue of the Home Miscellaneous Series* compiled by S. C. Hill (1927), six volumes of transcripts of the *Original Correspondence* series 1602–17 (1896–1902), and eleven volumes of calendars of the *Court Minutes* 1635–79 (1907–38), while the last two series are also calendared in the five volumes of *State Papers, Colonial, East Indies* covering 1513–1634 (1862–92).

The material listed below gives a representative if incomplete picture of the documents available relating to the Far East. Further relevant papers which are not picked out in the various lists and indexes will be found embedded in the more general series, necessitating much detailed research. The most fruitful place to begin any such research would be in the Secret and Foreign series of the Proceedings of the Bengal Presidency and of the Government of India, and in the correspondence volumes and files of the India Office Political and Secret Department.

ORIGINAL CORRESPONDENCE. *E/3/1–83*. 'Collection of original correspondence from India with collateral documents originating at any places between England and Japan', 1602–1709. This series contains material relating to China and Japan. Transcripts of all the items to the end of 1617 have been published as *Letters received by the East India Company from its servants in the East*, ed. William Foster (6 vols., 1896–1902). A catalogue of the Original Correspondence will be found in vols. 711–12 of the Home Miscellaneous series. A complete edition of documents on 'The English factory in Japan', drawn mainly from this series, is currently being prepared by A. J. Farrington and S. Iwao.

DESPATCH BOOKS. *E/3/84–111*. Copies of letters from the Company to its settlements in India and other places in the East, including China, 1626–1753.

DRAFTS OF DESPATCHES. *E/3/112–21*. 'Despatches to all Presidencies', 1703–53. This series of original drafts duplicates, to a certain extent, the latter portion of the preceeding collection.

FACTORY RECORDS: China and Japan. *G/12/1–291 Vols.*

1–10. Materials for a history of relations with China and Japan, 1596–1725 (the 1705–11 volume is missing).

[1] Joan C. Lancaster, 'The India Office Records' (*Archives* (British Records Association), ix (43) (1970), 130–41).

11–12.   Memoir on intercourse with China, 1518–1832 (in duplicate).

13.   Early papers on China, Japan, &c., 1623–99.

14.   Attempts to trade at Chusan, 1699–1759.

15.   Letter book of Richard Wickham in Japan and at Bantam, 1614–17.

16.   Consultations, letters, &c., China and Japan, including Weddell's China voyage of 1637, 1614–1703.

17.   Tonquin and Cochin China, 1672–97.

18.   China and Cochin China: miscellaneous papers, 1753–78.

19.   Miscellaneous correspondence, 1768–97.

20.   Miscellaneous documents, 1782–1815.

21–55.   China Supercargoes' Ship Diaries, 1721–42, 1745–7, 1749–51.

56–89.   Canton Diaries and Consultations, 1751, 1753, 1755–88, including Letter-books for 1776 and 1779.

90.   Col. Cathcart's Embassy to China, 1787–9.

91–3.   Lord Macartney's Embassy, 1787–1810.

94–194.   Canton Diaries and Consultations, 1788–1815.

195.   China and Japan: miscellaneous, 1710–1814.

196–8.   Lord Amherst's Embassy, 1815–17.

199–257.   Canton Diaries and Consultations, including Commercial Consultations for 1832–4 and Financial Consultations for 1834, 1815–34.

258–63.   Canton Agency Consultations, 1834–40.

264.   Superintending Committee's Consultations, 1792–4.

265–77.   China Secret Committee's Consultations, 1793, 1796–1832.

277A.   Abstracts of China Public Consultations, 1831–3, and of Factory Consultations, 1833–5.

278–83.   Letters received from China, 1823–34.

284–7.   Secret Letters received from China, 1821–7, 1830–2.

288–90.   Despatches to China, 1829–32.

291.   Secret Commercial Drafts to China, 1813–32.

FACTORY RECORDS: Miscellaneous. *G/40/1–24*, including:

1. Abstracts of letters received from various factories (including Japan), 1617–32.

8. Copies of letters, consultations, &c. regarding various factories (including Japan), 1608–24.

HOME MISCELLANEOUS. *H/1–860.*

Transcripts sent home for the use of the Company's historiographer, John Bruce (vols. 456a–456e). Including:

1. 'Japan Voyage', journal of the ship *Return* during its stay in Nagasaki, 29 June–28 August 1673 (vol. 456a, pp. 369–422). This journal has been printed as an appendix in vol. ii of J. G. Scheuchzer's translation (1728) of Kaempfer's *Japan*; also in the edition of Kaempfer published by Maclehose in 1906.

2. Bruce's letter-book (vol. 456e, pp. 1–372). Including:

(*a*) Emperor of China to the King, 21 December 1805 (pp. 278–82).

(*b*) His Majesty to the Emperor of China (pp. 288–94).

(*c*) President of the Board of Control to the Viceroy of Canton, March 1811 (pp. 296–304).

'A list of 52 English ships that sailed for E. Indies & China since the 10th Feb. 1698 [up to 25 April 1699]' (vol. 44, pp. 799–801, 804).

Papers of John Scattergood (1681–1723), merchant. These include material on trade with China, where he went on eight voyages between 1711 and 1722 (vols. 821–823a, including index vol.).

Captain William Fernell of the *Valentine* to the Court, recommending that the new passage from Batavia to Canton and back, discovered by Captain Wilson of the *Pitt*, should for political reasons not be used, 12 April 1760 (vol. 95, p. 683).

Correspondence, reports, &c. of George Bogle and Lieutenant Samuel Turner, relating to Assam, Bhutan, China, Nepal, and Tibet, 16 March 1768–2 March 1784 (vol. 219, pp. 325–522). *See* C. R. Markham, *Narratives of the mission of George Bogle to Tibet* (1786).

Advices from Canton: French force in the East, 20 November 1769 (vol. 102, pp. 111–12).

Memorandum relative to remittances to China, &c. (vol. 795, pp. 30–3).

Narrative of the remittances from Bengal to China, 1770–86 (vol. 795, pp. 65–72).

Extract from Court's letter to Bengal relative to China remittances (vol. 795, pp. 92–6).

Intelligence from Canton: arrival of Austrian ships, 21 December 1778 (vol. 143, p. 181).

Dutch Company's orders to Batavia for tea, silk, &c. from China, 20 November 1780 (vol. 149, pp. 399–405).

Case as to, and opinions of J. Wallace, Solicitor, General, and George Rous on the Company's action in seizing George Smith at Canton and sending him home, 3 and 8 January 1780 (vol. 411, pp. 55–79).

Capture at Macao of a vessel belonging to Baptiste Basilion, an Armenian, and Wandy Metree, a Greek, formerly merchants at Madras, by Captain John Taylor on 9 September 1780 (vol. 155, pp. 1–12).

Advices from Canton: debts of Chinese merchants, 29 October 1780 (vol. 155, p. 15).

Correspondence between Admiral Sir Edward Hughes and the Madras Council: convoy of Company's ships to China, 26–7 May 1780 (vol. 168, pp. 527–31).

Letters of Admiral Hughes to the Viceroy and Hoppo at Canton, with their reply: claims of Andrew Ross and other British merchants against Chinese merchants at Canton (vol. 168, pp. 535–70).

List of papers presented to Lord Hillsborough from Madras, Bombay and China, February 1781 (vol. 148, pp. 273–7).

Correspondence with the Marquis of Cordon regarding certain packets for the King of Sardinia transmitted by a missionary in Peking to Matthew Raper, 6–30 October 1781 (vol. 155, pp. 81–2, 433–7).

List of papers sent to Lord Hillsborough from Bengal, Madras, Canton, and St. Helena, 31 October 1781 (vol. 154, pp. 319–23).

Advices from Madras, including petitions from creditors of the Chinese merchants, &c., 9 January 1781 (vol. 154, pp. 575–664).

Papers concerning the Company's and private trade with India and the East Indies, including China, 1781–1809 (vols. 399–409).

Advices from Bengal: opium sent to China, &c., 9 February 1782 (vol. 163, pp. 393–402).

Draft of letter to Bengal submitted to Thomas Townshend, Secretary of State: ships taken up; Supracargoes at Canton; no prisoners to be sent to China, 23 December 1782 (vol. 164, pp. 363–72).

Draft of letter to Bombay submitted to Thomas Townshend: prohibition of private trade to Canton at Company's risk (vol. 169, p. 23).

Intelligence from St. Helena: naval and shipping news from the Cape, the Indies, and China, 17 May 1783 (vol. 175, pp. 629–31).

George Smith, Deputy Chairman, to Governor of Bombay: dispatch of French forces to China, 1 September 1783 (vol. 183, pp. 927–30).

William Perry, Naval Surgeon, to Bombay Council: complaint of ill usage at Macao by the Governor, Dom Francisco Xavier de Castro, 11 July 1783 (vol. 188, pp. 377–86).

Estimate of the prime cost of a China cargo purchased for the Company at Canton and sold in England at the prices of September and October 1784 (vol. 434, p. 145).

Papers regarding the trade in furs between the northwest coast of America and China and Japan, partly, apparently, by Alexander Dalrymple, 29 April 1785–23 February 1791 (vol. 494, pp. 359–457).

George Smith to Lord Cornwallis with plan for supplying the Treasury at Canton with money, 26 July 1787 (vol. 434, pp. 293–6).

'Historical sketch of the circumstances which led to the settlement of Penang and of the Trade to the Eastward previous to and since that period', 29 May 1795. This includes references to piracy, China trade, &c. (vol. 437, pp. 139–89).

Papers respecting the Portuguese settlements in India and China, 1799–1802 (vol. 60, pp. 353–571).

Papers relating to the impeachment of Warren Hastings (vol. 288), including:

1. Notes on the 7th, 10th, 11th, and 12th charges relating i.a. to the opium contract and opium sent to China, with printed copies (pp. 189–219).

2. Printed copies of Hastings's answers to charges 6, 7, 10, 11, 12 (pp. 221–8).

3. Appendix of papers in support of these charges (pp. 233–660, of which pp. 255–364 and 643–60 are printed).

'Selection of papers exhibiting a View of the East India Company's Commercial Concerns.' A series of tables giving statistics of trade to India and China and also details of Dutch, private, and coast trade, by R. Wissett (vol. 449, pp. 1–134).

Chops granted by the Hoppo of Whampoa to the Company's supercargoes (vol. 163, pp. 21–2).

Draft of circular letter to Ft. Marlborough submitted to Lord Shelburne: subjects include supercargoes at Canton (vol. 160, pp. 373–81).

Enclosures in Bengal Secret Letter of 30 November 1801, concerning protection against the French of Portuguese possessions in India and China (vol. 689, pp. 1–184).

'Papers respecting the supply of Tea and other Indian and China goods to the British Colonies on the Continent of North America and more particularly to the provinces of Upper and Lower Canada', c. 1802–24 (vol. 706, pp. 1–141).

Reference to Directors by the Bombay Government of a difference with the firms of Charles Forbes & Co. and Bruce Fawcett respecting the calculation of tonnage in the case of China ships, 6 August 1804 (vol. 333, pp. 605–60).

Plan for furnishing supplies for the provision of the China Investment without the exportation of bullion (vol. 340, pp. 359–67).

Correspondence concerning China hemp, June 1805 (vol. 375, pp. 673–87).

Memoirs dealing with the Portuguese settlements in

India and China, their occupation by British troops and the British expedition to Macao, 1807–9 (vol. 60, pp. 575–611).

Memorandum concerning the introduction of British troops into the Portuguese settlements in India and China (vol. 60, pp. 615–871).

FINANCIAL DEPARTMENT. *L/F*

L/F/6/811–22. Financial Papers: China Expedition, June 1900–December 1915.

MARINE RECORDS. *L/MAR*

Ships' Journals, 1605–1701. *L/MAR/A/*I–CLXXI. Including:

XIV. Journal kept by Captain John Saris on the *Clove* (8th Voyage), including a visit to Japan, 1611–13.

XXIII. Journal of the *Hoseander*, Captain Ralph Coppendale, from Pattani to Hirado and thence to Bantam, 1615–16.

XXIV. Journal kept by Edmund Sayers in the *Sea Adventure*, Captain William Adams, from Hirado to Thailand; accounts for presents and goods; journal of his return in a chartered junk, 1615–16.

XXVI. Journal kept by Edmund Sayers in William Adams's junk *Gift of God* from Hirado to Cochin China; rough cargo notes and accounts at Hirado; journal to the Ryūkyū Islands in a Chinese junk, William Adams pilot; notes of events at Hirado and Nagasaki, 1617–19.

XXXV. Journal kept by Edmund Sayers on the *Palsgrave* in the Japan Fleet of Defence and on the *Bull* from Hirado to Batavia, 1621–4.

LXIII. Portion of a journal [kept on the *Dragon*?] in Captain John Weddell's fleet (belonging to Courteen's Association) to Acheh, Macao, and Canton, and as far as Acheh on the return voyage, 1637–8.

LXVI. Journal kept by Richard Mathew in the *Hinde*, Captain William Broadbent, from Surat to Malacca and Macao and back, 1644–5.

LXXIV. Journal of the *Flying Eagle*, Captain John Shaw, from Bantam to Amoy and back, 1678–9.

LXXVIII. Journal of the *Carolina*, Captain John Harding, from England to Batavia, Macao, and other East Indian ports, 1682–3.

LXXX. Includes journal of the *Princess of Denmark*, Captain Joseph Haddock, from Madras to China and back, 1689–90.

XC. Journal of the *Defence*, Captain William Heath, from England to Madras, Macao and back, 1689–91.

CXVI. Journal of the *Fleet*, Captain John Merry, from England to Batavia and Amoy and back, 1698–1701.

CXXIII. Journal of the *Macclesfield*, Captain John Hurle, from England to China; with details of

transactions at Macao and Canton, kept by Robert Douglas, Supercargo, and his assistants, 1699–1700.

CXXXIII, CXXXIIIa. Journal of the *Rooke*, Captain George Simmonds, from England to several ports on the Malabar Coast, from Surat to Amoy and back, &c.; with ledger, 1699–1702.

CXXXIV. Journal of the *Dorrill*, Captain Samuel Hide, from England to Batavia and Amoy and back, 1699–1701.

CXXXVIII. Journal of the *Trumbal*, Captain Henry Duffield, from England to Borneo, several voyages between Borneo, Batavia, and China, and back from Borneo to England, kept by Richard Hooper (?), 1699–1702.

CXLIX, CXLIXa. Journal of the *Seaford*, Captain Martin Gardiner, from England to Batavia, Macao, Canton, &c. and back to England; with receipt book, 1700–2.

CLII, CLIIa. Journal of the *Rising Sun*, Captain Arthur Holford, from England to Batavia and Canton and back; with ledger, 1700–3.

CLVII, CLVIIa. Journal of the *Neptune*, Captain John Lesly, from England to Batavia and Amoy and back; with ledger, 1700–2.

CLX. Journal of the *Loyall Cook* from England to Batavia, Amoy and Madras and back, 1701–3.

Ships' Logs, 1702–1858. *L/MAR/B.* There are some 3,620 logs, of which a large number relate to voyages to China, including Canton, Whampoa, &c.

Marine Miscellaneous, 1600–1878. *L/MAR/C/1–900.* Including:

592. Steam communication with India and China: correspondence with Peninsular & Oriental Company, &c., 1839.

MILITARY DEPARTMENT. *L/MIL*

Compilations and Miscellaneous. *L/MIL/5*

Medal Rolls

67. China, 1842.

106–7. China, 1857–60.

Prize and Batta Rolls

262–72. China: Canton and Nanking Donation Batta, 1840–1.

Miscellaneous

489. Copy letters to India on various subjects: application of 1% commission on bullion from China; list of papers relating to intercourse with China; disposal of plate and furniture from Canton, 1827–35.

743. Proposed Anglo-Japanese intervention in Siberia, 1918.

1071. Far East Relief requirements, 1944.

Military Department Collections. *L/MIL*

17076–7. Anglo-Japanese alliance.

12272–85. Russo-Japanese War.

POLITICAL AND SECRET DEPARTMENT. *L/P&S*

Home Correspondence. *L/P&S/3*

Secret Home Correspondence, 1839–74. 82 vols. Including:

64. Central Asia, 1869.

Secret Correspondence with India. *L/P&S/5*

Enclosures to Secret Letters received from Bengal, 1784–1835. 46 vols. Including:

10a. Correspondence respecting the Portuguese settlements in India and China, 27 February 1802.

Secret Letters received from Bengal and India, Second Series, 1817–65. 19 vols. Including:

6. China, 3 April 1830–21 February 1832.

7. Portuguese authorities at Macao and affairs in China, 25 June–5 July 1832.

Secret Commercial Letters to India and China, 1 vol., 7 July 1815–10 April 1824.

Political and Secret Correspondence outside India. *L/P&S/9*

Secret Department China Correspondence, 10 vols., 1832–54.

1–4. China: Foreign Office instructions and correspondence, 1839–54.

5–6. China: Colonial Office instructions and correspondence, 1842–52.

7. China: Home correspondence, miscellaneous, 1832–41. Instructions to Lord Auckland, 1839–41.

8. China: Home correspondence, miscellaneous, 1842–3. Instructions to Lord Ellenborough, 1842–3.

9. China: Home correspondence, miscellaneous, 1844–54. Instructions to Lord Hardinge, 1844.

10. China: correspondence received from authorities in India, 1840–3.

Political and Secret Subject Files. *L/P&S/10*

The Subject Files, 1902–31, run parallel with other series which may contain further relevant material: Political and Secret Home Correspondence and Political and Secret Correspondence with India, 1902–11, supplemented, 1912–30, by a series of annual Files.

13. File 3379/1903 Pts. 1–3. China: railways, 1903–10.

16. 253/1904. Russian Central Asia: travellers, 1904–10.

54. 2342/1904. Central Asia: railways, 1904–7.

55. 2359/1904 Pts. 1–2. Chinese Turkestan, 1904–16.

72. 453/1905 Pts. 1–3. China, 1904–12.

137–9. 826/1908 Pts. 1–5. Tibet: trade, &c., 1907–16.

140. 932/1908 Pts. 1–3. Burma: Chinese officials, 1908–15.

145. 1638/1908 Pts. 1–2. China: travellers, 1909.

147–51. 2750/1908 Pts. 1–11. Tibet, including: Chinese Adhesion Convention; Chinese troops, 1904–13.

180–3. 1918/1910 Pts. 1–7. North-East Frontier, 1908–13.

186–7. 3658/1910 Pts. 1–5. Tibet: travellers, &c., 1906–12.

204–8. 51/1912 Pts. 1–9. Burma–China frontier, 1905–16.

218. 409/1912. Tibet: Trade Agency reports, 1912–25.

221–3. 505/1912 Pts. 1–7. Bhutan and Nepal, including: 1910 Treaty, Chinese interference, &c., 1904–16.

225. 539/1912. Mongolia, 1912–13.

241. 895–96/1912. Chinese revolution, situation at Kashgar, 1912.

265. 1349/1912. China and Tibet, 1912.

269. 1448/1912. Attitude of local authorities at Tengyueh, 1911–15.

276. 2342/1912. Burma–China frontier, 1912–13.

278–9. 2426/1912 Pts. 1–6. Northern Frontier, including: Hunza-China frontier, 1904–17.

282. 2597/1912. Burma–China frontier, 1912–13.

297. 3537/1912. Chinese Turkestan: revision of 1881 Treaty of St. Petersburg, 1910–24.

324. 4983/1912. China: miscellaneous prints, 1912.

330. 124/1913 Pts. 1–2. Chinese Turkestan, 1910–15.

331. 221/1913. Tibet: repatriation of Chinese, 1913.

337–8. 429/1913 Pts. 1–2. Burma–China frontier: annual meetings, 1912–27.

340–4. 464/1913 Pts. 1–6. Tibet: negotiations with China, 1913–16.

346–7. 591/1913 Pts. 1–2. China: railways, 1913–21.

352. 732/1913. North-East Frontier: Menilikrai post, 1913–19.

364–5. 1235/1913 Pts. 1–3. China: Mongolia situation; British commercial interests, 1913–16.

411. 3722/1913. Burma–China frontier, 1913–16.

431. 4922/1913. Anglo-Japanese alliance, 1911–21.

432–6. File 5062/1913 Pts. 1–6. Eastern Tibet affairs, 1913–19.

453. 2450/1914. Kashgar Consulate, 1914–25.

520. 4529/1914 Pts. 1–2. German War: German agents in China, 1914–19.

543. 544/1915 Pt. 2. German War: sedition in Far East—Germans in China, 1915–18.

545. 796/1915. Japanese policy in China, 1915.

553. 1875/1915 Pts. 1–2. German War: import of arms into Far East, 1915–16.

573. 4063/1915 Pts. 1–2. China: the Monarchy question, 1915–17.

578. 4830/1915. Japanese policy in the Far East, 1915–19.

627. 3839/1916 Pt. 2. China: Diplomatic and Consular expenditure, 1923–30.

654–5. 691/1917 Pts. 1–4. China: attitude towards German War; repatriation of enemy subjects, 1917–19.

721. 4377/1917 Pt. 1. The War: proposed mission to Russian Turkestan, 1917–21.

722. 4377/1917 Pts. 2–3. The War: mission to Kashgar—Lieutenant-Colonel F. M. Bailey, 1918–21.

741. 1735/1918. Central Asia: correspondence, 1917–20.

746. 2902/1918. Tibet: repatriation of Chinese soldiers, 1918–27.

825. 2273/1919. Kashgar monthly diaries, 1912–20.

873. 7139/1919. China: arms traffic, 1919–30.

878–9. 179/1920 Pts. 1–2. Burma–China frontier: disturbances; Namwam Triangle rent, 1919–31.

883–4. 876/1920 Pts. 1–3. Tibet: situation; Sino-Tibetan frontier, 1920–8.

949. 8512/1920. Chinese Turkestan: status and rights of British subjects, 1920–7.

950. 8926/1920 Pts. 1–3. Central Asia: Bokharan affairs, 1920–9.

976. 1743/1921. Kashgar diaries, 1921–30.

1011–14. 3971/1921 Pts. 1–10. Tibet: travellers, including Japanese, 1921–30.

1016. 4961/1921. China: Annual Reports, 1920–9.

1018. 5157/1921. Chinese Turkestan: travellers, 1921–9.

1032. 408/1922. Central Asia: travellers, 1922–32.

1092. 3504/1923. Japan: miscellaneous affairs, 1923–30.

1121–3. 3595/1924 Pts. 1–4. China: civil war, 1924–9.

1150. 1940/1925. Burma-China frontier, 1925–31.

1153. 3198/1925 Pt. 4. Northern Frontier: supply of arms to Sinkiang, 1928–32.

1156–8. 3936/1925 Pts. 1–3. China: Commission on Extra-territoriality, 1925–32.

1186. 3122/1926 Pts. 1–2. China: Tariff Conference, 1926–7.

1192. 3939/1926 Pt. 1. Revision of Aitchison's *Treaties*: Kashgar, Tibet, &c., 1926–31.

1197–1202. 1/1927 Pts. 1–19. China: situation; Yunnan affairs; war materials, &c., 1926–31.

1217–18. 3077/1927 Pts. 1–5. Chinese Turkestan: travellers, 1927–33.

1220. 3533/1927. China: proceedings of the Conference on the Chinese Customs Tariff, 1925–6.

1228. 5890/1927. Tibet: relations with China, 1927–32.

1283–4. 6413/1928 Pts. 1–3. North-East Frontier: delimitation of Burma-China frontier; Irrawaddy Triangle, 1928–32.

1296. 100/1929 Pt. 9. China: Shanghai Provisional Court, 1929–30.

1311. 333/1931 Pts. 1–2. China: extra-territoriality, 1931–2.

Political External Collections, c. 1930–47. *L/P&S/12.* Including:

2273–7. Collection 10—Central Asia.

2278–2330. Collection 11—China.

2331–2408. Collection 12—Chinese Turkestan.

2903–46. Collection 18—Japan.

Political and Secret Department Memoranda. *L/P&S/18*

The collection consists of post-1858 unpublished India Office memoranda, supplemented by some Foreign Office confidential prints. There is a printed list to 1899 with manuscript additions to 1947. Section 'B' contains material on the North-East Frontier, Tibet, China and Japan, and Chinese Central Asia is covered in sections 'A' and 'C'.

Political and Secret Department Library. *L/P&S/20*

The library consists mainly of post-1858 printed material, both published and unpublished, including Enclosures to Political and Secret Letters from India, &c., India Office memoranda, Foreign Office confidential prints, as well as standard reference works. Section 'D' contains material on the North-East Frontier, Tibet, China, Korea and Mongolia, and Chinese Central Asia is covered in section 'A'. There are also some miscellaneous East India Company records, including:

92. Papers relative to the affairs of China, 1839–41.

ECCLESIASTICAL RETURNS. *N*

N/9/1. Returns of baptisms, marriages, and burials of Europeans at Macao, 1820–33, and of burials at Whampoa, 1820–34.

PROCEEDINGS. *P*. Including:

Bengal Marine Board Proceedings: China Special Service, 9 January 1840–29 December 1842, with indexes (P/169/11–13, 25–7, 38–41).

Bengal Superintendent of Marine Proceedings: China Special Service, 3 January–14 August 1843, with index (P/169/57–9).

India Marine Proceedings: China, 1900–3, with index (P/6640).

India Military Proceedings: China, 1900–3 (P/6167, 6632).

CHINA RECORDS. *R/10*

This material was transferred to the India Office Records, through official channels, in 1931.

1. Extracts on trade with China, Japan, &c., 1623–83.
2. Extracts from Diaries and Consultations, 1727–40.
3. Diary and Consultations, 1741–55.
4. Diary and Consultations, 1755–60, with unconnected consultations, 1755–8.
5. Diaries, 1761–9.
6–8. Letter-books, 1763–9, 1769–75, 1775–9.
9. Diaries, 1771–7.
10–20. Consultations, 1779–92, except 1785–6 (vol. 17, 1788–9 has an index).
21. Index to Consultations, 1785–1803.

Select Committee's Secret Consultations

22. 1796–1800.
23. 1800–5.
24. 1806–9.
25. 1806–10.
26. 1811, 1813, 1816.
27. 1809–21.
28. 1819–29.
29. 1829–30.
30. 1831–4.
31. Index, 1799–1822.

32. Proceedings of the Secret Committee at Macao, 1808.

33–62. Court's Letters to China, 1784–1833, including (at vol. 27) Register of Letters, 1817–20 and 1827–30.

63–6. Secret Letters to the Court, 1810–18, 1820–7.

Miscellaneous

67. Instructions to Supercargoes, and Covenants, 1771–87, 1777–92.

68. Secret Consultations, Supercargoes, 1818–26.

69. Duplicate letters and instructions to Supercargoes, 1816–31.

70. Lindsay's journal of Lord Amherst's journey, 1832.

71–2. Letters to the Foreign Office, 1840–1.

73. Canton, 1829–36.

74–5. Memoir on intercourse with China, 1656–1832.

KING'S COLLEGE LONDON LIBRARY

Strand, WC2R 2LS

MARSDEN MSS.

Letter beginning 'In this I will give account to your Reverence of the peregrination which we made to the lands of Tibet'. *Portuguese.* Evidently the report made by Andrade after his return, which was first published at Lisbon in 1626, and subsequently translated into several languages.

Copy of a letter written by Pr. Antonio de Andrade from Tsaparang, Tibet, 24 September 1626.

The Centre for Military Archives at King's College London is collecting manuscript material on the military affairs of the present century, particularly on Britain's defence policy and her strategy in the two world wars. Certain of the papers already received deal with the recent military history of the Far East, but detailed lists are not yet available. Moreover, access to such papers is necessarily restricted owing to their highly confidential nature. Inquiries and applications to see these papers should be addressed in writing to the Librarian at the above address.

Papers of Major-General Sir Thompson Capper relating to the Indian Staff College, 1908–11, and including tactics in the Manchurian War, 1904–7. (*List of accessions to depositories in 1971*, p. 53.)

Diaries of Major-General N. W. Barnardiston on Tsing-Tao operations. 1914. (*List of additions to depositories in 1966*, p. 48.)

Papers of Major-General Sir W. R. C. Penney on Shanghai. 1932.

Memoirs of C. A. Vlieland, *Disaster in the Far East.* 1941–2. (*List of accessions to repositories in 1965*, p. 38.)

THE LABOUR PARTY

Transport House, Smith Square, S.W. 1

The Labour Party has a certain amount of material relating to the Far East, chiefly in the form of memoranda, which it is prepared to make available—though not for publication—to bona fide research students. They should apply to the Librarian, Overseas Department, at the above address.

Many lists of the voluminous records have been compiled by the Royal Commission of Historical Manuscripts (NRA 14863). Not all groups have as yet been indexed and many remain to be listed. The following have been noticed in the existing lists:

Labour Representation Committee, vols. 1 and 2. Among the relevant items are many references to Chinese labour in South Africa and a letter from F. Volkhovsky requesting the party to mobilize aid for the political prisoners in Japan, dated 13 August 1905.

Overseas correspondence. Manchuria. 1935. (Box 8.)

International Department. Countries and organizations, 1946 and 1947. China. 1946. (Box 1.) Japan, 1947. (Box 8.)

Subject files. Peace with China Council. LP/UN/51/ 14–16.

Arthur Henderson papers

Letter from C. Delisle Brown to A. L. Scott on the resumption of trade with China. 12 June *s.a.* (HEN/1/ 94.)

LAMBETH PALACE LIBRARY

London, S.E. 1

The manuscripts in Lambeth Palace Library are described in H. J. Todd, *Catalogue of the archiepiscopal manuscripts in the Library of Lambeth Palace*, 1812; M. R. James, *A descriptive catalogue of the manuscripts in the Library of Lambeth Palace*, 1932, and E. G. W. Bill, *A catalogue of manuscripts in Lambeth Palace Library. MSS. 1222–1860.* Oxford, 1972.

A letter from W. Adams written in Japan. 1611. (MS. 250, f. 397.)

'Mr Pound's letter from China [Chusan] giving some account of that Kingdom.' 19 November 1701. (MS. 933/94.)

Letter to M. Boehm relating chiefly to the state of Christianity in China. 10 January 1713. 4 pp. (MS. 933/116.)

FULHAM PAPERS

Papers of the Bishops of London, relating mainly to North America, but including in Box 30 some papers concerning China and Japan. 18th–19th centuries.

FACULTY OFFICE RECORDS

F. III *Public Notaries: notarial licences*

There are detailed records of these notarial licences, which probably contain material relating to notaries practising in Hong Kong. There is a calendar of foreign notaries, 1801–96.

SHANGHAI REGISTERS (MSS. 1564–84)

Registers of marriages, baptisms, confirmations, and burials at Shanghai, China, according to the rites of the Church of England. 1849–1951.

Letter to George Smith, Bishop of Victoria, Hong Kong. 1849. (MS. 1727, f. 171.)

ARCHBISHOP LONGLEY PAPERS (NRA. 8802)

Letters and papers of Charles Thomas Longley, Archbishop Longley, 1862–8, including (in vol. iii) correspondence concerning the appointment and consecration of a bishop for North China, ordination of clergy there, &c., letter about China from Earl Grey. 1859. (MS. 1841, ff. 73–5.)

File of correspondence of Archbishop Edward White Benson on Japan. 1886.

Letter to Charles Richard Alford, Bishop of Victoria, Hong Kong. (MS. 1727, f. 107.)

Diary of A. Faunce De Laune of Sharsted Court, Sittingbourne, Kent, describing a journey from Tokyo to England, via Vancouver, Chicago, and New York, 1892. i+153 pp. (MS. 1610.)

BURDETT COUTTS PAPERS (MSS. 1374–88)

Papers of Angela Georgina Burdett-Coutts (1814–1906), Baroness Burdett-Coutts of Highgate and Brookfield (1871) on the colonial church, including some relating to the diocese of Victoria, Hong Kong. 19th century. (MS. 1385, ff. 330–42), and a copy of a letter from Charles Richard Alford, Bishop of Victoria, Hong Kong to Archbishop Longley, 1867. (MS. 1385, f. 332.)

ARCHBISHOPS' CORRESPONDENCE

Correspondence of the Archbishops of Canterbury, including overseas correspondence. The papers of the first in the series, Archbishop Longley (1862–8), have been catalogued (*see above*), and those of the second in the series, Archbishop Tait (1868–82), have been partially catalogued (NRA. 8476). For these two as well as for the succeeding prelates, whose papers are as yet uncatalogued, there exists an annual register of letters in which, from 1871 onwards, the colonial and foreign correspondence is listed alphabetically at the end of each year. It is therefore easy to pick out any material relating to the area covered by this Guide. The fifty-year rule applies in this series.

RECORDS OF THE VICAR GENERAL'S OFFICE

These records are not listed in detail, but the section 'Colonial Bishops' is known to contain some material relating to China, Japan, and Korea. 19th–20th centuries.

Letter from William Awdry, Bishop of South Tokyo. 1904. (MS. 1616. ff. 109–11. *Church Quarterly Review* Papers.)

SHANTUNG REGISTERS (MSS. 1761–4)

Registers of baptisms, confirmations, births, and marriages in the diocese of Shantung, China, 1906–50.

Letters of Mark Napier Trollope, Bishop of Korea, 1: to the *Church Quarterly Review*, 1912 (MS. 1619, f. 247); 2: to the Revd. C. Jenkins, 1916 (MS. 1634, f. 278).

JENKINS PAPERS (MSS. 1590–1679)

Irrigation project in China, 1932. (MS. 1633, ff. 70–1)

LEPROSY MISSION

7 Bloomsbury Square, London, W.C. 1

The Mission to Lepers was founded in 1874, originally for the promotion of work among the sufferers of leprosy in India, but was later extended to other countries, including Hong Kong and Korea in the Far East. There are complete printed records going back many years, but many of the early manuscript records have not survived. Papers still in existence, including information of a confidential nature which is not normally available to students, may be described as follows:

1. Deeds relating to the Mission's property on the field: originals and photostats, in the English language and in local languages.

2. Minute books and account books covering the period.

3. Files relating to the work on the field and to the organization of the support of the Mission in Great Britain and other countries. There are about two thousand files of various kinds.

See also Marchant, p. 78; Keen, LM/1–14.

China

National Christian Council of China. 1926–35.

International Relief Committee of China. 1944–9.

Fukien North: Leprosy Committee. 1949–50.

China general: development, remittances, statement on work in China 1951, miscellaneous. 1943–51.

Formosa

Taiwan Leprosy Relief Association. 1961–3.

General correspondence. 1924–34.

Papers relating to individual stations. 1926–63.

Japan

Japan: general. 1918–60.

Papers relating to individual stations. 1912–39.

Korea

Representative in Korea. 1956–62.

Australian Presbyterian Mission. 1953–6.

Save the Children Fund. 1954–6.

Miscellaneous. 1957–62.

Papers relating to individual stations. 1910–42.

Hong Kong

Auxiliary. Minutes 1950–62; medical secretary 1951–62.

LINNEAN SOCIETY

Burlington House, Piccadilly, London, W1V 0LQ

See *Catalogue of the manuscripts in the Library of the Linnean Society*, London (1934–48). Part I (the Smith Papers), by Warren R. Dawson; Parts II, III, and IV (the Ellis Papers), by Spencer Savage.

SMITH PAPERS

Letter from Sir George Leonard Staunton in Canton about the culture of cotton in China. 5 May 1801. (Vol. 25, 181.)

ELLIS PAPERS

Three letters from John Bradby Blake in Canton to John Ellis. 12 February and 1/2 December 1770, 15 January 1772. Also three undated notes.

Two draft letters by Ellis to Thomas Fitzhugh in Canton, the first cancelled for the second. 28 November 1764. (Notebook no. 2. 44V–45R, 45R–46R.)

LONDON LIBRARY

14 St. James's Square, London, S.W. 1

Papers of John F. Baddeley, including an envelope containing miscellaneous manuscript notes, many relating to China.

LONDON SCHOOL OF HYGIENE AND TROPICAL MEDICINE

Keppel Street, London, WC1E 7HT

MANSON COLLECTION. Papers of Sir Patrick Manson (1844–1922), physician and parasitologist, who worked 1866–83 in China, being appointed Medical Officer for Formosa to the Chinese Imperial Maritime Customs in 1866, moving to Amoy in 1871, and later to Hong Kong. Including:

1. Case book kept by Manson in Formosa, 1865–8, containing descriptions of fifty-eight cases of leprosy and thirty-one cases of scrotal disease.

2. Extract of a letter from Manson in Amoy to T. S. Cobbold, together with some mosquitoes experimentally injected with filaria. 1879.

Report of a tour in the East for the study of rural hygiene, by D. B. Blacklock, 1935–6. The tour, financed by a Leverhulme Fellowship, included a visit to China, 16 August–7 September 1935. Hong Kong, Shanghai, Soochow, Nanking, Peiping are among the places he visited there. 2 vols., the second containing photographs. (SR 1935/6.)

Nutrition in civilian internment camps in the Far East January 1942–August 1945, compiled by Dean A. Smith, Medical Officer, Colonial Medical Service, Hong Kong. Together with a report on nutrition and the main causes of death, 'F' Force, Thailand, May 1943–April 1944, by T. Wilson and J. A. Reid, of the Colonial Medical Service, Malaya. 173 ff. 19 ff. The former was later published, with changes, in *Deficiency diseases in Japanese prison camps*, by D. A. Smith and M. F. A. Woodruft (Med. Res. Course. Spec. Rept. no. 274), London, H.M.S.O., 1951.

MARTINS BANK LIMITED

68 Lombard Street, London, E.C. 3

Catalogue of archives [1970?]. (NRA. 14254.)

29. Bank-note prepared by the Japanese Government for use by the Army in Manchuria.

431. Papers regarding the purchase of Chinese Russian 4% loan (A. G. Fullerton). 1895.

473. Papers regarding Chinese labour in the Transvaal. 1904.

METHODIST MISSIONARY SOCIETY

25 Marylebone Road, London, NW1 5JR

The Methodist Missionary Society was founded in 1817, although missionary work had begun at the end of the eighteenth century. The first missionary to China was George Piercy who arrived at Canton in 1851; and the first synod of the Methodist Church was held there in 1853. The Society has extensive records which are described in a number of typescript inventories, and they are open to students up to 1914. The manuscript records consist of minutes, correspondence, estate papers, legal papers, constitutions, maps and plans, home organization papers, candidates' papers, biographical material, the Coke MSS., ordination certificates, various miscellaneous papers, papers of local societies, financial records, ship records, and notes and transcripts. There are in addition numerous printed records. For an account of the work of the Society see G. G. Findlay and W. W. Holdsworth, *The history of the Wesleyan Methodist Missionary Society*, vols. i–v, London, 1921–4. (Marchant, pp. 68–77; Keen, MMS/1–17.)

CHINA AND HONG KONG

Synod minutes: China, 1853–1910; Hong Kong, 1952–4; Hong Kong and South-East Asia, 1955–8.

Correspondence

General: incoming, 1858–1915; outgoing, 1878–96, 1905–7.

Canton: incoming, 1858–1905.

Hupeh: incoming, 1905–17.

Wuchang: incoming, 1868–1905.

Correspondence with government departments.

Maps of districts.

Minutes of former branches of the Methodist Church:

Methodist New Connexion, North China. 1859/60.

Bible Christians. 1884– .

United Methodist Free Church. 1864– .

United Methodist Church: North, South-East, and South-West China. 1908–33.

BIOGRAPHICAL: CHINA

Papers of David Hill (d. 1896), missionary in China from 1864, with a few later papers. 6 boxes.

1. Bibles, &c., belonging to David Hill. *English, Greek*, and *Chinese*. 1 box.

2. Notes on the Old and New Testaments. 27 vols. in 1 box.

3. Journals, letters, and papers. 1 box, including:

a. Journals. 1865–76, 1879, 1885–9. 3 vols.

b. Memorandum book.

c. Notes on the opium trade.

d. 'The Sui Tsz Chin, its teaching, influence and uses.' May 1870.

e. Various papers including photographs of Hill,

notes on members at Wusueh, 1875, and notes on the Chinese classics.

f. 290 letters written by David Hill, the majority (248) to members of his family, including 74 to his father, 1866–76, and 147 to his brother J. R. Hill, 1857–96. There are also 13 letters, 1888–95, to G. G. Warren and 26, 1873–87, to A. Foster. 1847–8, 1857–96.

g. Seven letters addressed to David Hill. 1866–96.

h. Other letters, including 26 not addressed to Hill, 1847–1917, and 29 pages of letters (not identified); with four miscellaneous papers.

4. Various papers. 1 box, including:

a. Slides for a lantern lecture by David Hill, with notes.

b. Chinese book of proverbs arranged by David Hill. Wuchang 1870.

c. Cash book, Central Lay Mission. 1894–9.

d. Various printed booklets, including: Mission Work in Central China, 1882; Extracts from letters from David Hill, 1883; Sermon preached in Hankow, 1886; Hints to missionary evangelists in China, 1892; The Claims of Christ, 1896; Country life and itinerant evangelism in Central China; Three great cities in Central China; The Friend of China, 1917; Methodist Record, with report of a speech by David Hill, 1881, and other copies for 1859 and 1861.

e. Leaflets concerning events at York.

f. Various leaflets, newspaper cuttings, and other papers on the opium trade. 1877–81.

g. Paper relating to the China Famine Relief Fund, 1879.

h. Correspondence respecting anti-foreign riots in China, presented to the Houses of Parliament, July 1891.

i. Various pamphlets, articles on China, accounts, and missionary papers.

j. Map of Hupeh province.

k. Chinese manuscripts.

5. A box of notebooks, containing sermon notes.

6. A box of miscellaneous photographs, &c.

Papers of Josiah Cox, missionary in China. 1853–76. 1 box. (Box 8.)

1. Journals. January 1853–July 1861, August 1861–March 1876. 2 vols.

2. Minute book of 'Conversations' between personnel of the China Mission. March 1853–February 1860.

3. Letter-books containing flimsy carbon copies of letters. 1861–74. 4 vols.

4. Account book.

5. A book of notes entitled 'Looking into Jesus'.

Papers of N. Bridie, missionary in China. (Box 7.)

1. Ningpo cash book. 1864–81.

2. Manuscript account of the opening of Wuchan to the Wesleyan Methodist Missionary Society. 1897.

Account of travels in China by Jane C. Radcliffe, Women's Work missionary. 1867. (Box 7.)

Papers of W. E. Soothill, missionary in China. (Box 7.)

1. Letters from W. E. Soothill to his parents. 1882 and 1883. two packets.

2. Letters from W. E. Soothill. 1884–5. One packet.

3. Letters from Soothill to Dorothy Soothill (Lady Hoosie) and Lucy Soothill. 1885–1909. One packet.

4. Photographs of W. E. and Lucy Soothill.

Papers of W. A. Cornaby. missionary in China. (Box 7.)

1. Nineteen letters from W. A. Cornaby to his brother and others. 1885–93.

2. 'Notes of a missionary trip to the Lake District of Wuchang' with illustrations by Tsen Fah Shin and sepia drawings by Cornaby. 1887.

3. An account of the customs of the Nosu tribe, in Chinese script, with translation.

4. Typescripts and proofs of articles, &c.

5. Chinese passport. 1901–2.

Letters and papers of Samuel Pollard, missionary in China. *c.* 1909–15. (Box 7.)

Printed pamphlet on the Lord's Prayer, by G. W. Shepherd, missionary in China. (Box 7.)

Diary by the Revd. H. B. Rattenbury of his visit to China and Burma. 1939–40. (N/T 62.)

REGIMENTAL HEADQUARTERS, THE MIDDLESEX REGIMENT (DUKE OF CAMBRIDGE'S OWN)

T.A. Centre, Deansbrook Road, Edgware, Middlesex

Account of the part played by the 1st Battalion The Middlesex Regiment in the defence of Hong Kong, December 1941, by Lieutenant-Colonel S. F. Hedgecoe. Typescript, 12 pp. Included in a volume containing Records of the Officers' Mess 1757–1938.

MINISTRY OF DEFENCE NAVAL LIBRARY

Empress State Building, Little Road, Fulham, London, S.W. 6

A. Numerous maps and charts, including:

The English Pilot: Oriental Navigation. 1675.

Some Japanese maps. Various dates.

Plans of ports and passages including some relating to China and Japan. 1774–1822.

Chart showing the soundings off the coast of China. 1759.

B. Manuscripts

Journal by George Shelvoke (1690–1728) of a privateering voyage to the South Seas and finally to China, the voyage ending in Canton. 1719–21. 1 vol. (MS. 18.)

'Vocabulary of the language spoken at the Island called the great Lieoukieou or Lieuchew (by the natives Doo-Choo) in the Japan Sea.' This contains phonetic equivalents and some small sketches to illustrate words. By Hubert John Clifford, R.N., 1816. Two parts bound together: 137 pp. and 33 pp. (MS. 36.)

Commodore Anson's track from Acapulco to Tenian and thence to China. 1743. (290 Hf.)

Old Spanish [?] manuscript of the North Pacific between latitude 0° and 45° North and from China and Borneo to the Carolines, received from Sir T. Trowbridge. (488 P.)

THE MISSIONS TO SEAMEN

St. Michael Paternoster Royal, College Hill, London, E.C. 4

The Missions to Seamen was founded in 1856: it united with the Thames Church Mission in 1904, and with the St. Andrew's Waterside Church Mission in 1939. (Keen, MS/1–6.)

Correspondence files: Hong Kong, 1885; Kobe, 1895; Yokohama, 1880.

NATIONAL ARMY MUSEUM

Royal Hospital Road, London, SW3 4HT

The National Army Museum has a very large collection, which is continually being enlarged, of medals, weapons, uniforms, and other military relics as well as of books and manuscripts. (NRA. 18641.)

'Secret' memorandum to the Governor-General of India regarding actions in China (First China War). 1842. (6501/17.)

Miscellaneous documents, some connected with the First China War. c. 1842. (6401/17.)

Letters and documents of W. W. H. Greathed on the Second China War. 1860. (*List of accessions to repositories in 1967*, p. 70.)

Letter from Li Huy Chang to Miss M. A. Gordon. 1892. (6406/79.)

Extracts from the reports of various officers on manoeuvres in various fields including Japan, with some manuscript notes. 1897. (6412/151.)

Diary of H. B. Orpen-Palmer of travel in China. 1909. (6410/111–4.)

Journal of a trip to France, Russia, China, and South-East Asia. 1910. (14.)

Bound sketch-book, same trip. (57.)

Presentation volume to Colonel Orpen-Palmer on the completion of three years' command of the Shanghai Volunteer Corps, containing signatures. 1931. (6410/111–17.)

Maps relating to the Russo-Japanese War. n.d.

History of the 5th Battalion the 7th Rajputs, written by Lieutenant-Colonel R. J. F. Cadogan-Rawlinson, and illustrated by Lieutenant W. D. Pollock. The work was compiled and 'published' in an officers' prisoner-of-war camp in Hong Kong. 1943. Holograph. (Acc. 580/20.)

File of correspondence between General Molesworth and General Auchinleck, including: discussion on the Pacific War. Restricted. (6505/55.)

NATIONAL MARITIME MUSEUM

Greenwich, London, S.E. 10

ADMIRALTY RECORDS

This is a large collection, to some extent duplicating the Public Record Office series. It contains a little scattered material relating to the Far East, but it has not been possible in conducting the present survey to go through such a vast number of papers to extract and list the relevant material.

LLOYD'S REGISTER OF SHIPPING

These records consist of the original reports of first survey and plans of ships classed with Lloyd's from 1834. Until 1899 the arrangement is by port of survey, with an alphabetical index to ships' names. From 1900 individual ships are arranged alphabetically in groups, as the records fall due for transference from Lloyd's Register to the Museum. In the port series are included: Miramichi, 1856–69, Kobe, 1891–1901, Shanghai, 1894–1901, Yokohama, 1898–9, Nagasaki, 1898–1900.

SHIPS' LOGS AND JOURNALS

I. Official naval lieutenants' logs, largely duplicating the captains' and masters' logs in the Public Record Office. 1678–1809. 5205 vols. listed under the names of ships. An index of names is in progress.

II. Private Royal Navy logs and journals, including:
1. *Cruiser*. China Station in the First China War. Kept by Captain H. W. Giffard. 1839–41. (LOG/N/H/3.)
2. *Thalia*. China Station. Kept by Rear-Admiral Charles Hope. 1842–3. (JOD/61.)
3. *Vixen*. Commander H. Boyes, captain. In the East Indies, including China. 1842–3. (WAT/1.)
4. *Ringdove*. China Station. Kept by Captain U. C. Singleton. 1874. (LOG/N/R/31.)
5. *Audacious*. Chinese waters. 1887. (WRE/161.)
6. *Sapphire*. Chinese waters. 1888–9. (WRE/161.)
7. *Imperieuse*. China Station. Kept by Captain A. de K. L. May while a midshipman. 1891–3. (LOG/N/J/19–20.)

III. Logs in personal collections, listed with the collections (below) to which they belong.

IV. Merchant ships' logs and journals, including:
1. *Kelso*. London to Hong Kong and back. Kept by William Locke, 2nd mate. 1842–60. (LOG/M/25.)
2. *Osprey*. London to Shanghai. Captain Andrews. Kept by J. Peters, cabin passenger. 1863. (JOD/18.)
3. *Tamesa*. Account of a voyage to China by Robert Brown, 3rd mate. 1874–6. (JOD/64.)
4. *Glenroy*. Two voyages from London to China and back. Kept by G. A. Wilson. 1877–8. (LOG/M/31.)

V. Logs of East India Company ships. Including:
1. *Princess of Wales*. London to China and return. Captain Robert Mead. 1735–7. (WEL/46.)
2. *Ceres*. India to China and back. Robert Mylne, commander. 1743–5. (PHB/14.)
3. *Augusta*. Short log, India and China. c. 1744. (PHB/14.)
4. *St. Nicholas*. India and China. c. 1745. (PHB/14.)
5. *Walpole*. England to Bombay and China. Kept by Benjamin Lowe, commander. 1745–7. (LOG/C/27.)
6. *True Briton*. To China and back. Henry Broadley, commander. Kept by William Abdy, midshipman. List of officers and men. 1750–2. (CAL/201.)
7. *Essex*. England to Madras and China and back. George Jackson, commander. 1753–5. (LOG/C/5.)
8. *Lord Anson*. England to China and back. Charles Foulis, commander. 1753–5. (LOG/C/25.)

9. *Horsenden*. England to Madras and China and back. Alexander Jameson, commander. 1771–2. (LOG/C/21.)
10. *Melville Castle*. England to Bombay and Canton. Philip Dundas, commander. Water-colour landfalls and charts. 1786–8. (CLU/11.)
11. *Cuffnells*. England to China and back, maiden voyage. Kept by Francis Minnitt, 4th mate. Map of the world showing track. 1796–8. (LOG/C/42 a–c.)
12. *Walthamstow*. England to Madras and China. William T. Money, commander. 1800–1. (LOG/C/32.)
13. *Earl of Abergavenny*. Portsmouth to China. John Wordsworth, commander. Incomplete. 1801. (LOG/C/43.)
14. *Warley*. England to China. — Wilson, commander. 1803. (LOG/C/10.)
15. *Ceres*. England to China and back. Hugh Scott, commander. In verse, with explanatory notes. 1812–14. (PHB/7.)
16. *Cuffnells*. England to India and China and back. Robert Welbank, commander. Kept by William Kershall. 1814–16. (LOG/C/12.)
17. *General Hewitt*. China to England. Walter Campbell, commander. Diary kept by Campbell's brother, Colin. Descriptive. 1816–17. (LOG/C/19.)
18. *Bridgewater*. England to China and back. Philip Hughes, commander. 1817–18. (WEL/42.)
19. *Castle Huntly*. London to India and China and back. Andrew Drummond, commander. Kept by Henry Wise, midshipman. 1819–21. (LOG/C/47.)
20. *Thames*. London to India and China and back. Charles le Blanc, commander. Kept by George Wise, 5th officer. 1819–21. (LOG/C/22.)
21. *Castle Huntly*. London to India and China and back. Andrew Drummond, commander. Kept by Henry Wise, midshipman. 1822–3. (LOG/C/48.)
22. *Warren Hastings*. London to China and back. Richard Rawes, commander. Kept by William Lidderdale, 5th officer. List of officers, men, and dimensions of ship. 1823–4. (LOG/C/31.)
23. *Castle Huntly*. England to India and China and back. H. A. Drummond, commander. Kept by Henry Wise, 4th officer. List of officers, men, troops and passengers, and cargoes. 1823–5. (LOG/C/33.)
24. *Dunira*. To Bombay and China. Kept by George Davey. List of cargo, &c. 1824–5. (LOG/C/9.)
25. *Sir David Scott*. England to Bengal and China and back. Two voyages. J. O. McTaggart, commander. Kept by T. A. Gibb, purser. List of officers, men, passengers and troops. 1825–9. (LOG/C/6.)
26. *Castle Huntly*. London to China and back. H. A. Drummond, commander. Kept by Henry Wise, 3rd

officer. List of officers, men and passengers (incomplete). 1826–7. (LOG/C/49.)

27. *Castle Huntly*. England to China and back. Thomas Dunkin, commander. Kept by Henry Wise, 4th officer. List of officers, men, and passengers. 1828–9. (LOG/C/34.)

28. *George Fourth*. England to Bengal and China and back. Thomas William Barrow, commander. Kept by Jones Collins, midshipman. List of officers, men, and passengers. 1828–9. (LOG/C/2.)

29. *Duke of York*. England to Bengal and China and back. Robert Locke, commander. Kept by Thomas Gardiner, purser, 1829–30. (LOG/C/11.)

30. *William Fairlee*. England to Bengal and China and back. Thomas Blair, commander. Kept by T. A. Gibb, purser. 1829–31. (LOG/C/6.)

31. *Astell*. Blackwall to China and back. John Lawrence, commander. Kept by Henry Wise, chief officer. List of crew. 1830–1. (LOG/C/50.)

32. *Earl Balcarras*. England to Hong Kong and back. Bryan Broughton, commander. Probably kept by Jones Collins, midshipman. 1830–1. (LOG/C/1.)

33. *Sir David Scott*. England to India and China and back. D. J. Warr, commander. Kept by T. A. Gibb, purser. List of officers, men, and passengers. 1831–3. (LOG/C/6.)

34. *Warren Hastings*. England to China and back. H. B. Avarne, commander. Kept by William Lidderdale, chief officer. List of officers, men, and passengers. 1831–2. (LOG/C/30.)

35. *Asia*. England to Madras, Bengal and China and back. G. K. Bathie, commander. Kept by Thomas Gardiner, passenger. List of passengers, descriptions of ports. 1832–3. (LOG/C/11.)

36. *Broxbornebury*. England to China and back (by Quebec). Robert B. Shettler, commander. Kept by Frederick Alexander, midshipman. With flags of the East India Company, dimensions, cargo, rate of sailing, officers, men, and passengers, and pen and ink sketches of ships and landfalls. 1832–3. (LOG/C/7.)

37. *Edinburgh*. Blackwall to China and back. David Marshall, commander. Kept by Henry Wise, chief officer. List of crew and passengers. 1832–3. (LOG/C/51.)

38. *Warren Hastings*. England to India and China and back. Thomas Sands, commander. Kept by William Lidderdale, chief officer. List of officers, men, passengers and troops. 1832–4. (LOG/C/14.)

39. *Inglis*. To Bombay and China and back. Kept by George Wise, commander. 1836–7. (LOG/C/24.)

40. *Earl Balcarras*. To India and China. Kept by Richard Banks, purser. 1855–7. (Acc. 1692.)

PERSONAL PAPERS

'Nautical Observations on a voyage from England to China in His Majesty's ship *Lion* with the embassy under the Right Honourable Earl of Macartney in the years 1792, 1793 and 1794', by Sir Erasmus Gower [later Admiral], captain of the said ship. 2 vols. 132 pp., 127 pp., both with illustrations. (GOW/1–2.)

Letters received by Admiral John Elliot, including a description by Captain Erasmus Gower, H.M.S. *Lion*, of his voyage to China with Lord Macartney, 1793. (ELL/400.)

Papers of Admiral Sir Joseph Nias (1793–1879), who as captain commanded the *Herald*, being senior officer at Hong Kong, and took part in the First China War, 1840. (BAY/101–4.)

1. Commissions, certificates, &c. relating to his official career. 1820–67. (BAY/101.)

2. Official orders received. 1815–67. (BAY/102.)

3. Letters from Sir W. Parker. 1841–2. (BAY/103.)

4. Letters received, notes, and memoranda. (BAY/104.)

Journal kept by Mr. Stevens of the Indian Navy in the merchant ship *Lord Amherst* off the east coast of China. March 1838. (MAL/6/22.)

Papers of Sir Gilbert Elliot, 2nd Lord Minto, First Lord of the Admiralty, 1835–41, including:

1. Letters from Sir W. Parker (China). 1841–4. (ELL/226.)

2. Lord Minto's correspondence on the China War. 1839–41. (ELL/234.)

Letter written by Lieutenant Francis Meynell, R.N. while serving in China, 20 July 1840, together with press-cuttings about the China War, 1840–3. (MEY/4.)

Papers of Admiral Sir William Parker (1781–1866), as Commander-in-Chief East Indies (China station), 1841–4.

Log-books

1. May 1841–November 1844. 5 vols. (PAR/1a, 1b, 2a, 2b, 3.)

2. May 1841–May 1842. (PAR/15.)

3. April–October 1842. (PAR/14.)

Letter-books

1. Letters to Admiralty. Vols. 1 and 2. 1841–4, 1844–7. (PAR/16, 17.)

2. Letters to Departments. 1841–4. (PAR/22.)

3. Squadron letters. 1841–4, 1844–8. 2 vols. (PAR/24, 25.)

4. Miscellaneous letters. 1841–6. (PAR/27.)

5. East Indies (China station). 1842–4. 10 vols. (PAR/139–48.)

6. Private letter-book, East Indies and Mediterranean. 1841–5. (PAR/80.)

Order books

1. Sailing orders. 1841–4. (PAR/30.)

2. Memoranda, &c. 1841–4. 3 vols. (PAR/33–5.)

Loose documents

1. Letters from the Admiralty. 1841–5. (PAR/154 a and b.)

2. Letters from diplomats, including Sir Henry Pottinger, Plenipotentiary at Hong Kong. 1841–4. (PAR/155 a and b.)

3. Official papers relating to the Investiture held by Parker. 1842. (PAR/156.)

4. Letters received, semi-official and private. 1813–60. (PAR/163.)

Miscellaneous

Journal kept by Parker on his voyage to Hong Kong May–August 1841, describing the action at Amoy Bay. (PAR/177.)

Diary of Lieutenant Henry Thomas Dundas le Vesconte during the China War, in H.M.S. *Cornwallis*. 1841–4. (*list of accessions to repositories in 1969*, p. 66.)

Description of the Porcelain Tower at Nanking, translated from the Chinese in 1842. Also account by Rear-Admiral George Purvis of the action of the boats of H.M.S. *Highflyer* at Peking, June 1859. (BGY/5C/3.)

Log-book of H.M.S. *Vixen*, captain Commander H. Boyes, in the East Indies and China, kept by G. Waters. 1842–3. (WAT/1. 50. MS. 0015.)

Papers (copies) of Vice-Admiral George F. Hastings, including correspondence with other naval officers relating to his service in H.M.S. *Harlequin* in the China War and suppressing piracy off Sumatra, 1844–8. (TRN/10.)

Papers of Admiral Thomas Leeke Massie (1802–98)

1. A series of eighty-three numbered letters received and sent by Massie, as Captain of H.M.S. *Cleopatra* at Hong Kong and Singapore. August 1851–March 1852. (MAS/7.)

2. Diary kept by Massie as Captain of H.M.S. *Cleopatra* serving in the East Indies and Hong Kong. January–December 1850. (MAS/21.)

3. Journal of H.M.S. *Cleopatra* on a voyage from Hong Kong to Chatham. March–October 1853. (MAS/23.)

Letters written by Lieutenant W. H. Childers to his parents describing *i.a.* his service in the Second China War aboard H.M.S. *Tribune*. 1851–63. (CHI/4.)

Papers of Sir Edmund Fremantle (1836–1929)

I. *Logs and journals*

(a) Log-book of H.M.S. *Spartan*, Captain Sir William Hoste, China station, kept by Fremantle as midshipman. 1852–5. (FRE/115.)

(b) Log-book of H.M.S. *Spartan*, *Orion*, and other ships kept by Fremantle as acting Lieutenant. 1855–9. (FRE/116.)

(c) Private journal of H.M.S. *Spartan*, China station. 1856–7. (FRE/124.)

II. *Papers as Commander-in-Chief, China station. 1892–5*

(a) Selected general letters to the Admiralty reporting proceedings. Carbon copies signed by Fremantle. 1892–5. (FRE/140a.)

(b) Official papers sent to the Admiralty on the political situation. 1894–5. (FRE/140b.)

(c) Letters received from the Admiralty. 1892–5. (FRE/141a.)

(d) Letters received from Ambassadors and Ministers. 1893–5. (FRE/141b.)

(e) Letters received from senior naval officers. 1893–5. (FRE/141c.)

(f) Miscellaneous letters. 1892–5. (FRE/141d.)

Eighty-four letters written by Cuthbert Ward Burton (later Major-General, R.M.) to his mother, Mrs. Alfred Burton, during his service on the China station, where he was attached for a time to the Canton constabulary. 1853–8. (BUR/101.)

Papers of Commander Arthur Rodney Blane (d. 1891), who served as Lieutenant on H.M.S. *Niger* in operations during the Second China War. Including:

1. Seven acting commissions and commissions. February 1854–January 1866. (BLA/1–7.)

2. Sixteen certificates. February 1848–April 1863. (BLA/8–24.)

3. Series of nine maps and charts, referring to the 'Seat of war in the East, 1856–7', being chiefly plans of Canton and environs. (BLS/29/37.)

4. 'Order of anchoring off the Pei-ho'. c. 1859. (BLA/38.)

5. Extract 'News from Pei-ho' from the *North China Herald*. 9 July 1859. (BLA/39.)

6. Extract 'Battle of Kagosima' from the *Japan Commercial News*. 26 August 1863. (BLA/40.)

7. Two maps, both engravings, relating to a revolt in western Tartary. 1826. (BLA/41.)

Papers of Vice-Admiral Harry Edmund Edgell (1809–76) who commanded H.M.S. *Tribune* and H.M.S. *Bittern* in China waters, 1855–8, being appointed Senior Naval Officer at Hong Kong in 1857. In August 1858 he was promoted Commodore and transferred to India.

1. Out letter-book, including letters to the Admiralty,

E

the Commander-in-Chief, &c. written from H.M.S. *Tribune*, and H.M.S. *Bittern*. September 1855–February 1858. (EDG/1.)

2. Out letter-book, containing letters written from H.M.S. *Bittern*. March–September 1858. (EDG/4.)

3. Register of correspondence; being heads of letters received and sent, November 1857–January 1858. (EDG/2.)

4. Senior officer's book for gunboats working in the Canton River, December 1857–October 1858. (EDG/3.)

5. Register of letters received, June–August 1858. Being a summary of official correspondence received as Senior Naval Officer, Hong Kong. (EDG/5.)

6. Orders and letters received from the Commander-in-Chief, allied commissioners and diplomats. January–October 1858. Unbound. (EDG/10.)

7. General memoranda. December 1857–October 1858. Unbound. (EDG/11.)

Letters written home by Thomas Noakes during the outward voyage of the China tea clipper *Challenger*. 1856. (BGY/5C/4. MS. 60/014.)

Papers of Rear-Admiral Dawkins (1828–96), including journal kept in the steamship *Esk*, 1856–7, in *Calcutta*, 1857–8, and *Comus*, 1858, covering the attack on Canton, 1857–8. (DAW/4.)

HAMILTON PAPERS

I. Papers of Admiral Sir Henry Keppel (1809–1904), who was Commodore, China station, 1856–7, and Commander-in-Chief, China station, 1866–9. (HTN/1–68.)

1. Log of H.M.S. *Raleigh*, China station. 1856–7. (HTN/9.)

2. Logs of H.M.S. *Salamis*, and appendix to logs. 1867–9. 6 vols., 14 vols. (HTN/13a.)

3. Journals, China station. 1866–9. (HTN/13b, c, d.)

4. Diaries, China station. 1856–7. 2 vols. (HTN/15c and d.)

5. Diary, China station. 1866. (HTN/16c.)

6. Out letters to the Admiralty, China station. 1867–9. 2 vols. (HTN/59–60.)

II. Papers of Admiral Sir Louis Henry Hamilton, who served on the China station, 1927–8. (HTN/201–49.)

1. Log of H.M.S. *Wanderer*, Mediterranean and China station, February–May 1927, and H.M.S. *Wild Swan*, Commander Hamilton, at Hankow, May 1927–July 1928. (HTN/214.)

2. Log of H.M.S. *Wild Swan*, Commander Hamilton, on the China station and bound for England via Singapore, &c. July–September 1928. (HTN/215.)

3. Signal log of H.M.S. *Wanderer* at sea and Hong Kong. March–April 1927.

4. Memoranda and proceedings, China station, H.M.S. *Wild Swan*. 1927–8. (HTN/224b.)

Transcripts of letters written home by Rear-Admiral Victor Montagu (1841–1915), while serving as midshipman with Sir Henry Keppel in the Second China War. 1856–8. (SAN/T/101. MS. 60/008. The originals are the property of the Earl of Sandwich.)

papers relating to the career of Captain William Hans Blake (1832–74), including copy of letter from Commander-in-Chief China to the Commanding Officer H.M.S. *Niger*, expressing approval of gallantry displayed in proceeding against pirates at Hong Kong, 18 March 1857; and copy of letter of appreciation from the Hong Kong Government. (BLK/7.)

Papers of Vice-Admiral Philip Ruffle Sharpe (1831–92). (SHP/1–13.)

1. Personal journal, including a part in the *Magicienne*, China. 22 January 1857–19 October 1858. (SHP/5.)

2. Personal journal in the *Magicienne*, China. 21 October 1858–2 June 1859. (SHP/6.)

3. Letter from Sharpe to his mother after the reverse of the Taku forts, June 1859. (SHP/12.)

Report to the Admiralty by Sherard Osborn, captain of H.M.S. *Furious*, on the voyage of the *Furious* while taking the British Minister, Lord Elgin, down the Yangtse. Copy signed by Osborn. 23 December 1858. Also draft of report by Lieutenant-Commander W. H. Jones to Captain Sherard Osborn on the loss of the gunboat *Lee* during the attack on the Pei-ho forts, 25 June 1859. (JON/103.)

Papers of Rear-Admiral Edwin John Pollard.

1. Sailing orders received by Captain Pollard, 1858–78, including operations at Pei-ho and Hong Kong, 1858–61. (PDW/4.)

2. Miscellaneous papers, cuttings, &c., 1858–78, including a long letter about the attack on the Chinese forts in 1859. (PDW/5.)

Account of voyage on board the *Jura* in South China Seas, by Martin Bienvenu. 1859–62. (*List of accessions to repositories in 1968*.)

Journal kept by Captain Thomas H. Tizard in the surveying vessel H.M.S. *Rifleman* in the Far East. November 1861–April 1867. (TIZ/4.)

Papers of Vice-Admiral James Barlow (1848–1912), including:

1. Log-book of H.M.S. *Scylla*, Captain R. W. Courtenay, on a voyage to Singapore, China, and back to England, kept by C. J. Barlow, naval cadet and midshipman. 1863–7. (BAR/1.)

2. Miscellaneous papers about ships, including the Japanese ship *Mikasa*. 1900–2. (BAR/9.)

Papers of Vice-Admiral Charles Johnstone (1843–1927), including:

1. Log-book of H.M.S. *Serpent*, China station. June 1866–November 1867. (JOH/4.)

2. Log-book of H.M.S. *Juno*, China station. June 1871–June 1873. (JOH/5.)

3. Personal diaries, 1880–97 (except 1890 and 1895). (JOH/56/1–18.)

Papers of Admiral Sir Cyprian Bridge (1839–1924).

1. Watch bill and other papers relating to H.M.S. *Audacious*, flagship of Vice-Admiral A. P. Ryder, China station. 1874–7. (BRI/11.)

2. Letters received by Vice-Admiral Bridge while serving as Commander-in-Chief, China station, 1901–4. (BRI/14–19.)

Papers of Captain Henry L. Bethune, including:

1. Log of H.M.S. *Topaz*, Captain H. Thrupp, on a voyage to Bombay, Singapore, Nagasaki, and back to Singapore, kept by H. L. Bethune, midshipman. 1875–7. (BET/4.)

2. Log and journal of H.M.S. *Constance*, Captain Frederick Doughty, on a voyage in the Pacific, calling at Hong Kong, kept by H. L. Bethune. Also of H.M.S. *Orontes* to Singapore and England. 1883–6. (BET/8.)

Notebook written by Admiral Pelham Aldrich, while commanding the surveying vessel *Sylvia* in Japanese waters, 1877–80. (ALD/2.)

Papers of Admiral John F. L. P. Maclear (1838–1907), who in 1883–7 commanded the *Flying Fish* employed on surveying work on the China station.

1. Remark book, with notes on Japan and Korea, kept partly by Alfred Carpenter, captain of H.M.S. *Magpie*, and partly by Maclear. 1882. (MAC/8.)

2. Journal, H.M.S. *Flying Fish*, kept by Maclear. 1885–7. (MAC/9.)

3. Captain's letter-book, H.M.S. *Flying Fish*, with reports of proceedings to the Hydrographer of the Navy. January 1884–April 1887. (MAC/11.)

Papers of Admiral Richard Vesey Hamilton, Commander-in-Chief, China, 1885–8.

1. Admiral's private out letter-books, H.M.S. *Audacious*, Flagship China station. October 1885–6. June 1886–January 1887. Duplicated copies. 2 vols. (VHM/3–4.)

2. Admiral's private out letter-books, H.M.S. *Audacious* and H.M.S. *Alacrity*, Flagships China station. October–November 1887. November 1887–February 1888. Duplicated copies. 2 vols. (VHM/5–6.)

3. Official papers relating to China, the Admiralty, and the R.N. College, Greenwich. 1887–94. (VHM/7d.)

Scrapbook of Admiral A. H. Smith Dorrien including entries relating to his service on H.M.S. *Alacrity*, China station, 1897–1904. (SMD/3.)

Journal kept by Mrs. Harry Clegg during the Boxer rising, August 1900–January 1901. (JOD/68.)

Papers of Vice-Admiral Charles Blois Miller (d. 1926).

1. Log of H.M.S. *Audacious*, China station, C. B. Miller midshipman. Rough copy illustrated with drawings and sketches and a fair copy. (MIL/1.)

2. Log of H.M.S. *Talbot*, China station, illustrated with drawings, &c. April 1901–January 1903. (MIL/8.)

Papers of Commander Gerald William Vivian relating to H.M.S. *Rosario*, China station. 1904. (VIV/1.)

Confidential information for officers in the China Squadron during the Russo-Japanese War, June, 1904. (*List of accessions to repositories in 1970*, p. 69.)

Papers of Admiral Sir Gerard Henry Uctred Noel (1845–1918), Member of the Board of Admiralty, 1893–7, Commander-in-Chief, China station, 1904–6.

1. Correspondence; being letters to Noel throughout his service career. (NOE/1–5.)

2. Papers relating to the Russo-Japanese War. 1904–5. (NOE/8A, 8B.)

3. Enclosures to general letters, China. 1904–6. (NOE/20C.)

4. General letters, China. 1904–6. (NOE/20D.)

5. China correspondence. 1904–6. (NOE/20E.)

6. Diaries (Letts) kept by Noel. 1880–1918. (NOE/32.)

Papers, press cuttings, photographs, &c. of Vice-Admiral Sir Arthur Moore, relating to a visit made to the China station, 1906. (Acc. 1964.)

Papers of Admiral Sir William Archibald Howard Kelly (1873–1952), Commander-in-Chief China, 1931–3.

1. Journal as Commander-in-Chief, China, with photographs. 1931–3. 2 vols. (KEL/36–8.)

2. Letters and proceedings. 1931–3. 2 vols. (KEL/39–40.)

3. Miscellaneous loose papers, China station. 1932–3. (KEL/41.)

Diary of Captain Theobald John Claud Purcell-Buret written while in command of the troopship *Andes* on a voyage with 4,000 naval ratings from Marseilles to Hong Kong and intermediate ports, &c. January–June 1940. 2 vols. (PUR/2–3.)

Instrument of Surrender of the Japanese forces at Hong Kong, signed by Rear-Admiral Harcourt, Major-General Umekichi Okado, and Vice-Admiral Ruitaro Fujitia. 16 September 1945. (FD/58.)

Unpublished article on Chinese junks by W. J. King. *c.* 1949. (NOT/1.)

'The China and Japan (coast and river) S. N. Co., 1862', and 'Steam vessels sold to or reportedly sold to Japan up to 1870', both compiled by T. M. Milne. 1964. (Acc. 1964.)

Collection of notes, articles, and photographs on Chinese junks written or collected by Lieutenant-Commander D. W. Waters. (WTS/1–25. Five of the articles are printed in *Mariner's Mirror*, vols. xxiv, 49; xxv, 62; xxvi, 79; xxxii, 155; xxxiii, 28.)

NEW COLLEGE, LONDON

527 Finchley Road, Hampstead, London, NW3 7BE

CURWEN MSS.

Letter from Jonathan Lee about the translation of the first Chinese hymn. 1893. (C. 2/9/11.)

Letter from the Revd. Griffith John from Hankow. 1901. (C. 2/9/10.)

Letter from Sir Claude Macdonald, British Legation, Peking, to Dr. Curwen. 1915. (C. 2/3/25.)

Letter from R. Morrison to Thomas Wilson. 12 February 1814. (418/49.)

Four letters from R. Morrison in Canton to Thomas Wilson, Treasurer of the London Missionary Society. 1817–34. (L/52/2/5.)

Letter from the Revd. David Thorn to Trustees of Homerton College, presenting a copy of the posthumous publication of his brother Robert, formerly Consul at Ningpo. 1848. (316/15.)

NORTH CHINA AND SHANTUNG MISSIONARY ASSOCIATION

c/o U.S.P.G., 15 Tufton Street, London, S.W. 1

Formerly St. Peter's Missionary Guild, 1874–80, this organization was created to support a missionary already in China in 1874. Records in possession of the Association's Secretary are listed in Marchant (p. 88):

Letter of Bishop Norris to P. Tucker. 1899.

Photographs.

Tracts and pamphlets.

PENINSULAR AND ORIENT STEAM NAVIGATION CO. LTD.

122 Leadenhall Street, London, E.C.3

Papers relating to voyages of the company's vessels to China and other places in the Far East. (Mathias and Pearsall, pp. 69–79. Inquiries to the company's Public Relations Officer.)

PHARMACEUTICAL SOCIETY OF GREAT BRITAIN

17 Bloomsbury Square, London, WC1A 2NN

Papers and notes of Daniel Hanbury (1825–75), pharmacist, including:

Chinese materia medica: inorganic substances. Notes with letters from Berkeley, Guibourt, and others. Various dates.

POST OFFICE RECORDS

Headquarters Building, St. Martin's-le-Grand, London, EC1A 1HQ

The Post Office has a very large collection of records which are in the process of being listed. The documents are well arranged and easy of access, but apart from the Packet Minutes series for which there is a detailed index, it is possible here to give only a general description of the main series of records.

A. Cash books. 1672–1800.

B. General account books. 1685–1849.

C. Treasury letter-books.

1. There are many hundreds of Treasury letter-books, all indexed with entries concerning post offices and services in the Far East from 1686 to the present day.

2. Index 78: packet and mails. 1 vol.

3. Index 81: conveyance of mails. 1 vol.

D. Instructions relating to the packet service.

1. Instructions, including instructions to packet captains. 1760–1811. 1 vol.

2. Packet service instructions, being orders to officers at home and abroad about foreign mails, &c. The instructions are often very detailed. 1812–48. 1 vol.

3. Packet service instructions. 1949–66.

E. Various papers relating to packet boats. 1791–1846.

F. PACKET MINUTES. 1811–1900 and 1901–20. (Post 29.)

Amoy

Packet agent appointed. 1866. (Post 29/126.)

Proposed branch packet service. 1881. (Post 29/305.)

Canton

Post office agency established. 1853. (Post 29/58.)

China

Arrangements for receipt and delivery of mail at Consular ports. 1854. (Post 29/60.)

Management of postal agencies transferred to Hong Kong post office. 1861. (Post 29/100.)

Re-establishment of second monthly mail: postage on correspondence increased. 1862. (Post 29/105.)

Mails conveyed by French packets. 1863. (Post 29/111.)

Mails via Marseilles: postage rates altered. 1863. (Post 29/112.)

Contract with P. & O. 1868. (Post 29/143.)

Control of agencies transferred to Hong Kong. 1868. (Post 29/149.)

Postal agencies: use of registration system. 1868. (Post 29/149.)

New line of United States packets. 1868. (Post 29/152.)

Marine mail sorting on homeward Mediterranean packets continued. 1870. (Post 29/162.)

Experimental introduction of supplemental mails via Brindisi. 1870. (Post 29/162.)

Correspondence sent via Brindisi. Postage rates reduced. 1876. (Post 29/209.)

Shanghai: day of departure of packet revised during NE. monsoon. 1878. (Post 29/251.)

Route via Southampton abolished. Mails sent via Brindisi. New postage rates. 1880. (Post 29/275.)

Places to which letters, &c. may be forwarded through Hong Kong as if in postal union. 1881. (Post 29/303.)

Proposed branch packet service to Foochow, Amoy, and Swatow. 1881. (Post 29/305.)

Mails via San Francisco: time-table 1882–5. (Post 29/313.)

Report by Committee on the dates of arrival and dispatch of China mails. 1882. (Post 29/323–4.)

Time-tables. 1885. (Post 29/361.)

Time-tables. 1886. (Post 29/383.)

Time-tables. 1887. (Post 29/409.)

Provisional mail service via Montreal established. 1887. (Post 29/414.)

Time-tables. 1888. (Post 29/414.)

P. & O's claim for first quarter of 1889. Adjustment of penalties. 1889. (Post 29/480.)

Imperial post office: proposed entry into postal union. 1894. (Post 29/572.)

Mail service: new contract with P & O. Co. 1898. (Post 29/656–7.)

Mail service via Quebec. 1899. (Post 29/660.)

Chusan

Receipt and delivery of mails. 1854. (Post 29/60.)

Foochow

Appointment of packet agent. 1865. (Post 29/119.)

Proposed branch packet service. 1881 (Post 29/305.)

Hong Kong

Post office established. 1854. (Post 29/60.)

Book post established with East Indies, Ceylon, Mauritius, and Australia. 1857. (Post 29/79.)

Post office transferred to Colonial control. 1861. (Post 29/100.)

Mails via Marseilles. Postage rates reduced. 1863. (Post 29/112.)

Control of China and Japan agencies transferred to Hong Kong. 1868. (Post 29/149.)

Marine sorting established on packets to and from Singapore. 1868. (Post 29/149.)

Postal convention with U.S.A. 1868. (Post 29/152.)

Postal convention with Netherlands Indies. 1877. (Post 29/221.)

Admission into general postal union. Postage rates reduced. 1877. (Post 29/230.)

Postal Convention with Queensland. 1880. (Post 29/276.)

Insufficiently paid Postcards. Rate of accounting. 1881 (Post 29/294.)

Authority for giving up value of stamps on insufficiently paid letters from Hong Kong. 1881. (Post 29/299.)

Mail service with Japan. 1883. (Post 29/340.)

Sale of British postal orders. 1884. (Post 29/358.)

Parcel post service established. 1885. (Post 29/382–3.)

Exchange of parcels with certain West Indian Colonies. 1885. (Post 29/383.)

Postal accounts. Adoption of postal union system. 1886. (Post 29/395.)

Official correspondence from local naval and military authorities. 1886. (Post 29/395.)

Parcel post: maximum weight extended. 1886. (Post 29/408.)

Parcel service with Ceylon. 1887. (Post 29/440.)

Parcel post service with Belgium and Germany. 1887. (Post 29/445.)

Parcel post rates reduced. 1888. (Post 29/468.)

Postage rates revised. 1891. (Post 29/514.)

Direct parcel post service with France. 1900. (Post 29/694.)

Direct parcel post service with the United States. 1903. (Post 29/767.)

Parcel post service with Japan. 1908. (Post 29/966.)

Parcel post service via Siberia established. 1913. (Post 29/1155–7.)

Legislation affecting the post office. 1914. (Post 29/1204.)

Japan

Postal agencies: management transferred to Hong Kong post office. 1861. (Post 29/100.)

Mails via Marseilles; postage rates revised. 1863. (Post 29/112.)

Mail service. Contract with P. & O. Co. 1868. (Post 29/143.)

Use of registration system in agencies. 1868. (Post 29/149.)

New line of United States packets. 1868. (Post 29/152.)

Correspondence sent via Brindisi. 1876. (Post 29/209.)

Complaints regarding high rates of postage by British packet. (Copies of 1st, 2nd, 3rd, and 4th reports by the Japanese post office.) 1876. (Post 29/210.)

Letters sent via San Francisco. Postage rates reduced. 1876. (Post 29/219.)

Proposed postal convention. 1877. (Post 29/231.)

Entry into general postal union: postage rates revised. 1877. (Post 29/232.)

British post offices abolished. 1879. (Post 29/268.)

Money order convention. 1881. (Post 29/309.)

Mails via San Francisco: time-tables 1882–5. (Post 29/313.)

Mail service from Hong Kong. 1883. (Post 29/340.)

Reply postcards introduced. 1884. (Post 29/357.)

Mails via San Francisco: time-tables 1886–7. (Post 29/410.)

Provisional mail service via Montreal established. 1887. (Post 29/444.)

Amended money-order agreement. 1890. (Post 29/499.)

Sample post agreement. 1894. (Post 29/576.)

Parcel post service. (1898.) (Post 29/638.)

Mail service via Quebec. 1899. (Post 29/660.)

Postal agencies in China; money-order service established. 1901. (Post 29/702.)

Mail service via United States. Weight of mails. 1902. (Post 29/742–3.)

Insured letter services. 1903. (Post 29/752.)

Assumes control of Korean posts, telephones, and telegraphs. 1905. (Post 29/872.)

Russo-Japanese war. Japanese mail on board S.S. *Knight Commander* seized. 1905. (Post 29/874.)

Parcel post service. Proposed new agreement. 1907. (Post 29/939.)

Parcel post service with Hong Kong. 1908. (Post 29/966.)

Import prohibitions. 1911. (Post 29/1091.)

Mail service via Vancouver. 1912. (Post 29/1104.)

Mail service via Vancouver. Contracts with Canadian Pacific Railway Co. 1907–19. 1914. (Post 29/1206–7.)

Korea

Control of posts, telephones, and telegraphs assumed by Japan. 1905. (Post 29/872.)

Macao

Arrangements for receipt and delivery of mail. 1854. (Post 29/60.)

Shanghai

Day of departure of packet altered during NE. monsoon. 1878. (Post 29/251.)

Packet agency. Duties performed by Consular officer. 1854. (Post 29/60.)

Swatow

Proposed branch packet service. 1881. (Post 29/305.)

Tientsin

French postal agency: assimilation to postal union. 1893. (Post 29/562.)

G. Contracts

1. P. & O. Company contracts. 1837–1907. The contracts are printed but bound with them is some correspondence for the year 1836–7. 1 vol.

2. Contracts for foreign and colonial mail packet services, including contracts with the Union Steamship Company and British India Steamship Company. 1863–1907.

H. Admiralty Agents

1. Instructions to Admiralty agents at Falmouth and Southampton. 1837–63. 3 vols.

2. Order book to naval agents at Southampton for mails east, west, and south. 1850–79. 3 vols.

3. Admiralty agents' letters. Letters to the Admiralty agent at Southampton from the G.P.O. and from naval agents on ships and abroad. 1855–70. 40 vols.

I. Packet agents

1. 'Agents', being copies of letters sent to agents at home and abroad. 1849–71. 45 vols.

2. Letter-book of agent at Southampton. 1860–1. 1 vol.

3. Letter-book, Southampton packet office. 1861–70. 1 vol.

4. Daily journal of the Southampton agent. 1867–8. 1 vol.

J. Overseas mails: ships' time-bills. 1841–92. 5 boxes.

K. Colonial postmasters' letter-books, all indexed, with entries under Hong Kong, &c.

1. 1849–70. 45 vols. (Vols. 1–22, 24–46: vol. 23 is missing.)

2. 1876–1920. 10 vols have been retained to cover every fifth year.

L. Copies of letters sent from the General Post Office to contract packets. 1860–70. 20 vols.

M. P.M.G.'s Reports. 1792–1806.

N. Packet Reports. 1807–37, including: East Indies Packet Reports. 1816, 1818–20.

THE PUBLIC RECORD OFFICE

Chancery Lane, London, W.C. 1

The records in the Public Record Office have been described in the very comprehensive *Guide to the contents of the Public Record Office* (3 vols., H.M.S.O., 1963, 1968), upon which this list is mainly based. A further unpublished volume of the *Guide* is at present (1975) available in the Search Rooms, but it is intended that in future there will be produced, from the PROSPEC data base, a new *Guide to departmental records in the Public Record Office* in three editions a year, available initially for consultation only in the Search Rooms of the Office. PROSPEC is described in the *Thirteenth annual report of the Keeper of Public Records*, 1971, p. 7. The Office has also issued a series of Handbooks, of which the following are particularly relevant to the present project:

3. The Records of the Colonial and Dominions Offices. 1964.

4. List of Cabinet papers, 1880 to 1914. 1964.

6. List of papers of the Committee of Imperial Defence to 1914. 1964.

8. List of Colonial Office Confidential Print to 1916. 1965.

9. List of Cabinet papers, 1915 and 1916. 1966.

10. Classes of departmental papers for 1906–39. [Addendum to vol. iii of the *Guide*.]

11. The Records of the Cabinet Office to 1922, 1966.

12. The Records of the Foreign Office 1782–1939. 1969.

13. Records of interest to social scientists 1919 to 1939; introduction, by Brenda Swann and Maureen Turnbull. 1971.

14. The Second World War; a guide to documents in the Public Record Office. 1972.

These Handbooks, naturally, give more detail about the contents of the various groups and classes of records than does the general *Guide*, but there are also available in the Search Rooms numerous lists and indexes (printed, typescript, and manuscript), which give the most detailed descriptions of all. It was not possible for the compilers of the present work to examine all of these registers to locate relevant items.

Departmental records are constantly being transferred to the Office; lists of documents deposited form a regular feature of the *Annual Report of the Keeper of Public Records*. In general, papers less than thirty years old may not be consulted at present, but an exception is made in favour of the records of the Second World War, the majority of which were made accessible to the public in 1972.

STATE PAPER OFFICE

The State Paper Office was officially constituted in the early years of the seventeenth century, and its records consist of the State Papers, both domestic and foreign, from the beginning of the reign of Henry VIII to 1782, when the Home and Foreign Departments were established. These records are not complete, as many state papers were retained by the Secretaries of State and other Ministers, and are now to be found among the collections of many public and private libraries. From the reign of Edward VI onwards the state papers have been classified into Domestic and Foreign. There are papers about voyages of discovery in the State Papers, Domestic Series. The student is referred to the *Calendar of State Papers (Domestic Series): Edward VI to Anne, 1547–1704* where the papers are calendared in detail. Reference should also be made to the *Calendar of State Papers, Colonial Series.*

2. East Indies, China, and Japan, 1513–1616. 1862 (reprinted, Vaduz, 1964).

3. — — 1617–21. 1870.

4. — — 1622–24. 1878.

6. East Indies, China, and Persia, 1625–9. 1884.

8. East Indies and Persia, 1630–4. 1892.

ADMIRALTY

The records of the Navy before 1546 are to be found among the documents of the Privy Council, the Chancery, and the Exchequer; the records from 1546 to 1660 are much dispersed, many being in the records of the State Paper Office, some among the Exchequer records, some in public and private collections, and a few classified with Admiralty records proper. From 1660 all naval records will be found in this class.

Admiralty records are only exceptionally arranged according to geographical areas, and therefore anyone seeking material relating to the Far East must undertake a thorough search in the most likely categories.

ACCOUNTING DEPARTMENTS: including records of the Treasurer of the Navy, the Controller of Treasurer's Accounts, the Accountant General, and after 1832 of the Accountant General's Department of the reorganized Admiralty Board.

Adm. 14. In-letters. 1693–1835. 181 vols., &c.

Adm. 15. Out-letters. 1807–30. 7 vols.

Adm. 16. Treasurer's accounts. 1681–1836. 188 vols.

Adm. 17. Various accounts, including accounts of naval storekeepers at yards and stations abroad. 1615–1850. 226 vols., &c.

Adm. 18. Bill books. 1642–1831. 155 vols.

Adm. 19. Journal. 1826–60. 35 vols.

Adm. 20. Treasurer's ledgers. 1660–1836. 357 vols.

Adm. 21. Accountant-General's registers. 1826–60. 35 vols.

Adm. 117. Ships' ledgers. 1872–7, 1880–4. 1,036 vols.

Adm. 22–30, 139. Registers of salaries and pensions, services, &c. 1689–1902. 3,613 vols., &c.

Adm. 31–5, 42. Ships' pay books, and yard pay books. 1660–1857. 6,555 vols., &c.

Adm. 36–9, 41, and 119. Ships' musters. 1667–1878. 40,062 vols.

Adm. 43. Head money vouchers. 1710–1833. 80 bundles.

Adm. 44. Seamen's effects papers. 1800–60. 376 bundles.

Adm. 45. Officers' and civilians' effects papers. 1830–60. 39 bundles.

Adm. 48. Seamen's wills. 1786–1882. 107 bundles.

Adm. 141. Registers of seamen's effects papers. 1802–61. 9 vols.

Adm. 142. Registers of seamen's wills. 1786–1909. 19 vols.

Adm. 46. Admiralty orders. 1832–56. 197 vols.

Adm. 47. Record books. 1832–56. 25 vols.

Adm. 49. Various. 1658–1862. 176 vols., &c.

ADMIRALTY AND SECRETARIAT: including records of the Admiralty up to 1832, and thereafter records of the Secretary's Department of the reorganized Admiralty Board.

Adm. 1. Papers: this class contains papers relating to the China Station, and they are arranged under sub-headings up to 1840; from that date the papers are classified from Admirals, Captains, and other officers, and from various departments: to find relevant material it is necessary to use the indexes in Adm. 12. 1660–1934. 8,779 vols., &c.

Adm. 2. Out-letters: classified under sub-headings such as 'Orders and Instructions', 'Lords' letters', 'Secretary's letters (including letters to commanders-in-chief), 'Letters relating to Admiralty and Vice-Admiralty courts and business', 'Secret orders and letters', &c. 1656–1859. 1,756 vols.

Adm. 116. Cases: these are similar to the papers in Adm. 1. 1852–1926. 2,313 vols.

Adm. 3. Minutes. 1657–1881. 286 vols., &c.

Adm. 4 and 5. Original patents. 1707–1867. 229 cases, &c.

Adm. 8. List books, showing the disposition of ships. names of officers, &c. 1673–1893. 172 vols.

Adm. 9. Returns of officers' services. 1817–22, 1846. 61 vols.

Adm. 6. Various registers, returns, and certificates. 1673–1859. 428 vols., &c.

Adm. 7. Miscellanea: including letter-books of Admirals and others, 1796–1857; naval instructions, 1684–1830; cases, similar to those in Adm. 116, 1809–71; books of Vice-Admiral Sir E. Hughes, 1747–85; &c. 1563–1871. 773 vols., &c.

Adm. 13. Supplementary: records supplementing or in continuation of some of the preceding classes. 1803–1902. 250 vols.

Adm. 10–12. Indexes and compilations, Series I–III. Adm. 12 (1660–1926, 1668 vols.) includes Admiralty digests, which refer to subjects, and indexes, which refer to persons and ships, relating to the papers in Adm. 1, Adm. 3, and Adm. 116.

Adm. 50. Admirals' journals. 1702–1911. 413 vols., &c.

Adm. 51. Captains' logs. 1669–1852. 4,563 vols.

Adm. 52. Masters' logs. 1672–1840. 4,660 vols.

Adm. 53. Ships' logs. 1799–1920. 52,158 vols.

Adm. 54. Supplementary, Series I: Masters' logs preserved to fill gaps in the Ships' logs. 1837–71. 339 vols.

Adm. 55. Logs and journals relating to voyages of exploration. 1766–1861. 162 vols.

GREENWICH HOSPITAL: papers relating to Greenwich Hospital will be found in Adm. 65–80, 161–6.

HISTORICAL SECTION: a collection of documents forming material for the official history of the First World War, arranged chronologically and under areas of operations. 1900–24. 3,955 vols. Adm. 137.

MATERIAL DEPARTMENT: including records of the Surveyor and, from 1860, of the Controller of the Navy.

Adm. 83–90. In-letters. 1806–60. 247 vols., &c.

Adm. 91–4. Out-letters. 1688–1860. 63 vols.

Adm. 135–6. Ships' books. 1807–73, 1854–1962. 570 vols.

Adm. 95. Miscellanea. 1688–1867. 98 vols., &c.

MEDICAL DEPARTMENT: including records of the Sick and Hurt Board, the Physician General of the Navy, the Inspector General of Naval Hospitals and Fleets, the Medical Department and other bodies which at different times administered the medical affairs of the Navy.

Adm. 97. In-letters. 1702–1862. 259 vols., &c.

Adm. 132. Register of letters received. 1832–62. 31 vols.

Adm. 133. Digest and index of letters received. 1832–62. 31 vols.

Adm. 98. Out-letters. 1742–1833. 335 vols.

Adm. 99. Minutes. 1698–1816. 281 vols., &c.

Adm. 100. Accounts. 1810–22. 5 vols.

Adm. 101. Medical journals. 1785–1856. 127 bundles.

Adm. 102. Hospital musters. 1740–1860. 920 vols., &c.

Adm. 103. Prisoners of war. 1755–1831. 648 vols., &c.

Adm. 104. Various. 1774–1886. 29 vols., &c.

Adm. 105. Miscellanea, including reports of medical officers, inspectors of hospitals, &c. 1803–63; and minutes, &c., of Sir William Burnett, Physician-General of the Navy, 1832–53. 1696–1867, 1871. 74 vols., &c.

NAVY BOARD

Adm. 106. Navy Board records, comprising in-letters, out-letters, minutes, registers, and miscellanea. 1658–1837. 3,624 vols.

STATION RECORDS: CHINA

Adm. 125. Correspondence: records of the China Station, including the East Indies, Japan, Korea, Australasia, Pacific Islands, and the Behring Sea. They include correspondence relating to the East India Company in China, general service proceedings, piracy, and the Sino-Japanese War of 1894–5. 1828–1936. 148 vols.

Adm. 126. Indexes to correspondence. 1856–1914. 6 vols.

TRANSPORT DEPARTMENT

Adm. 108. Records. 1773–1837. 189 vols.

VICTUALLING DEPARTMENT

Adm. 109–114, 134. In-letters, out-letters, minutes, accounts, registers, miscellanea, and registers of letters received. 1660–1860. 1,214 vols., &c.

HIGH COURT OF ADMIRALTY

The High Court of Admiralty was originally concerned chiefly with cases of piracy and spoil, but it gradually acquired cognisance of all cases affecting piracy, privateering, ships and merchandise on the high seas or overseas. The records effectively begin from the year 1525.

CRIMINAL

H.C.A. 1. Oyer and terminer records: proceedings in trials for piracy and other crimes committed on the high seas. 1535–1834. 101 vols., and bundles.

INSTANCE AND PRIZE COURTS

H.C.A. 2. Accounts. 1628–1889. 567 vols., and bundles.

H.C.A. 3. Acts. 1524–1786. 290 vols., and bundles.

H.C.A. 4. Appraisements. 1626–1745. 24 files.

H.C.A. 5–7. Assignation Books (Instance). 1746–1864. 144 vols.

H.C.A. 8–11. Assignation Books (Prize). 1718–1840. 337 vols.

H.C.A. 28–9. Court Minute Books (Prize). 1777–1842. 93 vols.

H.C.A. 13. Examinations, &c. 1536–1826. 223 vols. and bundles.

H.C.A. 15–26. Instance papers. 1629–1943. 1,930 bundles.

H.C.A. 32. Prize papers. 1661–1855. 1,846 bundles.

H.C.A. 34. Sentences (prize). 1643–1854. 65 vols., and bundles.

H.C.A. 39. Warrants. 1515–1760. 55 files.

H.C.A. 40. Royal warrants. 1760–1853. 27 parcels.

H.C.A. 38. Warrant books. 1541–1772. 77 vols.

H.C.A. 30. Miscellanea: this class includes many subsidiary books and papers of the Court, with many other reports and other records. 1531–1888. 803 bundles and vols.

PRIZE APPEALS RECORDS

H.C.A. 41. Acts. 1689–1813. 18 bundles and vols.

H.C.A. 42. Appeals papers. 1689–1833. 574 bundles.

H.C.A. 43–8. Assignation books, case books, interlocutories, sentences, miscellanea. 1689–1844. 260 vols., and bundles.

APPOINTMENTS

H.C.A. 50. Admiralty muniment books: entry books relating to appointments, the establishment of Vice-Admiralty Courts in colonial possessions, &c. Eliz. I–1873. 24 vols.

H.C.A. 51. Indexes to Admiralty Muniment Books. Eliz. I–1955. 2 vols.

VICE-ADMIRALTY COURTS

H.C.A. 49. Proceedings. 106 bundles and papers.

AIR MINISTRY

AIR 23. Second World War. Overseas Commands: records of Air Force headquarters in Middle East and Far East Commands. c. 7,000 pieces.

CABINET OFFICE

The origin of the Cabinet Office is to be found in the secretariat of the Committee of Imperial Defence.

The Defence Committee of the Cabinet was formed in 1895, remodelled in 1902 as the Committee of Imperial Defence, and provided with a small permanent secretariat in 1904. In 1914 its functions were absorbed by the War Committee (later Council), which in December 1916 merged with the Cabinet to become the War Cabinet. It was then, in 1916, that a record of the proceedings of the Cabinet first began to be kept, and from that date there is preserved a complete set of Cabinet papers. [See *List of Cabinet Papers 1880–1914*, Public Record Office Handbook No. 4, H.M.S.O. 1964; *List of papers of the Committee of Imperial Defence to 1914*, P.R.O. Handbook No. 6, H.M.S.O. 1964; *List of Cabinet Papers 1915 and 1916*, P.R.O. Handbook No. 9, H.M.S.O. 1966; *The records of the Cabinet Office to 1922*, P.R.O. Handbook No. 11, 1966.]

CABINET PAPERS

Cab. 1. Miscellaneous records: printed Cabinet memoranda to December 1916. *c.* 800 papers.

Cab. 27. Committees. General Series includes the Eastern Committee (March 1918 to January 1919).

Cab. 37. Photographic copies of Cabinet papers, many relating to the Far East—Chinese claims in Burma, Hong Kong, Behring Sea, Opium, Japan, China, Wei-hai-wei, China Station, Boxer Rising, Railways in China, Anglo-Japanese Agreement, Russo-Japanese War, &c. 1880–1916. 162 vols. [See *List of Cabinet Papers, 1880–1914*, P.R.O. Handbooks, no. 4, 1964.]

COMMITTEE OF IMPERIAL DEFENCE PAPERS

Cab. 2. Minutes: some relating to the Far East. 1902–22. 3 folders (subject index).

Cab. 4. Memoranda, miscellaneous: some relating to the Far East. 1903–14. 5 folders and 30 vols.

Cab. 5. Memoranda, colonial defence: papers relating to the defence of particular overseas territories. 1902–22. 5 folders.

Cab. 17. Correspondence and miscellaneous papers. 1902–14. 11 folders.

Cab. 18. Miscellaneous volumes. 1875–1915, 1918–19. 96 vols. and 3 folders.

COLONIAL/OVERSEAS DEFENCE COMMITTEE PAPERS

Cab. 7. Minutes, &c. 1878–1916. 7 vols. and 1 folder.

Cab. 8. Memoranda: concerning the defence of the colonies. 1885–1914, 1916, 1919–22. 9 vols.

Cab. 9. Remarks: on memoranda and defence schemes prepared by the colonies. 1887–1914, 1919–22. 16 vols., and 5 folders.

Cab. 10. Minutes by the Committee: an incomplete collection. 1912–14. 3 folders.

Cab. 11. Defence schemes: relating to various colonies. 1863–1914. 153 folders.

Cab. 38. Committee of Imperial Defence: photographic copies of minutes and memoranda. 1888–1914. 28 pieces. (Hdbk. 6.)

C.I.D. *AD HOC* COMMITTEES OF INQUIRY PAPERS

Cab. 16. Reports of *ad hoc* subcommittees. 1905–14. 34 vols. and folders.

C.I.D. JOINT OVERSEAS AND HOME PORTS DEFENCE COMMITTEE PAPERS

Cab. 36. Minutes and memoranda of the Joint Committee. 1920–2. 2 folders.

CONFERENCES, ETC.

Cab. 30. Minutes and memoranda of the Washington Conference on Disarmament and on Pacific and Eastern questions held between November 1921 and February 1922; with minutes, memoranda, &c. of various committees, and with minutes and circulated papers of the British Empire Delegation. Other papers relating to this Conference are in Cab. 4, above.

HISTORICAL SECTION

Cab. 45. Official war histories 1904–18: correspondence and papers. Contains one file about the Russo-Japanese War of 1904–5.

WAR OF 1939–45

WAR CABINET COMMITTEES

Cab. 96. Far East. 1940–5. 10 vols.

Cab. 107. Co-ordination of departmental action in the event of war with certain countries. Minutes of meetings and memoranda (incl. Japan). 1940–2.

Cab. 72. Economic policy. 27 pieces.

Cab. 78. MISC and GEN series. 39 pieces.

Cab. 81. Chemical warfare against Japan.

Cab. 92. Supply, Production, Priority, and Manpower. 126 pieces.

The Second World War; a guide to documents in the Public Record Office (P.R.O. Handbooks, no. 15. 1972) includes a general index to War Cabinet Committees Cab. 69–Cab. 98 and Cab. 107.

CAPTURED ENEMY DOCUMENTS

GERMAN FOREIGN MINISTRY: comprising copies of the records of the Foreign Ministries of Prussia, the North German Federation, and, from 1871, of Germany. See *Catalogue of German Foreign Ministry files and microfilms, 1867–1920*.

G.F.M. 1. Repertoria, &c. 1866–1945. 14 vols. (photostats).

G.F.M. 2–5, 30. Projects H, K, L, M, C. 1863–1945.

G.F.M. 13. Florida State University Selection: including files relating to the Far East, 1867–1914. 150 reels.

G.F.M. 19. Miscellaneous. 1870–1945. 8 boxes of prints and 55 reels.

G.F.M. 21. American Committee for Study of War Documents Selection: covering parts of all continents. 1855–1920. 433 reels.

GERMAN NAVAL ARCHIVES: comprising copies of the records of the Admiralstab der Marine, Marine-Kabinett, Reichs-Marine-Amt, and Oberkommando der Marine/Seekriegsleitung, filmed by the Australian Government and the universities of Cambridge, Michigan, and Hawaii. G.F.M. 26–32.

G.F.M. 28, 29. Contain files relating to the Far East.

COLONIAL OFFICE

Before a separate Secretaryship of State for the Colonies was appointed in 1854 colonial affairs were dealt with by the Commissioners for Trade and Plantations (to 1782), the Home Secretary (1782–1801), and the Secretary of State for War and the Colonies (1801–54), but all papers relating to colonial affairs are now to be found among the archives of the Colonial Office. [See *The records of the Colonial and Dominions Office*, PUBLIC RECORD OFFICE Handbook no. 3, H.M.S.O., 1964.]

A printed list (Lists and indexes, xxxvi) covers the records down to 1837. There is also a Calendar of *State Papers Colonial relating to the East Indies, China, Japan and Persia* for the period 1513 to 1634, 5 vols., and including material in the British Museum and the India Office Records.

Eastern

C.O. 825. Original correspondence, relating in a general way to the Far Eastern colonies. 1927–43. 38 vols.

C.O. 537. Original correspondence, supplementary. 1914. 1 vol.

C.O. 872. Register of correspondence. 1927–41. 3 vols.

East Indies

C.O. 77. Original correspondence, entry books, &c., relating to the East India Company and its possessions, China, and to Lord Macartney's embassy to China in 1793–4. Also Meteorological Journal: Canton and Macao, 1807 (v. 64). 1570–1856. 66 vols.

Hong Kong

C.O. 129. Original correspondence. 1841–1943. 90 vols.

C.O. 537. Original correspondence, supplementary. 1873–98, 1907. 5 vols.

C.O. 349. Register of correspondence. 1849–1931. 29 vols.

C.O. 489. Register of out-letters. 1872–1926. 15 vols.

C.O. 403. Entry books. 1843–72. 21 vols.

C.O. 130. Acts, 1844–1939. 13 vols.

C.O. 131. Sessional papers. 1844–1939. 104 vols.

C.O. 132. Government gazettes. 1846–1940. 86 vols.

C.O. 133. Miscellanea: blue books of statistics, trade and shipping returns. 1844–1940. 111 vols.

Wei-hai-wei

C.O. 521. Original correspondence. 1898–1931. 32 vols.

C.O. 770. Register of correspondence. 1898–1931. 4 vols.

C.O. 771. Register of out-letters. 1901–26. 4 vols.

C.O. 841. Acts. 1903–30. 1 vol.

C.O. 744. Government gazettes. 1908–30. 3 vols.

C.O. 873. Commissioners' files: local records of the Commissioner in Wei-hai-wei taken over by the Colonial Office on rendition of the territory. 1899–1930. 779 files, &c.

Far Eastern Reconstruction

C.O. 865. Original correspondence. 1942–4. 5 boxes [of files].

C.O. 975. Registers of correspondence. 1942–4. 1 vol.

Supplementary

C.O. 537. Correspondence: relating to various colonies, incl. Hong Kong 1873–98, 1907 (noted under the Colonies concerned), and including correspondence relating to the Civil Service Commission, emoluments of governors and their staffs, secret service pensions, and other matters. 1759–1929. 156 vols.

Accounts Branch

C.O. 431. Original correspondence: correspondence with colonial Governors, the Treasury and other departments, and with individuals, relating to financial matters. 1868–1925. 152 vols.

C.O. 622. Register of correspondence. 1868–1921. 18 vols.

C.O. 621. Entry books and registers of out-letters. 1868–1908. 19 vols.

C.O. 701. Miscellanea. 1794–1913. 26 vols.

British North Borneo Company

C.O. 874. Papers include relations with Japan and the Japanese occupation. *c.* 200 pieces.

Chief Clerk

C.O. 523. Original correspondence: correspondence of the General Department on such matters as precedence, consecration of colonial bishops, medals, titles, the drafting of governors' instructions, &c. 1843–8, 1901–31. 88 vols.

C.O. 863. Register of correspondence. 1902–31. 8 vols.

C.O. 864. Register of out-letters. 1902–33. 4 vols.

Claims, 1914–18 War

C.O. 848. Original correspondence. 1920–38. 7 boxes.

Colonial Statistical Tables

C.O. 442. Command Papers: concerning trade with overseas territories. 1833–1912. 63 vols.

Colonies, General

C.O. 323. Original correspondence: including the series formerly known as 'Plantations General' among the Board of Trade correspondence (1689–1780), Law Officers' reports on colonial Acts, applications for passports and colonial appointments, semi-official correspondence and correspondence, including circular dispatches, relating to the colonies generally. Between 1801 and 1854 much of the correspondence concerns both the War and Colonial Departments which were then under the same Secretary of State. 1689–1943. 1,868 vols.

C.O. 324. Entry Books, Series I: entry books of commissions, instructions, petitions, grants, Orders in Council, warrants, Law Officers' Opinions, letters (many of a private and unofficial nature), précis of correspondence, &c. 1662–1872. 175 vols.

C.O. 381. Entry Books, Series II: similar to C.O. 324, but from 1816 arranged under the various colonies. 1740, 1791–1872. 93 vols.

C.O. 378. Register of correspondence. 1852–1931. 71 vols.

C.O. 379. Register of out-letters. 1871–1925. 24 vols.

C.O. 432. Register of general miscellaneous correspondence. 1860–70. 2 vols.

C.O. 652. Register of 'unregistered' correspondence. 1886–1927. 4 vols.

C.O. 694. Register of secret correspondence. 1865–1928. 25 vols.

C.O. 570. Secret entry books and registers of out-letters. 1870–95. 2 vols.

C.O. 854. Circular dispatches. 1808–1929. 74 vols.

C.O. 862. Register of replies to circular dispatches. 1862–1931. 25 vols.

C.O. 816. Original letters patent, warrants, &c. 1834–82. 7 docs.

C.O. 380. Draft letters patent, commissions, royal instructions, warrants, &c., bound under colonies.

1764–1882. 183 vols. (92. Hong Kong: Labuan. 1874–82).

C.O. 325. Miscellanea: historical sketches and tracts on the colonies, returns of colonial appointments, registers of applications for colonial appointments, statistical returns, précis and memoranda. 1744–1858. 46 vols.

Confidential Print

See List of Colonial Office Confidential Print to 1916 (P.R.O. handbooks, no. 8). 1965.

C.O. 882 (formerly C.O. 809). Eastern. 1847–1933. 12 vols.

C.O. 601. Catalogues. 1852–1915. 3 vols.

Correspondence

C.O. 714. Indexes to correspondence, arranged by colonies. 1795–1870. 165 vols.

Duplicates

C.O. 412. Duplicates of correspondence in the general series. 1605–1863. 247 bundles.

Economic

C.O. 852. Original correspondence. 1935–40. 353 vols.

Emigration

C.O. 384/133. Original correspondence. Dispatches: Hong Kong, &c. 1881.

Empire Marketing Board

C.O. 758. Original correspondence. 1922–34. 107 boxes.

C.O. 759. Card index. 134 packets.

C.O. 760. Minutes and papers. 1926–33. 39 vols.

Governors' Pensions

C.O. 449. Original correspondence. 1863–1925. 10 vols.

Honours

C.O. 448. Original correspondence. 1858–1943. 68 vols.

C.O. 728. Register of correspondence. 1859–1931. 10 vols.

C.O. 729. Register of out-letters. 1872–1934. 4 vols.

Imperial Service Order

C.O. 524. Original correspondence. 1902–32. 14 vols.

C.O. 834. Register of correspondence. 1902–26. 2 vols.

C.O. 835. Register of out-letters. 1902–26. 2 vols.

Maps and Plans
C.O. 700. Maps. 17th–19th centuries. *c.* 1600 maps.

Military
C.O. 820. Original correspondence. 1927–43. 51 vols.
C.O. 871. Register of correspondence. 1927–31. 5 vols.

Patronage
C.O. 429. Original correspondence. 1867–70, 1881–1919. 131 vols.
C.O. 430. Register of correspondence. 1867–70, 1887–1918. 13 vols.

Personnel
C.O. 850. Original correspondence. 1932–43. 195 boxes.

Precedence
C.O. 851. Original correspondence. 1873–85. 1 box.

Prisoners of war and civilian internees department
C.O. 980. Much of the class relates to civilians captured by the Japanese in Singapore and Hong Kong.

Registers (Miscellaneous)
C.O. 326. General: including Board of Trade registers and indexes, 1635–1787; and general registers of colonial letters received between 1810 and 1849, after which date see separate registers under each colony. 1623–1849. 358 vols.
C.O. 382. Daily correspondence. 1849–1929. 82 vols.
C.O. 668. Daily correspondence, out-letters. 1901–10. 9 vols.
C.O. 383. Acts. 1781–1892. 93 vols.
C.O. 600. Printing. 1864–1914. 26 vols.

Order of St. Michael and St. George
C.O. 447. Original correspondence. 1836–1932. 129 vols.
C.O. 845. Register of correspondence. 1869–1930. 5 vols.
C.O. 734. Entry books and register of out-letters. 1838–1934. 7 vols.
C.O. 844. Original warrants and letters patent. 1852–99. 8 vols.
C.O. 745. Miscellanea. 1818–1940. 5 vols.

Social Service
C.O. 859. Original correspondence: concerning labour conditions, nutrition, public health, housing, education, &c. 1939–43. 82 boxes.

Board of Trade
C.O. 388. Original correspondence: papers relating to foreign and domestic trade, &c. 1654–1792. 95 vols., &c.
C.O. 389. Entry books: commissions, instructions, petitions, correspondence, Orders in Council, &c. 1660–1803. 59 vols.
C.O. 390. Miscellanea: trade statistics, Custom House accounts, reports, &c. 1654–1799. 15 vols., &c.
C.O. 391. Minutes: journals of the Board, with the original minutes of the proceedings, &c. 1675–1782. 120 vols. [See *Calendar of State Papers, Colonial*, and *Journal of the Commissioners for Trade and Plantations*, 14 vols., 1920–38.]

Colonial Labour Advisory Committee
C.O. 888. Papers and minutes. 1931–61. 11 vols.

Colonial Economic Research Committee
C.O. 898. Papers of the Committee, appointed in 1947. 1947–61. 8 vols.

Colonial Products Research Council
C.O. 899. Papers of the Council, appointed in 1943. 1943–59. 6 vols.

Colonial Research Council
C.O. 900. Papers. 1943–59. 16 vols.

Colonial Social Science Research Council
C.O. 901. Papers. 1944–61. 40 vols.

Colonial Agricultural Animal Health and Forestry Research Committee
C.O. 908. Papers. 1944–61. 42 vols.

Colonial Fisheries Advisory Committee
C.O. 910. Minutes and papers. 1943–61. 5 vols.

Colonial Pesticides Research Committee
C.O. 911. Minutes and papers. 1947–61. 26 vols.

Treatment of Offenders in the Colonies, Advisory Committee
C.O. 912. Minutes and papers. 1937–61. 10 vols.

Colonial Medical Research Committee
C.O. 913. Minutes and papers. 1945–60. 17 vols.

Colonial Local Government Advisory Panel
C.O. 915. Papers. 1948–60. 3 vols.

Committee on the Deportation of British Subjects from the Colonies
C.O. 916. Papers. 1932–3. 1 vol.

BOARD OF CUSTOMS AND EXCISE

Many of the Customs records have been destroyed in a series of fires at the London Customs House, and most of the records transferred to the Public Record Office are compilations made, until 1871 in the office of the Inspector General of Imports and Exports, later in the Statistical Office. Many other records have been retained by the Board of Customs and Excise at King's Beam House. No excise records have been transferred.

Customs 3. Ledgers of imports and exports. 1697–1780. 80 vols.

Customs 4. Ledgers of imports under countries. 1792–1899. 94 vols.

Customs 6. Ledgers of imports into colonies, under countries. 1832–53. 22 vols.

Customs 8. Ledgers of exports of British merchandise, under countries. 1812–99. 140 vols.

Customs 10. Ledgers of exports of foreign and colonial merchandise, under countries. 1809–99. 97 vols.

Customs 12. Ledgers of exports from colonies, under countries. 1832–53. 22 vols.

Customs 17. States of navigation, commerce and revenue. 1772–1808. 30 vols.

Customs 21. Miscellaneous books; including entry books of letters and reports 1816–57, and registers of seizures, 1715–86. 1715–1857. 92 vols.

EXCHEQUER AND AUDIT DEPARTMENT

The Exchequer and Audit Department was created in 1866, but its records include many formerly belonging to the Commissioners of Audit (created 1785) and to various offices absorbed by them.

A.O. 1. Declared accounts in rolls: including army accounts. 1536–1828. 2,541 rolls.

A.O. 2. Declared and passed accounts in books: including accounts of Superintendents of British trade in China. 1803–48. 92 vols.

A.O. 20. Accounts declared before the Chancellor of the Exchequer. 1849–66. 124 vols. Incl. accounts of the China expedition, 1840 to 1848.

A.O. 22. Signed and passed accounts: including accounts of colonial treasurers. 1848–1912. 137 vols.

A.O. 3. Accounts various: including Admiralty, Army, including account of the China expedition 1840–8. Colonies and Dependencies, Consuls, Customs, &c. 1539–1886. 1,430 rolls, &c.

A.O. 19. Accounts current. c. 1828–1906. 123 bundles.

A.O. 4. Registers of accounts received. 1765–1834. 1845–68. 27 vols.

A.O. 5. Registers of papers received. 1806–1918. 86 vols.

A.O. 6. Minutes: including those of the Commissioners for Colonial Accounts, 1814–32. 1785–1867. 147 vols.

A.O. 7. Out-letters, general. 1785–1867. 91 vols.

A.O. 8. Reports and letters to the Treasury, some relating to the colonies, 1814–32. 1801–67. 89 vols., &c.

A.O. 9. In-letters, office of Comptroller-General of the Exchequer. 1840–67. 11 bundles.

A.O. 10. Reports to the Board. 1785–1867. 106 vols.

A.O. 16. Miscellanea: including papers relating to Admiralty courts, colonies and dependencies, &c. 1568–1910. 196 vols., &c.

A.O. 17. Absorbed departments: including the records of the Comptroller of Army Accounts, 1711–1835. 1580–1867. 499 vols., &c.

A.O. 23. Reports and letters. 1867–90. 23 vols.

FOREIGN OFFICE

The Foreign Office was created in the reorganization of 1782, and the records of the Foreign Department form a continuous series with the State Papers, Foreign. The majority of the Foreign Office papers belong to the two classes GENERAL CORRESPONDENCE and EMBASSY AND CONSULAR ARCHIVES, the rest being classified under TREATIES, ARCHIVES OF COMMISSION, CONFIDENTIAL PRINT, CHIEF CLERK'S DEPARTMENT, PASSPORT OFFICE, PEACE CONFERENCE OF 1919–20, WAR OF 1939–45, MISCELLANEOUS, and PRIVATE COLLECTIONS.

There is likely to be a great deal more material relating to the affairs of the Far East in these records than is apparent from the catalogues and lists. All the diplomatic exchanges between London and foreign capitals relating to Far Eastern affairs will be found in the files coming under the heading of the foreign state concerned: to this material there is no short-cut, although the Confidential Prints give some indication of the nature and volume of the material. Attention is therefore directed to the following headings: America, United States; France; Prussia and Germany; Russia, &c. See *The records of the Foreign Office 1782–1939* (P.R.O. Handbooks, no. 13, 1969).

GENERAL CORRESPONDENCE: original dispatches and reports from British diplomatic and consular representatives abroad, correspondence with foreign missions in England, miscellaneous correspondence with individuals, and drafts or copies of letters sent from the Office; arranged alphabetically under countries until 1905, and thereafter under the following subject-headings—Africa (New Series), Commercial, Consular, Dominions Information, Library, News, Political, and Treaty, with other headings included in time of war. See especially:

F.O. 5. *America, United States of, Series II.* 1793–1905. 2,625 vols.

F.O. 17. *China*: including dispatches from the consul-general at Seoul in Korea for the period 1890–1905. 1815–1905. 1,768 vols.

F.O. 27. *France.* 1781–1905. 3,772 vols.

F.O. 46. *Japan.* 1856–1905. 678 vols.

F.O. 64. *Prussia and Germany.* 1781–1905. 1,654 vols.

F.O. 65. *Russia.* 1781–1905. 1,739 vols.

F.O. 83. *Great Britain and General*: including correspondence with Government departments at home, and many matters not relating to any one foreign country. 1745–1930. 2,480 vols.

F.O. 97. *Supplement to General Correspondence*: correspondence, enclosures, papers relating to various cases and claims, memoranda, &c., supplementary to the general series of correspondence, arranged under countries. 1780–1905. 621 vols.

F.O. 368. *Commercial.* 1906–19. 2,269 vols.

F.O. 369. *Consular.* 1906–33. 2,340 vols.

F.O. 395. *News.* 1916–33. 443 vols.

F.O. 371. *Political.* 1906–32. 16,518 vols.

F.O. 372. *Treaty.* 1906–33. 2,981 vols.

F.O. 566. *Registers of General Correspondence.* 1817–1911. 1,081 vols.

F.O. 605. *Registers (Modern Series) and Indexes of General Correspondence*: microfilm copies of originals in the Foreign Office Library. 1810–90. 256 reels.

EMBASSY AND CONSULAR ARCHIVES: archives of British diplomatic and consular establishments overseas, arranged alphabetically under countries, and containing original letters from the Foreign Office and drafts of dispatches from envoys abroad. These records are complementary to the General Correspondence. See especially:

America, United States of

F.O. 115. Correspondence. 1791–1929. 3,392 vols.

F.O. 116. Letter-books. 1791–1823. 10 vols.

F.O. 117. Registers of correspondence. 1823–78, 1900–29. 40 vols.

China

F.O. 228. Correspondence: including correspondence relating to Korea up to 1896. 1834–1930. 4,371 vols., &c. See also F.O. 676, below.

F.O. 229. Correspondence, duplicates. 1836–53. 12 vols.

F.O. 230. Letter-books. 1834–1917. 185 vols.

F.O. 231. Registers of correspondence. 1836–1945. 117 vols.

F.O. 232. Indexes to correspondence. 1843–1937. 54 vols.

F.O. 233. Miscellanea: catalogue of embassy archives, 1727–1859; trade and intelligence reports; records of legal proceedings; miscellaneous papers of the Chinese Secretary's Office; entry book of papers relating to the East India Company in China; claims arising from Sino-Japanese hostilities (1927–32); accounts, circulars, &c. 1759–1935. 189 vols.

F.O. 917. China: Shanghai Supreme Court: Private records. Probate papers. 1857–1941. 3998 files.

F.O. 932. Chinese Secretary's Office.

F.O. 385. Chinkiang: correspondence. 1871–5, 1889–1925. 19 vols.

F.O. 386. Chinkiang: registers of correspondence. 1871–1927. 8 vols.

F.O. 387. Chinkiang: miscellanea, including registers of British subjects, ships and marriages, notices of marriages, and copies of powers of attorney. 1865–1927. 11 vols.

F.O. 562. Peking: correspondence. 1902–20. 13 vols.

F.O. 692. Peking: registers of correspondence. 1901–47. 9 vols.

F.O. 564. Peking: miscellaneous registers, &c. 1874–1926. 14 vols., &c.

F.O. 563. Peking: miscellanea, including fee cash books, military registration papers, and applications for passports. 1905–31. 8 boxes, &c.

F.O. 656. Shanghai Supreme Court: consular and other correspondence relating to court business; general correspondence of the Crown Advocate and his journal, recording visits made and cases heard. 1862–1939. 269 vols.

F.O. 924. China, Shanghai, Registrar of Companies, 1914–49. 54 files.

F.O. 663. Amoy: correspondence with Chief Superintendent of Trade, general correspondence, registers of correspondence, registers of births, deaths, and marriages. 1834–1951. 45 boxes and 50 vols.

F.O. 664. Chengtu: register of births, marriages, and deaths, lease, &c. 1902–45. 5 vols., &c.

F.O. 665. Foochow: correspondence, registers of births, deaths, and marriages, lists of British subjects. 1846–1946. 10 vols., &c.

F.O. 666. Hankow: correspondence, 1865, 1896–1921, and registers of births, deaths, and marriages. 1863–1951. 92 vols., &c.

F.O. 667. Ichang: correspondence, 1926, and registers of births, deaths, and marriages. 1879–1941. 3 vols., &c.

F.O. 668. Kunming: lease, registers of births, deaths, and marriages. 1945–51. 3 vols., &c.

F.O. 669. Newchang: correspondence. 1865–8. 1 box.

F.O. 670. Ningpo: correspondence, registers of births, deaths, and marriages, lists of British subjects.

1843–63. 256 vols., &c. Also correspondence of the Superintendent of Trade in China.

F.O. 671. Shanghai: correspondence, lists of British subjects. 1845–1948. 572 vols., &c.

F.O. 672. Shanghai: registers of births, deaths, and marriages. 1851–64. 3 vols.

F.O. 914. Shanghai.

F.O. 673. Taku: correspondence, registers of births, deaths, and marriages, Supreme Court records. 1862–76. 11 files, &c.

F.O. 674. Tientsin: correspondence, registers of births, deaths, and marriages, and Supreme Court records. 1860–1952. 344 files, &c.

F.O. 675. Tsingtao: correspondence, registers of correspondence, registers of births, deaths, and marriages, inventories of archives (1936–9). 1911–51. 19 files, &c.

F.O. 676. Correspondence Series II: files of the legation at Peking, 1875–1947; the Embassy at Nanking, 1929–48; the Embassy at Shanghai, 1937–40; the Embassy at Chungking, 1938–45. Correspondence before 1930 is complementary to that in F.O. 228. 1875–1948. 469 files.

F.O. 677. Records of the Superintendent of Trade, complementary to those in F.O. 228. 1759–1874. 17 boxes. 9 vols.

F.O. 678. Various consulates: deeds, agreements, wills, and other miscellaneous legal papers. 1837–1959. 2,952 files, &c.

F.O. 679. Various consulates: registers of deeds, &c. 1853–1953. 20 vols.

F.O. 680. Various consulates: land registers. 1854–1942. 50 vols.

F.O. 681. Various consulates: registers of births, deaths, and marriages from consulates and vice-consulates at Canton, Chansha, Chefoo, Chinanfu (Tsinan), Chungking, Daires, Kinkiang, Kweilin, Mukden, Nanking, Swatow, Taewan, Tamsuy, Tengyneh, Wei-hai-wei, Whampoa, and Yunnanfu. 1861–1951. 81 vols.

F.O. 692. Peking: registers of correspondence and (after 1920) of the Commercial Secretary. 1901–47. 9 vols.

F.O. 693. Chinanfu (Tsinan): record book of court cases, &c. 1907–37. 1 vol.

F.O. 694. Canton: list of British subjects; record of decrees issued by Chinese authorities. 1844–51. 2 files.

F.O. 735. Chefoo: inventories of archives, furniture and other government property; copies of correspondence relating to the Chinese Maritime Customs Service. 1860–1941. 6 boxes and 1 file.

F.O. 851. Wenchow: correspondence. 1878–1906. 6 vols.

F.O. 931. Kwantung provincial archives.

F.O. 932. Chinese Secretary's Office.

F.O. 682. Peking. Papers in the Chinese language. Archives of the Chinese Secretary's Office at the British Embassy in Peking, incl. diplomatic and commercial correspondence, official Chinese documents, some deeds, and much material relating to rebellions and their suppression, and missionaries. Certain parts of the MS. Peking Gazette were transferred to the State Paper Room at the British Museum. 1765–1951. 1,968 pieces.

F.O. 677. Superintendent of Trade: records. 1759–1874. 26 vols.

France

F.O. 146. Correspondence. 1814–1915. 4,604 vols.

F.O. 147. Registers of correspondence. 1815–1915. 108 vols.

F.O. 148. Miscellanea. 1782–1900. 38 vols., &c.

Germany

F.O. 244. Prussia and Germany: correspondence. 1784–1913. 825 vols.

F.O. 245. Prussia and Germany: letter-books. 1788–1860. 17 vols.

F.O. 246. Prussia and Germany: registers of correspondence. 1823–1913. 44 vols.

F.O. 340. Prussia and Germany: indexes to correspondence. 1909–13. 9 vols.

Japan

F.O. 262. Correspondence, with accounts from 1921. 1859–1940. 2,032 vols., &c.

F.O. 344. Letter-books. 1865–1907. 3 vols.

F.O. 263. Registers of correspondence. 1858–1941. 39 vols.

F.O. 276. Accounts. 1858–1920. 74 vols.

F.O. 345. Miscellanea: memoranda of interviews with the Japanese authorities, translations from Japanese newspapers and other publications, special cases and claims, papers and correspondence relating to the foreign settlements, marriage declarations and certificates (1870–87), correspondence concerning the visit of the Duke of Gloucester upon the investiture of the Emperor with the Order of the Garter, and various treaties, conventions and agreements. 1855–1923. 59 vols.

F.O. 721. Taiwan (Formosa): register of deaths. 1873–1901. 1 vol.

F.O. 763. Tamsui: correspondence, registers of correspondence. 1897–1939. 25 files, &c.

F.O. 796. Nagasaki: consular court records, correspondence, registers of correspondence, register of British subjects. 1859–1932. 202 vols, &c.

F.O. 797. Shimonoseki: correspondence, register of British subjects. 1901–22. 47 files, &c.

F.O. 798. Tokyo: consular court records, correspondence, registers of correspondence, indexes to correspondence. 1859–1928. 83 vols.

F.O. 908. Yokohama: papers on perpetual leases and the reconstruction of the Foreign Settlement of Yokohama after the earthquake and fire of 1923. 1924–7. 4 files.

Korea

F.O. 523. Correspondence of the consulate-general at Seoul. 1891–1902, 1909. 13 vols.

Portugal, Macao

F.O. 697. Correspondence. 1835–66. 2 boxes. The bulk of the consulate's records, which had been deposited in the Consulate-General in Canton, were destroyed when that building was burned down in 1949.

Russia and U.S.S.R.

F.O. 181. Correspondence. 1801–1918, 1941–7. 1030 vols., &c.

F.O. 182. Letter-books. 1820–53. 16 vols.

F.O. 183. Registers of correspondence. 1816–1918. 23 vols.

F.O. 184. Miscellanea. 1800–81. 14 vols.

F.O. 399. Miscellaneous consulates: registers from various consulates and vice-consulates, including Irkutsk. 1894–1919. 6 vols.

F.O. 537. Vladivostok: registers of correspondence. 1907–23. 3 vols.

F.O. 510. Vladivostok: miscellanea. 1908–26. 11 vols.

TREATIES

F.O. 93. Protocols of treaties, arranged in alphabetical order of countries. 1778–1946. 141 boxes.

F.O. 94. Ratification of treaties, arranged in alphabetical order of countries. 1782–1950. 1,559 boxes.

ARCHIVES OF COMMISSIONS

F.O. 538. Vladivostok Allied High Commission. Correspondence and papers of the Allied High Commission set up at Vladivostok in 1918 to render military assistance to the anti-Bolshevik forces in Siberia. 1918–21. 4 vols.

F.O. 317. Miscellaneous: including register of correspondence and notes of evidence of the Behring Sea Commission (on the sealing industry in the northern Pacific), 1891–2. 1868–92. 5 vols.

CONFIDENTIAL PRINT: duplicate set of certain important political papers specially printed by the Foreign Office and known as Further Correspondence, being collections of printed papers bound up annually for distribution within the Foreign Office

and Missions concerned. Correspondence before 1942 is arranged mainly under geographical areas, that from 1942 to 1946 arranged in eight classes (including *Far Eastern Affairs*), and correspondence from 1947 onwards is arranged under countries.

F.O. 539. *Asia, Central*, including Turkestan. 1834–1911. 96 vols.

F.O. 405. *China*. 1848–1937; 1947–57. 287 vols. Including after 1954 correspondence relating to Formosa.

F.O. 436. *Far Eastern Affairs*. 1937–56. 25 vols. Correspondence relating to China, Japan, Nepal, Siam, and South-East Asia.

F.O. 410. *Japan*. 1859–1937; 1947–56. 108 vols.

F.O. 483. *Korea*. 1947–56. 10 vols.

F.O. 415. *Opium*. 1910–41. 31 vols.

F.O. 418. *Russia and Soviet Union*. 1821–1941; 1947–56. 97 vols.

F.O. 535. *Tibet and Mongolia*. 1903–23. 27 vols.

WAR OF 1939 TO 1945

F.O. 648. *International Military Tribunal, Far East*: copies of papers relating to the trials of Japanese War Criminals held in Tokyo between April 1946 and December 1948, including daily transcripts of the proceedings by the United States against Hiroshi Tamura and Soemu Toyoda. 1946–8. 187 vols. and boxes.

MISCELLANEOUS

F.O. 96. *Miscellanea, Series II*. 1816–1929, 1937. 216 bundles, &c. Naturalists' Mission to Seal Island in Behring Sea, 1896; photographs.

PRIVATE COLLECTIONS: consisting mainly of the semi-official papers, presented to the Foreign Office, of persons formerly engaged in the Diplomatic Service.

F.O. 800/244–8. *Alston Papers*: papers of Sir Beilby Francis Alston relating to China and the Far East. 1908–15. 5 vols.

F.O. 800/199–217. *Balfour Papers*: papers of Arthur James Balfour, 1st Earl Balfour, as Foreign Secretary, 1916–19, and Lord President of the Council, 1919–22; some relating to the Far East. 1916–22. 14 vols.

F.O. 800/159–91. *Bertie Papers*: correspondence of Sir Francis Bertie, later Lord Bertie of Thame, as Assistant Under-Secretary for Foreign Affairs, 1894–1903, Ambassador to Rome, 1903–4, and Ambassador to Paris, 1905–18; some relating to the Far East. 1896–1918. 33 vols.

F.O. 800/293–4. *Cadogan Papers*: correspondence of Sir Alexander Cadogan, Minister, 1933–5, and Ambassador to China, 1935–6.

F.O. 361. *Clarendon Papers*: original private letters from ambassadors and others to Lord Clarendon, Foreign Secretary, and copies of letters sent by him. 1867–70. 1 vol.

F.O. 800/243. *Crowe Papers*: miscellaneous correspondence of Sir Eyre Crowe, Under-Secretary of State for Foreign Affairs from 1920 to 1925. 1907–25. 1 vol.

F.O. 800/28; 147–58. *Curzon Papers*: correspondence of Lord Curzon as Under-Secretary of State for Foreign Affairs, 1895–8, and as Foreign Secretary 1919–23, some relating to the Far East. 1895–8, 1919–24. 5 vols.

F.O. 800/255. *Elliot Papers*: correspondence of Sir Charles Elliot, Ambassador to Japan, 1920–6.

F.O. 800/25–7. *Fergusson Papers*: correspondence of Sir James Fergusson, as Parliamentary Under-Secretary of State for Foreign Affairs. 1886–91. 3 vols.

F.O. 800/28. Correspondence of Sir James Fergusson, J. W. Lowther, and Lord Curzon, as Under-Secretaries of State for Foreign Affairs. 1886–97. 1 vol.

F.O. 362. *Granville Papers*: letters to Lord Granville and others at the Foreign Office, with drafts and copies of letters sent by him. 1870–4. 5 vols.

F.O. 800/35–113. *Grey Papers*: correspondence of Sir Edward Grey as Foreign Under-Secretary, 1892–5, and as Foreign Secretary, 1905–16, some relating to China and Japan. 1892–5, 1905–16. 78 vols.

F.O. 391. *Hammond Papers*: private and semi-official correspondence of the Rt. Hon. Edmund (afterwards Lord) Hammond, as Permanent Under-Secretary of State for Foreign Affairs, 1854–73, with British representatives abroad (including those in China and Japan), and others. 1831–4, 1854–85. 30 vols., &c.

F.O. 800/298–303. *Inverchapel Papers*: Correspondence of Sir Archibald Clark-Kerr, first Baron Inverchapel, Ambassador to China, 1938–42.

F.O. 350. *Jordan Papers*: private correspondence, mainly with the Foreign Office, of Sir John Newell Jordan, as minister resident in Korea, 1901–6, and envoy to China, 1906–20. 1901–19. 16 vols.

F.O. 800/297. *Knatchbull-Hugessen papers*: correspondence of Sir Hughe Knatchbull-Hugessen, Ambassador to China, 1936–8.

F.O. 800/29–31 and 235. *Langley Papers*: correspondence of Sir Walter Langley as Assistant Under-Secretary of State for Foreign Affairs, 1886–1919, with miscellaneous Far East correspondence, 1908–15. 3 vols.

F.O. 800/115–46. *Lansdowne Papers*: correspondence of the fifth Marquis of Lansdowne, Secretary of State for Foreign Affairs, 1900–5, some relating to China and Japan. 1885–1926. 32 vols.

F.O. 800/6–20. *Lascelles Papers*: correspondence of Sir Frank Cavendish Lascelles, Ambassador to Russia, 1894, and Ambassador to Berlin, 1896–1908, some relating to China and Japan. 1874–1908. 15 vols.

F.O. 800/28; 34. *Lowther Papers*: correspondence of Sir J. W. Lowther as Parliamentary Under-Secretary of State for Foreign Affairs. 1891–4. 1 vol.

F.O. 800/218–19. *MacDonald Papers*: correspondence of James Ramsay MacDonald, as Prime Minister and Secretary of State for Foreign Affairs. 1923–4. 2 vols.

F.O. 800/336–81. *Nicholson Papers*: private papers of Sir Arthur Nicholson, Ambassador to Russia, 1906–10, and Permanent Under-Secretary for Foreign Affairs, 1910–16. (For details see our *Guide to . . . South and South East Asia*, p. 110.)

F.O. 705. *Pottinger Papers*: private and semi-official correspondence and papers of Sir Henry Pottinger (1789–1856), envoy, plenipotentiary and Superintendent of British trade in China and Governor of Hong Kong, 1841–3, &c. 1797–8, 1809–60, 1897. 129 packets, &c.

F.O. 800/1–2. *Sanderson Papers*: papers of Thomas Henry, Lord Sanderson, Permanent Under-Secretary of State for Foreign Affairs, 1894–1906. 1860–1922. 2 vols.

F.O. 363. *Tenterden Papers*: correspondence of Lord Tenterden, Under-Secretary of State for Foreign Affairs. 1873–82. 5 vols.

GIFTS AND DEPOSITS

P.R.O. 30/40. *Ardagh Papers*: papers of Sir John Charles Ardagh (1840–1907) consisting of drafts, proof-copies of War Office and Foreign Office memoranda, technical notes and monographs, diaries, collections of private memoranda, press-cuttings, and public and private correspondence. 1862–1908. 22 boxes.

P.R.O. 30/48. *Cardwell Papers*: papers of Edward, Viscount Cardwell, mainly as Secretary of War from 1868 to 1874. 1834–1911. 54 boxes.

P.R.O. 30/6. *Carnarvon Papers*: private and official papers of the 4th Earl of Carnarvon, Secretary of State for the Colonies from 1866 to 1867 and from 1874 to 1878, &c. 1833–98. 173 vols., &c.

P.R.O. 30/29. *Granville Papers*: private and semi-official correspondence of the 1st Earl Granville and his son the 2nd Earl, including Cabinet papers of the 2nd Earl, 1855–85, and an extensive series of private correspondence with British representatives abroad and foreign representatives accredited to the court of St. James. 1604–1909. 429 boxes and vols.

P.R.O. 30/22. *Russell Papers*: private and semi-official correspondence of Lord John, later earl, Russell. 1804–1913. 118 boxes and vols.

P.R.O. 30/33. *Satow Papers*: private, diplomatic, and other correspondence, letter-books, diaries, and papers of Sir Ernest Mason Satow, who served in the Japan consular service from 1861 to 1884, was envoy to Japan from 1895 to 1900 and to China from 1900 to 1906. The collection includes his diary covering the years 1861–1926. *c.* 1856–1927. 23 boxes.

P.R.O. 30/57. *Kitchener Papers*, including: Russo-Japanese War: dispatches from Sir Ian Hamilton with the Japanese field army in Manchuria (HH/1–43); Far East: correspondence. 1914–16.

The Far Eastern Department's private papers. 1908–15. 6 vols. (China 84.) Presumably transferred from Foreign Office Library.

HOME OFFICE

The Home Department was created in the reorganization of 1782, and although concerned mainly with internal affairs certain categories may contain material relevant to this *Guide*. See especially the following classes:

H.O. 28. Admiralty, correspondence. 1782–1840. 63 vols., &c.

H.O. 29. Admiralty, entry books. 1779–1836. 7 vols.

H.O. 32. Foreign Office, correspondence. 1782–1845. 20 vols., &c.

H.O. 35. Treasury and Customs, correspondence. 1781–1854. 33 vols., &c.

H.O. 36. Treasury entry books: out-letters. 1776–1871. 37 vols.

H.O. 30. War and Colonial Office, correspondence. 1794–1840. 5 bundles, &c.

H.O. 50. Correspondence and papers, military. 1782–1840. 462 vols., &c.

H.O. 118. Miscellaneous warrant books: including a volume of special commissions for seizing pirates (addressed to commanders of East India Company ships proceeding to India and the Far East), 1768–1827, and for determining prizes, in hostilities with Russia, China, and Japan successively (addressed to the Board of Admiralty), 1854–63.

PAYMASTER GENERAL'S OFFICE

The office of Paymaster-General was created in 1835, but among the records are many of earlier date, being those of predecessor departments. Information about particular individuals and regiments who served in the Far East can be obtained from the records of this department. The classes of documents listed below are those most likely to repay examination.

ARMY ESTABLISHMENT

P.M.G. 1. Letters. 1784–1867. 115 vols.

P.M.G. 2. Ledgers. 1757–1840. 227 vols.

P.M.G. 3. Retired full pay and General Officer's pay and allowances. 1813–1920. 118 vols.

P.M.G. 4. Half pay. 1737–1921. 277 vols.

P.M.G. 5. Commissariat: half pay, pensions, &c. 1834–55. 11 vols.

P.M.G. 9. Pensions for wounds. 1814–1920. 66 vols.

P.M.G. 10. Compassionate list and royal bounty. 1812–1920. 95 vols.

P.M.G. 11. Widows' pensions. 1810–1920. 104 vols.

P.M.G. 12. Ordnance: half pay, pensions, &c. 1836–75. 19 vols.

P.M.G. 13. Militia, Yeomanry, and Volunteers: allowances. 1793–1917. 50 vols.

P.M.G. 14. Miscellaneous books. 1721–1861. 187 vols.

P.M.G. 35. Rewards for distinguished services, &c. 1873–1941. 16 vols.

NAVAL ESTABLISHMENT

P.M.G. 15. Half pay, retired pay, and unattached pay. 1836–1920. 183 vols.

P.M.G. 16. Miscellaneous services, wounds, widows, &c.: pensions, &c. 1836–1920. 30 vols.

P.M.G. 18. Compassionate list. 1837–1921. 38 vols.

P.M.G. 19. Widows of naval officers: pensions. 1836–1929. 94 vols.

P.M.G. 20. Widows of Marine officers, &c.: pensions, &c. 1870–1920. 25 vols.

P.M.G. 24. Salaried officers: civil pensions, &c. 1836–1918. 36 vols.

P.M.G. 69. Engineers, subordinate and Warrant Officers, &c.: pensions, &c. 1874–1924. 29 vols.

P.M.G. 70. Greenwich Hospital pensions and civil superannuation allowances. 1866–1928. 30 vols.

P.M.G. 71. Naval pensions, &c. 1846–1921. 13 vols.

PRIVY COUNCIL OFFICE

The Privy Council acts as a court of final resort in Admiralty jurisdiction and in all civil and criminal appeals from the courts of the Crown's dominions overseas.

P.C. 1. Papers, mainly unbound: these papers are of a very varied character, and include petitions and letters to the Council, reports and memorials from Government departments, &c., law officers' opinions, papers in appeal cases (many from the colonies), orders and minutes of the Council, proclamations, &c. 1481–1946. 4,559 bundles, &c.

P.C. 2. Registers: the registers contain the minutes of proceedings of the Council, its orders, certain proclamations, and the reports of committees with the papers accompanying them. The volumes are fully indexed. 1540–1920. 445 vols.

P.C. 4. Minutes. 1670–1928. 27 vols.

P.C. 8. Original correspondence. 1860–1920. 901 files.

P.C. 9. Registers of correspondence. 1860–1920. 63 vols.

P.C. 7. Letter-books. 1825–99. 54 vols.

BOARD OF TRADE

The earlier records of the Board of Trade, concerned mainly with the American colonies, have been amalgamated with those of the Colonial Office.

GENERAL

B.T. 1. In-letters and files, general; among the subjects dealt with are commercial questions, tariffs, colonial questions, navigation laws, and merchant shipping and seamen. Some relating to the China trade. 1791–1863. 569 vols. and boxes.

B.T. 2. In-letters, Foreign Office. 1824–45. 14 vols.

B.T. 3. Out-letters, general. 1786–1863. 64 vols.

B.T. 4. Registers and indexes, general: these relate to the in-letters and files in B.T. 1 and B.T. 6. 1808–64. 40 vols.

B.T. 5. Minutes: recording the daily proceedings of the Board. 1784–1850. 59 vols., and bundles.

B.T. 6. Miscellanea: reports, accounts, and returns made to the Board including consular reports, 1786–1835; consular returns, 1816–21; customs and excise accounts, accounts of imports and exports, &c., 1780–1832; shipping and trade returns from consuls and naval officers, 1697–1850; Orders in Council referring to colonial laws, 1802–43; trade statistics, 1782–1831. 1697–1867. 292 vols. and bundles.

COMMERCIAL DEPARTMENT: before 1872 the main function of the department was the revision of the tariff and the negotiation of tariff agreements with foreign countries. In 1872 it was amalgamated with the Statistical Department. Few papers earlier than 1902 have survived.

B.T. 11. Correspondence and papers. 1866–72. 1 box.

B.T. 35. Indexes and registers of correspondence: the papers to which these relate have not survived. 1897–1902. 18 vols.

B.T. 12. Out-letters. 1864–1900. 42 vols.

B.T. 36. Indexes to out-letters. 1897–1902.

ESTABLISHMENT DEPARTMENT

B.T. 13. Correspondence and papers. 1865–1902. 34 boxes.

B.T. 14. Registers of correspondence. 1865–1904. 6 vols.

B.T. 20. Out-letters. 1865–1903. 17 vols.

B.T. 21. Indexes to out-letters. 1865–1906. 3 vols.

B.T. 1

463. File 1285. Mail steam conveyance between India and China. 1846.

472. File 948. Japan, Cochin China, &c.: memorial from certain merchants and manufacturers of Halifax. 1849.

498. File 1806/52. East India and China Association of Liverpool. 1852.

543. File 728/57. Chartered Mercantile Bank of India, London and China: charter considered. 1857.

550. File 1277/59. Cable: Rangoon to Hong Kong. 1859.

FINANCE DEPARTMENT

B.T. 15. Correspondence and papers. 1865–1902. 46 boxes.

B.T. 16. Indexes and registers of correspondence. 1864–1902. 163 vols.

B.T. 17. Out-letters. 1864–1902. 138 vols.

B.T. 18. Indexes to out-letters. 1869–1902. 34 vols.

RAILWAY DEPARTMENT

B.T. 22. Correspondence and papers. 1867–1900. 56 boxes.

REGISTRY

B.T. 19. Indexes to papers retained in B.T. 1, 11, 13, 15, and 22, and in M.T. 9 and 10. 1846–85. 17 vols.

COMPANIES REGISTRATION OFFICE

B.T. 41. Files of joint stock companies registered under the 1844 and 1856 Acts. 1844–c. 1860. 926 boxes.

B.T. 31. Files of dissolved companies. 1856–1948. 31,740 boxes.

B.T. 34. Dissolved companies, liquidators' accounts. 1890–1932. 5,221 boxes.

STATISTICAL DEPARTMENT

B.T. 24. Out-letters. 1832–8. 1 vol.

B.T. 26. Passenger lists, inward. 1878–88, 1890–1955. 1,347 boxes.

B.T. 27. Passenger lists, outwards. 1890–1955. 1,788 boxes.

B.T. 32. Registers of passenger lists. 1906–51. 15 vols.

DEPARTMENT OF OVERSEAS TRADE

B.T. 59. Overseas Trade and Development Council. 1930–9. 29 boxes.

B.T. 60. Correspondence and papers. 1918–46. 82 boxes.

B.T. 90. Advisory Committee to the Department of Overseas Trade (Development and Intelligence): minutes and papers. 1918–30. 26 files.

MINISTRY OF TRANSPORT

This department was created in 1919 and certain powers and duties were transferred to it from the Board of Trade and other departments: at the same time the Ministry took over the relevant records of those departments.

ADMIRALTY AND BOARD OF TRADE HARBOUR DEPARTMENTS

M.T. 19. Admiralty Harbour Department: correspondence and papers. *c.* 1842–65. 145 boxes.

M.T. 10. Board of Trade Harbour Department: correspondence and papers. The functions of the Admiralty Harbour Department passed to the Board of Trade in 1863. The papers in this class relate to harbours, lighthouses, pilotage, fisheries, and miscellaneous shipping questions. 1864–1919. 2,074 boxes.

M.T. 2. Out-letters. 1848–1919. 456 vols.

M.T. 3. Indexes to out-letters. 1915–16. 2 vols.

ADMIRALTY TRANSPORT DEPARTMENT

M.T. 23. Correspondence and papers: relating to the transport by sea of all military forces and their supplies. 1795–1917. 820 boxes.

Includes (File T. 7249/01), Dispatch of China Expeditionary Force from India to China, &c. 1901; (File T. 4028/07), Mail contract between the Postmaster-General and the Peninsular and Oriental Steam Navigation Company for the conveyance of the East India, China, and Australian mails, 1908–15. 1907.

M.T. 31. Letter-books. 1857–69. 31 vols.

BOARD OF TRADE MARINE DEPARTMENT

M.T. 9. Correspondence and papers: these papers relate to merchant shipping matters. 1854–1902. 747 boxes.

588. File M. 12104/96. Consuls: discretionary powers of Consuls in China, Japan and Siam to undertake arbitration; and affixing of fee stamps to ships' agreements. 1896.

M.T. 4. Out-letters. 1851–1939. 1,424 vols.

M.T. 5. Indexes to out-letters and registers of correspondence. 1864–1918. 58 vols.

M.T. 20. Minute book. 1857. 1 vol.

MINISTRY OF SHIPPING

M.T. 25. Correspondence and papers. 1917–26. Under arrangement.

TREASURY

The Treasury is responsible for the control and management of the entire public revenue and its expenditure, but the character and extent of this control have varied from time to time, developing with the extension of Parliamentary control over the finances of the country. It is the primary instrument for controlling the expenditure by Government departments of money voted by Parliament.

T. 1. Treasury Board papers: these papers contain the original correspondence of the Board, with occasional minutes, reports, &c. They are described in the *Calendar of Treasury Board Papers,* 1556 to 1728 (6 vols.) and in the *Calendar of Treasury Books and Papers,* 1729 to 1745 (5 vols.). For later periods the papers may be referred to by means of the registers and reference books listed below (T. 2, T. 3, T. 108, T. 4).

T. 98. Treasury Board papers, supplementary. 1599–1800. 3 vols.

T. 2. Registers of papers. 1777–1920. 502 vols.

T. 3. Skeleton registers. 1783–1920. 110 vols.

T. 108. Subject registers: these registers are subject indexes to T. 1. 1852–1909. 18 vols.

T. 4. Reference books, &c. 1680–1819. 43 vols.

T. 5. Out-letters: Admiralty. 1849–1920. 58 vols.

T. 7. Out-letters: colonial affairs. 1849–1921. 44 vols.

T. 11. Out-letters: customs. 1667–1922. 137 vols.

T. 12. Out-letters: Foreign Office. 1857–1920. 47 vols.

T. 27. Out-letters: general. 1668–1836. 97 vols.

T. 23. Out-letters: treasurers abroad. 1856–1913. 7 vols.

T. 28. Out-letters: various, including letters to consuls and ministers abroad, 1831–54; East India Company and India Office, 1849–56 and 1859–85; naval and military departments, 1811–35; secretaries of state, 1796–1856; war departments, &c., 1849–56. 1763–1885. 113 vols.

T. 24. Out-letters: War Departments. 1855–1920. 63 vols.

T. 29. Minute book. 1667–1870. 632 vols.

T. 99. Minute books, supplementary. 1690–1; 1831–2. 2 vols.

T. 38. Departmental accounts. 1636–1865. 53 vols., &c.

T. 39. Treasury chest; including accounts of foreign and colonial stations, 1846–76. 1838–78. 143 vols.

T. 63. Maps and plans, Series II: including material relating to the colonies and elsewhere abroad. 1838–82. 38 docs.

T. 64. Various: including papers relating to the army, 1685–1845, and the colonies, 1680–1867. 1547–1874. 401 vols., &c.

TREASURY SOLICITOR

Since 1842 the Treasury Solicitor has acted as legal adviser and solicitor to an increasing number of other departments, and he also acts as solicitor for those departments, including Foreign, Colonial, and Commonwealth Relations, which have a Legal Adviser but no solicitor as such. There are therefore among these records many relating to the Far East. Attention is drawn particularly to those classes listed below.

T.S. 5. Report books. 1806, 1899–1919. 88 vols.

T.S. 6. Report books, Admiralty. 1816, 1828–68. 15 vols.

T.S. 11. Papers: these are papers in the various legal proceedings dealt with by the Treasury Solicitor and King's (Queen's) Proctor, and relate to a great variety of business. 1584–1856. 1,147 boxes.

T.S. 8–T.S. 9. King's (Queen's) Proctor: reports, series I and II, including papers in prize causes. 1804–44. 148 vols.

T.S. 10. King's (Queen's) Proctor: reports, Admiralty, relating to prize and other matters. 1801–8, 1854–8. 3 vols.

T.S. 15. King's (Queen's) Proctor: assignation books, notes of proceedings in appeals from Admiralty Instance and Prize Courts and Vice-Admiralty courts. 1827–73. 5 vols.

WAR OFFICE

These records consist of the official papers of the Board of Ordnance (which ceased to exist in 1855), the Secretary-at-War (office abolished in 1863), the Commander-in-Chief (office abolished in 1904), and the Secretary of State for the War Department (which included the Colonies from 1801 to 1855). They contain many papers of interest scattered throughout the various classes. See *Alphabetical guide to War Office Records* . . . Between 1801 and 1855 letters on military matters will also be found in the Colonial Office Colonies (General) Series.

Correspondence

W.O. 1. In-letters: original dispatches, letters, and papers addressed to the Secretary-at-War and later to the Secretary of State for War, arranged under the various stations and public departments from which they were sent; including stations in the Far East. 1755–1868. 1,138 vols., &c.

461–72. China, Hong Kong, and India. 1841–4.

W.O. 40. Selected unnumbered papers: in-letters and reports addressed to the Secretary-at-War. 1753–1815. 32 bundles.

W.O. 43. Selected 'V.O.S.' and 'O.S.' papers: miscellaneous papers of the Secretary-at-War's office to 1857. 1809–57. 107 bundles.

W.O. 32. Registered papers, general series: documents relating to all aspects of War Office business. 1855–1925. 1,764 boxes.

W.O. 139. Subject indexes: these registers provide a digest of the chief correspondence of the department. 1826–1901. 13 vols.

W.O. 31. Memoranda papers. Commander-in-Chief, relating to appointments, promotions, and resignations, and including schedules and memorials from military commands abroad. 1793–1870. 1,565 bundles.

W.O. 107. Quartermaster-General: papers relating to trooping programmes and various expeditions including that to China, 1857–64. 1763–1914. 12 boxes.

W.O. 3. Out-letters: Commander-in-Chief. 1765–1868. 617 vols.

W.O. 4. Out-letters: Secretary-at-War; including letters to the colonies and places abroad, to other departments, &c. 1684–1861. 1,053 vols.

W.O. 2. Indexes of correspondence. 1759–1858. 107 vols.

W.O. 5. Marching orders. 1683–1852. 122 vols.

W.O. 6. Out-letters: Secretary of State, including letters to colonies and dependencies, and to public departments. 1793–1859. 214 vols. (96–102. Eastern colonies. 1841–54.)

W.O. 7. Departmental letter-books. 1715–1862. 130 vols.

RETURNS

W.O. 64. Manuscript army lists. 1702–1823. 13 vols.

W.O. 65. Printed annual army lists. 1754–1879. 168 vols.

W.O. 66. Printed quarterly army lists. 1879–1900. 86 vols.

W.O. 69. Artillery records of services, &c. of non-commissioned officers and men. 1765–1906. 314 vols.

W.O. 42. Certificates of birth, &c., with wills, administrations, statements of services, and personal papers of officers and their families. 1755–1908. 73 bundles.

W.O. 67. Depot description books. 1768–1908. 34 vols.

W.O. 24. Establishments: warrants authorizing the establishments of various regiments and of the military forces in the colonies. 1661–1846. 892 vols.

W.O. 27. Inspection returns. 1750–1912. 507 vols., &c.

W.O. 100. Campaign medals: original lists arranged under campaigns. 1793–1904. 371 vols.

W.O. 102. Long-service and good-conduct awards. 1831–1902. 16 vols.

W.O. 101. Meritorious service awards. 1846–1923. 7 vols.

W.O. 104. Order of the Bath. 1815–94. 13 vols.

W.O. 98. Victoria Cross. 1856–64. 2 boxes.

W.O. 17. Monthly returns. 1759–1865. 2,812 vols., &c.

W.O. 73. Monthly returns: distribution of the army. 1859–1938. 141 vols.

W.O. 10. Muster books and pay lists: artillery. 1708–1878. 2,876 vols.

W.O. 11. Muster books and pay lists: engineers. 1816–78. 432 vols.

W.O. 15. Muster books and pay lists: foreign legions. 1854–6. 102 vols., &c.

W.O. 12. Muster books and pay lists: general. 1732–78. 13,305 vols.

W.O. 16. Muster books and pay lists: new series, continuing W.O. 12. 1878–98. 3,049 vols.

W.O. 76. Records of officers' services. 1771–1919. 378 vols.

W.O. 116. Out-pensions records, Royal Hospital Chelsea: admission books. 1715–1882. 154 vols.

W.O. 23. Chelsea registers, &c. 1805–95. 123 vols.

W.O. 121. Out-pensions records, Royal Hospital Chelsea: discharge documents of pensioners. 1787–1813. 136 vols.

W.O. 122. Out-pensions records, Royal Chelsea Hospital: discharge documents of pensioners, Foreigners' regiments. 1816–17. 14 vols.

W.O. 28. Headquarters returns (302. Correspondence and papers: China (Boxer Rebellion) between Lieutenant-General Gaselee, commander of the British contingent, and government officials. 1900–1.

W.O. 131. Documents of soldiers awarded deferred pensions. 1838–96. 44 boxes, &c.

W.O. 22. Pension returns. 1842–83. 300 vols.

W.O. 120. Out-pensions records, Royal Hospital Chelsea: regimental registers. c. 1715–1857. 70 vols.

W.O. 97. Soldiers' documents: this is the main series of service documents of soldiers. 1760–1900. 4,231 boxes.

W.O. 117. Service pension books, recording award of pensions for length of service. 1823–82. 36 pieces.

W.O. 118. Out-pensions records, Royal Hospital Kilmainham: admission books. 1759–1863. 44 vols.

W.O. 119. Out-pensions records, Royal Hospital Kilmainham: discharge documents of pensioners. 1783–1822. 70 vols.

W.O. 25. Registers, various: including commission books, successions books, chaplains, medical, regimental description and succession books, staff pay books, staff returns, service returns, returns of soldiers' services, embarkation and disembarkation returns, casualty returns, deserters, discharges under special conditions, medical department, confidential reports on the proficiency of lieutenants of the Royal Engineers on completion of their courses at the School of Mechanical Engineers Chatham, military nursing establishment, War Department establishments, &c. 1660–1938. 3,992 vols., &c.

W.O. 19. Royal Garrison Regiment. 1901–6. 9 vols.

W.O. 138. Selected personal files. 1830–1914. 1 file.

W.O. 114. Strength returns of the Army. 1890–1920. 54 vols.

W.O. 70. Volunteer and territorial records. 1860–1912. 21 vols.

Miscellanea

W.O. 9. Accounts. 1679–1865. 48 vols., &c.

W.O. 123. Army circulars, memoranda, and orders. 1856–1907. 49 vols.

W.O. 112. Army estimates. 1876–88. 20 vols.

W.O. 111. Army Ordnance Corps. 1901–19. 13 vols.

W.O. 74. Army Purchase Commission papers. 1861–1908. 194 vols., &c.

W.O. 115. Directorate of Medical Services: reports, returns, and summaries. 1921–35. 47 vols.

W.O. 106. Directorate of Military Operations and Intelligence: papers, including correspondence and papers relating to China 1895–1920 and the Russo-Japanese war, 1904–5; inspection reports; letter-books, 1891–3, 1910–12; daily diaries, 1921–3; registers forming indexes to information on foreign countries, 1875–86. 1837, 1870–1925. 65 boxes.

W.O. 28. Headquarters Records: including, General Orders, 1811–57; records relating to the China Expedition, 1840–4; and correspondence of the Commander of the Chinese Field Force, Boxer Rebellion, and some private papers, 1900–1. 1746–1901. 346 vols., &c.

W.O. 78. Maps and plans. 1627–1946. 4,991 pieces.

W.O. 130. Military lands and buildings: printed copies of correspondence and reports relating to War Department lands and buildings in the Colonies. 1886–1935. 4 boxes.

W.O. 30. Miscellanea: including permanent and regimental order books of the Hong Kong Regiment, 1892–1902. 1684–1903. 132 vols., &c.

W.O. 26. Miscellany books. 1670–1817. 42 vols.

W.O. 109. Paymaster-General: miscellaneous. 1714–43. 106 vols.

W.O. 29. Prince Imperial deed: deed verifying the official identification of the Prince Imperial of France under the seals of a notary public and the Colonial Secretary of Natal, with the notary's letter. 1879. 1 box.

W.O. 33. Reports and miscellaneous papers: including reports of Select Committees and Commissions of Inquiry and operations and intelligence summaries. 1853–96. 56 vols.

W.O. 99. Royal Military College, Sandhurst. 1798–1866. 34 boxes.

W.O. 191. War diaries and H.Q. records: Minor campaigns. Includes Shanghai (1927–32).

W.O. 147. *Wolseley Papers*: private papers of Field-Marshal Viscount Wolseley, including accounts of the war with China, 1860. 1860, 1873–85. 14 vols., &c.

ORDNANCE OFFICE: mainly the records of the old Board of Ordnance, which was abolished in 1855.

W.O. 44. In-letters. 1682–1873 (but mainly nineteenth century). 732 vols., &c.

W.O. 45. Reference books: registers of the in-letters of the Board of Ordnance, 1783–1856, and of the Master-General, 1844–70. 1783–1870. 298 vols.

W.O. 46. Out-letters: entry books of out-letters. 1660–1861. 169 vols.

W.O. 47. Minutes. 1644–1856. 2,897 vols., &c.

W.O. 48. Accounts: ledgers. 1660–1847. 357 vols.

W.O. 49. Accounts: various. 1592–1858. 293 vols., &c.

W.O. 18. Vouchers for agents' disbursements, Artillery. 1770–1820. 213 vols., &c.

W.O. 50–W.O. 53. Bill books, Series I–IV. 1630–1859. 1,650 vols.

W.O. 54. Registers. 1594–1871. 947 vols., &c.

W.O. 55. Miscellanea: including general reports, 1753–1858; colonial reports, with correspondence and papers, 1808–59; warrants, 1568–1857; orders, 1744–1863; engineer papers, both home and colonial, 1785–1860; artillery letters and letter-books, home and abroad, 1773–1862; observations, &c. on defence and fortifications, home, Colonial, and foreign, 1681–1879; lands, rents, and buildings, home and abroad, 1732–1923; miscellaneous books and papers, 1568–1865. 1568–1923. 3,038 vols., &c. (1563 (1). Description of the coastline, &c. from the Cape of Good Hope to Japan, by Jean Corneille. French. 1746.)

JUDGE ADVOCATE GENERAL'S OFFICE

W.O. 71. Courts martial: proceedings. 1668–1850. 342 vols., &c.

W.O. 72. Courts martial: letters and miscellaneous documents. 1696–1850. 103 bundles.

W.O. 86. District courts martial. 1829–1913. 60 vols.

W.O. 89. General courts martial. 1666–1829. 5 vols.

W.O. 91. General courts martial: confirmed at home. 1806–1904. 51 vols.

W.O. 92. General courts martial: registers. 1666–1704, 1806–1917. 3 vols.

W.O. 81. Letter-books. 1715–1900. 133 vols.

W.O. 82. Office daybooks. 1817–99. 24 vols.

W.O. 83. Minute books. 1871–1900. 10 vols.

W.O. 84. Charge books. 1857–92. 4 vols.

W.O. 85. Deputation books. 1751–1910. 9 vols.

W.O. 93. Miscellaneous records. 1754–1904. 4 vols.

COMMISSARIAT DEPARTMENT

W.O. 57. In-letters. 1806–17. 58 bundles, &c.

W.O. 58. Out-letters. 1793–1888. 178 vols.

W.O. 59. Minutes. 1816–54. 76 vols.

W.O. 60. Accounts: 1774–1858. 112 vols., &c.

W.O. 61. Registers. 1791–1889. 135 vols.

W.O. 62. Miscellanea. 1798–1859. 50 vols., &c.

WAR OF 1914–18

W.O. 157. Intelligence summaries, and reports on military, economic, and political matters in Europe, Africa, the Middle East, and the Far East. 1914–21. 1,307 vols., &c.

W.O. 106. Directorate of Military Operations and Intelligence: papers. 1837; 1870–1939. 1,509 boxes, vols., and folders. Correspondence and papers relating to various theatres of war including the First World War, and to administration, defence, and other problems in Europe, Africa, and Asia.

WAR OF 1939–45

W.O. 172. War diaries, South-East Asia and Allied Land Forces, South-East Asia. Includes Hong Kong. 1939–45.

W.O. 203. Military headquarters papers: Far East. 1932–47. 5,734 files.

MINISTRY OF WORKS

Works 10. Public buildings overseas:

56/5. Contribution from the Indian Government on account of legation and consular rents in China. 1876–1900.

56/6. Reports (including original manuscripts) on legation and consular buildings in China, Korea, Japan, and Siam, by R. H. Boyle. 1899–1900.

ROYAL ANTHROPOLOGICAL INSTITUTE OF GREAT BRITAIN AND IRELAND

36 Craven Street, London, W.C. 2

'Report of a journey N. and E. of Peking made in Oct^r, Nov^r & Decr 1886', by E. T. C. Werner. [*c.* 1887]. 61, [i] pp. (MS. 122.)

L. Marillier, Anthropological notes and extracts on general subjects, some relating to China and Japan. 11 folders. *French, English*. (MS. 99.)

Neil Gordon Munro collection of Ainu material. This includes correspondence, the original typescript, but fuller than the published version, of Munro's *Ainu creed and cult* (edited with preface by B. Z. Seligman, 1962), notes, extracts, &c. 10 folders. (MS. 249.)

MUNIMENTS ROOM, ROYAL ARMY MEDICAL COLLEGE

Millbank, London, S.W. 1

The manuscripts belonging to the Royal Army Medical College are described in the cyclostyled 'Catalogue' issued in June 1958, with later supplements.

Copies of Japanese prison regulations, propaganda leaflets, &c. (237.)

Japanese Prisoner of War documents relating to Ex.-S.S.M. Mussett R.A.S.C., including case notes, camp orders, &c. (335.)

Papers of the late Brigadier Julian Taylor, M.D., F.R.C.S. describing the retirement on Singapore and his surgical experiences as a Japanese prisoner of war. (439.)

ROYAL ARTILLERY INSTITUTION

Woolwich, London, S.E. 18

Paper concerning passages from England to the Cape of Good Hope and China. Signed S. Dalrymple, Hydrographer of the Navy. 1799. (M/MS/245.)

General Order by Major-General D'Aguilar, commanding the troops in China. Hong Kong, 1846. (MS. 108. P. 1.)

'Royal Artillery at Canton—desultry notes at Takoo 1860', by R. E. Cane. (MD/13. See *Occasional papers of the R.A. Institution*, vol. 2, pp. 156–219.)

China war—1860: returns of captured ordnance, casualties Royal Artillery and Madras Artillery, ammunition expended, and officers and men brought to favourable notice. (MD/145.)

'My soldiering days', by General Sir John William Campbell, including (in vol. 1, pt. 2) an account of service in China, 1860–1. 1899. 3 vols., vol. 1 being in 2 pts. (MS. 33a.)

Notes on artillery of the Allied Forces, Peking. 1900–1. (M/MS/1015. Pipon Papers.)

Correspondence of Lieutenant-Colonel Everard Fer-guson Calthrop including some letters to his mother written in Japan, 1905. (D. 2/261.)

Report of the siege of Tsingtau, August–November 1914, by Major-General Machida. n.d. Typescript. (MD/259.)

Diary of a German soldier during the siege of Tsingtau, July–November 1914. Translation. (MD/259a.)

Messages of H.M. the King and Lieutenant-General Thomas J. Hutton on the disbandment of the Hong Kong–Singapore Royal Artillery Corps. 11 November 1946. Typescript, photostats, &c. (MD/210.)

ROYAL ASIATIC SOCIETY OF GREAT BRITAIN AND IRELAND

56 Queen Anne Street, London, W1M 9LA

Instructions of the Chinese Government to the Merchants trading with the Russians. English translation. 1823.

Letter from Thomas Weeding to the Royal Asiatic Society, enclosing the 'Grand Chop' or official clearance of an English ship, the *Sarah*, from the customs house at Canton, with explanation and translation. 24 May 1836.

'Translation of the Monumental Inscription in the Fa-hsing Temple at Canton made for the use of his Excellency Sir John Bowring Kt. &c.' by J. Gibson, 14 October 1858.

'A Sketch of Buddhist mythology as represented in a Chinese sheet-tract. Revd. J. Edkins. Read 22 January 1859.'

'The Intercourse of China with Eastern Turkestan and the adjacent countries in the second century B.C.', by Thomas W. Kingsmill, Shanghai. 1878. 38 ff.

Papers relating to the rendering of the Chinese word 'E'. [19th century.]

Notes on the Chinese game of chess. n.d.

ROYAL BOTANIC GARDENS

Kew, Richmond

The official papers of the Royal Botanic Gardens, Kew, fall mainly into two series (which occasionally overlap), consisting of a large number of bound volumes dating from the middle of the eighteenth century and continuing after about 1927 in registry files. The first series, relating largely to economic botany, covers Kew's participation in botanical and agricultural research projects all over the world, and consists of correspondence with Government Departments, local authorities, and individuals, as well as reports, &c. These papers are mainly in manuscript but some printed material is occasionally included. The second series comprises correspondence with botanists and collectors in all areas, together with related papers. The collection also includes a quantity of correspondence and papers of individual botanists, both officials at Kew and others. The fifty-year rule applies.

I. ECONOMIC BOTANY: CORRESPONDENCE AND REPORTS

China: correspondence, &c., relating to Henry Fletcher Hance. 1882–8.

China: economic products. [c. 1861–95.] 2 vols.

China: economic products, insect white wax.

China: foods, medicines, woods. 1869–1914.

China: grass. 1858–1900. 2 vols.

China: index to 'Flora Sinensis'. 1883–1905.

China: plant collections, cultural products, &c. 1853–1914.

China and Tibet: miscellaneous. 1861–1924.

Hong Kong: Botanic Gardens. 1870–1900. 2 vols.

Hong Kong: miscellaneous. 1874–1928.

Japan: lacquer. 1881–1902.

Japan: miscellaneous. 1861–1918.

II. KEW CORRESPONDENCE WITH BOTANISTS AND COLLECTORS

Asian letters (including China and Japan). 1909–28.

Chinese and Japanese letters. 1865–1900. 2 vols.

East Asian letters. 1866–1900.

East Indian, Chinese, and Mauritius letters. 1818–37 and 1851–6. 3 vols.

Foreign letters, miscellaneous (including Canton). 1822–9.

Indian and Chinese letters. 1858–65.

Japanese, Chinese, and Siberian letters. 1901–14.

Kew collectors (i.e. official collectors sent out by Kew). This series includes correspondence of and concerning Charles Wilford, China, 1857–63, and Richard Oldham, China and Japan, 1861–6. 16 vols.

III. PAPERS OF INDIVIDUAL BOTANISTS, ETC.

A few letters in the correspondence of Sir Joseph Banks (1743–1820), naturalist and explorer, are concerned with the areas covered by this *Guide*. These include letter of William Pigou, naturalist, at Canton, 31 December 1783, and two letters of Richard Cadman Etches, concerning trade with Japan, 1785, 1788. (See Warren R. Dawson, *The Banks letters*, London, 1958.)

Papers of George Bentham (1800–84), botanist, including:

1. Catalogue of collections in Bentham's herbarium, including plants from China. 1838–55.

2. Correspondence addressed to Bentham, arranged alphabetically under names of correspondents. Some of the letters may contain material relevant to this *Guide*. 10 vols.

Notes on plants of Hong Kong, by John George Champion (1815–54). [1848.]

Documents relating to the voyage of H.M.S. *Challenger*, 1872–6, including letters from H. N. Mosely and others written at Yokohama, Hong Kong, and on the China Sea, 1875.

Papers of Dr. Augustine Henry:

1. Lists and descriptive notes on Chinese plants. 1 vol.

2. Chinese–English and, English–Chinese vocabulary of plants, &c. 2 vols.

3. Letters from Henry to Hosen B. Morse on botanical subjects, written from various places in China, c. 1893–1907, together with lists of plants. 2 packets.

Lists of *Carices japonicae* supplied to Kew in 1896 by l'abbé Faurie, with notes by C. B. Clarke. 1896.

Hosen B. Morse. Lists, with illustrations, of flowers and plants from China and Formosa. [c. 1896–]. 18 vols.

Sketch of the botany of Kwantung, by Theophilus Sampson (1831–97). 98 ff.

Provincial tabulation of the vascular plants of China and Formosa, by Francis Blackwell Forbes (1839–1908), and William Botting Hemsley (1843–1924). 1904. 3 vols.

Notes on seeds collected by W. Purdom whilst travelling for J. Veitch & Sons Ltd. in China. 1909–12.

'Plant collecting in Formosa in 1912', by W. R. Price, together with list of species collected. 1961. 288 pp. Typescript.

ROYAL CENTRAL ASIAN SOCIETY

42 Devonshire Street, London, W. 1

Inclusion of a document on this list does not necessarily imply that it is available for study. Application to see any particular item should be made in writing to the Secretary, at the above address.

Memoirs of Kashgar: account of an unusual journey from Kashgar to Gilgit, by Dr. S. G. Tscherbakoff. With foreword dated Gilgit–Srinagar, March–April 1932. 111 ff. Typescript.

'Some episodes in the history of Amoy'; being translation of a chapter in the Hsia-men chih or topography of Amoy. No author or date. 2 pp.+50 ff.

Review by Oswald White, not published in the Society's Journal, of *Typhoon in Tokyo* (1954), a record of the U.S. occupation of Japan. 18 ff.

Some notes on the southern road of Chinese Turkestan. No author or date. 8 ff.

Texts of lectures given to the Society but not published in the Journal, and records of discussions. (Mostly typescript.)
Air communications with China, by Group Captain H. St. Clair Smallwood. 11 April 1945.
Beyond the Japanese lines in the Shan States, by Captain J. E. St. Clair Smallwood. 20 November 1946.
Shanghai and South China, by Henry Longhurst. 23 April 1947.
The future of British interests in China, by Trevor Powell. 15 October 1947.
Impressions of China today, by John Keswick. 18 April 1951.
Danish expeditions to Central Asia, by H.R.H. Prince Peter of Greece and Denmark. 14 December 1955.
Recent visits to Sinkiang and Outer Mongolia, by H. C. Taussig. 1 May 1957.
Formosa, by William Teeling, M.P. 30 April 1958.

ROYAL COLLEGE OF PHYSICIANS OF LONDON

11 St. Andrew's Place, Regent's Park, London, NW1 4LE

'The extraordinary history of a new method of inoculating practised in the kingdom of England.' In Chinese, translated into that language by Sir George Staunton. (Printed: 10 leaves.) Followed by the 'English copy which accompanied each corresponding page of the Chinese treatise sent to Dr Jenner'. This again is followed by 'The English copy which accompanied the Chinese treatise sent by Mr A. Pearson to Dr John Hunter & presented by him to the College'. The English copies are in the handwriting of E. Larken, Inspector of Tea to the East India Company, Macao. 1805. 26 ff. (No. 252.)

'The Pun-tsaou-Pe-yaou, which treats of Chinese medecine, &c. &c. Translated by P. P. Thoms. Macao, 1825.' Followed by an analysis of the 'E-tsung king-kan or Chinese Imperial Medical work'. At the end is an index to the 'Pun-tsau-Pe-yaou'. 1825. 71 ff. (No. 323.)

A volume containing 814 Chinese water-colour drawings of medicinal plants and animals with directions in Chinese and English for their preparation and use. At the beginning is the inscription 'This book was Sir Charles Raymond's, a present from Captain I. Hindman'. n.d. [? early 19th century]. 221 ff. (No. 50.)

ROYAL COMMONWEALTH SOCIETY

Northumberland Avenue, London, WC2A 3PN

Log of the ship *Houghton*, Captain John Edwards, England to China via Cape of Good Hope and return. 1786–8.

ROYAL ENTOMOLOGICAL SOCIETY OF LONDON

41 Queen's Gate, SW7 5HU

Narrative journal, by James John Walker (1851–1939), of the surveying voyage of H.M.S. *Penguin* in the Pacific. From September 1892–May 1893 the ship was anchored off various points on the China coast and the journal contains many observations and notes of the natural history of those parts. February 1890–July 1893. 3 vols in one.

ROYAL GEOGRAPHICAL SOCIETY

Kensington Gore, London, S.W. 7

Stephen Else: 'Journal of a Voyage to the E. Indies and an Historical Narrative of Lord Macartney's Embassy to the Court of Pekin . . . by a member of the Embassy', 1793. (Lib. Val. Bks, Case 260H.)

'Report of an Exploration of the New Course of the Yellow River, undertaken between Sept. and Dec. 1868', by Ney Elias, Jr. and H. G. Hollingsworth. Together with a letter from Hollingsworth to his father, dated 12 October 1868, and a reprint from the Journal of the North China branch of the Royal Asiatic Society of a report on the Yellow River by Ney Elias. (Lib. MS. file.)

Journal of John W. Stevenson, covering a circular tour beginning and ending at Bhamo, Upper Burma, 18 November 1879–5 January 1880; and journey from Bhamo across China to Shanghai, 29 November 1880–4 June 1881. (Lib. MS. file.)

Papers of Captain, later Colonel Sir, Francis E. Younghusband:

1. 'Hints to Travellers', used on his journey in Manchuria and from Peking to India, 1886–7. (Museum No. 191.)

2. Journal: Kashmir and Sinkiang. August–October 1889. 2 vols. (Lib. MS. file.)

'Observation files.' A collection of files containing observations and notes on geographical, geological, and meteorological, &c. subjects.

    F. S. A. Bourne. China—Upper Yang-tse Kiang. 1897.   No. 51.
      C. W. Campbell. Mongolia. 1902.   No. 68.
      Major H. R. Davies. Western China. 1894–1900.   No. 112.
      R. B. Shaw. Central Asia—Yarkand. No. 5.
      G. P. Tate. China—Kaulun. 1899–1901.   No. 61.
    E. C. Young. Yunnan to Assam.   No. 65.

Route books and books of meteorological observations of Major H. H. P. Deasy in Tibet and Sinkiang, 1896–9. (Museum No. 198.)

Copies of letters written by Captain W. A. Watts Jones to his mother during travels in China, 1898–1900. 1 vol. (Lib. MS. file.)

'Record of a journey from Moulmein, Burma, to Hanoi, Tongking, via the S. Shan States, Siam and S. Yunnan. 1899', by Captain Gerard C. Rigby. Typescript. Together with covering letter from donor/author, 13 June 1934. (Lib. MS. file.)

Papers of C. D. Bruce. (Lib. MS. file.)

1. 'Diary across Asia, 1901.' Typescript.

2. 'A Journey to the Far East.' Typescript copies of articles printed, in twelve instalments, in the *Evening Standard*, 1902–3.

3. 'A thousand Miles Ride across Asia from Pekin to Lake Baikal.' 7 December 1907. Typescript.

Diaries, roadbooks, and rough notes of Colonel W. H. Jeffery in eight small notebooks. (Corridor Case 400.)
(i) Hong Kong to Miao Feng Shan, &c. October 1902–December 1903.
(ii–v) Bhamo, Upper Burma, to Shanghai. 1905–6.
(vi–viii) Sadiya, Assam, and various short expeditions based on that centre.

'Diary of Manchurian Journey, Autumn 1912', by Sir Alexander Hosie. The entries are from 29 August, Peking, to 19 September, *en route* to Harbin from Tsitsikar. The diary is preceded by pages of notes. (Corridor Case 400.)

Journal of William Bensley Cotton of journey through Chinese Turkestan, 1914. Typescript copy. (Lib. MS. file.)

Road book, Chinese Turkestan, of Colonel R. C. F. Schomberg. October 1927–June 1928. 172 pp. (387 A.)

ROYAL HORTICULTURAL SOCIETY

Lindley Library, Vincent Square, London, SW1P 2PE

'Rough journal' and 'Fair journal' of John Potts (d. 1822), the first collector sent to China by the Horticultural Society. The first, and main, part of the journal is concerned with India where he stayed from June to August 1821. In November he arrived in China, and the last few pages of the journal deal with his stay there until March 1822. This part consists mainly of day-to-day jottings, together with some observations on Chinese gardens, methods of propagation, &c. 1821–2. 2 vols. (See *Transactions*, iv and v.)

'Rough journal of John Damper Parks relating to a plant collecting expedition for the Society to China, 1823–4. It consists of copies of five letters to the Society, and of observations and jottings, mainly about plants, on the voyage out on board the *Lowther Castle*, in China—Canton, Macao, &c.— and on the return voyage on board the *Hythe*. 1823–4. 1 vol. 188 pp., of which many are blank. (See *Transactions*, v.)

Papers concerning the botanical mission to China of Robert Fortune (1812–80), 1843–5. They include minutes of the Chinese Committee of the Horticultural Society, copy of instructions issued to Fortune, list of letters of introduction, and correspondence. The correspondence consists of letters dealing with arrangements for the expedition and also of letters sent by Fortune, mainly from Hong Kong but also from Shanghai and Fou-chou, together with his accounts. 1842–6. 2 vols.

List of collections made in northern China by William Purdom (1880–1912) for Messrs Veitch. 1909–12.

THE ROYAL SOCIETY

6 Carlton House Terrace, London, S.W. 1

The Royal Society has a large collection of archives and manuscripts, well arranged and easy of access. The main catalogue is a card catalogue of approximately 100,000 items arranged by authors, not subjects. The following list is not exhaustive, but merely indicates the various classes of documents, the relevant items within them being listed only wherever these have been separately catalogued. For a description of the available catalogues see R. K. Bluhm, 'A Guide to the archives of the Royal Society and to other manuscripts in its possession', in *Notes and records of the Royal Society of London*, vol. 12, no. 1, pp. 21–39 (August 1956). Students should also consult the published *Philosophical transactions*, and other numbers of *Notes and records* (1938 to date). The

Royal Society's manuscripts are available only to serious students by appointment.

MINUTES

The Journal Book: minutes of meetings of the Royal Society. 1660 to date, with a duplicate set, 1660–1826.

Council Minutes: minutes of meetings of the Council of the Royal Society. 1660 to date.

Committee Minute Books: minutes of *ad hoc* committees of the Royal Society in the nineteenth and early twentieth centuries.

EARLY LETTERS

Official correspondence of the Royal Society from its foundation in 1660 to about 1740. 4,237 items in 38 vols. (EL. The catalogue gives the name of the writer, place of origin of the letter, date, to whom addressed, and language.)

Fair copies of letters received to about 1740. The originals are in EL. *c.* 3,000 items in 30 vols., and duplicates. (LBC.)

CLASSIFIED PAPERS (CP)

Original papers, letters, and memoranda communicated to the Royal Society, and arranged in 1740–1 chiefly according to subject, but in part according to author. 2,500 items in 39 vols.

Observables of China, by [Isaacus] Vossius. 2 pp. (CP. 7 (1) 26.)

Of Cittay on the north side of the Great Wall of China, by — Noorderman. 1 p. (CP. 7 (1) 58.)

'China's observations [astronomical] at Pekin', by the Peking Fathers. *c.* 1694–5. 3 pp. *Latin.* (CP. 8 (1) 52.)

Eclipse of the sun at Peking, by Ignatius Kegler and Andreas Pereyra. 15 July 1730. 4 pp. (CP. 8 (2) 34.)

Immersions and emersions of Jupiter's satellites as observed at Peking from November 1730. Read 16 November 1732. 3 pp. (CP. 8 (2) 36. See *Phil. Trans.* no. 424.)

'Memoire sur la Nouvelle Table chronologique des Chinois', by [Jean François] Foucquet. Read 1 May 1729. 18 pp. 22 pp. English translation. (CP. 16. 16.)

An explanation of Chinese chronology [?by the same]. 30 pp. *French.* 38 pp. *English.* (CP. 16. 17.)

Chinese chronological table: the original text. Author unknown. (CP. 16. 55. See *Phil. Trans.*, No. 415.)

Questions and answers about Japan. Read 25 February 1668. 5 pp. *French.* (CP. 19. 42.)

THE REGISTER BOOK (RBC)

Fair copies of papers submitted to the Society to about 1740. The originals are in CP. *c.* 2,000 items in 21 vols., and duplicates.

LETTERS AND PAPERS (LP)

Letters and papers communicated to the Royal Society. 1741–1806. 3,651 items in 127 vols., arranged in decades.

Two letters, one from Theodoricus Pedrini, the other from Antonius Gogeisl, to John Hodson giving astronomical observations at Peking. 8 November 1738, 7 November 1741. Read 27 January 1743. 7 pp. *Latin.* 6 pp. English translation. (LP. 1. 153.)

Astronomical observations, by Augustin Hallerstein, together with a letter from the President of the Astronomical College at Peking. *Latin.* 4 pp., 2 pp. (LP. 2. 22. See *Phil. Trans.* xlvi. 305.)

Observations at Peking of a comet, &c. by Anthony Gaubil. 9 November 1748. Read 18 January 1750. *Latin.* 3 pp. (LP. 2. 23. See *Phil. Trans.* xlvi. 316.)

Of Geography among the Chinese and of paper-money current in China, by the same. Translation from the French by D. J. Slack. Read 1 February 1750. 4 pp. This paper is accompanied by a specimen of a note for 1,000 cash printed on grey paper and issued between A.D. 1368 and 1390. (LP. 2. 33. See *Phil. Trans.* xlvi. 327.)

Catalogue of plants from Peking, by Pierre D'Incarville. 9 November 1748. *French.* Together with letter, translated from the same. Read 21 June 1750. 14 pp., 3 pp. (LP. 2. 153.)

Letter of Augustin Hallerstein in Peking to Dr. C. Mortimer, Secretary, Royal Society. Read 19 December 1751. 4 pp. *Latin.* 7 pp. English translation (LP. 2. 247. See *Phil. Trans.* xlvii. 319.)

Letter of Pierre D'Incarville in Peking to same about various Chinese plants and seeds. 15 November 1751. 7 pp. *French.* 8 pp. English translation. (LP. 2. 359. See *Phil. Trans.* xlviii. 253.)

Two letters from Anthony Gaubil in Peking about Chinese astronomy and geography. 2 pp. (LP. 2. 385. See *Phil. Trans.* xlviii. 309.)

Of Chinese music, by the same, with 4 pp. in musical notation—'Cantilenae Sinicae Signis Europeis Expressae.' (LP. 2. 422.)

Of the eclipse of the sun observed at Peking, by the same. 25 May 1751. 6 pp. (LP. 2. 423.)

Of the shape of the several provinces of China, Tibet wanting, by the Jesuit Fathers at Peking. Read 30 June 1757. 1 p. *Latin.* 2 pp. English translation. (LP. 3. 261.)

Paper by Anthony Gaubil on a Chinese book on perspective published in 1735, and of which he had sent a copy to the Royal Society. Read 11 May 1758. 2 pp. (LP. 3. 319.)

Remarques sur le Ti-ouang-miao, by the same. 14 pp. (LP. 3. 322.)

A description of the plan of Peking, by the same. Read 1 June 1758. 37 pp. Translated from the French. (LP. 3. 323. See *Phil. Trans.* l. 704.)

Official report by Dr. James Parsons and three others on a large collection of stones sent from Siberia by Count S. Read 22 January 1761. 3 pp. (LP. 4. 40.)

A beautiful Chinese pheasant—the Angus, by George Edwards. Read 7 March 1765. 5 pp. (LP. 4. 255. See *Phil. Trans.* lv. 88.)

Letter from Stephen De Visne in Canton giving an account of an earthquake at Macao, and of tailless 'monkeys'. 7 January 1768. Read 9 March 1769. (LP. 5. 81. See *Phil. Trans.* lix. 71.)

Of Macao monkeys, by the Revd. [Sidney] Swinney. Read 6 April 1769. 1 p. (LP. 5. 88.)

Of Mr. Turberville Needham's conjecture as to the connection between Egyptian hieroglyphics and the Chinese characters, by C. M. D. Morton, Secretary, Royal Society. 14 pp. (LP. 5. 142. See *Phil. Trans.* lix. 489.)

Letter of Stephen de Visme [or De Visne] and paper by Père Gramont on the manner in which the Chinese heat their rooms. Read 31 January 1770. 3 pp. and 8 pp. *French*, with 11 pp. translation of Gramont's paper. (LP. 5. 213. See *Phil. Trans.* lxi. 59.)

'Resa til Japan', by C. P. Thunberg. Read 10 February 1780. 5 pp. *Swedish*. 18 pp. English translation, entitled 'Abstract of journal kept in Japan, a letter to the President, Royal Society'. (LP. 7. 139. See *Phil. Trans.* lxx. 143 for Swedish text.)

Letter from Keane Fitzgerald to Sir J. Banks on experiments with Chinese hempseed. Read 17 January 1782. 3 pp. (LP. 7. 229. See *Phil. Trans.* lxxii. 47.)

PHILOSOPHICAL TRANSACTIONS MSS. (PT)

Manuscripts (not complete) of papers published in the *Philosophical Transactions*, arranged as in the printed volumes, which should be consulted first. 1807–65. *c.* 600 items in 75 vols. and box files.

ARCHIVED PAPERS (AP)

Papers communicated to the Royal Society, but not published, or published in abstract only. These papers are catalogued in the card catalogue under the authors' names, and there is a list of contents in each volume. 1800 onwards. 1,499 items in 82 vols. and box files.

REFEREES' REPORTS [confidential] (RR)

Referees' reports on papers communicated to the Royal Society. These reports are confidential and not available for examination. 1832 to date.

ROYAL SOCIETY LETTERS (RS)

Official correspondence arranged in alphabetical order of writers' names. Late 18th and early 19th centuries. 3 vols.

MISCELLANEOUS CORRESPONDENCE (MC)

Letters addressed to the Royal Society. 1800–99. 6,435 items in 17 box files, and *c.* 2,000 items in 20 small box files.

NEW LETTER-BOOK

Copies of outgoing letters (uncatalogued). 1885 to early 20th century. 73 vols.

MANUSCRIPTS (GENERAL) (MS)

Life of Confucius, by Louis Poirot. 18th century. *Italian*. (MS. 167.)

Two tracts relating to Confucius and Confucianism (MS. 171):

1. Ta Hio. Confucius philosophus totius imperii Sinensis Universalis magister. Translation of a Chinese original by Johannes [?Juan] Rodriguez. 1763.

2. Traduzione del Touintzui di Confusio fatta da Luigi de Poirot. 18th century.

The journal of Mr. Samuel Holmes, Sergeant-Major of the 12th Light Dragoons during his attendance . . . on Lord Macartney's Embassy to China. (MS. 72. Published 1795.)

MISCELLANEOUS MANUSCRIPTS (MM)

Miscellaneous single letters and documents.

METEOROLOGICAL ARCHIVES (MA)

Sets of meteorological observations. 352 items in bound volumes and box files. Including:

China: Canton. 1771–4. (MA. 209.)
　　　　　1804. (MA. 180.)
　　　　　1840. (MA. 26.)

On board the East India Company ship *Elphinstone* on a voyage from China to England, 1811. (MA. 80.)

ROYAL SOCIETY OF TROPICAL MEDICINE AND HYGIENE

Manson House, 26 Portland Place, London, W. 1

MANSON PAPERS. Papers of Sir Patrick Manson (1844–1922), physician and parasitologist, who lived and worked in China from 1866 to 1883. Including:

1. Diary kept in Amoy and Hong Kong, containing a record of observations, experiments, &c., beginning June 1877. Some letters are inserted. (See Philip Manson-Bahr, 'A commentary on the diary kept by

Patrick Manson in China and now conserved at Manson House', in *Trans. Royal Soc. Trop. Med. and Hygiene*, vol. xxix, no. 1, pp. 79–90.)

2. Envelope containing miscellaneous papers relating to the Hong Kong College of Medicine.

3. 'Manson's notebook. 1875. British Museum.' This includes 'an account of the first 26 cases of filiariasis studied in Amoy 1877'.

4. Typescript of *Life and work of Sir Patrick Manson*, by Manson-Bahr and Alcock (1927), together with some correspondence, press-cuttings, &c.

ROYAL UNITED SERVICE INSTITUTION FOR DEFENCE STUDIES LIBRARY

Whitehall, London, SW1A 2ET

Papers and journals of Captain William Robert Broughton (1762–1821), navigator and explorer, some relating to his survey of the coast of Asia, 1794–8. (NM 132.)

Letters and papers of Assistant Surgeon C. Pine, including some written in China, 1840. Also Pine's private journal, 1841–5, of which the first part, August 1841–October 1842, covers service in Nanking, Chusan, and other parts of China. (MM 262 A and B.)

Journals and logs kept by Captain T. W. Oliver, 1848–66, including: (2) *Rapid*, 1851–3, and (3) *Rapid* and *Spartan*, 1853–5, both mainly in Chinese waters. (NM 150.)

Recollections by F. Parry, Royal Marines, of two expeditions to China, in 1858 and during the Boxer troubles in 1900. (MM 457.)

Embarkation state at Talein during Sir Hope Grant Johnson's expedition to China, 1860. (MM 453/10.)

Journals kept by an anonymous lieutenant R.N. on board H.M.S. *Iron Duke, London, Kite*, and *Valiant*, and the Chinese gunboat *Eta* on a passage to the East, 1879. 1874–9. 1 vol. (NM 167.)

Some notes on China. 19th century. (MM 148/vii.)

Coded dispatch from Peking. August 1900. (MM 475.)

Copy of the autobiography of Field-Marshal Sir Garnet Joseph Wolseley, *The Story of a soldier's Life*, 2 vols. (1903), with numerous manuscript corrections and additions by the author. Volume 2 contains seven chapters on the China War and on a visit to Japan, 1860–1. (In MM 385 A. Wolseley Papers.)

THE SALVATION ARMY

101 Queen Victoria Street, London, E.C. 4

Keen devotes a section to the Salvation Army (SA/1–2), mentioning that it has worked in China (since 1916), Japan (1895), Korea (1908), Taiwan (1928, reopened 1965), but does not indicate the existence of any records relating to these areas.

SCHOOL OF ORIENTAL AND AFRICAN STUDIES

Malet Street, London, WC1E 7HP

MARSDEN MSS.

Annuae Sinenses 1633 et 1634. (Missio Anamica, sive Tunquinensis. Anno 1634.) Reports on Jesuit missions and the state of Christianity in China, Annam, and Tongking. *c.* 1634. 77 ff. (MS. 11976.)

Juan de Paz, Quaesita missionariorum Tunkini et responsiones ad ipsa. [Copied from a book published in Manila, 1680.] 161 ff. (MS. 12215.)

Quaesita Missionariorum Chinae seu Sinarum, S. Congregationi de Propaganda Fide exhibita, cum Responsis ad ea. [1669.] (MS. 11455.)

William Marsden, English Luchu vocabulary compiled 16 September–27 October 1816. 24 ff. (MS. 41681.)

Herbert John Clifford, Vocabulary of the language spoken on the island called Great Lieou-Kieou or Lieuchew, to which are added sentences, proper names and other miscellaneous remarks illustrative of the language. (MS. 11117.)

Name and age of the Old Emperor (Ch'ien Lung). Name of the reigning Emperor (Ch'ia Ching). Written by a Chinese at the Admiralty. 11 April 1799. (MS. 12897.)

Basilio Brollo, vicar Apostolic of Shensi. Dictionarium Sinico-Latinum, cum variis appendicibus. A manuscript copy of this work. On 1a and 593b appears the signature 'Andr. Reid' in a nineteenth-century hand. [*c.* 1740.] V, 593 ff. of which I–V and 582–92 are blank. (MS. 12187.)

Philippe Masson, A book of philological and bibliographical notes in Latin and French on various oriental and other languages and literatures, with some notes in French on personal matters. The languages include Arabic, Persian, Chinese, &c. [18th century.] 155 ff. (MS. 42791.)

Manuscript catalogue of the Chinese collection which Robert Morrison brought back with him from China in 1824, and which was presented to University

College, London. This collection is now incorporated in the Library of S.O.A.S. (MS. 80823.)

Manuscript copy by Sir Thomas Wade, with his additions and corrections, of 'Vocabulary of the Canton dialect', by Robert Morrison. Hong Kong. 1843. (MS. 30368.)

'Voyage au Japon, par le Colonel d'état-major Du Pin, Chef du Service topographique en Chine.' An account of the author's tour in Japan in 1861 to study the topography of the country and the life of its people. With tables showing the administrative areas at that time, a section of a map, and illustrations. 2,387 pp., p. 34 missing. [1862.] (MS. 63179.)

CHINESE MARITIME CUSTOMS DOCUMENTS

Manuscript letter-book of George H. Fitzroy. Shanghai, 16 November 1860–25 May 1863. pp. 104. (MS. 258361.)

Correspondence between Sir Robert Hart and his personal representative J. D. Campbell, 1868–1906. 7 boxes. (MS. 191931.)

Typescript copies of Sir Robert Hart's letters to Sir Francis Arthur Aglen. Peking, 26 November 1888–14 September 1911. ff. 192, 45. (MS. 211081.)

Typescript copies of Sir Robert Hart's correspondence with J. D. Campbell. Peking, letter series Z, nos. 947–1102, 3 January 1903–14 October 1906, with an abstract of letter series Z, nos. 1103–1119, 28 October 1906–29 September 1907. ff. (48), 136, 147, 12. (MS. 211351.)

Copies of James Duncan Campbell's correspondence with Sir Robert Hart. London, letter series Z, nos. 1125–1564, 5 August 1898–21 December 1906. 2 vols. (MS. 211353.)

Papers of Edward Charles Macintosh Bowra and Cecil Arthur Verner Bowra relating to the family and its service with the Chinese Maritime Customs, 1840–1966. 4 boxes; 1 loose-leaf folder; 7 vols. (MS. 201813.)

Correspondence of Guy Francis Hamilton and Cecil Arthur Verner Bowra with Sir F. A. Aglen. London, letter series Z, nos. 309–86, 7 January 1921–23 December 1924. 1 vol. unfoliated. (MS. 211354.)

Confidential correspondence of Sir Francis Arthur Aglen with G. F. H. Acheson and C. A. V. Bowra. Peking, 2 January 1921–7 June 1926. With five later letters by A. F. H. Edwards, 3 July 1926–28 August 1926. 1 vol. unfoliated. (MS. 211355.)

For a detailed list of these papers, see *Papers relating to the Chinese Maritime Customs 1860–1943 in the Library of the School of Oriental & African Studies*, 1973.

N. St. V. Nepean, English–Chinese vocabulary, in Wade transcription. *c.* 1900. (MS. 65426.)

Copies of three pieces by Oswald Wallwyn Darch,

with photographs, descriptive of Kongmoon, Amoy, and Formosa, contributed to the manuscript magazine *The Beehive*. 1912–14. (MS. 283049.)

Photograph album of Richard Henry Lovelock Lee, with two envelopes of duplicate prints, mainly showing Chinese life and work in Shansi. 1905–10? (MS. 282377.)

ROYAL INSTITUTE OF INTERNATIONAL AFFAIRS: FAR EAST DEPARTMENT PAPERS

A collection of miscellaneous papers, including Embassy hand-outs, conference papers, background material, &c. accumulated by the Far East Department of the Royal Institute of International Affairs. *c.* 1927–62. MS., typescript, and print. Including:

1. British policy in the Far East and South-East Asia, Copies of statements and speeches made in Parliament, 1943–50. 1 box. (MS. 186387.)

2. China: economic. 1937–53. 2 boxes. (MS. 186362.)

3. China: political. This includes letters and speeches by Sir Austen Chamberlain, 1927 (Box IX) and Shanghai and Tientsin report, 1929 (Box X). 10 boxes. (MS. 186361.)

4. Economic development: Far East and South-East Asia. 1949–58. 2 boxes. (186374.)

5. Formosa. 1946–60. 2 boxes. (MS. 186480.)

6. General. 1936–62. 9 boxes. (MS. 186377.)

7. Japan: economic. 1939–62. 5 boxes. (MS. 186370.)

8. Japan: political. 1929–61. 4 boxes. (MS. 186371.)

9. Korea. 1938–61. 3 boxes. (MS. 186372.)

10. U.S. policy in the Far East. 1938–51. 2 boxes. (MS. 186386.)

Typescript letter from Ezra Pound to S.O.A.S. asking for advice on obtaining Chinese books. Rapallo, 17 September 1937. (MS. Guardbook 257288.)

Papers of Dr. E. D. Edwards, Professor of Chinese at London University 1939–55, mainly concerned with her work on producing a textbook of classical prose. Uncatalogued. 2 parcels. (MS. 145609.)

Papers of J. K. Rideout. Uncatalogued. 1 parcel. (MS. 145610.)

Undated

Kuei-chiao Kai-ssu. An anti-Catholic pamphlet. Chinese text with English translation. 13 ff., 2, 35 pp. (MS. 82537.)

Lecture notes taken down by G. W. Bonsall at Cambridge of Gustave Haloun's translation, interpretation, and notes concerning chapters 37, 49, and 55 of Chung Kuan, Kuan-tzŭ. MS. and typescript. 1, 141, 2 ff. (MS. 107005.)

The Confucian [Li-Chi] or Record of Ritual. Translated by . . . T. McClatchie. 17 parts. (MS. 105332.)

Papers of Sir Gerard Leslie Makins Clauson, comprising preliminary studies in the decipherment of the Hsi-hsia language, a skeleton dictionary and other manuscripts concerned with Hsi-hsia studies. 7 folders and an envelope containing miscellaneous manuscripts. (MS. 84335.)

Letters and other relics of Gladys Aylward, missionary to Shansi and Taiwan. (MS. 291591.)

ARCHIVES OF THE COUNCIL FOR WORLD MISSION

C. Stuart Craig, *The archives of the Council for World Mission (incorporating the London Missionary Society): an outline guide.* School of Oriental and African Studies. The Library, 1973. See also Marchant, pp. 63–76; Keen CCWM 1/6.

London Missionary Society Archives.

Board minutes. 1795–1942. 58 boxes.

Committee minutes, incl.:

Candidates. May 1799–1939. 16 boxes.

India and Ultra-Ganges. 1827–40. 2 boxes.

Finance. January 1837–September 1840, November, 1865–June 1910. 3 boxes.

Foreign occasional. 1840–5, 1882–1944. 7 boxes.

China. November 1856–1939. (Boxes 2–11. Box 1, 1840–56, missing.)

Ladies. October 1875–June 1907. 4 boxes.

Consultative and Finance. November 1895–1938. 9 boxes.

Special. Box 1, Joint L.M.S. Board of Union Medical College, Peking. 1908–16.

ULTRA-GANGES

Outgoing letters. China/Ultra-Ganges. 1822–54. 4 boxes in 3.

Journals. 1813–41. 1 box.

CHINA

Outgoing letters: China/Ultra-Ganges. 1822–54. 4 boxes in 3.

China. 1854–1914. Boxes 5–43.

Personal

1. R. Morrison—Letters (1)

2. R. Morrison—Letters (2)

3. R. Morrison—Papers (3); Anglo-Chinese Coll. documents and papers; Mission report; Notes on Chinese language.

4. J. Legge—Sermons (1)

5. J. Legge—Sermons (2)

6. J. Legge—Sermons (3); Address early Amoy Induction 1874.

7. J. Legge—Printed and typed articles; notes on literary and language work.

8. J. Legge—Letters to and from.

9. J. Legge—Draft life of JL; personal documents on JL; cuttings, reviews, obituaries, &c.

10. J. Legge—Letters to Mrs. L; letter-book; letters from Mrs. L.

11. Miscellaneous letters from missionaries to friends.

12. E. Hope-Bell—papers.

13. Marjorie Clements—letters from North China 1930/33; MS. 'Discipleship' arranged by Eric Liddell.

14. George and Dorothy Barbour—diary and letters North China. 1920/36.

15. F. A. Brown—autobiographical sketch—China 1935/51; India 1952/58.

16. Lockhart—records and a/cs; Terrell diaries; Dudgeon-note on Pekin hospital.

Odds

1. PUMC—minutes, letters; Siaokan hospital; Griffith John obit.; Nestorian Tablet rubbings.

2. Amoy Dist. Com. Min.—local 1903/24.

3. Amoy Dist. Com. Min.—1878/87; 1887/1912.

4. N. China Dist. Com. Min.—1874/94; 1895/1909 vols. 1 and 2.

5. N. China Dist. Com. Min.—1909/20 vol. 3.

6. Hong Kong and New Territories Evang. Soc.— 3 minute books (1904/1932).

7. F. H. Hawkins—Deputation 1917.

8. Central China Dist. Com. Min.—1932/37; political odds; letters re book M. Aldersey.

9. Hankow Med. Planning papers; Wuchang hosp. controversy; Chinese medal with history; Medhurst MS. notes 1848/52; Boxer Indemn. papers.

10. Miscellaneous notes on Chinese Church leaders.

FUKIEN

Incoming letters. 1845–1927. 14 boxes.

Correspondence files (in and out). 1928–39. Boxes 15–19.

Reports. 1866–1939. 6 boxes.

SOUTH CHINA

Incoming letters. 1803–1927. Boxes 1–17, 18A, 18B, 19–24.

Correspondence files (in and out). 1928–39. Boxes 25–30.

Reports. 1866–1939. 7 boxes.

Journals. 1807–42. 1 box.

1. R. Morrison. From England to Philadelphia. February–May 1807.

2. R. Morrison. New York to Canton. May–September 1807.

3–7. R. Morrison. Canton. September 1807–November 1808.

8. Mrs. W. Milne. From England to Cape Town. September–December 1812.

9. W. Milne. From England to Cape Town. September–December 1812.

10. W. Milne. From Cape Town to Canton including stay at Macao. December 1812–January 1814.

11. R. Morrison. Canton. February 1813–January 1814.

12. W. Milne. Canton. Journey among Malayan islands, distributing books. January 1814–February 1815.

13. W. Milne. Malacca. December 1815–January 1817.

14. Leang A-fa. Translated by R. Morrison. 1830.

15. W. C. Milne. Macao. December 1841–June 1842.

NORTH CHINA

Incoming letters. 1860–1927. Boxes 1–14, 15A, B, C, D, 16–25.

Correspondence files (in and out). 1928–39. Boxes 26–36.

Reports. 1866–1939. 12 boxes.

Journals. 1863–4. 1 box.

1. J. Lees. Tientsin. Journey to Peking and Kalgan. October–November 1863.

2. J. Lees. Tientsin. Journey to Pan Ting Fu. April–May 1864.

CENTRAL CHINA

Incoming letters. 1843–1927. Boxes 1–11, 12A, 12B, 13–32, 33A, 33B, 34–40, 41A, 41B.

Correspondence files (in and out). 1928–39. Boxes 42–65.

Reports. 1866–1940. 13 boxes.

Journal. Dr. C. J. Davenport. Hiao Kan. 1888–96. 1 box.

HOME

Personal

6. W. N. Bitton papers—China, South Seas, &c.

Odds

15. W. H. Somervell letters, B.F.B.S. Chinese Bible correspondence, L.M.S. maps 1895, two lectures 1919, 1929, Farquhar House.

Glass negatives

China. Box 4.

Pictures (mainly photographs)

China. 9 boxes.

Maps. China.

Miscellaneous

Morrison and Chinese writers; two prints.

Battles and ceremonies in China—costumes, architecture, &c. 1765.

Nouvel atlas de Chine et Tartar[ie].

Plates to the Chinese Embassy.

Sketches of China and the Chinese—Borget.

The China Mail, Hong Kong, 1854, 1855, 1858, 1859.

Designs of Chinese buildings, furniture, &c., by Chambers. 1757. 2 copies.

Scrapbooks—torture methods (Chinese).

10–15 Chinese water-colours with explanatory paragraphs.

Faits mémorables des empereurs de Chine. 1788.

The costume of China, Alexander. 1805.

Six views of Singapore and Macao. 1840.

Cloth paintings—Mongol god of Hell (Gilmour or Stallybrass).

Early Chinese Christian writings. 2 boxes.

Maps of coast of China.

Parcel of Chinese pictures.

Wooden box of Chinese writings, drawings, &c., marked 'valuable'.

Compare also the description given in Marchant, op. cit., pp. 63–7.

RUSSIA

Journals

1. C. Rahm. E. Stallybrass. Siberia. Irkutsk. Journey from St. Petersburg to Irkutsk. Incomplete. January 1818.

2. C. Rahm. Sarepta; journey to Astrachan. November–December 1819.

3. Richard Knill. From leaving India to within two years of leaving St. Petersburg. 1819–31.

4. W. Swann. Siberia. Selenginsk. Occurrences at the Tabungut Temple. March 1821.

5. E. Stallybrass. Siberia. Account of the burial festival of the White Month. February 1821.

6. C. Rahm. Sarepta. January 1821–March 1822.

7. E. Stallybrass. Siberia. Selenginsk. Tour with W. Swann in the country of the Chorinsky Buriats. January–February 1822.

8. R. Knill. St. Petersburg. March 1823.

9. R. Yuille. Siberia. Selenginsk. February–March 1824.

10. W. Swann. Siberia. 1827.

SOCIETY OF FRIENDS' LIBRARY

Friends House, Euston Road, London, NW1 2BJ

RECORDS OF THE SOCIETY (See also Marchant, pp. 95–7.)

1. *London Yearly Meeting Minutes.* 1668– . In progress.
The minutes of Yearly Meeting, the annual assembly of Quakers in Britain, contain reports and decisions of general moment covering a variety of subjects, including the traffic in opium. The minutes and proceedings are available in print from 1857. There is a printed index for the years 1857–1906.

2. *London Meeting for Sufferings Minutes.* 1675– . In progress.
Meeting for Sufferings, which met weekly until the close of the eighteenth century and has met monthly thereafter, is the representative body acting on behalf of the Yearly Meeting between its sessions. The minutes contain reports of committees appointed to carry out detailed work, accounts from Friends 'liberated' to travel in the ministry, and other official records. It must, however, be noted that especially during the nineteenth century many matters in which Friends were interested and which were discussed by members assembled for Meeting for Sufferings were not considered to be 'Society concerns' and no minute of decision in relation to them will be found.

3. *Continental Committee Minutes and Papers*
A committee, set up by Meeting for Sufferings in 1817 and later known as the Continental Committee, was responsible for maintaining oversight of Quaker groups overseas where there was no settled Yearly Meeting. China, which was a Friends Foreign Mission Association field, does not occur largely in the minutes (MS., vol. 65 ff.) but there is a file of epistles between Chinese Friends and the Continental Committee, 1894–1912 (Temp. boxes 84, 92/6).

4. *Anti-Opium Association Committee*
Minute books. 1858–60. (Box V.)
Executive Committee Minute book. 1860–3. (Box T.)
Account book. 1858–61. (Box V.)
Letters to Edward Newman, &c. and leaflets. (Box V.)

5. *Anti-Opium Urgency Committee*
Minute book. 1894–5. (Social Purity Box.)

6. *Anti-Opium Committee*
Minute books. 1895–6. (Box D.)

Minute Books. 1903–14. Together with correspondence and related papers.

7. *Far East Watching Committee*
Minute books. 1932–4. (MS. vol. 82.)

Reply of the Chinese Ambassador to address. (Kuo Sung tao to George S. Gibson and others. 1877. (MS. Box 11/4. 2.)

Letters from William and Katherine Jones in Japan. 1888–90. (MS. Box 16.)

Papers of Isaac Sharp (1806–97):

1. Diaries, vols. 83, 84, and 85, covering his visits to Japan and China in 1892–3.

2. A description of a presentation to Isaac Sharp by members of the Friends Mission on the occasion of his visit to Chungking, December 1892. (MS. Box 11/6. 1.)

3. Extract from diary of Isaac Sharp referring to a presentation from an ex-Taoist priest. December 1892. (Port. 41/173.)

Letter from the Quarterly Meeting at Chungking with translation, 1895. (MS. Box 11/5. 5.)

Epistle from Chungking to the Yearly Meeting, with translation. 1896. (MS. Box 11/5. 4.)

Journal, consisting of a series of letters, written by J. Gundry Alexander describing his visit to China, by way of Malaya, on an anti-opium mission. Places visited in China include Hong Kong, Canton, Foochow, Soochow, &c. 2 October 1906–18 June 1907. MS. and typescript. (Box R.)

Letter from Szechwan Yearly Meeting to Young Friends of military age in Great Britain and Ireland. *Chinese*, with a number of signatures. February 1917. Also English translation. (Box P.)

Letters and notes of Henry T. Hodgkin about his work in China. 24 November 1920–1 June 1922. (Box W.)

FRIENDS' FOREIGN MISSION ASSOCIATION (Marchant, pp. 60–1)

Executive Committee. Minutes. 1874–91. 2 vols.

China Subcommittee. Minutes. 1883–1905. 2 vols.

THE SOCIETY FOR PROMOTING CHRISTIAN KNOWLEDGE

Holy Trinity Church, Marylebone Road, London, NW1 4DU

Since its foundation in 1698, the main activities of the S.P.C.K. have been in the fields of education and the printed word. The influence of the Society in China, Japan, and Korea has been largely through its support of the various Anglican dioceses set up in these countries from the mid nineteenth century onwards, through the allocation of grants, and through the translation, publication, and distribution of Christian literature. There is a name and subject card index compiled from the tables of contents in many of the individual volumes. The records listed below are those known to contain, or thought most likely to contain, material relevant to this *Guide*. Application to consult these records should be made to the Public Relations Officer at the above address. (Marchant, pp. 100–2; Keen, SPCK/1–7.)

I. MINUTES

General Board minutes. 1698–1939. 76 vols, indexed, continuing to date. (GM 1–76.)

General Board: draft minutes. 1708–53. 44 vols. (GM 1/1–44.)

General Board: duplicate minute books. 1699–1859. 32 vols. (GM 1b–32b.)

Standing Committee minutes. 1705–25. 4 vols. (SM 01–04.)

Standing Committee minutes. 1825–1929. 49 vols., indexed. (SM 1/1–49.)

Finance Committee minutes. 1838–1926. 28 vols., indexed from 1852. (FC m/1–28.)

Committee of General Literature and Education minute books. 1832–1909. 12 vols., some of them indexed. (PG m/1–13.)

Foreign Translation Committee minute books, 1834–1955. 10 vols., indexed. (PF m/1–10.)

Medical Missions Committee and Subcommittee minute books. 1888–1947. 5 vols.

II. CORRESPONDENCE

Abstract letter-books, containing abstracts of letters received and sent. 1699–1701, 1708–83. 27 vols., indexed. (CR 1/01–26.) One of the earliest references to China in this series is a letter to Mr. Boehm from 'a gentleman in the East Indies that conceals his name' which describes the state of religion in China, with much criticism of the Jesuits; read before committee 10 September 1713.

Copies of the abstract letter-books. 1699–1701, 1708–9, 1711–15. 4 vols. (CR 1/01a–3a.)

III. FINANCE

Money Grants (overseas) voted. 1825–1923, 1924–date. 2 vols.

Grants Books (home and overseas). 1907–47. 11 vols. Bills payable. 1914–26. 1 vol. (FT 3.)

ARCHIVES OF *THE TIMES*

Times Newspapers Ltd., P.O. Box no. 7, New Printing House Square, Gray's Inn Road, London, WC1X 8EZ

In addition to the papers of the Correspondents from the territories listed below, the resources of this Archive on the Far East include a lengthy series of volumes entitled Managerial Letter Books, which comprise out-letters from the Manager to these Correspondents and certain of their deputies and stand-ins, as well as to the public in general, and cover the period 1849–1915. A similar set of volumes from the Foreign Editor, addressed almost solely to staff writers overseas, cover 1891–1910.

Letters of a personal nature to the Editor and designed as background appraisals and policy justifications, include some from persons in public life in the Far East of the stature of Lord Irwin, 1926–31, and Sir Harcourt Butler, written from Burma in 1923–8. Earlier letters to J. T. Delane, Editor of *The Times*, 1841–77, and the Walter family, former Proprietors of the paper, treat also on the Far East, especially India.

There are, in addition, folders devoted to editorial policy on certain questions and countries, as well as the more contemporary confidential memoranda and briefings from Correspondents in the field, which remain closed under the thirty-year rule operating elsewhere in the U.K. There is also an interesting small section on the Russo-Japanese War of 1904.

This Archive is attempting to collect all the commercially published works by *The Times* staff writers, *ab initio*, and obviously these will include books on the Far East by a wide range of writers, including Laurence Oliphant and Sir Valentine Chirol. Biographical clippings files are also held and an effort is made on an international basis to discover the whereabouts of documents relevant to *The Times* and its former writers, contained in other libraries and repositories.

A prior requisite for any researcher wishing to visit this Archive is a familiarity with the printed *History of The Times*, published in 5 volumes from 1935 to 1952 and reviewing the world as seen from Printing House Square from 1785 to 1948.

Papers of various staff correspondents, assistant correspondents, special writers, 'stringers', &c.

China. Peking, 1857 to date, including George Wingrove Cooke, 1857–8; George Ernest Morrison, 1897–1912; and David Fraser, 1912 onwards.

Hankow, 1910–1938.

Shanghai, 1863 onwards, notably J. O. P. Bland, 1897–1910.

Hong Kong. 1847 to date.

Japan. Tokyo, Kobe, 1890 onwards, notably D. S. Fraser, 1915–21, Hugh F. Byas, 1926–41.

Korea. 1920 onwards.

The amount of material for each country varies enormously, from a mere identity and date of service, where known, of a Correspondent, to complete boxes and folders ranging over the whole period of service for *The Times.*

See also an article by the Archivist in *Business archives,* no. 41, Jan. 1976, pp. 20–4.

UNITED REFORMED CHURCH

Historical Library and Muniment Room,
86 Tavistock Place, London, WC1H 9RT

The United Reformed Church results from a union of the Presbyterian Church of England with the Congregational Church in England and Wales. The Presbyterian Church of England opened its first mission station on the Chinese mainland at Amoy in 1847, and was active in different parts of Fukien for over 100 years—the last missionary leaving the province in 1951. The Formosa mission, founded in 1865, continues actively to date. There is an interesting collection of Church archives (although many records were destroyed during the Second World War), but the mission papers are only partially sorted and arranged, and the following list, though representative, is not complete. It seems unlikely, however, that there still exists more of the early material than is shown below. As well as the manuscript material there is a large quantity of printed material, including reports, minutes, pamphlets, &c. For a history of the mission see Edward Band, *Working his purpose out: the history of the English Presbyterian Mission, 1847–1947.* See also Marchant, pp. 92–5; Keen, PRES/1–4.

BOUND VOLUMES, I. General Records

Minutes of the Foreign Missions Committee of Synod. 1841–99. 4 vols. Later minutes are printed.

Minutes of the Advisory Committee of Foreign Missions. 1886–93. 2 vols.

Minute books of the financial sub-committee of the Foreign Mission Executive. 1904–20. 6 vols.

Minutes of the Synod's special committee on the relations between the Foreign Missions Committee and the Woman's Missionary Association. 1913–16. 1 vol.

Minutes of the W.M.A. [Women's Missionary Association] Committee. 1878–1964. 26 vols., continuing.

Minutes of W.M.A. Council. 1950–64. 3 vols.

Minutes of W.M.A. Executive Committee [becoming, 1926, W.M.A. Advisory Committee]. 1901–52. 14 vols.

Minutes of joint W.M.A. and F.M. [Foreign Missions] Advisory Committee. 1899–1917. 1 vol.

Minutes of W.M.A. Candidates Committee. 1945–61. 1 vol.

BOUND VOLUMES, II. China records.

E.P.M. [Evangelical Presbyterian Mission]. Amoy Council Minutes 1880–96, 1895–1902, 1902–5. 3 vols.

W.M.A. Amoy Council. 1911–26. 2 vols.

Hakka Council Minutes. Vol. 1. 1911–23; vol. 2. 1923–32; vol. 3. 1933–44; vol. 4. 1911–40.

Centenary Conference Committee. No. I. The Chinese Church. 1 vol.

LOOSE PAPERS, I (including correspondence, reports, &c., arranged in folders)

American Baptist Foreign Missions Society. 1943–6.

Amoy papers. 1912–28, 1917–44, 1919–40, 1925–7, 1925–8, 1928–30, 1929–34, 1942–4. 8 folders.

Amoy Council minutes. 1903–22.

Amoy Minutes. 1928–30, 1931–3. 2 folders.

Amoy Minutes, W.M.A. 1929–30.

Annual field reports. 1930, 1935–63. *c.* 34 folders including several duplicates.

Associated Mission. Treasurers. 1944–7, 1948. 2 folders.

Bible, book, and tract depot, H.K. 1953–6.

British United Aid to China Fund. 1940–9, 1942–4, 1953–9. 3 folders.

Budget. 1949/50–1963/4. 15 folders.

Canadian Presbyterian Church. 1935–47.

Candidates and personnel correspondence. 1948–57. 4 folders.

Candidates and personnel committee minutes. 1949–60. 3 folders.

Centenary correspondence. 1946–7.

China Christian Universities. 1948–9, 1950–1. 2 folders.

China, Medical. 1930–2.

China, News. 1949–52.

China, Papers. 1925.

China, Situation. 1926–9.

Chuanchow. 1926–8.

Chuanchow. Hospital. 1946–51.

Chuangpu. 1919–28, 1938–53.

Church of Christ in China. 1928–33, 1934–40, 1943–7, 1948–50. 4 folders.

Church overseas [magazine]: correspondence. 1945–51.

Church of Scotland F.M.C. [Foreign Mission Committee]. 1941–9.

— statistics. 1936.

Circular letters to Councils. 1930–42.

Compensation for missionaries. *c.* 1942–9, 1952–3. 2 folders.

Conference of British Missionary Societies Insurance. 1945–54.

Correspondence of Dr. Maclaglan, Secretary of the Foreign Missions Committee. 1926–7.

— with relatives of missionaries. 1937–45.

Cost of living (China): correspondence. 1942–8.

Council on Christian medical work—China. 1943–9.

Cyclostyled papers. 1950–2. 5 folders.

Donations and gifts. 1943–8.

Educational returns for Councils. 1936.

Edinburgh House
    Far East Committee. 1929–38.
    Far East Literature Committee.
    Grants, finance. 1944–9, 1947–9. 2 folders.
    Miscellaneous. 1944–9.
    Minutes and circulars (China). 1924–8.

Formosa
    (Papers, general). 1924–6, 1927–9, 1931–4, 1940–6. 4 folders.
    Correspondence with the Revd. C. H. Hwang. 1950–8. 3 folders.
    Council minutes. 1917–25.
    English Committee. 1959–63. 5 folders.
    Floods. 1959.
    General Assembly. 1951–63. 6 folders.
    Minutes of joint meetings of English and Canadian Presbyterian Mission Councils. 1957–9.
    Mission Council papers. 1950–9. 22 folders.
    Mountain work, including correspondence with the Revd. J. N. Whitehorn. 1959–63. 2 folders.
    Political situation and correspondence with the Revd. Bruce Copland through Hong Kong, &c., 1960–1.
    School for missionary children. 1955–62.
    South Synod. 1946–56.
    Tainan papers—miscellaneous. 1929–37.
    Tainan theological college property. 1960–1.
    United conference: North and South Formosa Councils. 1950–7.

Hakka papers, correspondence and reports. 1919–41.

Hakka Council Minutes. 1911–44.

Hong Kong Bible, book and tract depot. 1953–6.

Insurance of mission property. 1917–36.

Inter Council conference. 1928–32.

Lintung [i.e. Swatow–Hakka]
    Council papers. 1950–2.
    Council. Special file. Letters to and from **Mr. and Mrs.** Graf. 1951.
    Council. Synod business. 1949–51.
    Finances. 1950.
    Letters. 1943–5.
    Synod business. 1949–52.
    Synod papers. 1938–48, 1946–50.

Medical work
    Survey of field. 1936.
    Miscellaneous papers. 1943–9.

Miscellaneous papers, including Wukingu incident. 1925.

Mission institutions (China). 1927.

Missionaries (files of correspondence and papers relating to):
    A. S. M. Anderson. 1928–45.
    The Revd. E. Bruce Copland. 1929–44.
    Dr. R. A. Elder. 1940–6.
    Dr. N. D. Fraser. 1929–43.
    The Revd. T. C. Gibson. Swatow. 1926–32.
    The Revd. T. W. D. James. *c.* 1936–44.
    Dr. David Landsborough. Chuanchow hospital. 1937–41.
    The Revd. C. C. Lu. 1947–9.
    Dr. Duncan MacLeod. 1930–44.
    Dr. J. L. Maxwell. 1926–49.
    The Revd. G. F. Mobbs. 1931–45. 3 folders.
    The Revd. W. E. Montgomery. Formosa. 1927–32, 1933–43. 2 folders.
    The Revd. A. B. Neilson. 1927–38.
    E. H. Scott. 1930–42.
    The Revd. W. Short. 1939–44.
    Dr. S. L. Strange. 1934–46.
    The Revd. Tsai Yung Ch'un. 1946–9.
    R. Tully. Amoy. 1930–46. 2 folders.
    Dr. N. Tunnell. 1938–50. 2 folders.
    The Revd. J. Waddell. Swatow. 1931–44. 2 folders.
    R. C. P. Weighton. 1939–45.

Missionaries and personnel (1 drawer, containing approximately 40 folders).

Missions, extraterritoriality, medical mission work, &c. 1926.

Ordination of missionaries. 1936–43.

Overseas Mission
    Convenor's conferences. 1937–49.
    Committee: correspondence with presbyterian Church of Australia. 1941–5.
    Committee: correspondence with United Church of Canada. 1931–49.

Plans and policy. 1929.

Register of Schools (China). 1927–9.

Reports, statistics sheets, &c. Swabue. 1918.

Scottish Auxiliary to F.P.M. [Foreign Presbyterian Mission].
    China. 1928–44, 1945–9. 2 folders.
    Minutes. 1924–7.

South Fukien
    Mission Council. 1947–51.
    Church and Missions Joint Committee. 1946–8.
    Missionary Committee. 1946–51.
    Synod. 1950–1.

Statistics. 1936–44.

Swatow
    Hospital. 1946–50.
    Hospital. Medical work papers. 1930–4. 2 folders.
    Medical. 1930–1, 1932. 2 folders.
    Medical correspondence. 1930–1.
    Medical, hospital reconstruction. 1930–1, 1934–5.
        2 folders.
    Minutes (and correspondence). 1928–33.
    Minutes. United Council. 1925–30.
    Papers. 1922–36, 1928–30, 1931–4. 3 folders.
    Presbytery. 1945–6.

Swatow–Hakka, Intercouncil Conference. 1930–2.

Theological education. 1920.

Westminster College
    Missionary Society. 1911–14.
    Students. 1945–9.

Wukingfu papers. 1931–4.

LOOSE PAPERS, II

Swatow correspondence. c. 1861–1906. (In a large cardboard container, with the letters arranged in packets.)

Two small box files labelled 'MS letters in connection with the China Mission of the Presbyterian Church of England'. Box I contains: (1) discharged accounts, 1858; (2) China Mission vouchers, 1858–9; (3 and 4) remittances, 1857–9; (5) folder containing a few miscellaneous papers. Box II contains correspondence of G. F. Barbour, 1855–79, some of it relating to the China Mission. Correspondents include Donald Matheson, H. M. Matheson, John MacPherson, &c. Included is a calendar of the letters compiled in 1952 by P. J. MacLayan.

Cardboard box containing miscellaneous papers, including letters to the Revd. W. Dale, some from Shanghai, 1902–6; letter from David Masson (who was drowned within sight of China), 8 August [18]66.

LOOSE PAPERS, III

Material for a history of the Presbyterian Church

arranged in a series of metal filing cabinets. The papers, both printed and manuscript, cover all activities of the Church and they are arranged in large (labelled) envelopes. Several drawers are devoted to ministers and missionaries arranged alphabetically ('Fasti'), and one in particular is devoted exclusively to missionaries. Each envelope has on the outside the name and dates, &c. of the minister or missionary, and contains biographical material such as photographs, cuttings, letters, &c.

UNITED SOCIETY FOR CHRISTIAN LITERATURE

4 Bouverie Street, London, E.C.4

Founded in 1935, taking over the work of the Religious Tract Society. (Marchant, pp. 113–16.)

UNITED SOCIETY FOR THE PROPAGATION OF THE GOSPEL

15 Tufton Street, London, SW1P 3QQ

The United Society for the Propagation of the Gospel was formed in 1965 when the Society for the Propagation of the Gospel in Foreign Parts (S.P.G.) amalgamated with the Universities' Mission to Central Africa (U.M.C.A.) (Marchant, pp. 103–7; Keen, USPG/1–14.)

RECORDS OF THE S.P.G.

The S.P.G., which was founded in 1701, was active in North China, Mongolia, Japan, and Korea from the second half of the nineteenth century onwards. The Society has a rich collection of archives, now in process of being recatalogued, which are open to students fifty years after the date of issue. For information about the work of the S.P.G. see C. F. Pascoe, *Two hundred years of the S.P.G.* (1901), and H. P. Thompson, *Into all lands, the history of the Society for the Propagation of the Gospel . . .* (1951).

MINUTES OF THE SOCIETY AND OF COMMITTEES

The various minutes of the Society often contain digests of, or extracts from, correspondence received and sent (or to be sent) in addition to records of business at meetings.

1. Journal of the Society, that is, minutes of the meetings of the Society as a whole. Vol. I to present day (more than 200 volumes, including signed originals and fair copies).

2. Minutes of the Standing Committee. Over the years the Standing Committee has gradually increased in importance. Its powers were officially

recognized in the S.P.G. Supplementary Charter of 1882, and at least from that date its minutes become a more important source of information than the Journal mentioned above. Vol. I (begins 1702) to present day.

3. Minutes of special committees, including:

(a) Agenda of foreign subcommittees. 1868–84. 3 vols. (X. 64a–c.)

(b) Foreign subcommittee, rough minutes. 1870–7. 7 vols. (X. 64–70.)

(c) Foreign subcommittee, rough minutes: Straits, Japan, China. 1878–80. 1 vol. (X. 73.)

(d) Foreign subcommittee, rough minutes. 1879–80. (X. 72.)

CORRESPONDENCE AND REPORTS

I. Letters and papers, mostly originals and unbound, kept in boxes. (C. MSS.) Including:

(a) China and Japan. This contains miscellaneous letters and papers of which the early ones relate mainly to Hong Kong. c. 1842–1959. 1 box.

II. Original letters (and papers) received, bound. 1850–date. (D. MSS.) This series is arranged geographically and chronologically. Its contents frequently overlap with that of the E. MSS. series (Missionaries' reports) below.

1. Letters received 1850–74, including:

(a) Bombay, Colombo, Victoria (Hong Kong), Borneo. 1850–9. 1 vol.

(b) Bombay, Colombo, Labuan, North China. 1868–74. 1 vol.

2. Letters received 1875 to date. During this period incoming letters were bound annually in two or more volumes of which at least one contains material relating to Asia and the Far East.

III. Copies of letters received, bound. 1833–1928. Fair copies, with an occasional original, of select incoming letters, i.e. those read before the Society. The volumes are arranged geographically and subdivided by dioceses. Most of them contain indexes. (G. MSS.) They include:

(a) China. 1872–1928. 7 vols.

(b) Korea. 1889–1928. 3 vols.

(c) Japan. 1873–1927. 6 vols.

IV. Missionaries' reports. 1840–1944. Annual reports to the Society from missionaries in the field, including the various dioceses in China, Japan, &c.; bound annually since 1858. (E. MSS.)

V. Letter-books of the Society. 1833–date. Copies of letters sent. The volumes are arranged geographically and the material is subdivided by dioceses in alphabetical order. Each volume contains an index. This series is only listed to 1928, but continues thereafter with a slightly different form of binding (F. MSS.) Including:

(a) China. 1889–1928. 6 vols.

(b) Japan. 1874–1928. 5 vols.

(c) Korea. 1889–1928. 3 vols.

VI. Royal letters. 1831–44, 1848–51. 2 vols. (X. 139–40.)

VII. Far East reports and letters. 1941–5. (X. 237.)

CANDIDATES' PAPERS. These papers relate to both successful and unsuccessful candidates. Information about the former will also be found in the general missionary correspondence, especially in the series C, D, and E. MSS., described above.

(a) Candidates' correspondence, with testimonials: a general series, unbound. 1761–1906. 11 boxes. (C. MSS. Home.)

(b) Board of Examiners' minutes. 1848–1950. 8 vols. (X. 116–122b.)

(c) Board of Examiners' minutes and Chaplaincies' Committee minutes. 1879–81. 1 vol. (X. 123.)

(d) Candidates; list with notes. 1848–68. 1 vol. (X. 113.)

(e) Missionary candidates subcommittee books. 1904–38. 5 vols. (X. 205a–e.)

MISCELLANEOUS PAPERS AND BOOKS

1. Missionary Roll. 1846–1911. 4 vols. (X. 124–7.)

2. Letters patent incorporating the diocese of Hong Kong. 1849. (X. 183.)

3. Colonial Bishopric's fund: centenary memorial volume. 1941. (X. 215.)

4. Extracts from the diaries of the Revd. R. D. M. Shaw and E. M. Shaw relating to mission work in the diocese of South Tokyo, Japan. 1908–20. 119 ff. Typescript. (X. 240. Another copy is with the author, the Revd. R. D. M. Shaw, at Steeple Langford Rectory, Nr. Salisbury, Wilts., as noted below.)

WOMEN'S WORK (formerly S.P.G. LADIES ASSOCIATION) RECORDS

1. Roll of women missionaries. 1866– .

2. File of women missionaries (deceased).

3. Minutes, including:

(a) Ladies Association Committee minutes. 1866–1903. 11 vols.

(b) Women's Work Committee minutes. 1908–13. 2 vols.

(c) Finance Subcommittee minutes. 1903–21. 7 vols.

(d) Advisory Subcommittee minutes. 1906–20. 2 vols.

(*e*) Furlough groups from Foreign Subcommittees. 1910–19. 1 vol.

(*f*) Foreign Group (became Overseas Group in 1928) minutes. 1921–31. 3 vols.

(*g*) Burma and Far East Subcommittee minute books. 1901–21. 6 vols.

(*h*) Women's Far East Subcommittee minute book. 1920.

4. Copies of letters received. 1861–95. 42 vols. Including:

(*a*) India and China. 1869.

(*b*) India and Japan. 1876–83, 1885–8. 12 vols.

(*c*) India, Japan, and North China. 1884, 1889–94. 7 vols.

5. Original letters received. 1894–1926. 63 vols. Including:

(*a*) Far East. 1901–3, 1911–25. 9 vols.

(*b*) Far East, China, Straits Settlements. 1904–10, 1916–18. 3 vols.

(*c*) Far East, Osaka, South Tokyo. 1904–10. 2 vols.

6. Foreign letters sent. 1867–1926. 48 vols. Including:

(*a*) General. 1867–9.

(*b*) Miscellaneous. 1876, 1895–1905. 8 vols. 1 parcel.

(*c*) India, Africa, and Japan. 1875, 1877–87. 7 vols.

(*d*) India, Africa, Japan, North China. 1888–94. 4 vols.

(*e*) Far East. 1904–25. 5 vols.

7. Reports, including:

(*a*) South Tokyo. 1875–1907.

(*b*) Burma and the Far East. 1908–10.

(*c*) Annual reports for 1866–94 (in 1 vol.), 1876, 1886, 1888, 1889, 1898, 1936–51.

8. Candidates:

(*a*) Candidates department, ledger. 1906–18. 2 vols.

(*b*) Candidates training fund. 1919–30. 2 vols.

(*c*) Candidates training ledger. 1921–6.

(*d*) Probationers training fund. 1921–30.

MEDICAL MISSIONS PAPERS

These papers have not been listed and the entries below give an incomplete though probably representative picture of the material available.

1. Bound volumes

(*a*) Medical Missions minutes. 1908–36. 6 vols.

(*b*) Receipts. 1909–32. 3 vols. each with index.

(*c*) Grants and payments. 1910–14. 1 vol.

(*d*) Ledger. 1918–30. 2 vols.

(*e*) 'Formation of Medical Missions Department, S.P.G., 1907–8.' Beginning with list of applications for medical missionaries, 1882–1907. 1 vol.

(*f*) Advice book. 1921–30. 1 vol.

2. Loose papers in boxes

(*a*) Medical dossiers. *c*. 11 boxes.

(*b*) Medical missions—dioceses. Several boxes of letters and papers filed alphabetically.

(*c*) Correspondence with Bishops, commissaries, and diocesan officers: (i) North China. 1930–51. 1 box. (No. 11.); (ii) Far East, including: Shantung, 1930–51, Kobe, 1928–40, Korea, 1930–54, Tokyo, 1933–6. 1 box. (No. 9.)

UNIVERSITY COLLEGE LONDON
LIBRARY

Gower Street, London, WC1E 6BT

S.D.U.K. PAPERS

The papers of the Society for the Diffusion of Useful Knowledge, 1826–46, include an essay on the opium trade entitled 'Dum vigilo tutus', n.d., submitted for a competition by an unknown author and received 24 December 1840; 55 pp., with 'notes and references'. (This Collection is uncatalogued but the contents are listed in a thesis submitted to London University in 1932 by Monica C. Grobel: 'S.D.U.K. 1826–1846'.)

UNIVERSITY OF LONDON
LIBRARY

Senate House, Malet Street, London, WC1E 7HU

A collection of reports, letters, advices, tables, &c. relating to trade in the East, including China. 1691–1732. (MS. 56.)

Papers of Patrick Lawson, Master of the *Lord Holland*. 3 vols. (MS. 395.)

1. Accounts of goods bought by Captain Lawson in London, Madras, Canton, between December 1768 and July 1771.

2. Accounts of goods purchased by Captain Lawson in Canton in the last quarter of 1776, and notes of goods packed for shipment.

3. Memoranda and accounts concerning the debts of Captain Lawson, and the administration of his estate on behalf of his creditors from 1777 to 1799; together with transcripts of letters between his trustees and the holders of bills, &c. owing to Captain Lawson in Canton. 1768–99.

Notes on the Japanese exchanges and markets made for Professor H. S. Foxwell by Juichi Soyeda. 1885–6. 33 ff. (MSS. 412, 502.)

Papers and notebooks of Dr. Herbert Chatley, sometime Engineer-in-Chief, Whangpoo Conservancy Board. The papers, mainly on technical questions, include material on Chinese rivers, railways, ports, &c. The notebooks contain notes on Chinese Buddhism and mysticism, as well as on astronomy and other subjects. *c.* 1895–*c.* 1947. 4 pamphlet boxes. (MS. 420.)

INSTITUTE OF COMMONWEALTH STUDIES

University of London, 27 Russell Square, London, WCɪB 5DS

Papers of Richard Jebb, being mostly letters and documents about imperial defence, especially naval policy. *c.* 1907–10. (NRA 18529.) Including:

Letter from A. R. Atkinson on *Morning Post* matters and its rejection of an article on Chinese labour. 6 March 1907.

Letter from Martin Burrell about Japanese immigration into Canada. 23 December 1908.

Letter of W. L. Mackenzie King on Japanese migration to Canada. 30 December 1907.

Letter of Alfred Milner, mentioning Chinese migration to Western Australia. 13 March 1908.

UNIVERSITY OF LONDON INSTITUTE OF EDUCATION LIBRARY

11–13 Ridgmount Street, London, WCɪE 7AH

Papers of the World Education Fellowship. (NRA 17720.)

II. Section papers

China correspondence. 1937–49. (77.)

Japan section. (132.)
　　Correspondence and some reports of meetings. 1935–60.
　　Correspondence. 1960–5.
　　Japan. Japanese subscribers. 1900–6.
　　Japan conferences. Printed matter. 1935–61.

THE LIBRARY, VICTORIA AND ALBERT MUSEUM

South Kensington, London, SW7 2RL

Letter of Thomas Manning, traveller and botanical collector, in Canton, to Sir Joseph Banks, with observations on Chinese porcelain. 2 ff. 1 March 1809. (Reserve K. 9.)

'The tea ceremonies of Japan', condensed from a work by Dr. Funk, with additions, by Mr. Kasawara. *c.* 1875. 8 ff. (86. N. 29.)

English translation by T. Asami of M. Shioda's 'Report on Japanese ceramics with reference to the exhibits at the Philadelphia Exhibition, 1876.' (Imperial Japanese Commission, Philadelphia.) 1876. 85 ff. Printed in A. W. Franks, *Japanese pottery*, 1880. (86. N. 32.)

Notes on four Japanese ceilings, of which copies were presented to Dr. Dresser by the Japanese Minister of the Interior; with the Minister's letter, and a description of the preparation of lacquer. 11th year Meiji (1879). 5 ff. (86. N. 37.)

An essay on a mythical stone age in China, by A. Terrien de Lacouperie. 1893. 62 ff. (86. K. 43.)

Copies of lectures (French) given by E. Deshayes, Musée Guimet, on Japanese and Chinese art. Cyclostyled text and illustrations, with English translation in manuscript. 1897–1905. 30 parts in 4 vols. The original text of the first lecture is missing. (86. P. 17–20.)

'Brief explanations of Ukiyo-ye' [by H. Hutchinson]. *c.* 1900. 16 ff. (MS. Box. 86K.)

'Chinese and Japanese Sennin', by R. G. Smith. Half-title, title, and 22 ff. of manuscript, 199 pen drawings, some coloured or tinted, and 1 colour print inserted. [*c.* 1900–10.] (86. o. 15.)

Typescript copy of above, with photographs. 6 pp. 127 ff. (5. G. 39.)

Notes and statistics on the manufacture of Japanese sword-blades, by Alfred Dobrée. [1905.] 51 rubbings. (Dept. of Metalwork.)

'Materials for a history of industrial arts', translated from the Japanese (Kōgei Shiriō) of Kurokawa Mayori by H. Inada. Comprising: (1) Japanese textiles (Typescript. 65 ff.); (2) Stonework (34 ff.); (3) Ceramics (63 ff.); (4) Woodwork (80 ff.); (5) Leatherwork (23 ff.); (6) Swords (30 ff.); (7) Lacquer (2 pts. 69 ff.). [1912.] 8 vols. (72D. 26–33.)

English translation of parts 5, 6, and 7 of another version of Kōgei Shiriō by Kurokawa Mayori, above. 1913. Comprising:

5. Leatherworking. Translator A. J. Koop. (86. K. 50.)

6. The sword in Japan. Translator H. Inada; editor A. J. Koop. 54 ff. Typescript. (72. D. 12.)

7. Lacquer. Translator H. Inada; editor A. J. Koop. 123 ff. Typescript. (72. D. 13.)

'Japanese textile designs': a commentary by A. J. Koop on the *Karakusa movo hinagata* of Kiyoshi Takizawa. 1913. 24 ff. (Box IV 86. DD.)

A key to the Mangwa of Hokusai. With transliteration and translation of all the text therein included and an index of names and subjects, by T. Wakameda and H. Inada. Edited by A. J. Koop. 1914. 2 vols. (86. K. 57–8.)

English translation by T. Wakameda and A. J. Koop of Kōko-shūran. Kakuzen-dzukō, by Ikeda Minamoto no Yoshinobu (1844.) (An antiquarian's collection. An illustrated treatise on leathers.) With a preface by Tojō Kōshi. 1914. 55 ff. (86. K. 50.)

Notes on a bygone Japanese craft, with special reference to materials and technique, by W. A. Young. For the Newcomen Society for the Study of the History of Engineering and Technology. 1937. 17 ff. Typescript. (72. C. 17.)

WELLCOME INSTITUTE FOR THE HISTORY OF MEDICINE: LIBRARY

183 Euston Road, London, NW1 2BP

In this Library there are nearly 6,000 Western manuscripts. 801 of these, written before A.D. 1650, are described in Volume I of the printed catalogue, and a further volume to appear shortly will cover manuscripts written after this date. A card catalogue for the whole collection can also be consulted. Approximately 100,000 autograph letters are arranged alphabetically in folders, and the more important of these will be indexed in the above-mentioned printed catalogue.

'Trattato de Medici Chinesi, e del The.' This is probably the work of a Jesuit missionary. The writer mentions his travels in Siam, Macao, and China. 12 ff. Late 17th century. (Miscellanea Medica I. MS. 531.)

'A relation of the Grand Tartary, drawn up from the original memoirs of the Suedes, who were prisoners in Siberia during the warr between Sueden and Russia.' This is an unpublished translation by William Farrington of the anonymous *Relation de la Grande Tartarie dressée sur les mémoires originales des Suédois prisonniers en Sibérie*, printed at Amsterdam in 1737. 1738. 5 ff. 462 pp. and 4 blank leaves. (MS. 2712.)

An account by John Fothergill (1712–80) of some observations and experiments made in Siberia, extracted from the preface to the *Flora Sibirica, sive historia plantarum Sibiriae* . . . by D. Gmelin, Professor of Chemistry and Natural History, published at St. Petersburg in 1747; with an attached holograph covering letter by Peter Collinson, F.R.S. The manuscript is endorsed by Martin Folkes as read before the Royal Society and printed in the *Transactions*, no. 486. 1748. 1 f. and 18 pp. (MS. 3948.)

An account of sales by a general merchant in the China trade, containing entries of various drugs,

opium, ginseng, &c., and of medicines supplied to ships. 1774–7. 16 ff. and 6 blank. (MS. 1837.)

Proposal for a better mode of victualling the Navy in warm climates, applicable also to East India ships, by Thomas Forrest (?1729–?1802), navigator in the service of the East India Company. 1789. 4 ff. (MS. 1509.)

'Segreti della vernice alla Chinese . . .' illustrated with rough pen drawings of apparatus, &c.; with receipts for dyes and colours. Incomplete. Mid 18th century. 40 pp. (MS. 2918.)

Notes in French on Genghiz Khan. Late 18th century. 6 ff. (In MS. 2261.)

'Kwaji oft Kruydboek. Explication du Livre du fleurs ou aromates en hollandois.' Followed by 'Japanse naemen van de in Japan groeyende boomen, struyken, heeters, planten en Kruyden.' Translator's holograph manuscript with corrections and additions; by Isaac Titsingh (1749–1812). 2 blank ff., 69 pp., and 14 ff. (MS. 886.)

Copy of the journal of George, 1st Earl Macartney, from 11 September 1792 to 15 June 1793, written during his voyage to China in the *Lion*. c. 1805. 2 ff., 230 pp.—pp. 95–6 and 119–26 are missing. (MS. 1754.)

'Note sur la peste: Orient et Egypte', by Etienne Pariset (1770–1847). Paris, 1828. 16 ff. (MS. 3106.)

'The Eight diagrams.' Notes on Chinese divination and fortune-telling. c. 1865. 26 ff. (MS. 91.)

Examination papers of the Hong Kong College of Medicine for Chinese:

1. Examination papers in Anatomy answered by Chinese students, 9 December 1887. 30 papers, including one by Sun Yat Sen, later first President of the Chinese Republic, who was one of the first pupils at the College, which was established on the initiative of Sir James Cantlie. (MS. 4408.)

2. Examination papers in Anatomy and Osteology answered by Chinese students, 31 March 1888. 16 papers. (MS. 4409.)

PAPERS OF SIR JAMES CANTLIE (1851–1926), Dean of the Hong Kong College of Medicine for Chinese from 1889 to 1896, and Founder and President (1921, 1922, and 1923) of the Royal Society of Tropical Medicine and Hygiene.

1. Papers in connection with an inquiry into the life history of Eurasians, including a paper on the subject by Cantlie, and a number of filled-in questionnaire forms with covering letters. The paper is apparently unfinished; the forms and letters are from various medical officers and others, mainly from China, Japan, Malaya, and New Zealand. 1888. 36 ff. and 48 ff. (MS. 4341.)

2. Fragment of a holograph diary, from 20 January to 3 June 1888, containing lists of patients and their ailments: Hong Kong. 2 ff. (MS. 4342.)

3. 'Pain in muscle in the febrile state': author's holograph manuscript, with two preliminary drafts. Hong Kong, 1889. 27 ff., 14 ff., and 5 ff. (MS. 4343. Published in *Transactions of the Hong Kong Medical Society*, vol. i, 1889.)

4. 'Vaccination amongst the Chinese': a preliminary draft and an expanded version headed 'Information supplied to the Sanitary Board concerning the method in practice amongst the Chinese in Hong Kong (and presumably in China generally) for the purpose of preventing smallpox (variola)'. It is stated that the information was gathered from the vaccinator at the Tung Wu Hospital. There is also a revised draft, with a new title 'Smallpox. Inoculation and Vaccination in China'. Hong Kong, 1889. 5 ff., 16 ff., 11 ff. (MS. 4344.)

5. A paper entitled 'Supernumerary Fingers' for reading to the Hong Kong Medical Society, but apparently unfinished. 1889. 6 ff. (MS. 4345.)

6. Fragment of a cash book, with entries of professional fees received in Hong Kong from 1 July to 15 October 1889. During this period the fees amounted to £531. 8s. 0d. 11 ff. (MS. 4346.)

7. Fragments from Hong Kong medical diaries, with dates ranging from 28 January 1889 to 8 January 1890. 298 ff. (MS. 4347.)

8. 'Reminiscences of William Pirrie M.D. . . . .' consisting of holograph manuscripts, corrected typescripts and proofs, but apparently never published. Hong Kong, 1889–90. (MSS. 4644–7.)

9. Clinical reports on six cases of Chinese patients suffering from leprosy and treated with Koch's tuberculin. Hong Kong, 1889–94. 32 ff. (MS. 4348.)

10. Fragments, from 12 January to 22 March 1890, of a register of patients: Hong Kong. 53 ff. (MS. 4349.)

11. An incomplete paper entitled 'Influenza in Hong Kong'. 1890. 16 ff. (MS. 4350.)

12. A paper read before the Hong Kong branch of the British Medical Association entitled 'The balance of temperature' and written on sheets from a 'Patients' Register Book'. *c.* 1890. 16 ff. (MS. 4351.)

13. Two incomplete holograph drafts of a paper entitled 'The temperature of food'. Hong Kong, *c.* 1890. 4 pp., 4 ff. (MS. 4352.)

14. An unfinished paper on 'Exercise in warm climates'. Hong Kong, *c.* 1890. 54 ff., 7 ff., 11 ff. (MS. 4353.)

15. Fragment of a history of the Volunteer Medical Staff Corps. Hong Kong, 1891. 10 pp. (MS. 4356.)

16. A paper entitled 'Two leper settlements in China:

Canton and Macao'. Hong Kong, 1891. 24 ff. (MS. 4357.)

17. A paper read before the Medical Society, Hong Kong, entitled 'On the advisability of adopting the term "tropical measles"'. Hong Kong, 1891. 24 ff. (MS. 4358. Published in *The Lancet* 1892, vol. 1, pp. 1413–16.)

18. A paper entitled 'Matinal (Hill) diarrhoea' and endorsed 'sent Indian Medical Gazette, Oct. 5, 1892'. Hong Kong, 1892. 5 ff. (MS. 4359.)

19. Two case books compiled during his residence in Hong Kong, covering the periods 4 July 1892 to 10 October 1893, and 22 July 1895 to 7 February 1896. 188 ff., 182 ff. (MSS. 4360 and 4361.)

20. Drafts of answers to a questionnaire of the Royal Commission on Opium. Hong Kong, 14 December 1893. 2 ff., 2 ff., 1 f. (MS. 4362.)

21. Fragments of three letters by Cantlie on the plague in Hong Kong. Hong Kong, 1894. 10 pp., 1 f., 6 ff. (MS. 4363.)

22. Three short papers on tropical liver abscess, with corrected typescripts. Hong Kong, 1894–8. 9 ff., 3 ff.; 12 ff.; 4 ff., 3 ff. (MS. 4364.)

23. A paper entitled 'An enquiry into the resemblance of the tubercle and leprous bacilli: with conclusions drawn therefrom', with five odd leaves of a paper on leprosy. Pencil. *c.* 1895. 6 ff., 5 ff. (MS. 4365.)

24. A lecture on the spread of plague delivered before the Hampstead Medical Society on 22 March 1897. This is possibly a draft of his essay on plague published in 1901, and is partly holograph, partly corrected typescript, and partly printed extracts from the reprint of the original lecture published in *The Lancet*, 2 and 9 June 1897. Incomplete. 43 ff. (MS. 4366.)

25. Report on the conditions under which leprosy occurs in China, Indo-China, Malaya, the Archipelago, and Oceania. This manuscript contains the first section only (on China), and is partly typescript and partly author's holograph manuscript. The complete report was published in the *Transactions of the Epidemiological Society*, 1897/8, N.S. No. XVII. 95 ff. (MS. 4367.)

26. Dummy copy of the first number of the *Journal of Tropical Medicine* with specimen layouts for advertisements: author's holograph manuscript. 1898. 18 ff. (MS. 4368.)

27. An incomplete lecture on Hong Kong: typescript with holograph corrections. London, 1898. 49 ff. (MS. 4369.)

28. Lectures on tropical surgery, originally delivered at the London School of Tropical Medicine and Hygiene and published in Gould and Warren's *International text-book of surgery*, 1900. The manuscript is incomplete and consists of typescript with copious

holograph additions and corrections. London. 1899.
ff. 15–85. (MS. 4371.)

29. Case book from 2 October 1899 to 31 December 1900, compiled during his residence in London. Many of the patients were people who had lived in the East and suffered from tropical diseases. 136 ff. (MS. 4372.)

30. Rough notes in pencil taken at the sixty-eighth annual meeting of the British Medical Association, section of tropical medicine, held at Ipswich, 31 July to 3 August 1900. 74 ff. (MS. 4373.)

31. A paper entitled 'Subhepatic abscess', read at the British Medical Association, section of tropical diseases, August 1900, and published in the *British Medical Journal*, 1900, vol. ii, pp. 548 and 549. Typescript. 5 ff. (MS. 4374.)

32. Contributions to Allchin's *Manual of medicine*, 1900: (1) Epidemic dropsy (6 ff.); (2) Kala-azar (11 ff.); (3) Leprosy (14 ff.); (4) Beri-beri (13 ff.); (5) Cholera (23 ff.); (6) Malarial and hepatic dysentery (3 ff.). Typescript and holograph manuscript. (MS. 4375.)

33. A paper in pencil entitled 'Colonial Nursing Association'. 1911. 8 ff. (MS. 4378.)

Reports on cases in the Alice Memorial Hospital, Hong Kong, partly by John Christopher Thomson (d. 1924) and partly by Sir James Cantlie, with a letter dated 13 January 1891 from Thomson to Cantlie. 1891. 2 ff., 10 ff. (MS. 4429.)

A collection of holograph and typescript material, notes, extracts, &c., compiled by William Lauzan Brown (d. 1919) for an unpublished and unfinished work on 'The employment of animal substances for the cure of disease'. The work is in eight parts, and included in Part IV is a section on Chinese medicine (2 drafts; 29 ff., 21 ff.). *c.* 1900. (MSS. 5255–62.)

A collection of seven transcripts of alchemical tracts, mostly abbreviated versions, including 'La sapience alchimique en Chine. Un antique recueil d'hiéro-glyphes hermétiques; avec sa grammaire secrète selon les explication d'un initié chinois' (32 ff.), illustrated with Chinese symbols and ideographs in red and purple. (MS. 2668. Miscellanea Alchemica XXX.)

Letter to the Editor of the *Journal of Tropical Medicine and Hygiene* on the relative prevalence of cancer in tropical and temperate regions, by George Herbert Fink (1860–1950). *c.* 1905. 16 ff. (MS. 4398.)

An article by George Herbert Fink on 'Epidemic malaria and the great pale plague' to the editor of the *Journal of Tropical Medicine and Hygiene. c.* 1905. 5 ff. (MS. 4399.)

A paper entitled 'Experiments upon the transmission of plague by fleas' apparently part of a draft of the paper published in the *Journal of Hygiene*, Cambridge,

1906, pp. 425–82. Incomplete. Typescript. 16 ff. (MS. 4397.)

BURROUGHS, WELLCOME & CO., PAPERS

1. History of the Portuguese explorers: papers prepared for the Fifteenth International Medical Congress held at Lisbon in 1906. Typescript and manuscript. 179 ff. (MS. 5283.)

2. A brief history of missionary enterprise in ancient and modern times. This work was published as 'Lecture Memoranda' for the World Missionary Conference held at Edinburgh in 1910. 5 vols. (MSS. 5284–8.)

Wellcome Chemical Research Laboratories: visitors' address book used at the exhibit of the Laboratories at the Japan–British Exhibition of 1910. London, 1911. 156 ff. (MS. 5669.)

Report of the first two weeks of the International Plague Conference, by Reuter's correspondent with manuscript cross-headings by Sir James Cantlie. 1911. Typescript. 7 ff. (MS. 4411.)

An article by Thomas L. L. Sandes (1882–1955) entitled 'The mode of transmission of leprosy.' 9 ff. Typescript with holograph corrections. (MS. 4426. Published in the *Journal of Tropical Medicine and Hygiene*, 1911, vol. xiv, pp. 223–35.)

An indignant letter to the Editor of the *Journal of Tropical Medicine and Hygiene* from William Leonard Braddon claiming the discovery of the cause of beri-beri, as against Dr. Henry Fraser and Sir Ambrose Thomas Stanton. (MS. 4405. Printed in vol. xiv, p. 153.)

Diaries of Donald Mars Morphett Ross (1865–1921), medical officer of the coolie ship *Hong Bee.* 1913–15.

1. Diary containing notes of voyages between Penang and the China coast. January–April 1913. 180 pp. (MS. 4122.)

2. Diary containing accounts of voyages between Singapore and the China coast, with rough drafts of letters, &c. 1914–15. 9 ff., 5 ff. (MS. 4020.)

A contribution to the history of pellagra and its connection with maize, by Charles J. S. Thompson (1862–1943) and others. There are two typescript drafts, the first with numerous holograph additions and corrections in pencil, with a collection of translations, extracts, and notes by various hands relating to pellagra and maize, and including two letters (1914) relating to maize in China from Herbert Allen Giles (1845–1935), sinologist. The projected two-volume work on pellagra was never published. London, 1914. 3 parts. (MSS. 4482–4.)

A report on Chinese poison (gelsemium), by Edward Morell Holmes (1843–1930). 1920. 5 ff. (MS. 4840/2.)

A collection of Chinese cookery receipts. *c.* 1925. 45 ff. (9 blank). (MS. 3975.)

Some suggestions for the Chinese edition of *Poverty and its vicious circles*, by Jamison Boyd Hurry (1857–1930): first and second instalment, with a second incomplete copy of the typescript, with holograph corrections. [1927.] 13 ff., 12 ff., and ff. 3–8. (MS. 4446.)

Unpublished work by Max Neuberger (1868–1955) on Chinese medicine (22 ff.) and Japanese medicine (4 ff.) [London, 1941]. (In MS. 5157.)

AUTOGRAPH LETTERS

The library has a very large collection of autograph letters of medical men, which are not catalogued, but arranged alphabetically in folders, and therefore easily accessible to anyone with a particular person in mind.

WORLD COUNCIL OF CHURCHES, DIVISION OF WORLD MISSION AND EVANGELISM

Edinburgh House, 2 Eaton Gate, London, S.W.1

RECORDS OF THE INTERNATIONAL MISSIONARY COUNCIL[1]

The International Missionary Council, which affiliated with the World Council of Churches in 1961 to become its Division of World Mission and Evangelism, had its roots in the World Missionary Conference held in Edinburgh in 1910 to co-ordinate work in the missionary field. The Edinburgh Conference appointed a Continuation Committee to carry on its work, and at a further meeting in 1921 the International Missionary Council was formally instituted. The records of the Council, consisting of correspondence, reports, minutes, &c., are arranged in labelled files in boxes. They are incompletely catalogued and the list below may not give a full picture of the material available which is of relevance to this *Guide*. As well as the papers noted here, which are mainly in manuscript or typescript, there is a quantity of printed material in the form of pamphlets, &c. It should be noted that inclusion of material on this list does not necessarily imply that it is available for study.

East Asia (general)
IMC/WCC East Asia Christian Conference, Bangkok, December 1949. 2 boxes.

China. 10 boxes

1. German and Swiss missions, 1914; Church unity conference, 1935; Japanese Christian work in China; communism, 1933.

2. China Continuation Committee, 1913–19.

3. Sino-Japanese relations, 1936; Sino-Japanese War, 1937–40: correspondence and reports, including representations to British Government; Manchuria correspondence, 1931–42; Japan and Manchuria, 1931–2.

4. Political situation, 1925–8.

5. Treaties, &c., 1917–27; Boxer indemnity, 1921–4; missionary freedom, East Turkestan, 1923–4; &c.

6. National Christian Council, Shanghai conference, 1922, &c.; Hong Kong child slavery, 1919–22.

7. National Christian Council, Jerusalem meeting, 1928, &c., correspondence, minutes, and reports.

8. N.C.C. bulletins, 1922–30. (Printed.) Information about China, issued by the Foreign Missions Conference of North America in duplicated news-sheets, 1925–8.

9. United Board for Christian colleges in China: news-letters from Yenching University, Huachung University, Nanking University, Soochow University, &c., 1949–51 (Duplicated).

10. Correspondence of the China Continuation Committee of the National missionary conference, Shanghai, 1913, 1914– ; general correspondence, 1920–7; Moukden Medical College 1922–5, letters from Dr. Harold Balme, Shantung Christian University, 1923–6; &c.

Japan. 3 boxes

1. Japan Continuation Committee, 1913–20; conference of federated missions in Japan, 1914; German missions, 1921–2; Kingdom of God campaign, 1929–32; Christian education commission, 1932–5.

2. National Christian Council, 1922– .

3. Sino-Japanese relations, 1936–8; nationalization of Church, &c. (China and Japan), 1936–43; Kagawa co-operators, 1930–7; &c.

Japan and Korea
Japan: shrine worship, 1936–41; Korea: shrine worship, 1936–7. 1 box.

Korea
Korean conspiracy case, 1912–13; federal council of Protestant missions, 1915–27; education in Chosen, 1915; &c.

---

[1] Some of the records of the former International Missionary Council were recently transferred to the archives of the World Council of Churches in Geneva. Much of the material here listed is therefore likely to be kept now at the World Council of Churches, 150 Route de Ferney, Geneva 20.

War and Missions, 1939–45

1. Financial aid. 2 boxes.

2. Early plans. 1 box.

3. Germany. 1 box.

4. First German missionaries going out. This includes Hong Kong. 1 box.

5. Director's postwar visits to fields, including Japan. 1 box.

Foreign Missions Conference of North America. 17 boxes (mainly duplicated material), including:

1. East Asia committee (general). 1942–6. 2 boxes.

2. East Asia committee: China. 1944–9. 1 box.

3. East Asia committee: Japan. 1945–9. 1 box.

I.M.C. Inter-Mission aid

China. 1940–53. This also includes material relating to Japan and the Pacific. 1 box.

I.M.C. (Organization). The following may contain relevant material:

1. Council and committee meetings, especially the big assemblies: Jerusalem, 1928, Tambaram, 1938, Whitby, Ontario, 1947; Willingen, 1952, Ghana, 1957–8.

2. Officers.

3. Finance.

Documents from the Field. A series of bound volumes containing informatory background material (typescript) sent in from all over the world for the various commissions of the World Missionary Conference, Edinburgh, 1910. The titles include:

1. Commission on Education: Japan, Korea, and Dutch East Indies. 1 vol. 464 ff.

2. Commission on Education: China. 2 vols. 444 ff. and 407 ff.

3. Commission on Missions and Governments. This includes material from China and Japan. 1 vol. 604 ff.

4. Commission on the Missionary Message: Japanese Religions. 1 vol. 315 ff.

5. Commission on the Missionary Message: Chinese Religions. 1 vol. 456 ff.

6. Commission on Co-operation and Unity. This includes material from China, Japan, and Korea. 1 vol. 475 ff.

WORLDWIDE EVANGELIZATION CRUSADE

19 Highland Road, London, S.E. 19

Mukyokai: a brief appraisal of the 'No-Church' movement in Japan, by John Kennedy. October 1960. Duplicated copy.

REST OF ENGLAND

AYLESBURY

BUCKINGHAMSHIRE RECORD OFFICE

County Offices, Aylesbury, HP20 1UA

RAMSDEN COLLECTION

Papers of Edward Adolphus Seymour, 12th Duke of Somerset (1804–85), 1st Lord of the Admiralty, 1859–66, including letters from:

(a) Admiral Sir James Hope, written from the China station. 1859–62. 85 letters.

(b) Vice-Admiral Sir Augustus L. Kuper, written from the China station. 1862–4. 19 letters.

(c) Earl of Elgin and Kincardine relating to his mission to China and to his treaty negotiations with the Emperor. 25 October 1860. 1 letter.

(d) Sir Rutherford Alcock from Yeddo to Admiral Hope about the political situation in Japan. 4 May 1860. 1 letter.

Log-book of ship *Stafford*, Felix Baker, commander, on voyage from England to Canton, China. 22 February 1746–21 July 1747. (3/67.)

BARROW IN FURNESS

PUBLIC LIBRARY

Ramsden Square, Barrow in Furness, Cumbria

A manuscript book containing letters and papers of John Leyden (1775–1811), including 'List of Manuscripts belonging to the Estate of Dr. John Leyden, that were received by Wm. Erskine Esq. from Mrs. Cholmondeley, the Executrix of the late Richard Heber Esq.' This list was copied from the original in the possession of Dr. John Morton of Guildford, Surrey. It contains fifty-one items, the majority relating to the languages of India, Persia, China, &c., and to Indian and Asian history.

BEDFORD

COUNTY RECORD OFFICE

County Hall, Bedford, MK42 9AP

Record of inheritance of copyhold property by 'Edward Pettit of Canton in the empire of China, merchant'. 1865. (In X 233/22.)

BERWICK-UPON-TWEED

THE KING'S OWN SCOTTISH BORDERERS REGIMENTAL MUSEUM

Berwick-upon-Tweed

[Inquiries to the Regimental Secretary]

'The Borderers in Korea', by Major-General J. F. M. MacDonald. A diary of events during the Korean War from April 1951 to August 1952. Original manuscript and typescript copy.

Korean War Diary, 1952. This includes casualty returns and Honours and Awards.

Letter from General Mark Clark, U.N. Commander-in-Chief to the Officer Commanding the 1st Battalion King's Own Scottish Borderers, on leaving Korea. 1952. (666. D. 4.)

BEVERLEY

HUMBERSIDE COUNTY RECORD OFFICE

County Hall, Beverley

Copy of a letter from an army officer in Tungku to his mother giving an account of the taking of the Taku forts from the Chinese. 25 August 1860.

BIRMINGHAM

THE ASSAY OFFICE

Newhall Street, Birmingham 3

MATTHEW BOULTON COLLECTION

Letter from James Cobb, at East India House, to Matthew Boulton (1728–1809), manufacturer and businessman, concerning the interest of members of the Chinese Embassy in articles of Birmingham manufacture. 22 October 1794.

CITY LIBRARY

Reference Library, Birmingham, B3 3HQ

A collection of specimens and drawings of Japanese plants with a manuscript index. Compiled by Amy Inglis. *c.* 1880–1900. (394940.)

Travel diaries of Helen Caddick. Typescript with illustrations, cuttings, &c. (336851–336862). Including:

Canada, Japan, vol. 1. 1891–2. (336852.)

Cape Colony, India, Japan, vol. 2. 1893. (336853.)

Cambodia, Yangtze, Korea, vol. 1. 1908–9. (336859.)

Cambodia, Yangtze, Korea, vol. 2. 1909. (336860.)

Philippines, China, Burma. 1913–14. (336862.)

Bibliography of Japanese translations of Shakespeare's works and Japanese works relating to Shakespeare, 1870–1918. Compiled by Ian Mutsu. [1932.] (395762.)

Japanese tsuba: photographs with descriptions and notes by Richard Hancock. 1950. 3 vols. (670169–71.)

'In Japanese Hands', a list of books dealing with prisoner-of-war and internment camps in the Far East, 1941–5, with a supplementary list of other works written in prison camps. Compiled by John Charles Sharp. 22 pp. Typescript. With complimentary list no. 1.

'Japanese documentary': a collection of papers from Japanese sources relating to prisoner-of-war camps in the Far East. Compiled by J. C. Sharp. 29 pp. Typescript. [No. 10 of edition limited to 100 copies.] (572735.)

UNIVERSITY OF BIRMINGHAM

Main Library, P.O. Box 363, The University, Edgbaston, Birmingham, B12 2TT

CHAMBERLAIN PAPERS (NRA 12604)

Papers of Joseph Chamberlain (1836–1914), statesman, including:

1. Hong Kong. 1898–9. (J.C. 9/3/3/1–7.)

2. Hong Kong. 1901. (J.C. 14/2/5/1–6.)

3. China and Hong Kong. 1902–3. (J.C. 18/5.)

Papers of Austen Chamberlain (1863–1937), Secretary of State for India 1915–17, including:

Japan and India. 1916. Confidential print. (A.C. 21 Pkt. 88.)

Papers of Sir Charles Raymond Beazley (1868–1955), geographer and historiographer, including:

Box 2. Account of opening up by Europeans of Central Asia.

Box 7. Early Asiatic embassies and treaties of Russia. Russia and China; the Kulja incident. Russia in Central Asia.

Box 8. Russia in Asia. [Article in another hand.] Chronology of Russia in Central Asia, after 1800, from Curzon, *Russia in Central Asia.*

Box 13. The discovery of the Far East and of Inner Asia, 1245–95, &c. 'History'. Annotated typescript.

Letter from Chia-Hua Yuan, of Oxford, to Alan Strode Campbell Ross, in connection with the latter's book, *Ginger; a loan word study* (1952). 6 June 1949. (L. add. 789.)

Extracts from letters and copies of memoranda written by I. J. F. Bandinel during the Sino-Japanese war. 1894–5. (1958/iii/11.)

BLACKBURN

PUBLIC LIBRARY, MUSEUM, AND ART GALLERY

Blackburn, Lancs.

Confidential report by Mr. F. S. A. Bourne, H.M. Consul, head of the Blackburn Commercial Mission to China, to the Blackburn Chamber of Commerce, 20 March 1898. Printed. Blackburn, 1898.

Report of the mission to China of the Blackburn Chamber of Commerce, 1896–7. F. S. A. Bourne's section. Printed. Blackburn, 1898.

STONYHURST COLLEGE

Near Blackburn, Lancs.

A few documents relating to Jesuit missions in China and Japan:

1. 'Of the glorious death of nine Christian Japonians Martyred for the faith of Christ in the Kingdoms of Fingo, Sassuma and Firando.' English translation [? 17th century] of a Relation sent by the Jesuit Provincial in Japan to the Jesuit General (Aquaviva) in March 1609 and 1610. n.d. 28 ff.

2. Letter of Fr. Ferdinand Verbiest (d. 1688), Vice-Provincial of the Chinese Jesuit Mission, written to his fellow Jesuits in Europe from Peking. 15 August 1678. *Latin.* Copy. 10 ff.

3. A Grammar (and Vade Mecum) for the use of

Jesuit missionaries in China, based apparently on a work by Fr. Jose Monteiro (d. 1718). 1757. *Portuguese, Latin,* and *Chinese* (Lingua Sinica Mandarina). 173 pp.

4. A Relation of the arrest of the Jesuit Fathers at Macao in 1762, of their sea journey, and of their imprisonment 'in arce Juliani' near Lisbon. *Latin.* A contemporary copy. 14 pp.

BRENTWOOD

THE ESSEX REGIMENT ASSOCIATION

Eagle Way, Warley, Brentwood, Essex

The museum of the Essex Regiment (formerly the 44th and 56th Regiments of Foot) has numerous photograph albums, scrapbooks, pictures, and other relics in addition to the documents listed below. The regiment served in China in 1860, in Korea in 1953, and in Hong Kong in 1954.

Access to these records is by appointment only.

A. Records of service. 1741–1954.

1. Draft of the historical records of the Forty-fourth or the East Essex Regiment of Foot, 1741–1864, by Thomas Carter of the Adjutant-General's office and published in London in 1864.

2. Historical records of the 44th Regiment of Foot, being a duplicate copy of Carter's history up to 1865 and from then continued up to 1894.

3. Historical records of the 1st Battalion The Essex Regiment from 1741 to 1910, with additions up to 1914.

4. A modern account of the 1st Battalion The Essex Regiment up to 1902. One exercise book.

B. Miscellaneous papers including notes on the regiment's service in Korea in 1953 and transfer to Hong Kong in 1954.

BRISTOL

BRISTOL ARCHIVES OFFICE

Council House, Bristol, BS1 5TR

PRIDEAUX COLLECTION

Letter from Mary Hinton in Japan to Miss M. V. Prideaux in London, referring to the life and customs of the Ainus. 1889. (20535/215.)

FORD COLLECTION

Letter, Alexander Ford in Hong Kong to Edward Henry Ford, *re* fighting in China. 1842.

BURY ST. EDMUNDS

WEST SUFFOLK RECORD OFFICE

School Hall Street, Bury St. Edmunds, Suffolk, IP33 1RX

BARNARDISTON ARCHIVES (NRA 2582)

Papers of Brigadier-General Barnardiston at Tsingtao. (613/3/1–13.)

1. Letter (*French*) from General Akashi, Tokio. 25 December 1914. Also postcards and letters in Japanese, and news-cuttings. 1914.

2–3. Letters in Japanese.

4–9. Postcards written in Japanese.

10. Note from Seichi Uda.

11. News-cutting concerning Brigadier-General Barnardiston. 27 October 1914.

12. News-cutting giving letter of Sarah H. Barnardiston. Tientsin. 16 October (?1914).

13. Itinerary for General Barnardiston in Japan. December 1914.

CAMBRIDGE

CHESHUNT COLLEGE

Cambridge

Archives of Cheshunt College, Cambridge (NRA 12352)

SPARHAM PAPERS (B6)

Diaries of the Revd. C. G. Sparham of Hankow. 1885–1905.

Letters to Mrs. Sparham. 1882–1930.

Miscellanea. 1885–1931.

Reports on Chinese mission. 1887–1928.

Papers about the Revd. Griffith John (Sparham's father-in-law). 1883–1931.

THE LIBRARY, CHURCHILL COLLEGE

Cambridge, CB3 0DS

Letters of C. A. Spring Rice to Theodore Roosevelt concerning China and other countries, including the Russo-Japanese War. 1887–1918.

Archives of Lord Lloyd of Dolobran (NRA 12663):
Slavery—Chinese labour. 1907–9. (16/61.)

Oriental languages school. 1910. (16/60.)

Public and political papers, Japan. 1909–10. (16/34.)

Central Asia. Foreign Office and Cabinet papers,
and correspondence. 1879–84. (Esher papers 13/4.)

FITZWILLIAM MUSEUM
Cambridge

The Manuscripts in the Fitzwilliam Museum are
described by M. R. James in *A descriptive catalogue of
the manuscripts in the Fitzwilliam Museum* (Cambridge,
1895) and in *A descriptive catalogue of the McClean
Collection of manuscripts in the Fitzwilliam Museum* (1912),
and by F. Wormald and P. M. Giles in *A handlist
of the Additional Manuscripts in the Fitzwilliam Museum*,
parts 1–4 (1951–4).

Letter of the King of Siam to John Charles Bowring
(eldest son of the Governor of Hong Kong), concerning the trade of Siam with Hong Kong and Canton,
and other matters. 27 May 1856. (Ashcombe Collection, I. 17.)

Letter of H.M. Queen Mary to the Director of the
Fitzwilliam Museum, offering three pieces of Chinese
embroidery to the Museum; and enclosing a descriptive list of the three pieces. 11 October 1946.

PEPYSIAN LIBRARY
Magdalene College, Cambridge

Journal of the voyage of Benjamin Waters, a mate in
the service of the East India Company, on the *Formosa*,
Captain James Merriner, commander, including the
passage from Bantam 'to Emoy upon the coast
of China', 12 June–15 July 1677, thence back again
to Bantam, 24 December 1677–11 January 1678.
MS. 2584.)

'The Voyage of William Ambrose Cowley, Mariner',
who travelled from the 'Ladroones' to China and
thence to Java between 1683 and 1686. (MS. 2826.)

THE LIBRARY, TRINITY COLLEGE
Cambridge

See M. R. James, *A descriptive catalogue of the Western
Manuscripts in the library of Trinity College, Cambridge*,
4 vols. (Cambridge, 1900–4.)

'Miscellanea de Re Musica', on Chinese, Indian,
Egyptian, Russian, &c. national music, instruments,
&c. (R. 2. 53.)

UNIVERSITY LIBRARY
West Road, Cambridge, CB3 9DR

See *Catalogue of the manuscripts preserved in the library
of the University of Cambridge*, 6 vols., including index
(Cambridge, 1856–67), and *Summary guide to accessions
of Western Manuscripts (other than medieval) since 1867*,
by A. E. B. Owen (Cambridge, 1966).

CONWAY TRANSCRIPTS. (Add. 7226–7306. See J.
Street, 'The G. R. G. Conway collection in Cam-
bridge University Library: A checklist', *Hispanic
American Historical Review*, 37 (1957).) Including:

Don Rodrigo de Vivero, 'Narrative of a Journey
through Japan and Description of that Kingdom
together with certain Recommendations and Projects
for the better Government of the Spanish Dominions',
1609. (English translation, 230 pp.) This is bound
together with an appendix comprising: (*a*) translation of a speech by H. E. Don Pedro Quartin,
Minister of Spain in Japan, 7 November 1926
(3 pp.); (*b*) 'Project for the Erection of a Monument
Commemorative of the Initiation of Relations between Japan, Spain and Mexico' (4 pp. + 1 map);
(*c*) 'Iwada, port of the highest importance in the
history of the International Relations of Japan',
by Noajiro Murakami, Doctor of Historical Sciences
(English translation, 12 pp.). (Vol. 78. Add. 7302.)

'Relacion y Noticias de el Reino del Japan Cn. otros
Abisos y Proiectos para el buen Govierno de la
Monarchia Española de Don Rodrigo de Vivero . . .
1609'; transcribed from B.M. Add. MS. 18287.
(Translation in proceeding volume.) 211 pp. and 10
photographs. (Vol. 79. Add. 7303.)

ACTON COLLECTION

Log-book of the *Cadogan*, Captain John Hill, commander, from England to China and return, 1721–2,
also log of the *Morice* from the Cape towards Canton,
1721. (Add. 4619.)

Log-book of the *Lyell* from England to Canton and
Whampoa and return. 1721–3. 'Some Remarks on a
Voyage to China by Captain Edward Harrison to
Captain Cook'; 'Some Directions usefull in a Voyage
to China.' (Add. 4621.)

Log-book of the *Lynn* from England to Canton and
Whampoa and return. 1728–30. (Add. 4622.)

Log of a voyage from England to Canton and return.
1729–31. (Add. 4623.)

Log-book of the *Lynn* from England to China and
return. 1731–3. (Add. 4624.)

Dutch translation of an edict of Chien Lung, Emperor of China, 9 November 1785. (Add. 105/1.)

JARDINE MATHESON ARCHIVE. (For permission to see these papers apply in writing to Matheson & Co. Ltd., 3 Lombard St., London, E.C.3.)

I. ACCOUNTS, ETC.

1. Ledgers. 1798–1886. Series incomplete. 96 vols+ separate indices.

2. Journals. 1811–89. Series incomplete. 172 vols.

3. Cash books. 1819–1911. Series incomplete. 113 vols.

4. Accounts current. 1812–90. 107 vols.

5. Accounts sales. 1810–73. Series incomplete. 56 vols.

6. Invoice Books. 1810–1900. Series incomplete. 70 vols.

7. Miscellaneous accounts; ledgers, journals, and account books of subsidiary companies, including insurance companies; accounts of opium, tea, silk; freight books; lists of cargoes; manifests; diaries. Most of these last series are incomplete and consist of a few odd books in each case. c. 600 vols.

8. A large collection of loose papers and unbound material, arranged under provisional headings. 284 boxes.

II. CORRESPONDENCE

A. Unbound correspondence

1. Correspondence in: from America, Australia, Great Britain and Europe, India, East Indies, Siam, Malaya, Africa. c. 1814–98. 82,009 letters.

2. Correspondence local: Amoy, Canton, Chapoo, Chefoo, Chinchu, Chinchin, Chinhai, Chinkiang, Chuc Chau, Chuempeh, Chusan, Coast, Foochow, Hankow, Hoihow, Honan, Hong Kong, Ichang, Kiukiang, Kowloon, Kumsingmun, Lema, Li-chow, Lintin, Lukon, Macao, Newchang, Ningpo, Pakhoi, Peking, Port Arthur, Shanghai, Shanking, Sunghong, Swatow, Tientsin, Whampoa, Wanchai, Wenchow, Woosung, Wuhu. 1814–1904. 71,862 letters.

3. Letters from (a) Formosa. 1856–1901. 1,277 letters; (b) Korea. 1883–4. 191 letters; (c) Japan. 1859–92. 5,870 letters.

4. Unplaced. 1813–1900. 5,723 letters.

5. Private letters. 9,244 letters.

B. Letter-books

1. India letter-books (i.e. to India, East Indies, Australia, &c. from Canton, Hong Kong, Macao). 1800–83. 67 vols.

2. Europe letter-books. (Mainly to Europe, but also to America, Australia, &c. Mainly from Hong Kong, but including two volumes from Canton, and two volumes from Macao.) 1810–98. 58 vols.

3. Coast letter-books. (To ships and places on the China Coast, Japan, &c. Volume I is from Macao and Hong Kong, the rest from Hong Kong.) 1842–83. 29 vols.

4. Local letter-books. (To ships and places on the China Coast &c. Volume I is from Macao and Hong Kong, the rest from Hong Kong.) 1842–82. c. 11 vols.

5. Miscellaneous letter-books. 65 vols.

a. General series from Shanghai. 1858–85. 35 vols.

b. Shanghai to Coast. 1856–68. 6 vols.

c. Shanghai to Hong Kong. 1847–70. 5 vols.

d. Shanghai to Japan. 1859–69. 2 vols.

e. Danish Consulate, Shanghai. 1863–8. 2 vols.

f. Canton, general. 1847–53. 3 vols.

g. Canton to Hong Kong. Insurance. 1850–3. 1 vol.

h. Hong Kong to London. Piece Goods. 1868–83. 2 vols.

i. Hong Kong to Coast. Insurance. 1852–9. 2 vols.

j. Hong Kong to America. 1877–82. 1 vol.

k. Hankow to Shanghai. 1866–7. 1 vol.

l. Augustus Howell at Hong Kong. 1842–7. 2 vols.

m. W. S. Boyd at Canton. 1841. 1 vol.

n. Danish Consulate, Hong Kong and Canton. 1845–8. 1 vol.

o. Petitions to authorities in China, and replies. 1829–32. 1 vol.

6. Private letter-books. c. 43 vols.

a. Miscellaneous, early. Writers include R. Taylor, James Matheson, Yrisarri & Co., W. Jardine, James B. Compton—all at Canton. c. 1818–36. c. 5 vols.

b. William Jardine. 1830–9. 7 vols.

c. James Matheson. 1831–41. 7 vols.

d. Alexander Matheson. 1841–6. 4 vols.

e. Coast—mainly from Macao. 1839–42. 2 vols.

f. Canton letter-books. (Hong Kong to Canton.) 1844–55. 8 vols.

g. Hong Kong to India. 1846–85. 10 vols.

7. Insurance letter-books (mainly Canton and Hong Kong). 1823–59. 26 vols.

8. Press Copy letter-books. 219 vols.

  1. Hong Kong Times. 1874–6. 3 vols.

  2. Insurance. 1868–94. 29 vols.

  3. Hong Kong to Swatow. 1879–83. 1 vol.

  4. Hong Kong to Coast. 1871–96. 41 vols.

  5. Hong Kong to Coast (2nd series). 1879–96. 25 vols.

  6. Hong Kong to Australasia. 1883–5. 1 vol.

  7. Hong Kong to Straits and India. 1882–1905. 5 vols.

8. Hong Kong, local. 1871–1901. 7 vols.

9. Hong Kong to America. 1883–98. 6 vols.

10. Hong Kong—'General Foreign'. 1878–99. 16 vols.

11. Hong Kong to Great Britain. 1870–87. 3 vols.

12. Hong Kong, banking and financial (Book Office). 1881–1912. 9 vols.

13. Hong Kong, local (sugar). 1880–1. 1 vol.

14. China Sugar Refinery. 1883–1913. 3 vols.

15. Hong Kong Charbonnages. 1893–9. 2 vols.

16. Steam Navigation Companies (From Hong Kong). 1883–1903. 12 vols.

17. Hong Kong Tea Company. 1881–96. 1 vol.

18. Hong Kong House Properties. 1890–1902. 1 vol.

19. Hong Kong. Agreements and Contracts. 1887–1903. 1 vol.

20. Hong Kong, shares, dividends, &c. 1892–1902. 1 vol.

21. Thomas Hunt & Co. 1865–8. 3 vols.

22. Augustus Heard & Co. 1865–75. 9 vols.

23. Foochow Tea Circulars. 1871–3. 1 vol.

24. From Korea. 1883–4. 1 vol.

25. Shanghai. Banking and financial (Book Office). 1870–91. 4 vols.

26. Shanghai Piece Goods. 1889. 5 vols.

27. Shanghai. China Coast Steam Navigation Co. 1881–3. 1 vol.

28. Shanghai. Alexander Bird. 1859–60. 1 vol.

29. Shanghai (general). 1908. 1 vol.

30. Manila to Hong Kong. 1883. 1 vol.

31. Private. Shanghai to Hong Kong. 1876–95. 14 vols.

32. Private. Shanghai local. 1873–90. 2 vols.

33. Private. Shanghai to Coast. 1872–86. 2 vols.

34. Private. Shanghai to Foochow. 1877–83. 1 vol.

35. Private. Shanghai to Tientsin, Hankow, Foochow. 1886–90. 2 vols.

36. Private. Shanghai to Tientsin, Foochow, Hankow, Amoy. 1890–2. 1 vol.

37. Private. Shanghai to Korea. 1884. 1 vol.

38. Private. Shanghai to Japan. 1872–9. 1 vol.

39. Private. Shanghai. J. J. Keswick. 1880. 1 vol.

C. Bound volumes of original letters (all to Hong Kong). 78 vols.

1. From America. 1879–1912. 1 vol.

2. From Jardine, Skinner & Co. Calcutta. 1893–6 (incomplete). 1 vol.

3. From Amoy. 1885–95. 10 vols.

4. From Canton. 1885–95. 11 vols.

5. From Herbert Dent & Co. Canton and Macao. 1888–90. 1 vol.

6. 'Coast miscellaneous.' 1884–95. 5 vols.

7. 'Coast Reports.' 1898–1900. 1 vol.

8. From Foochow. 1885–95. 10 vols.

9. 'Local' (Hong Kong). 1885–91. 4 vols.

10. From Margesson & Co. Macao. 1885–7. 1 vol.

11. From Shanghai. 1885–95. 11 vols.

12. From Swatow. 1885–8, 1892–4. 3 vols.

13. From Formosa. 1884–90. 2 vols.

14. From Kobe. 1888–93. 4 vols.

15. From Nagasaki. 1887–94. 2 vols.

16. From Yokohama. 1885–1902. 8 vols.

17. Indo-China Steam Navigation Co. 1886–9. 1 vol.

18. Hong Kong Tea Co. Ltd. 1886–1901. 1 vol.

19. London & Pacific Petroleum Co. Ltd. 1890–4. 1 vol.

D. Telegram Books. 1875–91. 16 vols.

E. Documents, unsorted. 13 boxes.

F. Two diaries. James Innes on *Jamesina*, and *Fairy*. 1832–3.

G. Unbound duplicates. Only roughly sorted. 139 boxes.

H. Miscellaneous

1. Material in Chinese. 1 box.

2. Miscellaneous printed material. 4 boxes.

3. Miscellaneous manuscript material. 1 box.

4. Telegrams. 1 box.

III. PRICES CURRENT AND MARKET REPORTS. Bound and unbound; print and manuscript. Arranged under localities. 83 boxes

IV. BOOKS SENT TO CAMBRIDGE IN 1950 Accounts current. 1808–1900. 17 vols.

Bound volumes of semi-official correspondence:

1. W. B. Walter. 1886–96.

2. Calcutta to New York. 1891–9.

3. Hong Kong to New York S/O. 1891–4.

4. William Keswick; official correspondence to New York. 1888–1910.

5. William Keswick; semi-official correspondence to New York. 1891–1903.

6. Miscellaneous letters to Jardine Matheson & Co., New York. 1897–1912.

Parcel containing:

Plans of old China Sugar Refinery at East Point. Swatow Sugar Refinery.

Admiralty Chart of Hong Kong Waters East. 1923.

Letters (original and copies) and extracts from letters and diaries of the Revd. John Scarth (1826–1909), relating mainly to his life in China where he was employed by the firm of Jardine, Matheson. 1847–59. 2 vols. (Add. 7084.)

Letters of William Hancock of the Chinese Maritime Customs. 1847–1908. (*List of accessions to depositories in 1971*, p. 16.)

Memoirs of Admiral Charles G. Dicken (1854–1937), including an account of his service in China, 1875–7, and of his service as Commodore-in-Charge, Hong Kong, 1903–5. *c.* 1863–1934. (Add. 7351.)

Archimandrite Palladius, Ancient traces of Christianity in China. A section transcribed from a book entitled *Eastern Miscellany* (vol. 1), St. Petersburg, 1877. 157 ff. *Russian.* (Add. 6403.)

Journals of F. H. H. Guillemard, naturalist, in East Indies, Japan, Kamchatka. 1882–3. (*List of accessions to repositories in 1969*, p. 19.)

Notes on Chinese affairs, by Sir T. F. Wade (d. 1895). (Add. 6318.)

Papers and correspondence of Lionel Charles Hopkins (1854–1952), Consul-General at Tientsin, 1901–8, &c., relating to ancient Chinese inscriptions. (Add. 7629.)

Papers and correspondence of Arthur Christopher Moule (1873–1957), Professor of Chinese at Cambridge, 1933–8. (Add. 7648.)

BALDWIN PAPERS (A. E. B. Owen, *Handlist of the political papers of Stanley Baldwin, first Earl Baldwin of Bewdley.* Cambridge, 1973.)

Foreign affairs 7: Japan, 1923; China, 1925–7. (vol. 108.)

Foreign affairs, series B. Mainly personal letters: China in 1926, 1927, 1930, 1931, 1932, 1933/1; Japan in 1932, 1933/1. (vol. 115.)

HALOUN PAPERS. Papers of Professor G. Haloun (1898–1951), Professor of Chinese at Cambridge University. 6 boxes. (Add. 7575.)

LECTURES

1. Chinese script. (Given to Oriental Ceramic Society, 2 February 1944.)
2. The Beginnings of Chinese History.
3. Some early Relations of China with the West.
4. Entwicklung des Gottesgedankens im alten China.
5. The Chinese Language. *German.*
6. Chinese Textual Criticism. *German.*
7. Die Rassen Ostturkestans.
8. Das Tocharerproblem.
9. Chinese and Indo-Europeans. *German.* Halle, 1927.
10. Early relations between East and West Asia. *German.*

LECTURE COURSES

1. Chinese Grammar: Particles (= Personal Pronouns).

2. Chung-Yung.
3. Li-Chi.
4. Hsün-tzu, Chapter 23.
5. Chuang-tzu, Chapters 1, 17, 2.
6. Lun-yü, Books III–VII.
7. Shih-chi, Book VII.
8. Meng-tzu, I A, III A, VI A.
9. Mo-tzu, 14, 15, 16.
10. Li-Sao.
11. Chinese Religion. *German.*
12. Early Chinese History. *German.*
13. The earliest Period of Chinese History. *German.*
14. Chinese Institutions. *German.*

MATERIAL FOR ARTICLES, NOTES, ETC.

1. Sven Hedin Documents 15, 16. ('To be published in series of Sino-Swedish Expedition by Professor H. W. Bailey'.)
2. Material for Professor Minorsky's book *Marvazi.*
3. Notes for Professor Henning's article 'Date of the Early Sogdian Letters', in *Bulletin S.O.A.S.*
4. A.B.C. Kuan-tzu 49 (Nei yeh).
5. Legalistic Fragments 2 and 3: Shen Pu-hai and Shen Tao.
6. Hua-i i-yü.
7. A and B. I-chou-shu.
8. Legend of the great Yü. (The flood legend.)
9. Biography of Chang Ch'ien.
10. The Life of Huan-kung (Duke Huan). (Kuan-tzu 20 and related texts.)
11. The Blondins.
12A and B. Meng-tzu wai shu.
13. The Burning of the Books.
14. Bone and Bronze Inscriptions.
15. The Stael-Holstein Roll.

Copies of original texts of passages translated in *Christians in China before the year 1550* (London, 1930), by Arthur Christopher Moule. *Italian, Latin, Chinese.* (Add. 7012–13.)

WESTMINSTER STUDENTS' MISSIONARY SOCIETY

Westminster College, Cambridge

The Society was interested in China since its foundation in 1879. (Marchant, pp. 117–18)

Minutes. 1879–1916. 1 vol.

CARLISLE

CUMBRIA COUNTY RECORD OFFICE

The Castle, Carlisle, CA3 8UR

Log-book (1799–1800), and account books (1783–1800) of the *Earl of Abergavenny*, East India Company ship travelling to China (J. Wordsworth, master).

Personal and trading documents of the *Earl of Sandwich* on voyage to China (J. Wordsworth, master). 1783–4.

(Mathias and Pearsall, pp. 107–8.)

THE KING'S OWN ROYAL BORDER REGIMENT

The Castle, Carlisle

'A Record of the Services of the Fifty-Fifth or Westmoreland Regiment of Foot' being the original digest of service, with inserted documents, maps, &c. There is a long and detailed account of the part played by the regiment in the China campaign, 1841–3, with water-colour drawings of Chinhae, Ching Kiang Foo (also spelt Tching-kiang-Fu and Cheng Keang Fool) and plans of towns, with copies of letters relating to the China campaign, 1842–4, in an Appendix. There is also some account of the service of the regiment with the Shanghai Defence Force in 1927. 1 vol. (large folio).

CAVERSHAM

BRITISH BROADCASTING CORPORATION, WRITTEN ARCHIVES CENTRE

Caversham, Reading, Berks.

Correspondence files
China, 1939–54.
Japan, 1935–54.
Eastern Service, 1941–5.
Far Eastern Service, 1940–55.
Certain files are subject to restrictions.

Programmes-as-Broadcast
Daily schedule, available from commencement of broadcasting.

London Calling
Bound volumes of B.B.C. Overseas Programmes, 1939– . Re-prints of talks, also shows reception areas of programme services.

Scripts
On microfilm—talks on foreign affairs include Far Eastern coverage.

News Bulletins
On microfilm—Home Service available in sequence from October 1939; incomplete before that date.

External Services News Bulletins and News Stories (English Text)
B.B.C. Japanese Service News Bulletins, 1 July–31 August 1945.

News Stories
On microfilm—Far Eastern coverage (China) from about 1950.

Monitoring Service
Daily Digest now called Summary of World Broadcasts—available from 1939 (China and Japan): current material can be seen by arrangement at the Written Archives Centre.

CHATHAM

INSTITUTION OF ROYAL ENGINEERS

Chatham, Kent

Museum

GORDON RELIC COLLECTION

Letters, papers, &c. of and concerning Major-General Charles George Gordon (1833–85), who served *i.a.* in the China War, 1860–2, including:

83. Maps of the Chinese campaign, with pencil notes by Gordon.

84. Maps of the 'Ever Victorious Army' drawn and painted by Gordon on silk.

89. Rough sketch drawn by Gordon for Colonel Du Cane, after his survey of the thirty mile radius about Shanghai, to explain the current positions of the Imperialists and rebels. The sketch was drawn at the Astor House Hotel, Shanghai, on 16 June 1862. It is accompanied by an explanatory note and a letter of Colonel Du Cane, dated 10 and 11 February 1885.

114. Military plan of the country round Shanghai, from surveys made in 1862–5.

118. Maps of Shanghai and environs drawn by Gordon on silk.

146. Letters about survey duties in China. 1862, 1863.

Library

File of papers and photographs relating to the Shanghai Defence Force. 1927. (951 '1927': 779 (51).)

CHELMSFORD

ESSEX RECORD OFFICE

County Hall, Chelmsford, CM1 1LX

Business papers of William and Samuel Braund of Upminster Hall, merchants, relating to Portuguese trade, the East India Company, and early transactions in marine insurance, including papers relating to voyages to the East Indies and China. (D/DRu B1–B26. See L. S. Sutherland, *A London merchant, 1695–1774*, 1933.)

Including:

B9. Tradesmen's bills for the first voyage of the *Grantham* to the East Indies, with a brief log of the voyage, a list of tradesmen and detailed accounts, a list of the crew and details of wages, and a balance sheet for the voyage. 1746–9. 1 vol.

B10. A similar volume to B9 relating to the second voyage of the *Grantham* to the East Indies. 1749–52. 1 vol.

B11. A similar volume to B9 relating to the first voyage of the *Boscawen* to the East Indies. 1748–52. 1 vol.

B15. Disbursements of the commander of the *Boscawen* on its second voyage to the East Indies, with separate detailed lists for disbursements for food and other stores in England, at the Cape, at Madras, Canton, St. Helena, &c. 1752–4. 1 vol.

B16. Disbursements of the commander of the *Grantham* on its second voyage to the East Indies, similar to B15. 1749–51. 1 vol.

B18 & 19. Copies of charter-parties for all Samuel Braund's ships. 1749–58. 2 vols.

B20. Various loose papers relating to the voyages of Samuel Braund's ships to the East Indies, including: contracts for the building of merchantmen; copy of the charter-party and of the orders to the captain of the *Grantham* on its third voyage, 1753; abstracts of journals and correspondence from the captains of various ships (*Boscawen*, *Grantham*, *Suffolk*, *Edgecote*, *Warren*) written from various ports in England, India, Africa, &c., giving details of sailings, provisions and commercial transactions, 1748–54; copy of the correspondence between the owners and captain of the *Warren*, 1755; copies of owners' instructions to captains; &c. 1 box.

Accounts of Samuel Braund relating to the East India Trade, viz.:

B21 and 22. Journals. 1746–64. 2 vols.

B23. Cash book. 1746–61. 1 vol.

B24. Journal, arranged by ships. 1746–61. 1 vol.

B25. Rough ledger for all ships, and bank account. 1748–60. 1 vol.

B26. Fair ledger arranged by ships and including accounts for the *Grantham*, *Edgecote*, *Warren*, *Suffolk*, and *Boscawen*. 1746–60. 1 vol.

Copy of the will of John Searle (died *c.* 1768), of Readings in Norton Mandeville, captain of the *Essex* on a voyage to China for the East India Company. 1768. (D/DCc T48.)

Letters from Richard Hall in Canton to his uncle, John Perry, sen., of Blackwall (Middlesex), with some comment on trade. 1795–7. (D/DEs T47.)

A narrative description, with accounts of China and the Chinese, of some Chinese drawings belonging to Mr. Drummond which were seized at Dover by the Customs for the non-payment of duty. *c.* 1830. 4 pp. (folio). (D/DVv 114.)

Letters from W. Luard on H.M.S. *Semarang* off Formosa. 1840. (D/DU 316.)

Note in diary of John Round of Danbury Park of the end of the China War. 21 November 1842. (D/DRh F25/24.)

Correspondence of the Revd. John Jessopp, chiefly applications for various appointments including that of Consular Chaplain at Shanghai in 1862, with various testimonials and other papers. 1861–77. 1 bundle. (D/DJg F24.)

Printed company prospectus, Chinese Imperial Railways (plan). 1899. (D/DU 559/19.)

Copy of a letter from C. J. Eyres describing an audience with the Tsar Nicholas II at Tsarskoe-Selo at which was mentioned the Russo-Japanese War, and Eyres's coming journey to Port Arthur via Lake Baikal. 5 May 1904. 4 pp. (D/DVv 107.)

Business records of Samuel Courtauld & Co., silk manufacturers. 1809–21. These records may be consulted only with the permission of the Company. (D/F 3.)

Log-book of Captain H. E. Laver, Master of the S.S. *Kalgan* of the China Navigation Co. Ltd., trading on the coast of China from Tientsin to Hong Kong. The log begins on 1 February 1917 and is written in the form of a diary containing, apart from navigational and cargo information, personal and general comments including family news, accounts of his activities on leave in harbour, observations on the Hong Kong reservoir and on Chinese fishing methods, &c. There is a reference to rumours of a German raider on 26 March and on 27 March to the reactions of the Russian postmaster at Chefoo to the early stages of the Russian revolution. The log ends on 27 June 1917 on which date orders came for the ship to proceed to Hong Kong as it had been chartered by the Admiralty as a transport. February–June 1917. 1 vol. (D/DMb B2.)

CHICHESTER

WEST SUSSEX RECORD OFFICE

County Hall, Chichester, PO19 1RN

COBDEN PAPERS. Papers of Richard Cobden (1804–65), statesman. (See Francis W. Steer, *The Cobden Papers*, Chichester, 1964.)

1. Newspaper cutting giving Yokohama shipping intelligence. 23 July 1864. (245.)

2. Printed memoranda about ships in Chinese waters. 1844–50. (480.)

3. Printed letter of the U.S. Minister at Peking containing opinions on various disputed points and also remarks concerning the co-operative policy. [1864.] (483.)

4. Notes and extracts, mainly in Cobden's hand, on China, India, and the Far East. Bound together. (484.)

5. Newspaper cuttings and extracts from periodicals about India, Burma, China, Japan, Singapore, the East Indies, and the colonies generally. Mostly undated but some 1844–64. (486.)

ROUS PAPERS. Copy of Overland China Mail. (A4/1.)

DARLINGTON

SIR R. ROPNER COMPANY (MANAGEMENT), LTD.

Ropner Holdings Ltd., 140 Coniscliffe Road, Darlington

Shipping papers relating to Company's vessels voyaging to the Far East. (Mathias and Pearsall, pp. 81–3.)

DEVIZES

WILTSHIRE REGIMENT MUSEUM

Regimental Headquarters (Devizes Branch), Duke of Edinburgh's Royal Regiment (Berkshire and Wiltshire), Le Marchant Barracks, Devizes, Wiltshire

Digests of service of the Wiltshire Regiment, formerly the 62nd and 99th Regiments of Foot, including accounts of service in China. 1860.

'From Calcutta to Pekin.' Diary of Captain Dunne of the 99th Regiment, covering his service with the 62nd Regiment in the China War, 1860. (B. 317.)

DORCHESTER

DORSET RECORD OFFICE

County Hall, Dorchester, DT1 1XJ

Papers concerning bales of fishing nets sent from Kobe, Japan. (Bridport-Gundry papers, A. 53.)

DURHAM

THE PRIOR'S KITCHEN

The College, Durham, DH1 3EQ

GREY OF HOWICK PAPERS

I. Papers of Charles, 2nd Earl Grey, Prime Minister 1830–4.

A. Personal and family correspondence. 1762–1875. There is available a list of this correspondence (1957), arranged under correspondents.

B. Political and public correspondence. 1787–1843. There is available a list of this correspondence (1956), arranged under correspondents. Although the correspondence must contain relevant material, it was not possible to search through such a large collection for the purpose of this *Guide*.

C. Subject files, including:
China
Abstract of proceedings at Canton, 1828–31; and memorandum of events in China in May and June 1831.

India and East India Company. Including:
Extract from a memorial presented to the Viceroy of Canton by the Hong merchants in January 1831.

Statement of the average annual profit of the China trade during five periods of three years each, 1814–29.

II. Papers of Henry George, 3rd Earl Grey (1802–94), Colonial Secretary 1846–52. The 3rd Earl retained a life-long interest in colonial affairs, and his papers include many relating to colonies in Asia and Africa, but as they are arranged under correspondents, not subjects, the description given below cannot claim to be complete. There is available a list of the correspondence, 1818–94 (1960), and a list of enclosures in the correspondence (1962). Among the correspondents are the following:

1st Marquess Anglesey

Thirty-nine letters from 1st Marquess Anglesey, Ordnance Office, to Lord Grey, Colonial Office, 1837–52; with copies of thirteen letters from Grey to Anglesey, 1846–50, including:

Copy of a letter from Grey to Anglesey on the operations in the Canton River. 15 March 1848.

Letter from Anglesey to Grey about Hong Kong. 12 September 1849.

Letter from Anglesey to Grey about Hong Kong, enclosing memoranda on the dispatch, relating to reductions in the forces in Hong Kong, from Governor Bonham to Earl Grey dated 23 May 1849; signed by J. F. Burgoyne, 12 September 1849 (13 pp.). 20 September 1849.

1st Earl of Auckland. 63 items, including:

Two letters relating to Hong Kong; candidates for the Governorship, and boats for Hong Kong. 6 and 11 November 1847.

Sir Samuel George Bonham

Thirteen letters from Sir Samuel George Bonham, Governor of Hong Kong, to Lord Grey, the first, 9 November 1847, applying for the Governorship of Hong Kong, and eleven, with enclosures, from Hong Kong, 25 April 1848–28 January 1851; with copies of eight letters from Grey to Bonham relating to the affairs of Hong Kong, 23 September 1848–21 October 1851.

4th Earl of Carnarvon. 13 items, including:

Letter from Lord Carnarvon to Lord Grey on Japan, Richardson's murder, &c. 28 June 1863.

G. Crawshay

Two letters from G. Crawshay, Chairman of the Newcastle Foreign Affairs Committee, to Lord Grey, concerning British conduct in China, the first, 17 November 1858, including a draft of a petition against the treaty with China; with Grey's draft reply, 23 November 1858. The second letter is dated 26 January 1863.

14th Earl of Derby

Twenty-nine letters to Lord Grey from the Earl of Derby, 1833–67, including two relating to China, 11 February 1857 and 23 January 1860, and one on

relations with Japan, 12 June 1864; with fifteen letters from Grey to Derby, including one, 23 January 1860, on China affairs.

John George Dunn

Letter from John George Dunn to Lord Grey, dated Tientsin, 21 September 1875, and forwarding two enclosures:

A private memorandum written by Dunn at the request of H. E. Tomomi Iwakura, prime minister of Japan, on the politics of China. Yokohama, 1 July 1875. 6 pp.

A confidential memorandum written by Dunn for Mr. T. F. Wade, H.M. Minister, relating to the consideration of matters of defence by the council in Peking, and containing much information on China's defence, policies, and proposals. Foochow, 12 January 1875. 9 pp.

Thomas Newton

Two letters to Lord Grey from Thmoas Newton, Foreign Affairs Association, Newcastle-upon-Tyne, on British action in China and Japan, with a memorandum (22 pp.) on the legality of the measures of the Chinese Government in attempting to arrest the opium trade. 26 February and 19 April 1861.

Lord Raglan

Forty-nine letters from Lord Raglan to Lord Grey, 1836–52, relating to troops, including one, 2 August 1847, on troops for China; with copies of seventeen letters from Grey to Raglan, 1831–51.

EASTNEY

ROYAL MARINES CORPS MUSEUM

Royal Marines Barracks, Eastney, Southsea, Hants.

Diaries of Lieutenant Francis Lean, R.M.L.I., covering voyages to many parts of the world including Hong Kong, Canton, Yokohama, Simono-Seki, and other parts of Japan. 1855–65. 2 vols.

Journal of Lieutenant F. Hutchinson, R.M.L.I., on a voyage from England to Japan. 1864.

ECCLES

ECCLES PUBLIC LIBRARIES, CENTRAL LIBRARY

Eccles, Manchester

JAMES NASMYTH COLLECTION (see *Catalogue of the James Nasmyth Collection*, 1958)

Papers of Nasmyth, Gaskell & Co., engineers of Patricroft, Lancashire, and exporters of machinery and locomotives to the Far East.

1. Order books. 1836–59. 2 vols.

2. Sales books. 1837–77. 5 vols.

3. Accounts day-book. 1837–54. 1 vol.

4. Letter-books, 2–7. 1838–40. 6 vols.

5. Specifications. 1875–8.

6. Notes, descriptions, &c. of locomotives built. 402 pp.

EDGWARE

REGIMENTAL HEADQUARTERS, THE MIDDLESEX REGIMENT (DUKE OF CAMBRIDGE'S OWN)

T.A. Centre, Deansbrook Road, Edgware, Middlesex

The museum of the Middlesex Regiment (formerly the 57th and 77th Regiments of Foot) has, in addition to the records described below, numerous albums of photographs, scrapbooks, pictures, and other relics. Many of the records of the 1st Battalion (the 57th Regiment) were destroyed by the Japanese in 1941. The regiment served in Hong Kong, 1908–11 and 1936–41, and in Shanghai in 1927.

1. Middlesex historical records, 1st, 2nd, 3rd, and 4th battalions to 1913, including service in Hong Kong. Typescript. 1 file.

2. Middlesex historical records including accounts of service in China. 1914–39. Typescript. 1 file.

3. A regimental scrapbook presented in 1931 containing cuttings, pictures, maps, &c. covering the whole history of the regiment. 1931. 1 vol.

4. Records of the Officers' Mess the 1st battalion, the Middlesex Regiment (the 57th Foot), 1757–1938: a historical summary of trophies, pictures, medals, and interesting relics, the property of the officers' mess, compiled by Major H. W. M. Stewart from records, letters, and memory. Many of the items described were lost in the fall of Hong Kong. Later additions include an 'Account of the part played by the 1st Battalion The Middlesex Regiment in the defence of Hong Kong, December 1941.' by Lieutenant-Colonel S. F. Hedgecoe. Typescript. 1 vol.

EXETER

CITY LIBRARY

Castle Street, Exeter

MISCELLANEOUS MS. COLLECTION

Volume containing: (1) Log of the ship *Townshend*, Captain Charles Keser, on a voyage from England to Canton via the Cape of Good Hope and return; apparently written by Daniel Ireson. 28 September 1716–15 August 1718. (2) Journal of the ship *Montague* on a voyage from England to China and return. 17 November 1719–31 December 1720.

Private journal of Richard de la Bère Granville, written sporadically aboard H.M.S. *Meander* in the East Indies, &c. with a short account of a stay at Hong Kong where the ship arrived on 30 March [1849]. 2 February 1848–August 1851.

Journal and letters, bound in one volume, of Richard de la Bère Granville. The letters, written by Granville from the time of his schooldays to December 1854, include four written aboard H.M.S. *Meander* at Hong Kong, April–May 1849. The journal describes the early days of the Crimean War, 1854.

DEVON RECORD OFFICE

Concord House, South Street, Exeter, EX1 1DX

SEYMOUR OF BERRY POMEROY PAPERS (NRA 12798)

Military contributions from Hong Kong. 1864. (Public office 6.)

Two letters on Japanese affairs. 1861. (p. 73.)

EXETER UNIVERSITY LIBRARY

The University, Prince of Wales Road, Exeter, EX4 4PT

Manuscripts at Exeter University Library (by C. F. Scott). (June, 1972.)

H. E. HILLMAN COLLECTION

Diaries of life in Shanghai. 1920–1, 1923–6.

Articles. Map of Hong Kong.

GLOUCESTER

GLOUCESTERSHIRE RECORDS OFFICE

Shire Hall, Gloucester, GL1 2TG

HUNTLEY (BOXWELL) MSS. (D 48. NRA 9215)

Letters mainly to Captain H. Huntley, R.N., while in the Gambia, some from J. Dorney-Harding on various subjects including the Chinese expedition. 1840–59. 57 docs. (C 8.)

Letters to same from J. Dorney-Harding, W. B. Brodie, R. Vernon Smith, and others on various subjects including China. 1840–59. 31 docs. (C 9).

BLATHWAYT (DYRHAM) MSS. (D 1799. NRA 9217) Personal correspondence of Miss Charlotte A. Baker [later Mrs. Blathwayt], 1864, including references to naval engagement against Japan. 3 bundles. (C 58–60.)

Log of *William Fairlie*, kept by J. Tombes, on journey London–China via Bengal, Penang, Singapore, and return by St. Helena. (D 1292, Acc. 2010. Mathias and Pearsall, p. 114.)

REGIMENTAL HEADQUARTERS, THE GLOUCESTERSHIRE REGIMENT

Robinswood Barracks, Gloucester

Digest of service of the 61st Regiment and 2nd Battalion the Gloucestershire Regiment. This includes a short reference to service in China, 1913.

GUILDFORD

GUILDFORD MUNIMENT ROOM

Castle Arch, Guildford, GU1 3SX

The parish records of Stoke, near Guildford, include the record of the baptisms in April 1792, of two children of George and Charlotte Smith who had been 'born at Macao in China' in 1779 and 1781. (PSH/STK/1/2.)

Part of account of a voyage in H.M.S. *Horatio* to China, India, &c. [Early 19th century.] Very bad condition. (L.M. 1327/38.)

HEREFORD

HEREFORD CITY LIBRARY, MUSEUM, ART GALLERY, AND OLD HOUSE

Hereford

Letters from Robert Biddulph to his brother Michael, including one written from Hong Kong, 1860. (Biddulph Collection, no. 529.)

HEREFORD COUNTY RECORD OFFICE

The Old Barracks, Harold Street, Hereford, HR1 2QX

'Diary of a journey from India to England by Japan and Canada', by John Biddulph, March–September 1889, giving an account of the situation in the Straits Settlements and Hong Kong as observed by the writer. Bound volume. Typescript. (A87/10.)

Chinese scroll, labelled 'Chinese Order, E. M. Dunne'. n.d. (F 76/IV/577.)

HERTFORD

HERTFORDSHIRE COUNTY RECORD OFFICE

County Hall, Hertford, SG13 8DE

Draft of a bill to prohibit the importation of silks and calicoes from Persia, China, or East India after 29 September 1701. 1701. (12538.)

GOLDSMITHS HALL COLLECTION

Account books for supplying Robert Williams's ship, the *General Coote*, for two voyages to Madras, Malacca, Viadore Islands, Macao, and China. 1780–5. (GH 1675–7.)

MARTIN-LEAKE PAPERS

Letters written by Vice-Admiral Francis Martin-Leake to his mother, including:

1. Two letters from H.M.S. *Bramble* at Hong Kong. 24 January, 28 February 1900. (87370–1.)

2. Eight letters written from H.M.S. *Bramble* with accounts of a visit to Manila, and the 'general muddle' in China, Hong Kong, the presence of German warships, gunnery practice off Wuhu, the Chinese fleet, &c. (87387–94.)

3. Six letters written from H.M.S. *Bramble* with a description of a visit to Bangkok, and accounts of the marking of new territory round Hong Kong, of Foochow, Wei-hei-wei, and Suiko. 16 February–9 April 1902. (87395–400.)

4. 111 similar letters, the latter part from England. 22 April 1902–4 July 1907. (87401–511.)

5. Copy of a letter of sympathy from Prince Enshimi of Japan to Mrs. Martin-Leake, on the death of her son Theodore in a balloon accident. 22 June 1907. (87565.)

HOVE

HOVE CENTRAL LIBRARY

Church Road, Hove, BN3 2EG

WOLSELEY PAPERS (NRA 10471)

Some original correspondence of Garnet Joseph, 1st Viscount Wolseley (1833–1913), field-marshal, who served in China in 1860, and in the Crimea, Africa, Egypt, &c. Including:

Sixteen letters to his family from China. (p. 180.)

Four letters from Admiral Sir James Hope. 1861, 1876. (p. 77.)

Notes and drafts by Wolseley for articles or lectures on current affairs, including China. (M1/12/27. i–x.)

Letter to Lady Wolseley from Mme Kati, 'the Japanese ambassadress'. 1898. (LW/P24/1–95.)

HULL

THE BRYNMOR JONES LIBRARY

The University, Hull, HU6 7RX

UNION OF DEMOCRATIC CONTROL PAPERS (NRA 13535)

Photographs of China. *c.* 1934. (4/35, 41.)

Files relating to Japan. 1943–4. (4/7.)

File relating to Far East. 1960–1. (3/50.)

PAPERS OF J. HENRY LLOYD (NRA 13532)

Correspondence on China. 1937–49. (3b.)

HUNTINGDON

CAMBRIDGESHIRE COUNTY RECORD OFFICE

Grammar School Walk, Huntingdon, PE18 6LF

MANCHESTER MSS. (NRA 0902)

Maps relating to various areas, including Russian Empire, Asia. 1750–1850. (Acc. 1. dd M1/4.)

Letters on miscellaneous subjects including the insurrection in China. 1839–57. (Acc. 1. dd M10/12.)

Copy of letter about employment of Chinese labour by Company Surveyor on road-making in Huntingdonshire. (NRA 9006. 839: 1.)

IPSWICH

SUFFOLK RECORD OFFICE. IPSWICH BRANCH

County Hall, Ipswich, IP4 2JS

ALBERMARLE MSS. (HA 67. NRA 4050)

Naval papers of Admiral Viscount Augustus Keppel (1725–86), including: 'Log book of Lord Anson's celebrated voyages round the world in the years 1740–1741, 1742 and 1744. Kept by Augustus Keppel himself on board the *Centurion*.' The entries include Canton. (461/228.)

KINGSTON UPON THAMES

THE QUEEN'S ROYAL SURREY REGIMENT MUSEUM

T.A. Centre, Portsmouth Road, Kingston upon Thames

Digest of service, 1st Battalion the East Surrey Regiment, including service in China. 1850–1931, 1931–9. 2 vols. Typescript and MS.

LANCASTER

LANCASTER PUBLIC LIBRARIES

Central Library, Market Square, Lancaster, LA1 1HY

Notarial books of *Favorite*, *Victoria*, and *Jane*, all for voyage Miramichi–Glasson. 1863, 1875, 1886. (Mathias and Pearsall, pp. 127–9.)

LEEDS

LEEDS PUBLIC LIBRARIES

Sheepcar Branch Library, Chapeltown Road, Leeds, LS7 3AP

CANNING PAPERS (Manuscripts belonging to the Earl of Harewood. NRA 7618)

Papers of Charles John Canning (1812–62), as Governor-General of India 1856–62. Including:

1. Volume of letters to China, the Colonies, &c. 1856–62. (57.)

2. Letter from Major-General C. T. van Straubenzie, C.B., commanding China Expeditionary Force, Hong Kong. (5839.)

3. Packet of dispatches about events in China received from Mr. Waterfield. 1857. (Misc. 143.)

4. Copies of dispatches, &c., relating to the China Expedition. 1859–60. (Misc. 469.)

——(NRA 9205)
Papers on China. (141.)

ARTHINGTON TRUST COLLECTION (AT/A–G)
Papers relating to the administration of approximately £1 million left by Robert Arthington (1823–1900) to be used for missionary enterprise and to be disbursed in twenty-five years. Five-tenths of the Arthington money was administered by the Baptist Missionary Society (Fund No. 1) and four-tenths by the London Missionary Society (Fund No. 2). The distribution of the estate took place in August 1910 and the Fund was wound up in 1936. The money was used in missionary activities throughout the world, including China and Japan. See A. M. Chirgwin, *Arthington's million: the romance of the Arthington Trust.*

A. *Minute Books*

1. 1905–17. 1 vol.

2. 1917–33. 1 vol.

3. 1917–36. 1 vol.

4–8. Rough minute books. 1905–36. 5 vols.

B. *Legal papers, accounts and correspondence arising from the administration of the Arthington Funds at source and dealing with the Trustees in general*

1. Copy of Robert Arthington's will. 1900.

2. Correspondence from relations of Robert Arthington claiming under the will.

3. Investment accounts, Arthington estate. 1901–9.

4. Litigation arising out of Robert Arthington's will. 1902–9.

5. Mortgages, lists, agreements and litigation. 1900, 1903, 1910, 1920.

6. Scheme for the application of the shares in the residuary estate bequeathed to the Baptist Missionary Society and the London Missionary Society. 1905. 4 copies.

7. Several copies of the Interim Report of the Trustees (to 1905), of the Final Report of the Trustees, 1910, of the release by the Baptist Missionary Society and the London Missionary Society and the Scheme trustees.

8. Estimates, balance sheets, and various general reports relating to Arthington Fund No. 2 (London Missionary Society): with special reports relating to

Ting Chow, 1918, 1921–2, and 1924; Poklo (Kuong Tung), 1925; Hwangpei, n.d.

9. Refused applications for grants from Fund No. 3. 1905–27.

10. Income account and missionary society account, with reports on accounts. 1918–20.

11. Financial statements relating to Fund No. 3. 1906–36.

12. Miscellaneous printed reports, &c., relating to Fund No. 2 (London Missionary Society). 1906–16.

13. Copies of deeds of release and indemnity terminating the Arthington Trust, 1937: with other papers including papers relating to the termination of No. 3 Fund, and papers concerning the handing over of the archives of the Trust to the Leeds Public Library. 1933–6.

14. Miscellaneous reports and correspondence relating to Fund No. 1 (Baptist Missionary Society). 1905–36.

15. Statement of conditions for application for Arthington grants.

C. *Files of correspondence and papers* (arranged in three series), including the following:

Series 1: Correspondence and papers from and relating to:

2. J. Fothergill Clarke and Edward Little, Secretary. 1912–15.

3. Agenda of Trustees' meetings. 1900–35. 4 files.

4. American Friends Mission, Nanking. 1908–33.

10. Correspondence with the Midland Bank. 1906–35.

11. Baptist Colonial Society. 1905–29.

12. Baptist Missionary Society. 1911–35.

13. Baptist Missionary Society Medical Mission Auxiliary. 1922–33.

14. Women's Missionary Association. 1911–34.

17. British and Foreign Bible Society. 1905–20.

18. China Inland Mission. 1906–20.

19. Christian Literature Society for China: the Revd. W. Hopkyn Rees, D.D., the Revd. D. McGillivray, D.D. 1919–31.

20. Christian Literature Society for China: Dr. Timothy Richard. 1905–35.

22. Church Missionary Society. 1908–34.

25. Church Missionary Society: Kienning Women's Hospital, Fukien. 1908–35.

30. East and West Friendship Committee. 1922–34.

33. Dr. Walter Fisher. 1911–28.

34. Friends Foreign Mission Association: Friends Service Council. 1905–34.

36. Friends Foreign Mission Association: Chentu University College. 1906–35.

46. London Missionary Society: general. 1908–35.

63. Methodist Missionary Society. 1933.

64. Minutes of Trustees' meetings. Typescript. 1904–34.

73. Postal and Telegraph Christian Association. 1908–34.

74. Primitive Methodist Missionary Society. 1909–33.

76. Record of the work of the Arthington Funds Nos. 1–3. 1917–35.

77. Religious Tract Society. 1932–5.

80. Scripture Gift Mission. 1914–35.

90–101. Correspondence with Trustees. 1908–35.

102. Miss Tseng: Champsa, Hunan, I Fang Girls' Collegiate School. 1918–34.

105. United Free Church of Scotland: Mukden Christian Medical College. 1910–35.

106. United Free Church of Scotland: Women's Foreign Mission. 1910–16.

109. Wesleyan Methodist Missionary Society. 1912–30.

112. West China Religious Tract Society: L. Wigham. 1908–23.

113. William Whiting. 1928–31.

114. Frank Livingstone Wilson. 1906–17.

115. Dr. William Wilson. 1909–11.

118. Y.W.C.A. Foreign Department. 1911–18.

119. Y.W.C.A. Hostel in Tokyo. 1907–17.

120. Y.W.C.A.: W. M. Vories, Japan. 1911–35.

121. Y.W.C.A.: Chinese labourers in France. 1917.

C. *Series 2*

128. American Baptists Foreign Mission Society. 1905–19.

129. American Friends Mission, Nanking. 1910–34.

131. Baptist Missionary Society: Tsi-Nan-Fu Soldiers Institute. 1905–11.

132. Bishop Cassels: Paoning Hospital, Dr. Elliott. 1908–13.

133. Bishop Cassels: Paoning Training Home. 1908–22.

134. China: aboriginal tribes of the West. 1916–33.

135. China: Miaos, &c. 1906–16.

136. China Emergency Appeal Committee. 1902–12.

137. China Inland Mission: Dr. J. C. Carr, Pingyang, reports. 1910–14.

138. China Inland Mission Hospital for Miaos, Anhseiw. 1906–8.

140. Christian Literature Society for China: Miss H. C. Bowser. 1911–31.

141. Christian Literature Society for China: Dr. Timothy Richard. 1907–19.

142. Chungking Missionary Association. 1908–10.

143. Church Missionary Society: Kienning Women's Hospital; Churches of Kien Yang, Masa, Men Suoing. 1908–31.

145. China Sunday School Union. 1908–15.

146. Central China Religious Tract Society: Arthington Press, Hankow. 1910.

147. Central China Religious Tract Society: colportage. 1908.

148. Chinese Tract Society. 1911–14.

149. West China Religious Tract Society. 1910–16.

153. Friends Foreign Mission Association. 1910–31.

154. Friends Foreign Mission Association: China. 1910–31.

155. Friends Foreign Mission Association: Chungking, International Friends Institute. 1909–21.

156. The same. 1917–31.

160. London Mission Hospital Hankow: reports. 1925–35.

163. International Y.M.C.A. Tokyo: Waseda Hostel. 1910–14.

169. Mukden Medical College, Manchuria: Dr. Dougald Christie, reports. 1910–34.

172. Post Office Christian Association, China. 1903–34.

173. Primitive Methodist Missionary Society, 1909–33.

175. Presbyterian Church of Ireland: Mukden Christian Union College. 1910–31.

177. Railway Mission, Japan. 1908, 1924.

178. Various reports sent to the Trustees. 1908–35.

179. Robert Morrison Memorial Institute, Canton. 1910–12.

181. Scripture Gift Mission: reports. 1913–27.

184. Miss Tseng, Changsha (? Champsa), Hunan: I Fang Girls' Collegiate School.

185. Various maps. 1918–34.

191. Bible Christian Methodist Mission. 1905–32.

192. Bible Translation Society. 1911–23.

194. Miss Flora Butcher. 1909–28.

195. Bishop Cassels. 1906–19.

196. Central China Religious Tract Society, 1908–18; China Emergency Appeal Committee, 1909–11; China Inland Mission, Dr. John C. Carr, 1910–13; China Inland Mission, Hospital for Miao, 1906–12; China Inland Mission, Batabg, 1908–14.

197. China Medical Missionary Association. 1907–10.

198. China Sunday School Union. 1907–15.

199. Chinese Tract Society, Shanghai. 1911–15.

200. Christian Literature Society for China: H. C. Bowser. 1907–30.

203. Chungking Missionary Association. 1908–10.

205. Church Missionary Society: Chengtu College, 1908; Kweilinfu, Bishop Banister, 1910–11.

207. Japan: Doshisha, 1910–20. Chungking International Friends Institute, 1911–30.

215. London Missionary Society: Hong Kong Christian High School. 1911–22.

216. London Missionary Society: Nanking Exhibition. 1910.

217. Robert Morrison Memorial, Canton. 1907–15.

223. Nurses' Association of China: Miss E. Hope Bell. 1924–9.

224. Peking Union Medical College Hospital. 1907–30.

227. Presbyterian Church of Ireland Foreign Missions. 1910–31.

228. Presbyterian Church of England Foreign Missions Committee. 1906–11.

231. Railway Mission, Japan: Miss Elizabeth Gillett. 1906–25.

244. Tientsin College: S. Lavington Hart. 1908–9.

248. Wesleyan Methodist Missionary Society: reports, the Revd. J. K. Hill, Hupeh, China. 1908–18.

249. West China Union University, Chengtu. 1907–34.

250. Dr. William Wilson: Chengtu. 1909–11.

251. Y.M.C.A. Japan: Baba Railway Y.M.C.A. Otsu, Omi: W. M. Vories. 1911–28.

252. Y.M.C.A. Hostel for Korean Students, Tokyo. 1912.

253. Y.M.C.A. International: China, Japan.

256. London Missionary Society: India and China. 1936.

258–60. China packets, No. 1–3.
    1. 1909–17. Shantung Province; Ching-Chu-Fu; Chinanfu; Chowstun; Chonping.
    2. 1913–20. Hsinchow; Tai-Yuan Fu; Wenshui; Shou Yang; Tai Chow; Fan Ssu; Khoa Hsieu.
    3. 1911–14. Shensi Province; San Yuan; Sianfu; Yenanfu; Suitechow.

C. *Series 3.* Additional files

276 *b.* China C.M.S. Fukhien. 1937.
    c. Changsha, Hunan: I Fang Girls' Collegiate School. 1937.
    d. Mukden Medical College Reports, &c. 1936–7.
    e. Shantung. 1909–19.
    s. Friends Service Council, Chengtu. 1937–8.
    cc. London Missionary Society Anglo-Chinese College, Tientsin. n.d. *c.* 1935.

277 *c.* Post Office Christian Association, China. 1936–7.
    o. Friends Service Council: the Union University, Chengtu. 1935–6.
    t. Japanese Book and Tract Society. 1934.
    x. Church Missionary Society: Kien Yang Fuh Kien. 1936.
    y. Friends India and China Missions. 1934, 1936.
    aa. The Methodist General Hospital, Hankow (circular letter). 1934.

278. National Committee of Y.M.C.A., China. 1911–15.

280. East and West Friendship Council Annual Report. 1933.

D. *Reports, pamphlets, and other printed papers*

1. *a–jj.* Annual Reports. 1902–37.

10. Baptist Missionary Society: Shantung Protestant University, comprising Shangtung Union College, Weihsien, Union Theological College, Ching-chou-fu, and Union Medical College, Chi-nan-fu. 1908.

11. Baptist Missionary Society: Shantung Christian University, pictures. 1922 (?).

12. Baptist Missionary Society: Imperial University Shansi, calendar. 1910.

15. Baptist Missionary Society: report on China missions. 1908. 3 copies.

19. Baptist Missionary Society: The Challenge of China, a deputation report. 1919–20.

26. 'Arthington and China.' 2 copies.

28. 'The Story of Tsinanfu.' 3 copies.

46. Friends Foreign Mission Association: annual reports. 1905–26.

54. Friends Foreign Mission Association: Chinese ladies in the Treaty Port. 1921.

56. The Christian Educational Union of West China, 2nd Annual Meeting, Chentu, 1907, and 4th, 1909.

57. West China Missionary Conference, Chentu. January–February 1908.

58. West China Missionary News. March 1908.

59. West China Union University, Chentu: A Proposal to found a college in Chentu. 1907.

62. 'An Open Door': a review of ten years' progress, 1909–19. 2 copies.

63. American Friends Board of Foreign Missions: History of Friends Work in China, by George De Vol, Nanking and Luho. 1904.

66. Reports of the West China Religious Tract Society, Chungking. 1906, 1908–12, 1914, 1915, 1915–16, 1917–18, 1918–19, 1919–20.

68. Annual reports of the Central China Religious Tract Society, Hankow. 1909–14.

69. Annual reports of the Chinese Tract Society, Shanghai. 1909–13.

70. Reports of the Religious Tract Society of North and Central China. 1917–18, 1919–20.

71. Reports of the Korean Religious Tract Society. 1911–13.

72. Report of the Japan Book and Tract Society. 1921.

83. Church Missionary Society: report of Fukien Church day schools. 1925.

84. Church Missionary Society Kienning-Fu Medical Mission: maps of prefecture. 1909, 1910.

98 a–y. Mukden Medical College: annual statements. 1911–35.

105. 'Present Day Conditions in China' by Marshall Broomhall, with maps, diagrams, and illustrations. 1908.

106 a–c. Reports of the China Inland Mission. 1913–15, 1921–2.

107. 'In touch with China's scholars' by Dr. William Wilson, with supplement. 1909. 2 copies.

108. Christian Literature Society for China: the Society for the Diffusion of Christian and General Knowledge among the Chinese, catalogue of publications. 1904.

109 a–u. Christian Literature Society: annual reports. 1907–11, 1914–24, 1926–8, 1930–2.

112. Presbyterian Church in Ireland: annual reports of mission, including Mukden Christian College. 1911.

113 a–c. Reports of the Irish Presbyterian Mission in Manchuria. 1912–14.

116. Presbyterian Church of England: Eng-Chhun. 1906.

117. United Free Church of Scotland: ninth report of foreign missions, including Mukden. 1908.

136. London Missionary Society: annual reports. 1901–37.

139. London Missionary Society: report of a deputation to China. 1903–4.

143. London Missionary Society: report of a deputation to China. 1909–10.

165. London Missionary Society: report of the Union Medical College, Peking. 1906, 1909, 1910, 1912, 1913.

166 a–w. London Missionary Society: Nurses Association of China, Miss Hope Bell, Quarterly Journals. January 1925–October 1930.

167 a–b. London Missionary Society: Nurses Association of China, reports of conferences. 1926, 1928.

168. London Missionary Society: report on the Men's Hospital, Hankow. 1924.

169. a–c. London Missionary Society: reports of Miss G. E. Stephenson, Nurses' Superintendent, Union Hospital, Hankow. 1928–30.

170 a–c. Primitive Methodist Missionary Society: annual reports. 1913–27.

171 a–g. United Methodist Church: reports. 1911–17.

173. 'Chinese Students in Japan' by D. W. Lyon. 1906.

174. 'Among young men of the Middle Kingdom': report of the Y.M.C.A. for China and Korea. 1911.

175. Progress reports of the Y.M.C.A. for China and Korea, 1907–12. 2 copies.

187. Handbook of London Missionary Society work in Shanghai District. n.d.

188. Fukien Diocesan Magazine. 1928, 1911, 1912.

190. Reports and prospectus for the Doshisha University, Japan. 1910–18.

191. 'The Great Opportunity in Yunnan': United Methodist Church. 1918?

209. Baptist Missionary Society: general committee reports. 1901–5.

210. Baptist Missionary Society: special Arthington committee (Fund No. 1) reports. 1905–19.

212. Baptist Missionary Society: 'The China Problem' by Timothy Richard. 1905.

216. 'A Mustard Seed in Japan' by William Merrell Vories, embodying the Japanese experience of a Japanese teacher. Omi-Hachiman, 1911.

217. The same.

218. The China Mission Year Book, 1914, edited by the Revd. D. MacGillivray, Shanghai.

219. 'Samuel Pollard, Pioneer Missionary in China' by the Revd. W. A. Grist. 1920.

220. 'The Story of the Miao' by Samuel Pollard. London 1919.

221. 'Light corners in China' by Samuel Pollard.

223. 'The Marches of the Mantze' by J. H. Edgar, missionary on the Tibetan border, China Inland Mission. 1908.

259. 'The Omi Brotherhood in Nippon' by William Merrell Vories.

266. 'The Omi Mustard Seed.' 1910–35, 1937.

270. Bulletin of the Diocese of Western China. 1912–22.

281. The Bulletin, Paoing, West China. 1923.

E. *Photographs*

Photographs of missions, &c., in China, Japan, Korea, and other parts of the world.

F. *Maps and Plans*

1. Blue-print, plans, and elevation of the Chinese Students' Hostel, Tokyo.

G. *Miscellaneous*

3. Letters to and from Robert Arthington and his family. 19th century.

LEICESTER

LEICESTER MUSEUMS, ART GALLERIES AND RECORDS SERVICE

The Museum and Art Gallery, New Walk, Leicester, LE1 6TD

Log-book, the *Sea Horse*, Gravesend to China. 1767–9. (15/1860.)

LEWES

EAST SUSSEX COUNTY RECORD OFFICE

Pelham House, St. Andrews Lane, Lewes, BN7 1UN

LOCKER-LAMPSON MSS. (NRA 12288)

Two letters from Laurence Oliphant, Shanghai and H.M.S. *Furious* off Canton. 1857–8. (p. 237. IV/12 xx and xviii.)

Letter from Hon. Sir Frederick William Adolphus Bruce in Shanghai. 1859. (p. 93. IV/12 viii.)

LICHFIELD

THE STAFFORDSHIRE REGIMENT MUSEUM

Whittington Barracks, Lichfield, Staffs.

RECORDS of the 1st and 2nd North Staffordshire Regiments, formerly the 64th and 98th Foot, and of the 1st and 2nd South Staffordshire Regiments, formerly the 38th and 80th Foot. Including:

1. Digest of Service, the 98th Regiment, later the 2nd Battalion North Staffordshire Regiment, including service in China, 1842–6. 1825–1910.

2. Diary of moves of 98th Foot, including Hong Kong, 1843–6. 1843–58.

3. Digest of Service of 80th Foot including service in Hong Kong, 1872–6. 1793–1899.

4. Nominal Roll of enlistments into 80th Regiment, with details of those joining and struck off strength in Burma 1852–3, Singapore and Malaya 1872 and 1875–7, Hong Kong 1872–6. 1804–81.

5. Copy of letter referring to circumstances of finding relics of 98th Regiment, at Stanley, Hong Kong. *c.* 1948.

LINCOLN

LINCOLNSHIRE ARCHIVES OFFICE

The Castle, Lincoln, LN1 3AB

MONSON DEPOSIT

Papers of Edmund Larken, father-in-law of the sixth Lord Monson, who was in the service of the East India Company at Canton from 1804 to 1811.

1. Copies of nine reports on the teas examined at Canton by Edmund Larken, sent to the President and Select Committee of the East India Company, dated February 1804 to January 1808. Inside the cover of the volume is a printed list of East India ships with owners, masters and officers for the season 1803–4. 1 vol. (Monson 7/46.)

2. Letter-book containing copies of letters written by Edmund Larken to various correspondents in England and the United States relating to the export of tea from Canton, 1804–7. The volume reversed contains lists of personal letters written and received and lists of presents dispatched, 1804–7; with brief journals for January to July 1804, 30 December to 2 January 1805, 3 March to 5 March 1805, 26 February to 4 March 1806, 4 January to 12 January 1807, 29 April to 11 October 1807; a list of articles left at Canton in 1807, and a list of letters written to China in 1809, 1810, 1811, and 1811–12. In the cover are a number of loose letters and papers relating to the export of tea from Canton. (Monson 7/47.)

3. Letters addressed to Edmund Larken at Canton mainly by business associates relating to the tea trade and trade in general, with some East India Company and general news from home. The letters are endorsed with the senders' names, dates, and means of arrival (often including the names of the ships), the dates answered, and by what means the replies were sent. 1806. 1 bundle (54 items). (Monson 25/5/1–54.)

4. Letters addressed to Edmund Larken at Canton, with other documents. Among the letters are several from persons returning to England with accounts of travelling in convoy with the China fleet; letters from business associates (as in 3 above) concerning the tea trade, some from Macao and Whampoa; numerous letters from Charles Magniac, banker at Canton; letters from Thomas Beale & Co. of Canton;

and a letter from the East India Company concerning Larken's retirement in 1811 on a pension of £500 per annum. There is also included a statement of the circumstances connected with and which caused the bankruptcy of Thomas Beale at Macao in January 1816 which gives information concerning Beale's twenty-five years as a merchant in China (7 pp.). 1804–28. 1 bundle (63 items). (Monson 25/6/1–63.)

5. Letters addressed to Edmund Larken after his retirement, mostly from Canton by Charles Magniac of Magniac & Co. and from Thomas Dent & Co., concerning trade and Larken's investments in China. One letter dated 23 July 1823 gives details of factories at Canton in which Larken and Magniac were interested (No. 2). 1823–9. 1 bundle (28 items). (Monson 25/7/1–28.)

6. Letter wrappers, mostly addressed to Mrs. Larken from Edmund Larken in China. 1803–7. 58 items. (Monson 25/8/1–58.)

Papers relating to the estate of Sir Theophilus John Metcalfe, 2nd Bart. (d. 1822), consisting of a limited administration of his goods with related accounts and papers, including a copy of a memorandum by Sir T. J. Metcalfe, dated 1819, concerning his claim on the insolvent Hong Kong merchants. 1819–29. 6 items. (Monson 28B/23/3.)

WELBY OF ALLINGTON DEPOSIT (Lind. Dep. 24)

Papers of R. E. Welby, later Lord Welby, who entered the Treasury in 1856, was assistant financial secretary from 1880 to 1885, and permanent secretary from 1885 to 1894. Among the papers are a series of working papers bound into volumes by subject (19 vols.) containing departmental reports, minutes, returns to orders and memoranda (printed and manuscript), newspaper cuttings, notes, and summaries by Welby, and some correspondence, including the following:

'Telegraphs & Mails': a volume of original letters and papers, manuscript and printed, relating to telegraphs and mails in the Mediterranean, India, China, Japan, Australia, West Indies, and North and South America. There are included notes, memoranda, letters, and papers concerning the mail packet service to India, China, and Japan. 1853–72. 1 vol. (Lind. Dep. 24/3/2/8.)

'China and Japan': a volume of original letters and papers, manuscript and printed, relating to Far Eastern trade and to legations and consular buildings in China and Japan. The printed papers consist of Treasury Minutes, Parliamentary Papers, Confidential Print, &c., with manuscript memoranda, notes, and correspondence. Many of the papers relate to the tour of inspection of consulates in China and

Japan made by Captain (later Major) W. Crossman, R.E., including his draft instructions (1866), about twenty-two original letters written by Crossman in Shanghai, Hong Kong, Peking, Nagasaki, Taku, and Yokohama reporting on his visits to legations and consulates (1866–9), various manuscript reports on legations and consular buildings (1870–2), with other notes and memoranda, manuscript and printed, on the same subject and an interleaved and annotated copy of the report on China consulates (1869). There are also papers relating to trade, including a manuscript report from Robert Boyce, H.M. Office of Works, Shanghai, to Major Crossman concerning open ports in Japan (1870), and a long letter from A. Davenport, Hankow, on trade in China (January, 1870). 1863–72. 1 vol. (Lind. Dep. 24/3/2/9.)

'China and Japan': a volume of original papers, manuscript and printed, relating to currency, foreign trade, and the treaty ports. There are papers concerning diplomatic and consular expenditure in China, Japan, and Siam (1870–1); reports on Japanese currency (1866), on foreign trade in China (1864–71), the trade of the Treaty Ports, &c. (c. 1872–4), on trade with Japan; papers concerning British troops in Japan (1867), the revision of the treaty of Tientsin (1868), the revision of the Japanese commercial tariff (1867), affairs in Japan (1868–70): a translation of the reports of the Japanese Minister of Finance for 1875–6, interleaved with shorter statistical reports and articles from various departments; and trade statistics of the Treaty Ports for the period 1863 to 1872 prepared by the Imperial Maritime Customs and printed at Shanghai in 1873. There is also a copy of the instructions given to Sir J. Walsham for his inquiry into consular and judicial establishments in Japan (1889). 1866–89. 1 vol. (Lind. Dep. 24/3/2/10.)

Account of travels in China for Ruston & Hornsby, engineers. 1934–5. (Bergne-Coupland papers. *List of accessions to repositories in 1970*, p. 57.)

THE ROYAL LINCOLNSHIRE REGIMENT MUSEUM

Sobraon Barracks, Lincoln

The Royal Lincolnshire Regiment, formerly the 10th Regiment of Foot, was raised in 1685, and served in the Far East from 1868 to 1876 and again between the two world wars. The museum has a large collection of records, photographs, and relics, including the following:

Records of service. 1784–1940.

1. Digest of service of the 1st Battalion The Royal Lincolnshire Regiment from 1784 to 1893, and of the 2nd Battalion from 1887 to 1892. 1 vol.

2. Digest of service of the 1st and 2nd Battalions from 1882 to 1910. 1 vol.

3. Digest of service of the 2nd Battalion from 1858 to 1883. 1 vol.

4. Digest of service of the 2nd Battalion from 1858 to 1936. 1 vol.

5. Historical records of the 1st Battalion from 1910 to 1940 and of the 2nd Battalion from 1910 to 1939, including documents relating to service in China in the 1930s.

6. War diary, or intelligence summary, of the 1st Battalion during the Shanghai area operation of 1932: with appendices. 'Secret'. 27 January–31 March 1932. MS. and typescript.

Photograph album containing photographs of people and views in Cape Town, Singapore, and Yokohama: with manuscript notes. 1865–70. 1 vol.

Officers' confidential letter-book, containing copies of letters written in Yokohama from 13 October 1869 to 14 April 1871, then in Hong Kong from 7 April 1871 to 30 October 1872, then in Singapore (some addressed to Hong Kong) from February 1873 to December 1876, then on the voyage home in 1877. 13 October 1869–June 1896. 1 vol.

Album containing photographs of the regiment in Japan, China, Singapore and Malaya, and England: with manuscript notes. 1 vol.

LIVERPOOL

CITY OF LIVERPOOL PUBLIC LIBRARIES

William Brown Street, Liverpool, 3

BROCKLEBANK PAPERS

A selection of the records of Thos. & Jno. Brockle-bank Ltd., which sent its first ship to the East in 1816, is deposited on permanent loan with the Liverpool City Library: the rest remains in the Company's offices. For a history of the firm based on its records see John Frederic Gibson, *Brocklebanks 1770–1950*, 2 vols., Liverpool, 1953. There is a rough list describing the whole collection, both deposited and non-deposited, and including the following:

I. *Whitehaven records*

A. Accounts.

1(*a*). Ledgers. 1808–20 (deposited); 1820–38; 1839–55.

1(*b*). Yard ledgers, journals, cash books, wages books, &c.

2. Apprentices book. 1809–40 (deposited).

B. Correspondence.

1. Letter-books. 1801–66. 9 vols. (The volume for 1815–17 is deposited: it is the letter-book of Thomas and John Brocklebank and includes correspondence relating to voyages to the East.)

2. Early letters. 1829–64. 1 bundle.

C. Log-books of the *Boyton*, 1811; the *Princess Charlotte*, 1826; and the *Ariel*, 1831.

II. *Liverpool records*

A. Letter-books. 1882–1916. 4 vols.

B. Store book. 1895–1900. 1 vol.

C. Staff

1. Apprentices books. 1820–98. 16 vols.

2. Officers and apprentices books. 1851–67. 3 vols. The volumes for 1851–7 and 1863–7 are deposited: they give name of ship, destination, date of sailing, number of men, and lists of officers and apprentices with their birthplaces, ages, remarks about their service and character, and include voyages to and from China—Hong Kong, Shanghai, Macao, Foo-chow, Whampoa, &c.

3. Officers and engineers books, listed under voyages. 1891–1919. 3 vols.

4. Officers and engineers records. *c.* 1900–33. 1 vol.

5. Engineers only, records. *c.* 1918–33. 1 vol.

III. *Miscellaneous records*

IV. *Maps and plans*: there is a large collection of ships' plans, and miscellaneous maps and plans.

V. *Historical notes*

1. Movements, &c. of Brocklebank ships, taken from Liverpool papers. 1770–1858, 1859–1901. 2 vols.

2. Brocklebank history papers, including extracts and copies. 1 parcel.

3. Letters of Colonel D. A. Bates concerning Brocklebank history. 1 bundle.

4. Notes for a history of Brocklebanks compiled by Captain Jefferson, including extensive lists, extracts from records, correspondence, &c. 1 parcel.

5. Papers concerning the history of Brocklebanks, filed in envelopes marked A–P.

6. News-cuttings. 1906–46. 1 vol.

Log of the *Jumna* (built in 1833 and the last Brockle-bank vessel to trade regularly to Bombay) kept by the captain, Joseph Pinder, on a voyage from Liverpool to Calcutta, June to October 1833, from Calcutta to Liverpool, November 1833 to February

1834, from Liverpool to Canton, May to September 1834, and from Canton towards Liverpool, December 1834 to January 1835. 1 vol. (Kf. 50.)

PAPERS OF MESSRS. WRIGHT, CROSSBY AND CO. (MD 285/1-4)

1. Details of rice cargoes from Rangoon, Bassein, Akyab, Moulmein, Japan (from 1878), Bombay, Saigon, Siam, Arakan. 1876-1904. 1 vol.

2. Table of Japanese weights.

3. Review of the rice trade. 1885.

4. Arrivals of white pepper. 5 September 1892.

LIVERPOOL CHAMBER OF COMMERCE

1 Old Hall Street, Liverpool, 3

The papers of Liverpool Chamber of Commerce contain much information on Liverpool trade with China and Japan. The East India and China Trade Section was inaugurated in 1882.

I. Annual Reports of the Council, including reports of sections. 1851 to present day. Printed.

(1) 1851-63. 1 vol. 758 pp.

(2) 1864-73, including reports on trade with China, and with Japan. 1 vol. 922 pp.

(3) 1874-83, including reports on trade with China, Japan, and Central Asia.

(4) 1886 to present day. 1 volume for each year, with much information on Far Eastern trade.

II. Reports of the Liverpool East India and China Association, 8th to 21st Reports. 1848-62. Printed. Bound in two volumes.

III. Magazines published monthly by the Chamber of Commerce and giving an account of the work being done by the Chamber.

(1) *Chamber of Commerce Magazine*. 1902-18. Vols. 1-17.

(2) *Chamber of Commerce Monthly Journal*. 1919-26. Vols. 18-25.

(3) *The Liverpool Trade Review*. 1928-55. Vols. 26-54.

(4) *The Liverpool Review*. 1956-61. Vols. 55-60.

LIVERPOOL RECORD OFFICE

City Libraries, William Brown Street, Liverpool, L3 8EW

LIVERPOOL: MUSEUM OF JAPANESE ART (708 BOW. NRA 16259)

Set up by James Lord Bowes and opened to the public in 1890, the collections were sold in 1901.

Scrapbook of the Japanese Fancy Fair at Streatlam Towers, Liverpool. 1891.

Committee minutes. 10 December 1890-25 April 1891.

Treasurer's accounts. 1891.

Printed circulars, accounts, &c.

THE UNIVERSITY LIBRARY

Harold Cohen Library, Ashton Street, P.O. Box 123, Liverpool, L69 3DA

See *A guide to the manuscript collections in Liverpool University Library*, Liverpool University Press, 1962.

RATHBONE PAPERS

Family and business papers of the Rathbones of Greenbank, Liverpool. (See *Catalogue of the Rathbone papers in the University Library, Liverpool*, 2 parts, 1959 and 1960.

I. Family papers, including letters to Samuel Greg Rathbone (1823-1903) from his parents and other relatives during his stay in China and India. The letters are mainly to him in China and relate partly to business matters. September 1843-April 1846. (XI. 1. 1-93.) There is also one letter to Samuel Greg Rathbone from his nephew Thomas Ashton Rathbone in Shanghai, dated 1 June 1880. (XI. 1. 100.)

II. Business papers, chiefly private business letters received by Rathbone Bros. & Co. during the latter half of the nineteenth century, with some accounts. Including the following relating to the China trade:

(1) Accounts and miscellaneous papers, 1843-55. *c.* 125 items. (XXI. 3. 1.)

(2) Files of general correspondence, 1844-72, consisting of eight large bundles arranged by years, viz. 1844-6, 1847-8, 1849, 1850, 1851, 1852-4, 1855-7, 1858-72. XXI. 3. 2-9.)

(3) Letter-book containing copies of letters written by S. G. Rathbone in Canton: the letters are addressed to Wm. Rathbone & Co., Liverpool, Thomas Moncrieff, Messrs. Rathbone, Worthington & Co. (Shanghai), and others. 1850. 318 ff. (ff. 198-237 blank). (XXI. 3. 10.)

(4) File of correspondence and papers relating to Thomas Moncrieff's withdrawal from Rathbone, Worthington & Co., the branch house in China of Rathbone, Bros. & Co. 1851-2. (XXI. 3. 11.)

MAIDSTONE

MAIDSTONE MUSEUM

Faith Street, Maidstone

Annotated catalogue by Henry Marsham of Japanese pottery presented by him to Maidstone Museum, with a letter to the curator, dated Kyoto, 18 February 1906.

KENT ARCHIVES OFFICE

County Hall, Maidstone, ME14 1XQ1 XH

Letter from Richard Cock, Firando, to Sir Thomas Wilson: description of places visited in Japan and of the new Emperor; curtailment of privileges of foreigners as a result of the activity of Jesuits. 1618–19, 1620. (Sackville MSS., Cranfield, p. 395; p. 424.)

Papers relating to China Expedition. 1857–60. (O. 13–15.)

RECORDS OF THE ROYAL WEST KENT REGIMENT, 1765–1961. (NRA 15264)
Commonplace book of the 8th Battalion, consisting principally of an account of work with Chinese coolies engaged on transport duties in France during the First World War. *c.* 1914. (B8/Z1.)

MANCHESTER

CENTRAL LIBRARY

St. Peter's Square, Manchester, M2 5PD

ARCHIVES OF THE MANCHESTER CHAMBER OF COMMERCE. (1794–1945.) 130 vols.
(M8/1–M8/7. For permission to consult these papers application should be made in writing to the Secretary of the Chamber of Commerce, Manchester.)

A. Proceedings of the Manchester Chamber of Commerce, including information on trade with China and Japan. 1821–1926. 17 vols. (M8/2/1–17.)

B. Minutes of Committee of the Manchester Chamber of Commerce. 1889–1926. 12 vols. (M8/3/1–12.)

C. Minutes of Sectional Committees. 1890–1926. 34 vols.
(M8/4/1–34). See especially the following volumes:
9. Minutes of the Executive Committee, 1890–1, and of the Chemical Sectional Committee, 1891–1901.

10 and 11. Minutes of the Chemical Sectional Committee. 1901–26. 2 vols.

12. Minutes of the China and Far East Section. 1916–26.

14 and 15. Minutes of the Engineering and Metal Sectional Committee. 1901–26. 2 vols.

17. Minutes of the Grey Cloth Section. 1916–26.

18. Minutes of the Home and Colonial Committee. 1910–26.

23. Minutes of the Leather Sectional Committee. 1909–25.

24 and 25. Minutes of the Produce Sectional Committee. 1894–1926. 2 vols.

28 and 29. Minutes of the Testing House Management Committee. 1899–1926. 2 vols.

30. Minutes of the Textile Exports Shipping Committee. 1918.

31–3. Minutes of the Yarn Sectional Committee. 1890–1926. 2 vols.

34. Minutes of the Manchester Yarn Contract Conference. 1896–1913.

D. Minutes of the Board of Directors, of Committees, and of Sections. 1927–45. 53 vols. (M8/5/1–53.)

These volumes are arranged chronologically, the minutes of the various sections not being bound together as they are in M8/4 above. They all contain much information (reports, &c.) on trade with the Far East. Included among the sections are the following:

Chemical and Allied Trades Section
China and Far East Section
Engineering and Metals Section
Finishing and Allied Trades Section
Furnishing Fabrics Section
Garment Manufacturers Section
General Importers and Exporters Section
Hosiery and Knitwear Section
Rayon Trade Section
Yarn Section
Japanese Competition. 1933 and 1934. (M8/5/18 and 22.)

E. Minute books of the Manchester Association of Importers and Exporters, including information on Far East trade. 1907–35. 11 vols. (M8/6/1–11.)

F. Minutes of the Manchester Commercial Association. 1845–58. (M8/7/1.)

Papers of George Robinson and Company of Manchester, a cotton firm which exported goods to the East. 1839–1880. (MS. F. 382. 2. R. 1.)

1. Contract book. 1847–55.

2. Cash book. 1847–52.

3. Petty cash books. 1847–79. 3 vols.

4. Stock book. 1848–73.

5. Wages book. 1865–76.

6. A volume listing exports of yarns, plain and coloured cottons, to various places in the East, including Shanghai, Hong Kong, and Japan. c. 1839–80.

'Cotton Fabrics'. A book of references for those who are engaged in the cotton industry, by Walter Hough, being a description of fabrics, with samples affixed, and including notes as to where the fabrics are shipped: this includes all parts of Asia. 1922. Typescript. 83 ff. and index. (B.R. 677. 1. H. 37.)

MANCHESTER REGIMENT PAPERS

The 1st Battalion The Manchester Regiment, formerly the 63rd Regiment of Foot, was raised in 1758 and has served in many parts of the world. Members of the Battalion were prisoners of the Japanese for three years, after the fall of Singapore, from 1942 to 1945. There is a large collection of records, both printed and manuscript, and many photographs, maps, drawings, newspaper cuttings, and other relics, formerly kept in the regimental museum at Ashton-under-Lyne. Among the manuscript records are the following:

Letter from F. G. Taylor in Shanghai to Colonel H. L. James. 27 July 1898. (609.)

Records of service

1. War diaries, and various documents, 1939–45.

2. War diaries and miscellaneous correspondence relating to the 1st Battalion. Singapore, 1942.

Account of the 1st Battalion. 1942–5.

Various documents and relics relating to prisoners of war of the Japanese. 1942–5.

Diary written by Major Hyde while a prisoner of war of the Japanese: with sundry documents. July 1942–December 1943. (1744.)

THE JOHN RYLANDS UNIVERSITY LIBRARY OF MANCHESTER

Manuscript Department, Oxford Road, Manchester, M13 9PP

The English manuscripts in the John Rylands Library have been described in a series of *Handlists* published between 1928 and 1951. See *Publications of the John Rylands Library* (Manchester 1956) and supplementary cyclostyled lists (to date). Accessions are noted in the *Bulletin of the John Rylands Library*.

MELVILLE PAPERS

Calendars of letters from China, St. Helena, and the Cape of Good Hope, in 'Miscellaneous Correspondence: Calendars and Indexes, I.' 18th–19th centuries. 100 ff. (Eng. MS. 697.)

BOWRING PAPERS (Eng. MSS. 1228–34. See G. F. Bartle, *Sir John Bowring and the 'Arrow' War in China*, Manchester, 1961, and *Sir John Bowring and the Chinese and Siamese commercial treaties*, Manchester, 1962.)

Personal and political correspondence of Sir John Bowring (1792–1872) and his family, including the following:

1. Letters from Sir John Bowring to his son Edgar A. Bowring at the Board of Trade, mainly concerning political and commercial affairs in the Far East at the time when Sir John was Consul at Canton, Plenipotentiary to China, and, from 1854, Governor of Hong Kong and Chief Superintendent of Trade. February 1849–May 1859. 239 items.

2. Correspondence of Sir John Bowring with his son Frederick H. Bowring at Trinity College, Cambridge, and Lincoln's Inn, London. Nos. 1–230 are letters from Sir John, 1837–58 (nos. 157–230 being from the Far East): and nos. 231–95 are letters from Frederick to Sir John. 1837–64. 295 items.

3. Miscellaneous papers of Sir John Bowring including letters to his wife, 1818–43 (nos. 1–11); letters and papers addressed to Sir John, the bulk relating to his Governorship of Hong Kong (nos. 12–234, nos. 12–181 being bound in one volume); and miscellaneous printed papers, 1844–77 (nos. 235–62). 1818–77. 262 items.

4. Correspondence of Frederick H. Bowring, consisting mainly of letters to members of his family. 1828–94. 262 items.

5. Diaries of Frederick H. Bowring. 1845–74, *passim*. 118 ff.

6. Miscellaneous letters to Edgar Alfred Bowring, mainly concerning the Shanghai duty question, from various correspondents, including five from Joseph Hume, 1854–5 (nos. 10–14). 1854–8. 18 items.

SPRING RICE PAPERS

Letters from Persia and Japan exchanged between Cecil and Stephen Spring Rice and Julia, Stephen's wife. 1873–1902. (Eng. MS. 1188.)

BROMLEY DAVENPORT MUNIMENTS

Letters of John Francis Campbell of Islay, mainly to his mother, from America, Japan, China, Hong Kong, Malaya, Java, and Ceylon. 1 vol.

'Copy Book' of Thomas Ashton & Sons, containing triplicates of eighteen business letters, one to Shanghai. 1850–1. 35 ff. (Eng. MS. 870.)

NEWCASTLE UPON TYNE

CITY LIBRARIES

Central Library, P.O. Box 1MC, Newcastle upon Tyne, NE99 1MC

SIR W. G. ARMSTRONG & CO. PAPERS. (Persons using this material must give an undertaking not to publish any information without first obtaining the approval of the Newcastle upon Tyne branch of the Bank of England.)

Correspondence and papers relating to the original Armstrong Company, and more particularly to the company of Armstrong, Whitworth. Armstrong guns were used in China and Japan, and between 1897 and 1914 foreign subsidiaries were created in a number of countries including Japan. This collection includes committee minutes, registers, ledgers, journals, cash books, and reports. See J. D. Scott, *Vickers: a history*, London 1962, which is equally a history of Sir W. G. Armstrong, Whitworth & Co. 1847–1949.

Schedule A

1–5. Share registers. 153 loose-leaf folders, 70 bound volumes.

Schedule B

1. Cash book. 1847–52.

2–15. Papers relating to stock, stockholders, insurance, &c.

16–26. Papers relating to accidents, compensation, &c.

27. Balance books. 1883–1912. 5 vols.

28. Various general books of accounts. 1920–48. 34 vols.

Schedule C

1–3. Annual reports. 1883–1943. 3 parcels.

4–7. Final accounts. 1925–43. 23 vols.

8. Minutes of meetings of shareholders. 1882–1949. 2 vols.

9–10. Reports to the Directors by J. Frater Taylor and Sir Gilbert Garnsey. 1926. 1 vol. and 2 files.

11–13. Reports and papers relating to Company Meetings. 1883–1943. 2 parcels, 1 file.

14–26. Papers relating to the financial affairs of the Company, and other internal matters.

27. Board agenda. 1882–1924. 5 vols.

28. Minutes. 1882–96. 2 vols.

29. Minutes. 1896–1929. 5 vols.

30. Minutes. 1929–43. 2 vols.

31. Minute book index. 3 vols.

32. Shareholders' and Directors' Attendance Books. 1883–1940. 3 vols.

33. Executive Committee minutes. 1912–33. 9 vols. and 1 loose-leaf binder.

34. Minutes of various committees. 1897–1935. 11 vols. and 4 loose-leaf binders.

35–9. Private journals and ledgers. 1847–1939. 14 vols.

40. Private minutes and papers. 1910–29. 1 vol.

41–4. Papers relating to salaries. 6 vols.

45. List of Directors.

46. Register of Directors or Managers. 2 vols.

47. Register of agreements, referring back to 1885. 1913–29. 2 vols.

48. Register of documents sealed by order of the Board. 1882–1947. 4 vols.

49 and 50. Old agreements. 4 parcels.

51. Packets of commercial and other agreements from about 1860 onwards. 1 tin box.

52–7. Correspondence, agreements, deeds, and other papers relating to the home affairs of the Company.

UNIVERSITY OF NEWCASTLE UPON TYNE

The University Library, Queen Victoria Road, Newcastle upon Tyne, NE1 7RU

TREVELYAN OF WALLINGTON MSS.

A. Elliot and G. Williams, *Catalogue of the papers of Sir Charles Edward Trevelyan, Bt. (1807–1886)*. Newcastle University Library, 1972. (NRA 12238.)

Memoranda by Sir C. E. Trevelyan and G. Arbuthnot on the legal valuation of the dollar at Hong Kong. 2 printed items. (CET 47.)

A. Elliot and G. Williams, *Catalogue of the papers of Sir Charles Philips Trevelyan, Bt. (1870–1958)*. Newcastle University Library, 1973. (NRA 12238.)

References to China in the index lead back to the following 'Record' entries:

Manuscript notes for speeches. 1925. (Record 117.)

Letters to and from. 1927. (Record 124.)

Letters to and from. 1928. (Record 125.)

Manuscript notes for speeches on Russia and China. 6 items. (Record 177.)

RUNCIMAN OF DOXFORD PAPERS

A. Elliot and G. Williams, *Catalogue of the papers of Walter Runciman, 1st Viscount Runciman of Doxford*

(1870–1949). Reproduced for Newcastle University Library by the Royal Commission on Historical Manuscripts, 1973.

References to China and Chinese labour will be found in the index, leading back to the following sections:

Letters and papers, mainly political. 59 items. 1904. (WR 9.)

Cabinet papers about Japan and China, including draft of treaty of commerce and navigation between Japan and the U.K. 1911. 24 items. (WR 55.)

Letters, mainly political. 144 items. (WR 177.)

Letters about China. 1932–9. 9 items. (WR 263.)

Letters, mainly political. 1934. 60 items. (WR 272.)

Press-cuttings about the Dewsbury by-election. April–May 1908. 1 vol. (WR 323.)

TYNE AND WEAR COUNTY RECORD OFFICE

109 Pilgrim Street, Newcastle upon Tyne, NE1 6QF

RENDEL PAPERS

1. Letters of Sir W. G. Armstrong & Co., consisting of about 1,500 reports, accounts, and letters, mostly relating to breakwaters and guns, largely the correspondence of G. W. Rendel, manager of the Ordnance Works at Elswick, and Stuart, later Lord Rendel. The firm had business dealings throughout the world, including China and Korea, and among the correspondence are letters from China, 1882–3. 1856–83. 1 box.

2. Business correspondence and papers of W. G. Armstrong and Stuart Rendel. This is a very large collection, not yet (1963) catalogued, consisting of twenty-six foolscap drawers of papers, and nine boxes of correspondence, &c. There are letters and papers relating to business dealings with China and Japan, including one box labelled 'China' which contains correspondence and papers of J. D. Campbell concerning gun-boats for China, 1878–82.

NORTHUMBERLAND COUNTY RECORD OFFICE

Melton Park, Gosforth, Newcastle upon Tyne, NE3 5QX

Large bundle of manuscript extracts from various histories and accounts of travellers, with notes on historical, geographical, and literary subjects: they relate to various parts of the world, including China and Japan, and were probably made by Sir John

E. Swinburne. (Swinburne (Capheaton) MSS. ZSw 643.)

Letters from Thomas Wallace (created Baron Wallace of Knaresdale, 1828), including one about the first shipment of tea grown in India and its effects on British relations with China (11 December). January–December 1838. (Middleton (Belsay) MSS. ZMI/S 77/11/1–22.)

The Brooks collection of autographs, containing letters written by many famous people, some having connections with the Far East. There is an index available, arranged by author. (Society of Antiquaries Papers.)

THE ROYAL NORTHUMBERLAND FUSILIERS

Fenham Barracks, Newcastle upon Tyne, 2

The Royal Northumberland Fusiliers, 'The Fifth', was raised in 1674 as 'The Irish Regiment' later becoming the Fifth Regiment of Foot, and in 1836, The Fifth or Northumberland Fusiliers. The regiment has served in many campaigns, including the Korean War in 1950 and 1951 followed by service in Hong Kong. The regimental museum has a large collection of the records of the regiment, both manuscript and printed, and many albums of photographs and loose photographs. The following records relate to service in the Far East:

The Circle News: Journal of the 29th Independent Brigade Group Korea, beginning with No. 1, 26 November 1950 and ending with No. 307, 20 September 1951. Some copies are missing. 1950–1. (No. 145.)

Roll of Honour, The Royal Northumberland Fusiliers, including the Korean War. 1939–51. (No. 131.)

Box file containing maps and other documents including the script of a B.B.C. broadcast in 1952 about the regiment including its exploits in the Korean War. (Box File 217.)

NEWTON LE WILLOWS

THE ENGLISH ELECTRIC COMPANY LIMITED

Vulcan Works, Newton le Willows, Lancashire

(For permission to consult these papers apply in writing to the Personnel and Education Officer at the above address.)

Papers of The Vulcan Foundry Ltd., builders of locomotives, some of which were exported to Japan from 1871.

1. List of all locomotives built. A modern compilation.

2. Cost ledgers, detailing the costs of building the locomotives. 1844–1930. 2 vols.

3. Letter-books, containing copies of out-letters. 1864–1955. 344 vols. (complete).

NORTHALLERTON

NORTH RIDING COUNTY RECORD OFFICE

County Hall, Northallerton, DL7 8SG

Album of photographs, British Army in Tibet. *c.* 1906. (2FW 16, 3.)

ZETLAND (DUNDAS) ARCHIVE

Papers of Sir Lawrence Dundas deposited by the Marquess of Zetland, July 1965. 1972. (NRA 16269/1.)

Detailed estimate of the value of the China tea trade to the East India Company. n.d. (X1/21/24.)

NORTHAMPTON

NORTHAMPTONSHIRE RECORD OFFICE

Delapré Abbey, Northampton, NN4 9AW

FITZWILLIAM (MILTON) MSS. Papers of Edmund Burke (1729–97), statesman. (NRA 4120.) Including: Account of population, revenues, &c. of China in the seventeenth century. *French.* (A. XXV. 39.)

Extract of a General Letter of the supercargoes at Canton to the Court of Directors. 28 December 1782. (A. XXV. 101.)

Account of dividends from ships from China, 1707. (Stopford Sackville 3447.)

DRYDEN (CANONS ASHBY) COLLECTION

Letter from John Slade in Canton to Sir Henry Dryden, describing a brush with the Chinese, 1822. (D/C. A. 377.)

NORWICH

NORFOLK RECORD OFFICE

Central Library, Norwich, NR2 1NJ

Letter from Edward Stacy at Hong Kong to his sisters at Norwich about the breaking up of the family through religion. 29 November 1844. (MS. 20628. 164 X 1.)

NOTTINGHAM

CITY OF NOTTINGHAM PUBLIC LIBRARIES

Nottingham, NG1 4BT

Author's typescript, with manuscript corrections, of *The Red Army of China* by Edgar O'Ballance, London, 1962. *c.* 1962. 345 ff.

Helen McAlpine, Japanese tales and legends, translations for a book. [*c.* 1955?] (M. 10,788.)

NOTTINGHAMSHIRE RECORD OFFICE

County House, High Pavement, Nottingham, NG1 1HR

See P. A. Kennedy, *Guide to the Nottinghamshire County Records Office*, 1960.

BRISTOWE PAPERS

Nine letters of Orlando Bridgman to his mother, Lady Selina Bridgman, and his sister Selina while on service in China at the time of the Opium War. Mainly personal, with some comments on events and surroundings. 1842–3. (DD. BB 113/31–39.)

Letter of H. K. Davenport, *The Portsmouth*, Hong Kong, to John Saville Lumley. 1857. (DDSR 226/16/73.)

Three journals of the Revd. Charles Craven of journeys to Calcutta, China, and England. 1825–8. (held by owner, Mr. R. A. Craven Smith Milner of Hockerton Manor, who deposited other papers on 21 January 1959, NRA 6898.)

REGIMENTAL HEADQUARTERS THE SHERWOOD FORESTERS (NOTTINGHAMSHIRE AND DERBYSHIRE REGIMENT)

Triumph Road, Lenton, Nottingham

Digest of service the 95th Regiment, 1823–82, including service in China, 1847–50.

MANUSCRIPTS DEPARTMENT UNIVERSITY OF NOTTINGHAM LIBRARY

University Park, Nottingham, NG7 2RD

PORTLAND COLLECTION (NRA 7628)

Notes on the Chinese marks on some of the china-ware of the 2nd Duchess of Portland. 18th century. (Pw E 77.)

Letter to Robert Harley from George Cornwall in Canton: thanks for favours received. 1704. (Pw 2 Hy/537.)

Journal of the Embassy to China. 1792–4. (Pw V/131.)

Papers of Lord William Henry Cavendish Bentinck (1774–1839), Governor-General of India 1827–35. Including:

(a) Memoranda on dissolution of commercial establishment in China. 1833. (Pw Jf 2701.)

(b) Memorandum to Select Committee on supra-cargoes at Canton. 1833. (Pw Jf 2702.)

Papers of Lord William George Frederick Bentinck (1802–48). Including:

(a) Letter from L. H. Wray enclosing notes on the emigration of Chinese labourers from China to the British West Indies. 7 December 1847. (Pw L 262, 263.)

NEWCASTLE MSS. Papers of Henry Pelham Clinton, 5th Duke of Newcastle (1811–64, Secretary of State for the Colonial and War Departments 1852–4, and for the War Department 1854–5, Secretary of State for the Colonies 1859–64. (NRA 7411.)

Political papers, Colonial Office (1852–4) and War Department (1854–5). (Ne. C. 9552–10884.) Including:

1. Letter-book (incomplete): private letters, Colonial Department, including Hong Kong. 1852–4. (Ne. C. 9555.)

2. Miscellaneous papers, memoranda concerning military establishments, including Hong Kong. c. 1853–4. (Ne. C. 9658–65.)

3. Colonial Office (a) notebook of official appoint-ments made by the Duke of Newcastle; (b) register of persons seeking employment in the Colonial service. 1853–4. (Ne. C. 9684.)

4. Correspondence with Prince Albert and Queen Victoria. 1853–5. (Ne. C. 9685–9786.)

Political papers, Colonial Office. (1859–64). (Ne. C. 10885–11653.) Including:

1. Private letter-books, series B. (B2. B3. B4. B5.) containing copies of letters to Colonial Governors. 1860–4. (Ne. C. 10885–8.)

2. Private letter-books, series C. (C. C2. C3.) containing copies of letters to miscellaneous persons, including Ministers. 1859–64. (Ne. C. 10889–91.)

3. Papers concerning Hong Kong and China, including letter from Lord Grey, information from Hong Kong about movements of Russians and Chinese, &c. 1859–63. (Ne. C. 11102–6.)

4. Papers concerning military expedition to China, especially relating to native regiments from India. 1860. (Ne. C. 11107–20.)

5. Albums of photographs of Hong Kong and Canton. 1860. (Ne. C. 11121–2.)

OXFORD

BODLEIAN LIBRARY

Oxford, OX1 3BG

There are two series of printed catalogues of manuscripts in the Bodleian Library covering collections acquired before the end of 1915. Accessions since 1915 are described in typescript catalogues available in the Library and listed in the Library's *Annual report*. The printed catalogues are as follows:

1. The Quarto Series: the volumes covering MSS. Ashmole, and Rawlinson A–D, contain material relevant to this survey, viz.:

A descriptive, analytical, and critical catalogue of the manuscripts bequeathed unto the University of Oxford by Elias Ashmole, compiled by William H. Black (Oxford, 1845).

Catalogi codicum manuscriptorum Bibliothecae Bodleianae, vol. v, parts 1–5, compiled by William D. Macray (Oxford, 1862–1900).

2. *A summary catalogue of western manuscripts in the Bodleian Library at Oxford* (Oxford, 1895–1953).

This covers collections (other than those described in the Quarto Catalogues) which were acquired before the end of 1915.

It should be noted that manuscripts with shelfmarks which include the word 'dep.' (either alone or in combination with other words, e.g. 'MSS. Clarendon dep.') are not the property of the Library but have been placed there on revocable deposit.

'Itinerarium Mundii, that is a memoriall . . . of certaine voiages . . . passed . . . into some parts of . . . China . . . ettc., to the south and east parts of the world . . .', 1611 to 1639, by Peter Mundy. Illustrated with maps and pen and ink sketches. Followed by an appendix which includes (at f. 209) 'Of Sir Wm. Courteene's designe, or voiage to China', 1636'. (MS. Rawl. A. 315. Mundy's Itinerary has been printed by the Hakluyt Society: series 2, nos. 17, 35, 45, 46, 55, 70; 1907–36.)

The original log-book of William Adams made during four voyages to Japan, Siam, and Cochin China. 1614–19. ii+81 ff. (MS. Savile 48. see C. J. Purnell, ed., *The Log Book of William Adams*, 1916.)

Copy of a report of the proceedings of the fleet sent home by the *Katherine* from Macao. 19 December 1637. (MS. Rawl. A. 299, f. 218.)

Maps of the coasts and islands in the Chinese and Indian seas, including Hainan and Tonquin, both by John Blaew of Amsterdam, drawn in the years 1663–9. (Corpus Christi deposit, MS. CCCXCII. See Henry O. Coxe, *Catalogus Codicum MSS. qui in Collegiis Aulisque Oxoniensibus hodie adservantur*, vol. ii, 1852.)

'A relation of a voyage for the discovery of a passage by the north-east to Japan and China; performed in his majesties shipp the Speedwell, and Prosperous pinck, anno Domini 1676 . . . by capt. John Wood.' (MS. Rawl. A. 467. The voyage was printed in 1694 and again in 1711 with that of Sir John Narborough and others.)

Transcript [by Samuel Pepys] of Captain John Wood's journal of his voyage in H.M.S. *Speedwell* 'bound for the discovery of a passage to the East Indies by the north-east, sayleing about Nova Zembla and Tartary, and soe to Japan, 1676.' The last page has been cut out. (MS. Rawl. C. 967, f. 1. Printed with the voyages of Narbrough, Tasman, and Marten, London, 1694 and 1711.)

Table of coins current in various parts of the world including Japan, with their weights and values; dated at Fort St. George, 1 January 1680 (MS. Rawl. C. 841, f. 1.)

'Grammatica Mallayo-Anglica. The Malayan Grammar, composed . . . 1682', with appendix including (pp. 33–4, 55–7): Chinese numeral words and figures from 1 to 1,000,000; and a short Anglo-Chinese vocabulary. (MS. Ashmole 1808.)

Copy of a letter from J. Dolben, merchant at Canton, 11 November 1695, included among papers relating to the East India Company. (MS. Rawl. A. 302, f. 126.)

'A breefe Catalogue or Illust[ratio]n of the . . . Revenewes of all the Nobles of Japon, the Emperour and his sonne . . . wᵗʰ somme few other petty Lordes, rated by the numbers of cokes of ryce h[ereafte]r described: every cokees of ryce being in value 7ˢ 6ᵈ in sterling money; the number of shires whereunto Japon is divided being 66.' n.d. (MS. Ashmole 1787. III, f. 99a.)

A collection of small charts of sea ports and coasts of islands including: (at f. 29) sketch of the town of Macao in China as seen from the sea; (at f. 30) sketch of the mouth of the Chin-cheu river in China, showing the situation of Amoy, Quemoy, and various islands and other towns. 17th century. (MS. Rawl. D. 813.)

SHERARD MSS. (MSS. Sherard 1–476, NRA 6305)

Water-colours of Japanese plants, with inscriptions in Dutch by N. Witsen, 1700. Book-plate 'E. lib. J. Sibthorp'. ii+181, ii+125, ii+404 ff. (MSS. Sherard 253–5.)

Water-colours of Chinese plants. Book-plate 'E. Bibl. Sherard.' i+104, i+104, i+151 ff. (MSS. Sherard 256–8.)

Twelve folded maps of parts of the Indian Ocean and Malaysia, including: (*e*) Cochin China, Formosa, Borneo, c. 1700, *English*; (*f*) north-west Formosa and a long stretch of the Chinese coast opposite, by John Thornton, 1701; (*g*) as *f*, late 17th century, *Dutch*; (*h*) Canton and the river, coast, and islands in the neighbourhood, Dutch notes but made by Samuel Thornton, 1707. (MS. maps Indian Ocean a. 1, ff. 5, 6, 7, 8.)

Papers relating to the East India Company, including (at f. 83) the case of Adam Cocley on behalf of his son, William Cocley, a supercargo in China, respecting chinaware, &c. bought by him (printed); also (at f. 144) directions about purchasing some jars, cups, &c. in China, with rough sketches of patterns. 17th–18th centuries. (MS. Rawl. A. 303.)

Letter from Antonio Barros, missionary in Peking, to padre Alex. Barros. 18 September 1701. *Spanish*. (MS. Rawl. A. 289, f. 276.)

Original letters, reports, &c., relating to Jesuit missionary work in China in 1701. The reports are signed by Giraldin Figeralx, Bouuet de la Touche, Martineau, and Boizard, all in Canton, Antonio de Barros in Peking, Carlos de Rezenda, ? in Chintimfu, and Ant. Beauvollier. (MS. Add. D. 74.)

Letter from Francis Terne, engaged in the trade with China, to his brother [?-in-law, Dr. Edward Browne who married a daughter of Christopher Terne, M.D.], giving a full account of the island of Amoy, the manners of the Chinese, &c.; dated 'off Anicugo', 25 April 1703. (MS. Rawl. D. 391, ff. 95–8.)

'Au nom de Dueu soit bien commance de la travercé de la Chine pour a ler [aller] en France et autre part, dans le vaisseau La rainne Despagne, commandé par monsieur Brunet, armé de 24p. de canon, 100 homme dequipage', November 1713–January 1714. Below the above title is written in another hand, 'A monsieur Hardancour, directeur general de compagnie Royale des Inde, en son autel [hôtel] ru Neuve St. Eustache, Paris.' On the outside cover of the volume is written 'Journal de la Chine, appartien a Pierre Gauchet'. (MS. Rawl. D. 592, f. 1.)

Journal of a voyage in the ship *Tounshend* through the Ladrones towards Macao, 18 June 1717 to 11 January 1718. (MS. Rawl. C. 869.)

Journal of a voyage in the ship *Bridgewater*, Edward Wilson, commander, to China and homewards, kept by Nicholas Jackson. 17 December 1719–29 August 1721. (MS. Rawl. A. 324.)

Correspondence and miscellaneous papers of Philip Henry Zollman, some relating to the Japanese manuscripts of Dr. E. Kaempfer, &c. *c.* 1723–31. (MS. Rawl. D. 871. Zollman Papers vol. iii.)

Log-book kept on board the ship *St. Joseph*, Charles Pike, commander, on a voyage from Canton homewards. 30 November 1723–21 May 1724. (MS. Rawl. C. 970.)

Letters to and from John Tucker, Member of Parliament, 1701–79, comprising, *a* (f. 1), correspondence prior to his voyage to China with the East India Company, 1725, and *b* (f. 36), correspondence 1728–37, including some letters from his father and brother. (MS. Don. b. 18, NRA 18512.)

Captain Patrick Lawson's account book of trading in Canton, October–December 1778, and in Madras, Malacca, and China, May–August 1778. ii+30 ff. (MS. Eng. hist. c. 331.)

Description of the chief ports and commercial cities in Arabia, East India, Sumatra, Malacca, Siam, and China, from Cape 'Russelgate', i.e. Ras-al-had, to Nanking and Amoy; headed 'Memoirs of East India'. 18th century. (MS. Rawl. A. 334. f. 72.)

'Les observations de Monsr. d'Haucarville sur le premier volume du Voyage aux Indes Orientales et à la Chine par Mr. Sonnerat . . .' (MS. Add. C. 204, p. 365.) 18th century?

Queries by Francis Douce about the Chinese language, with answers (1) in Portuguese by father Marchini, (2) translated into French by the abbé Devay. A note by Douce, dated 1805, states that a Mr. Lance forwarded the queries to China. *c.* 1800. (MS. Douce 75.)

CLARENDON DEPOSIT (MSS. Clar. dep. NRA 6302)

Papers of George William Frederick Villiers, 4th Earl of Clarendon (1800–70), Foreign Secretary, 1853–8, 1865–6, and 1868–70. *c.* 1840–70.

I. Papers as Foreign Secretary

1. In-letters, 1853–8, 1861–6. (MSS. Clar. dep. c. 1–104.) There is material relating to China, 1854–8, in c. 19, c. 37, c. 57, c. 71, and c. 85.

2. Letter-books. Copies of out-letters. 1853–8, 1865–6, 1868–9. (MSS. Clar. dep. c. 125–49.)

3. Papers printed for the use of the Foreign Office. 1848–58. (MSS. Clar. dep. c. 246–78.) Including (in c. 274): Papers relating to the proceedings of Her Majesty's naval forces at Canton, October–December 1856. 5 January 1857.

4. Correspondence as Foreign Secretary, 1868–70. (MSS. Clar. dep. c. 474–510.) There is a letter from Sir Rutherford Alcock in Peking, 27 February 1869, and a dispatch from Sir Harry Parkes, at Yedo, 20 June 1869 (in c. 490); also a letter from Colonel Showers to Clarendon about affairs in China, 8 April 1870 (in c. 510).

II. General correspondence and miscellaneous papers, 1820–70. (MSS. Clar. dep. c. 520–61.) Including:

(*a*) Memorandum on the opium trade. 26 May 1840. (c. 555/6.)

(*b*) Part of a letter in Clarendon's hand to —? on the new Government's attitude to China. [1868.] (c. 555/33.)

(*c*) Student interpreters on China and Japan. 1861. (c. 558, folder 10.)

(*d*) Letters from Sir John Bowring to Clarendon, mostly written from the Far East. 1855–9, 1869. (c. 559, folder 1.)

(*e*) Two letters from Lord Elgin to Clarendon. 22 May 1858, 14 July 1858. (c. 559, in folders 2 and 3.)

Letters to his wife of Sir Robert Hart, Inspector-General of the Chinese customs. 1866–1908. (MSS. Eng. lett. c. 304, d. 319–27, e. 124–7; Eng. misc. b. 108–9, c. 530–1.)

Journal of James Legge, later first Professor of Chinese at Oxford, with a list of certain expenses incurred in 1869. 1846–7. (MS. Eng. misc. e. 556.)

Letters from Gother F. Mann (1817–81) from China to his wife Margaret in Guernsey. 1857–62. (NRA 14156, Courtney-Mann MSS., 37/1–103.)

'Translations of documents found in the palace of Yuen Ming Yuen [at Peking] on the 8th October 1860', consisting of seven petitions to the Emperor of China, 26 August–13 September 1860, on the subject of his leaving the capital. The translations are in the hand of Major-General Gibbes Rigaud, who contributes a short general account of the campaign in China, dated 27 January 1861. (MS. Eng. hist. c. 2.)

Papers relating to the foundation of the Professorship of Chinese at Oxford and its first holder, James Legge, 1863–94. (MS. Top. Oxon. c. 528.)

Draft address of Richard Congreve, positivist, to the Chinese Ambassador. [1877.] (MS. Eng. lett. c. 185. I, f. 100.)

H. A. L. FISHER PAPERS. Papers of H. A. L. Fisher (1865–1940), statesman and historian.

1. Miscellaneous letters to Fisher grouped alphabetically. 1894–1940. (Boxes 1–2.)

2. Letters to Fisher 'on special occasions on special subjects from special people.' (Box 3.)

3. Copies of letters from Fisher. 1926–40. (Box 4.)

4. Letters from Fisher to his wife, 1904, 1907–40, together with (in box 6) packets of letters written while abroad. (Boxes 5–6.)

5. Letters from Fisher to Gilbert and Lady M. Murray. 1890–1939. (Box 7.)

6. Papers relating to various subjects, including Chinese Universities Relief Committee. (Box 29.)

ASQUITH PAPERS. Papers of Herbert Henry Asquith, 1st Earl of Asquith and Oxford (1852–1928), Home Secretary, 1895–1905, Chancellor of the Exchequer, 1905–8, Prime Minister, 1908–16, &c. (MSS. Asquith. NRA 12685.)

I. Correspondence

1. Royal Correspondence: letters to Asquith or to his (or Sir Henry Campbell Bannerman's) private secretaries, from Edward VII and George V, or their private secretaries. 1907–16. (MSS. Asquith 1–4.)

2. Cabinet letters: copies of Asquith's Cabinet letters to the King. 1908–16. (MSS. Asquith 5–8.)

3. Miscellaneous correspondence: letters to Asquith or to his private secretaries. 1891–1928. (MSS. Asquith 9–18.)

II. Miscellaneous letters, memoranda, &c. including:

1. 'Memo. as to the advisability of receiving a Deputation on the Opium question from the Colonial point of view.' [? October 1910.] (MS. Asquith 23. f. 304.)

Memorandum signed by Asquith, headed 'Ceding of territory' and endorsed 'China 1898'. (MS. Asquith 19. f. 37.)

MONK BRETTON PAPERS. (Dep. Monk Bretton. NRA 9224)

Papers of John William Dodson, 2nd Baron Monk Bretton (1869–1933), assistant private secretary to the Foreign Secretary, 1898–1900, private Secretary to the Colonial Secretary, 1900–3, &c. (Boxes 81–115.) Including:

1. Foreign Office and Colonial Office correspondence. 1895–1904. (Box 85.)

2. Papers relating to Australia, New Zealand, the Pacific, and Far East, 1895–1904, including: (h) references to command papers, &c. concerning Hong Kong, Wei-Hai-Wei, and other parts; (i) papers, manuscript and printed, relating to Wei-Hai-Wei, 1899–1903. (Box 98.)

3. Printed Colonial Office correspondence relating to Wei-Hai-Wei. 1901–2. (Box 102.)

BRYCE PAPERS. Papers of James Bryce, Viscount Bryce (1838–1922), jurist, historian, and statesman. (NRA 6716.)

Letters re bad behaviour of Sikhs and Sepoys in China. 1901. (MS. Bryce 16, English 160–2.)

See also index to the Calendar of papers relating to the United States of America by D. S. Porter (part of NRA 6716) S.vv. China, Japan, &c.

Letters from Goldwin Smith on possible immigration of Japanese to Canada. 1907. (MS. Boyce 17, English 103, 108.)

NATHAN PAPERS. Papers of Sir Matthew Nathan (1862–1939), soldier, colonial administrator &c., Governor of Hong Kong, 1903–7. (MSS. Nathan. NRA 8981. These papers are arranged chronologically in sections corresponding to Nathan's career. The section relating specifically to the Governorship of Hong Kong is in Rhodes House (q.v.), but the diaries and general correspondence noted below also cover the period.)

1. Diaries. 1881–1939. (MSS. Nathan 1–75.)

2. Private correspondence. 1868–1939. (MSS. Nathan 102–213.) Including: letters from Nathan to his mother, 1880–1909 (102–20); selected letters of congratulation including Hong Kong, 1903. (140.)

GILBERT MURRAY PAPERS. Letters, papers, &c. of Gilbert Murray (1866–1957), Greek scholar and author, chairman of the League of Nations Union, 1923–38. Permission to consult these papers must be obtained from the surviving literary executor: Mrs. M. I. Henderson, Somerville College, Oxford. See Gilbert Murray papers: inventory (NRA 16865).

Correspondence and papers arranged by subject. (China and Japan, G.M. 68.)

PAPERS OF EDWARD JONAH NATHAN, of the Chinese Engineering and Mining Company, and

Kailan Mining Administration, 1898–1962. (MSS. Eng. hist. a. 16, 17; c. 418–64; d. 280; e. 223–6; g. 20. NRA 12711.)

1. Correspondence. 1898–1955.

2. Papers referring to Nathan's activities during the Japanese occupation of Northern China, 1939–45.

3. Three diaries kept by Nathan during the Japanese occupation. 1941–3.

4. Miscellaneous papers relating to the history of the Chinese Engineering and Mining Company and its associate, the Kailan Mining Administration.

5. Map of China, with particular reference to the mining areas. c. 1900–1947.

Family correspondence of the Mann family, chiefly of Gother Frederick Mann and his wife Margaret, including some written in China. 19th century. (MSS. Eng. lett. b. 9; c. 292–4; d. 303–6; e. 119.)

PAPERS OF THE REVD. L. B. CHOLMONDELEY, chaplain to the British Embassy in Tokio.

1. 'Stories to kindle Patriotism, written for Japanese boys during the Russo-Japan War.' Translation by Cholmondeley, with preface, and letter dated 20 February 1909, &c. 102 ff. Typescript and MS. (MS. Eng. misc. 45.)

2. Correspondence. 1914–20. i+238 ff. (MS. Eng. lett. d. 99.)

Official papers relating to Japan, October 1917–July 1918, included among the papers of Viscount Milner (1854–1925). (Milner Deposit. These papers are the property of New College, Oxford.)

Copy of an English version of Lao-Tse's Tao-te-king, with comments, by John Gustav Weiss. 1923. Typescript. iii+105 ff. (MS. Eng. misc. e. 116. A German version is in MS. German e. 6.)

Papers of Ernest Richard Hughes concerning Anglo-Chinese cultural co-operation. 1939–47. (MSS. Eng. misc. c. 516.)

PAPERS OF GERALD W. BULLETT, poet

1. Holograph translations of the poems of Fan Cheng-Ta: *The Golden Year of Fan Cheng-Ta*, published 1946, with calligraphic examples by Tsui Chi and seven letters from him to Bullett, August 1945–January 1948. 58 ff, of which 35–7 are blank. (MS. Eng. misc. e. 458.)

2. Literal translations of the Chinese poems of Fan Cheng-Ta in the hand of G. W. Bullett. 22 leaves, of which 14–22 are blank. (MS. Eng. misc. e. 357.)

3. Drafts of a letter of Tsui Chi about a review of *The Golden Year of Fan Cheng-Ta*. (MS. Eng. misc. c. 354, f. 329.)

RHODES HOUSE LIBRARY
Oxford

Inclusion of a manuscript on the list below does not necessarily imply that it is available for study. For a list of manuscripts in the Library see Louis B. Frewer, *Manuscript collections (excluding Africana) in Rhodes House Library, Oxford* (Oxford, 1970).

PAPERS OF THE BRITISH AND FOREIGN ANTI-SLAVERY AND ABORIGINES PROTECTION SOCIETY. 1820–1951. (MSS. Brit. Emp. s. 16–24, NRA. 1095.) Including:

1. Nineteenth-century correspondence arranged in volumes under the names of the officers of the societies receiving the letters. There is an author index and a territorial index on cards. (MSS. Brit. Emp. s. 18, C 1–166.)

2. Twentieth-century letters. (MSS. Brit. Emp. s. 19, D 1–6.)

3. Paying-in books, China account, July 1933–January 1935 and March 1935–December 1938. (MSS. Brit. Emp. s. 21, F 2/2, 26, 27.)

4. Papers relating to China. 19th century. (MSS. Brit. Emp. s. 22, G 89.)

5. Papers relating to Hong Kong. 1920–37. (MSS. Brit. Emp. s. 22, G 361–8.)

6. Papers relating to Korea. 1920–2. (MSS. Brit. Emp. s. 22, G 372.)

7. Papers relating to League of Nations: opium traffic. 1922–3. (MSS. Brit. Emp. s. 22, G 469.)

8. Files on coolie labour. (G 476–81.)

9. Miscellaneous correspondence, some relating to Hong Kong. 20th century. (MSS. Brit. Emp. s. 22, G 490.)

10. Maltreatment of prisoners by Japanese in Korea. (NRA 1075, f. 43.)

11. Letters from Hong Kong. 1941–51. (G 505, 509.)

Notes by Sir William Peel on colonial service in Malaya, Singapore, and Hong Kong, 1897–1935. 1937. Typescript. (MSS. Brit. Emp. s. 208.)

Article by George Ormsby: The land of the Boxers, from Pekin to Kalgau. [c. 1900?] (MSS. Brit. Emp. s. 287.)

Letter of introduction of Frederick William A. Bruce, as Envoy Extraordinary and Minister Plenipotentiary, to the Emperor of China, signed by Queen Victoria. 1859. (MSS. Ind. Ocn. s. 176 (4).)

W. J. Watts, Chinese affairs in Malaya: review of the history of the Department of Chinese affairs; Notes on Chinese secret societies, &c. 1879–1956. (*Access restricted.*)

Papers of the Overseas Nursing Association. (MSS. Brit. Emp. s. 400.)

Private nurses: early correspondence. (Hong Kong Nursing Association. Japan Branch cf C.N.A.) 1896–1902. (Box 125.)

Private nurses: terms, conditions, and reports. (Hong Kong Nursing Association. The Peak Hospital in Hong Kong. Japan Branch.) 1902–5. (Box 126.)

Private nurses: terms, conditions, and reports. (The same organizations as in Box 126, plus Shanghai Municipal Hospital and Victoria Nursing Home in the same city.) (Box 127.)

Territorial files (4: Shanghai Municipal Council and Country Hospital, 1913–49. 6: Hong Kong, 1923–34.) (Box 134.)

The Far East (2: Hong Kong, 1916–63). (Box 137.)

Letters from nurses overseas, 1910–50. (3: Shanghai, 1919–49. 4: Hong Kong, 1925–37. Japan, 1926–31.) (Box 140.)

War casualties. 'Malaya, Hong Kong, and non-government Far East': letters and accounts of war casualties and nurses escaped. 1942–6. (Box 142.)

NATHAN PAPERS (MSS. Nathan 231–656. NRA 8981)

Papers of Sir Matthew Nathan (1862–1939), soldier and civil servant, as Governor of Hong Kong, 1903–7.

a. Note books, containing notes, photographs, accounts, &c. (322–7.)

b. Correspondence, including 'Out letter book', 19 August 1903–4 July 1907, index of addresses, and letters. (328.)

c. 'D.O. letters before 29 July, 1904.' (329.)

d. Miscellaneous official in-letters, arranged alphabetically. Correspondents include: Major-General Sir Owen Burne, Sir Cecil Clementi, General Hatton, Sir John Jordan, Lieutenant-Colonel Josling, Lieutenant-Colonel Kent, Colonel J. F. Lewis, C. M. Macowald, the Governor of Macao, Sir Gerard Noel, Sir M. Ommaney, Colonel Sir Herbert C. Perrott, Sir Francis Piggott, Sir Ernest Satow, Sir Edward Ward, Sir Pelham Warren, and Colonel Western. (330–7.)

e. Correspondence about the Hong Kong regatta and Nathan's accident, 1906. (338.)

f. Correspondence about guests at Government House, 1903–7. (339.)

g. Personal correspondence. (340–2.)

h. Letters from Hong Kong friends. 1905–7. (343–5.)

i. Letters from Hong Kong friends. 1907–19. (346–7.)

j. Semi-official correspondence from Hong Kong acquaintances and institutions, chiefly relating to the granting of commissions and other problems arising from the First World War. 1914–19. (348.)

k. Miscellaneous correspondence about the Universities' China Committee, the Kowloon–Canton Railway, and press-cuttings, 1931–7. Also letters from Hong Kong friends, including Sir John Simon. (349.)

l. Papers relating to trade and industries. (350A.)

m. Copies of correspondence about inaccuracies found by Nathan in 'Correspondence on the subject of the salaries of European civil servants' in Hong Kong, which was sent to Nathan at the request of the Chief Justice concerned, and miscellaneous papers on Chinese affairs, &c. 1904–5. (350B.)

n. Letters from friends associated with China, including Sir Cecil and Lady Clementi, 1924–6, W. G. Blunt, 1926, &c. together with other letters, telegrams, and drafts of letters from Nathan, 1925–6. Also letters from officers during the China War addressed to J. H. Dent of Messrs. Dent & Co. of Canton, 1838–42. (351.)

o. Miscellaneous correspondence about China and Hong Kong, together with reports, minutes, and correspondence of the Universities' China Committee. 1925–31. (352.)

p. Copies of the *Yellow Dragon*, 1904–7, and of the *South China Morning Post*, November 1904, January 1906, February 1907; together with miscellaneous papers relating to entertainments and clubs, 1903–7. (353.)

q. Volumes showing seating plans and arrangements for dinners at Government House. 1904–7. (354–5.)

r. Visitors' books (Hong Kong, 1903–4, 1904–6, Hong Kong and Natal, 1906–9). (356–8.)

Reminiscences of Hong Kong, mainly personal, by Colonel H. B. L. Dowbiggin. 1906–65. (MSS. Ind. Ocn. s. 151.)

LUGARD PAPERS. Papers of Frederick John Dealtry Lugard, Baron Lugard (1858–1945), soldier, administrator and author, including correspondence and papers as Governor of Hong Kong, 1907–12 (MSS. Brit. Emp. s. 66–s. 68) and Visitors' Book, Hong Kong (MSS. Brit. Emp. s. 80). (MSS. Brit. Emp. s. 30–99. NRA 8555. See Margery Perham, *Lugard*, 2 vols. London, 1956 and 1960.)

Report by A. G. Fraser on his visit to Japan while on the World Tour Education Commission. (MSS. Brit. Emp. s. 283, Box 2, File 1. ff. 22–7.)

PAPERS OF KATHLEEN LADY SIMON (1927–52). Including:

Papers on Mui Tsai, system of slavery. (K 25.)

Letters to his wife by Sir Claud Severn as Colonial Secretary, Hong Kong; miscellaneous correspondence, 1913–29; documents dealing with Chinese land tax and tariff duties, 1896. Letters home of Lady Severn from Hong Kong, 12 January 1921–4 March 1925. (MSS. Ind. Ocn. s. 176 (1–2).)

Miscellaneous articles on Hong Kong, 1914–45, by Lancelot Forster as Professor of Education, University of Hong Kong, including: Reflections on the cause of the Hong Kong strike, 1925; Journeys to and from Hong Kong; Stanley internment camp, 1942–5. 5 files. (MSS. Ind. Ocn. s. 177.)

Correspondence of Sir Francis Henry May as Governor, Hong Kong, mainly with Sir Charles Eliot on the appointment of Vice-Chancellor, University of Hong Kong, 1918, and with Sir Claud Severn as Acting-Governor, 1919. (MSS. Ind. Ocn. s. 176(3).)

Walter Schofield: Hong Kong. Memories of the District Office South, and other administrative papers, 1919–66; Chinese living conditions, 1950; Prehistory in Hong Kong. 8 pts. (MSS. Ind. Ocn. s. 61.)

Correspondence and memoranda on legal matters of Sir Henry William B. Blackall, including Hong Kong. 1919–50. (*Access restricted.*)

Recollections of Hong Kong by Sir Alexander William G. H. Grantham as Cadet, 1922–35 and as Governor, 1947–57. Tape recording and typescript of an interview with D. J. Crozier. (MSS. Brit. Emp. s. 288.)

Notes and reports by K. M. Anderson, headmistress, on kindergarten and transition classes, Stanley internment camp, Hong Kong; suggestions for reorganization of primary and pre-primary education in Hong Kong; reminiscences of service in the colony. 1923–45. (MSS. Ind. Ocn. s. 110.)

Letter by Frederick George Bourne to the Colonial Secretary on the death-rate of Chinese infants in Singapore. 22 January 1934. MSS. Ind. Ocn. s. 147.)

PAPERS OF ARTHUR CREECH JONES (1891–1964) (NRA 14026. MSS. Brit. Emp. s. 332)

Lectures, letters, and articles on China. 1934–9. (Box 27, file 2.)

Education in Hong Kong. 1937–9. (Box 40, file 2.)

Official papers on Hong Kong. 1946–9. (Box 57, file 1.)

Letters to his wife from Japan. 1960. (Box 13, file 4. *May be consulted only with permission of Mrs. Creech Jones.*)

Brochures collected in connection with his visit to Japan, 1960. (Box 13, file 9.)

Diary of Thomas Jackson Houston while in colonial administration, Hong Kong. 1936–8. *On long loan.* (MSS. Ind. Ocn. s. 141.)

The fall of Hong Kong, 25 December 1941, by A. Hill, with Stanley internment camp scrapbook, 1942–5, press-cuttings and photographs. (MSS. Ind. Ocn. s. 73.)

Reports on Chinese affairs in Singapore by Victor Purcell, 1946. Articles by W. L. Blythe on secret societies, and Blythe's replies to Lennox A. Mills's questionnaire on the recruitment of Chinese and Malays, 1941, &c. (MSS. Ind. Ocn. s. 116.)

Memorandum on the Chinese in Malaya, by George William Webb, as Acting-Secretary for Chinese Affairs, Singapore, 1948; with a note on the Memorandum by W. L. Blythe. (*Access restricted.*)

Circular letters home, and diary entitled 'Chinese assault team, 1949' written from Macao and Malacca by John C. Litton as Officer-in-charge of the Secretariat of Chinese affairs, 1948–51, describing the emergency and operations against the Communists. (MSS. Ind. Ocn. s. 113.)

Notes by William Donald Horne, Special branch, Federation of Malaya, on Communism and Chinese schools, the bandit movement, outlook of the overseas Chinese, squatters, and aspects of the political situation. 1949–51. (MSS. Ind. Ocn. s. 128.)

Notes by A. J. Mitchell as a controller of the Colonial Development Corporation in various areas, including the Far East. 1949–53. (MSS. Brit. Emp. r. 7.)

Note by H. J. Barnard on the activities of the Nationalist Chinese Military Organization (K.M.T.) in northern Perak after the Japanese surrender in 1945. (MSS. Ind. Ocn. s. 26.)

Papers of the Colonial Civil Servants Association, including constitution, minutes of conferences, circulars, bulletins, and correspondence, some relating to Hong Kong. 1947–61. (MSS. Brit. Emp. s. 100–21.)

Speech and report of Robin W. Band, 6th session of the Economic Commission for Asia and the Far East, as Adviser, Malaya and British Borneo group. 1950. (*Access restricted.*)

Conference documents of the *ad hoc* committee of experts on inland transport. Oct.–Nov. 1950, of ECAFE, with report by E. A. Gardiner. 1950. (MSS. Ind. Ocn. s. 170, 171.)

Family letters of G. B. Endacott, Hong Kong. 1953–66.

Memoranda on the recruitment of Chinese seamen for British vessels, and on the proposal to construct a runway in Yaumati or in Kowloon, by T. B. Low. 1953. (MSS. Ind. Ocn. s. 209.)

Lecture by H. A. de Barros Botelho on the Royal Hong Kong Defence Force, delivered 1955. Photostat. (MSS. Ind. Ocn. s. 108.)

Report by W. G. Morison on marketing and co-operatives in Hong Kong and Malaya. December 1961. (MSS. Ind. Ocn. s. 180.)

Facts and famous cases of the Hong Kong police, collected by Mr. Perdue. (MSS. Ind. Ocn. s. 76.)

Triad societies in Hong Kong, by Mrs. L. G. Dewar. n.d. (MSS. Ind. Ocn. s. 85.)

The Rhodes House collections contain many documents relating to the Japanese invasion and occupation of Malaya, Singapore, Hong Kong, and other parts of Asia, during the Second World War, together with accounts of internment or imprisonment in various jails or internment camps. Nothing of this type of material is included here: much of it can be found in L. B. Frewer, *Manuscript collections (excluding Africana) in Rhodes House Library, Oxford.* (Bodleian Library, 1970).

BALFOUR LIBRARY, PITT RIVERS MUSEUM

Oxford

Far Eastern diaries of Robert Gossett Woodthorpe. (1844–98.)

HOPE DEPARTMENT OF ZOOLOGY (ENTOMOLOGY)

University Museum, Parks Road, Oxford

Index to collections of insects made in India, Ceylon, and China, October 1903–April 1904, and in China, Japan, and Canada, April–June 1904, by G. B. Longstaff. 2 vols.

MUSEUM OF THE HISTORY OF SCIENCE

Old Ashmolean, Oxford

Notes on Japanese art by H. M. Underhill. (MSS. Underhill 2.)

THE ORIENTAL INSTITUTE

Pusey Lane, Oxford

English–Chinese dictionary by W. E. Soothill. 1 vol.

Microfilm of a manuscript translation from the Chinese, by Bunno Katō and W. E. Soothill, of the Lotus-sutra.

Draft book reviews by Dr. James Legge, the Chinese scholar.

THE LIBRARY, ALL SOULS COLLEGE

Oxford

See Henry O. Coxe, *Catalogus Codicum MSS. qui in Collegiis Aulisque Oxoniensibus hodie adservantur*, vol. ii (1852).

Diary of Simon Dolboo, Hans Gibbon, and W. Ramsden on their voyage to Japan. 1673. (MS. CCXXXIX. f. 185.)

THE LIBRARY, BALLIOL COLLEGE

Oxford

URQUHART BEQUEST. Papers of David Urquhart (1805–77), including correspondence of the Working Men's Committees. (NRA 11691.)

Memorial of the Gaythorn Public Affairs Committee to the Earl of Derby on Lord Elgin's visit to Japan. n.d. (G. 3/5b.)

Letter to Urquhart from the Gloucester Working Men's Committee about a meeting on China. (G. 5/6.)

Protest by working man against the bombardment of China, addressed to Lord Elgin. 1858. (G. 14.)

Letter of Francis Butterfield to Lord John Russell about China. 8 October 1859. (G. 10/5.)

Letters from J. Duce about China. 1859. (G. 11b.)

Pamphlet on crime and government at Hong Kong. 1859. (III/4.)

Letter of Joseph Foden about China. January, 1860. (In G. 14.)

Report of a meeting in Newcastle upon Tyne about China. July 1860. (In G. 15.)

Letter to W. Singleton about questions and replies on Russia and China addressed to and received from F. Marx. n.d. (G. 17/4.)

THE LIBRARY, CHRIST CHURCH

Oxford

See G. W. Kitchin, *Catalogus Codicum MSS qui in Bibliotheca Aedis Christi apud Oxonienses adservantur*, 1867.

'Chinese matters', included in vol. xxviii, 'Foreign Churches and Ministers: from 1715-1718', of Archbishop Wake's MSS. (MS. CCLXI.)

SALISBURY PAPERS

Papers of Robert Arthur Gascoyne-Cecil, 3rd Marquis of Salisbury (1830-1903), Secretary of State for India, 1866-7, 1874-8, Foreign Secretary, 1878-80, 1885-6, 1887-92, 1895-1900, Prime Minister, 1885-6, 1886-92, 1895-1902. These papers were used by Lady Gwendolen Cecil in the four published volumes (1921-32) and one unpublished volume of her father's biography.

I. Private correspondence, Foreign Office. 140 vols. This section, for which a detailed calendar is available (NRA 9226), is arranged to correspond to Salisbury's four periods of office, and subdivided mainly under country headings.

Correspondence 1878-80
China and Japan. (In A/19.)

Correspondence 1885-6
China. (In A/38-44.)

Correspondence. 1895-1900
India Office: China. (In A/91.)
Colonial Office: China. (In A/92.)
Lord Charles Beresford (mission to China, 1898-9). (A/97.)
China and Siam. (A/106.)
Japan. (A/126.)

There are also scattered references to China, Japan, &c. in volumes of correspondence with the Queen, with Ambassadors and others in France, Germany, Italy, Russia, U.S.A., &c., and with Under-Secretaries, &c.

II. Special correspondence, at present unbound, arranged alphabetically by correspondents, for which a card index is available in the Library. Correspondents include Sir Claud MacDonald, Sir N. R. O'Conor, Sir F. R. Plunkett, Sir J. Walsham, &c. *c.* 217 boxes.

III. Residual correspondence, political. Loose papers, arranged mainly chronologically in boxes. 1866-1903. *c.* 47 boxes.

IV. An artificial collection of copies of letters from Salisbury to eighty-six correspondents, arranged alphabetically. 21 vols., including index vol.

V. Three artificially created letter-books containing copies of letters from Salisbury all headed 'From Secretary's notebook'. There is a list of letters at the beginning of each volume. 1868-80, 1881-7, 1887-93.

VI. A collection of Cabinet and other official papers, nearly all printed, arranged by ministries (1866-7,

1874-80, 1885-6, 1886-92, 1895-1902) and within ministries roughly by subjects. There are microfilm or other copies of these papers at the Public Record Office. 36 boxes.

VII. Telegrams *re* trial of Portuguese Ozorio for murder at Hong Kong. 1898. (Vol. 83/97-107.)

THE LIBRARY, MANCHESTER COLLEGE

Oxford

Letters and papers of Sir John Bowring (1792-1872).

ST. ANTONY'S COLLEGE

Oxford

Papers of Sir Owen O'Malley on his service in China in the 1920s. (St. Antony's College, Middle East Centre: *Report for 1970 on the private papers collection.* 'Lodged in the Far Eastern section in the College library.')

Record of the expedition to Peking in 1900. (With the papers of Sir G. K. Scott Moncrieff in the Middle East Centre.)

PLYMOUTH

CITY LIBRARY

Central Library, Plymouth, PL4 8AL

Record of game killed in China, 8 February 1913-29 August 1915, and in Wales, 30 October-11 December 1915. Places named in China include Fengtai, Wang hai Lo, Peitaho, Nankou, Ningpo, Summer Palace, &c. The author is unknown. 1 vol. (Acc. 51.)

PRESTON

LANCASHIRE RECORD OFFICE

Bow Lane, Preston, PR1 2RE

See R. Sharpe France, *Guide to the Lancashire Record Office*, 2nd edn., Preston, 1962.

Illuminated letter from Elizabeth I to the Emperor of Cathay, proposing trade and sending an expedition of two ships under George Weymouth. 4 May 1602. (DDSh 15/3.)

Correspondence describing W. J. Garnett's travels in China, the Middle East, &c. 1905–18. (DDQ.)

Experiences of a prisoner of war in China, 1939–46. (DDX 525.)

REGIMENTAL HEADQUARTERS, THE LANCASHIRE REGIMENT (PRINCE OF WALES'S VOLUNTEERS)

Fulwood Barracks, Preston, Lancs.

The museum of The East Lancashire Regiment (formerly the 30th and 59th Regiments of Foot) has numerous albums of photographs, pictures, and other relics, in addition to the following records.

Digest of service of the 30th Regiment of Foot, later the 1st Battalion The East Lancashire Regiment, 1702–1905. This is a copy made in 1880 and then continued to 1905. 1 vol.

Digest of service of the 59th Regiment of Foot, later the 2nd Battalion The East Lancashire Regiment, 1755–1939. This is the original volume begun in 1830, with a historical account from 1782, and including detailed accounts of campaigns, battles, &c., with copies of documents, and some comment. The Regiment served in Hong Kong from 1850–8, and there is a detailed account of the part it played in the China War, 1857–8, and the capture of Canton. The Regiment was again in the Far East (Shanghai and Hong Kong) from 1933–7. 1 large folio vol.

Scrapbook containing pictures, cuttings, &c., relating to the history of the Regiment, with a large section (40 pp.) devoted to the China campaign, 1857–9, and the capture of Canton. 1 vol.

READING

BERKSHIRE RECORD OFFICE

Shire Hall, Reading, RG1 3EY

See *Guide to the Berkshire Record Office.* Reading, 1952.

DUNDAS FAMILY PAPERS. (D/EDd. NRA 1205.)
Letters from James Dundas Crawford in China to his sister, Janet Willis, containing much information about the Far East. 1870–8. (F4.)

PRESTON FAMILY PAPERS. (D/EP8.)
Diary of A. E. Preston containing account of a world tour, November 1912–October 1913, and including description of travels in China and Japan. 3 notebooks bound in 1 vol. (F4.)

Diary of Mrs. Lydia Preston, wife of the above, covering the same tour up to June 1913, and including account of journeys through China and Japan. November 1912–June 1913. (F6 and F7.)

Account of expenses while travelling on world tour. 1912–13. (F8.)

Notes by A. E. Preston on Japanese curios and deities. n.d. Typescript. 1 bundle. (F14.)

Typed lists of names and addresses of people— jewellers, curio dealers, &c.—in countries visited by the Prestons. 1914–15. 1 bundle. (F16.)

UNIVERSITY LIBRARY

Whiteknights, Reading, RG6 2AE

Journal and album of a cruise to the Far East by Lady Kinsore. 1926–7. (Eynsham Hall estate papers, box 29.)

RICHMOND (SURREY)

CENTRAL LIBRARY

The Green, Richmond, Surrey

Papers of Douglas Sladen about a literary agency for a group of Japanese writers, Yoshio Markino, Yone Nogushi, Gonnosuke Komai, and Shinji Ishi. 1913–21. (SLA. 40.)

Letters to Douglas Sladen from Yoshio Markino, author and artist, his collaborator. (NRA 14252, index.)

RICHMOND (YORKS.)

THE GREEN HOWARDS REGIMENTAL MUSEUM

Gallowgate Road, Richmond, Yorks.

The regiment was raised in 1688, and later became the 19th Regiment of Foot. It served in Shanghai from 1928 to 1931. The museum has a large collection of regimental records, other documents, photographs, relics, and printed books. Among the manuscript records are the following:

Records of service (1688–1942)

1. Original digest of service of the 1st Battalion The

19th Regiment, with various documents inserted. 1688–1906. 1 vol.

2. Historical records of the 1st Battalion, including accounts of service in Shanghai, 1928. 1919–39.

3. Historical records of the 2nd Battalion from the beginning in 1858 to September 1942, including accounts of service in Shanghai from 1929 to 1931. 1858–1942. 1 vol.

SELBORNE

THE WAKES MUSEUM

Selborne, Hants.

Diary of J. A. White in India and the East. 1801–2. (82.)

SHEFFIELD

CITY LIBRARIES

Central Library, Surrey Street, Sheffield, S1 1XZ

BARKER PAPERS (Bar. D.)

Papers of Captain Charles Barker, R.N. (1811–60). He entered the Royal Navy in 1826, being commissioned as Lieutenant in June 1838; Commander 1845; Captain 1850. (Bar. D. 801.) (NRA 6730.) Including:

54. Translation of communication from the insurgent prince at Nanking to Lord Elgin. c. 1858.

56. Report of the Harbour Master, Hong Kong, of a typhoon on the 13 and 14 September. 24 September 1849.

57. Letter from Lord Elgin, H.M.S. *Furious* to Captain Barker, enclosing a copy of a report from his Chinese secretary, Mr. Wade. 23 November 1858.

58. Report of Captain Osborn, R.N., commanding H.M.S. Frigate *Furious*, off Kew-Keang, to Captain Barker, H.M.S. *Retribution*, on the grounding of the *Furious* in the river Yang-tse-Kiang, and the silencing of the guns of the forts at Ngan-King. 23 December 1858.

81. Letter from Charles Barker, H.M.S. *Amazon*, to his mother from Hong Kong. 17 November 1850.

102–10. Nine letters from Charles Barker to his mother, on the passage to Hong Kong, off the Peiho, in the Yellow Sea and Shanghai, off Yeddo (Japan) and from Shanghai. 2–20 June, 4 and 7 July, 16–29 July, 18–26 August, 20 September, 3 October, 30 October, 2 November, and 29 November 1858–6 January 1859.

111. Extract from a letter received by Captain Barker at Woohoo on Christmas Day 1858 from the Chinese General at Nankin apologizing for the forts having opened fire on the British ships. c. 1858.

112. Extract from a letter from Frederic Bower of Shanghai to his brother describing Captain Barker's conduct when the British ships were fired on by the forts at Nankin. c. 1859. 2 copies.

113. Report from a correspondent in *The Times* of 2 March 1859 of the expedition to Hankow. 2 March 1859.

115. Galley proof of part of an article describing the visit of H.M.S. *Reynard* to the Great Wall of China. n.d.

Translation of a letter from Lin, Assistant-Controller-General, Adjutant-General of the Household Troops and Supporter of the Celestial Institutes, to Captain Charles Barker. c. 1858. (Bar. D. 804.)

WHARNCLIFFE MUNIMENTS

General correspondence of the 3rd Baron (1st Earl) of Wharncliffe, including letters from John G. Thirkell, about to take up a post in Shanghai, 1875. (Wh. M. 418, xx.)

Correspondence with the Japanese ambassador about the Russo-Japanese War. Letter to Sir Henry Bemrose about the visit of Japanese representatives to Sheffield. 1905. (Bagshawe collection, 778(v). NRA 7871, p. 228.)

Order book of Edgar Allen & Co. Ltd., steel manufacturers (founded 1867), containing orders for shipments of steel, &c. to Japan. 1924–35. 1 large folio vol. (MD 2327.)

CARPENTER COLLECTION

See *A Bibliography of Edward Carpenter: a catalogue of books, manuscripts, letters, etc. by and about Edward Carpenter in the Carpenter Collection . . . 1949*. There is also a typescript list of additional manuscripts presented in 1958.

Social and political life in China. 1901. (MS. 91.)

Manuscript notes for a lecture on the Chinese Academy. February 1907. (MS. 137.)

The Awakening of China. 1907. (MS. 140.)

A manuscript copy of The Awakening of China, altered and prepared for *Towards Industrial Freedom*. (MS. 209.)

Letters to Edward Carpenter from Japanese admirers and friends 1909–19. (MS. 380/1–45.)

1–8 Letters from Kiyoshi Sato, all except the last written in London. 19 December 1917–29 March 1919.

9–10 Letters from Ito Kei, written in London. 18 July and 13 October 1916.

11–15 Letters from Saikwa Tomita, written in Japan. 15 August 1915–3 September 1916.

16–19 Letters from Yone Noguchi, written in Japan. 12 December 1911–28 May 1915.

20–44 Letters from, or on behalf of, Sanshiro Ishikawa, Japanese socialist who translated *Never Again*, written from Japan, Brussels, England, and France. 14 December 1909–17 October 1919. Sanshiro Ishikawa was imprisoned in Japan in 1910, and lived in Europe from 1913 to 1919 working as a decorator and gardener.

STAFFORD

STAFFORDSHIRE RECORD OFFICE

Eastgate Street, Stafford, ST16 2LZ

DUKE OF SUTHERLAND MSS. (D593)

Letters and papers concerning a scheme organized by Richard M. Rapier (of Ransomes and Rapier) at a committee meeting at Stafford House for presenting the Emperor of China with a small line of railway and rolling stock as a belated wedding present, and to encourage trade. 1873. MS. and print. (D593/P/26/1.)

WILLIAM SALT LIBRARY

Eastgate Street, Stafford, ST16 2LZ

DARTMOUTH MSS. (D. 1778 V. NRA 5197)

Papers of William, 2nd Earl of Dartmouth, Secretary for the Colonies 1772–5, including:

1. Letter from G. L. Scott concerning North-West passage. 28 December 1772. (284.)

2. Letter from Beat Tavel concerning a passage to the East Indies and China. 27 August 1774. (285.)

3. Observations of John Hanson on the failure to find a North-West passage, and advising pursuit of a North-East passage. January 1774. (286.)

4. Letter from R. Valltravers concerning North-East passage and the value of Eastern countries. 30 November 1773. (287.)

Miscellaneous papers, including list of seeds from China per Captain Graham. 1801. (967.)

Elphinstone's voyages to Bombay and China. 1802–3, 1805–6, 1807–8. (162.)

TAUNTON

MINISTRY OF DEFENCE, HYDROGRAPHIC DEPARTMENT

Taunton, Somerset

The Hydrographic Department of the Admiralty possesses a unique collection of about half a million original documents relating to all parts of the world, including the areas covered by this *Guide*. Among the documents, which date from the seventeenth century, are the original surveys, the record copies of charts, the data books of the original surveys, minute books [not open to students], correspondence [not open to students], and view books. There is no published catalogue, but the documents may be inspected upon application in writing to the Hydrographer of the Navy at the above address.

SOMERSET LIGHT INFANTRY REGIMENTAL MUSEUM

Regimental Headquarters, The Somerset and Cornwall Light Infantry, 14 Mount Street, Taunton, Somerset

Records of service of the Somerset Light Infantry, formerly the 13th Regiment of Foot, including:

1. Record of service 2nd Battalion 13th Light Infantry, 1858–1928, including service in North China (Tientsin and Peking), October 1911–October 1913.

2. Digest of service 1st Battalion Somerset Light Infantry, 1910–41, including service at Hong Kong, 11 January 1929–26 November 1930.

Diary of Lieutenant-Colonel [later Major-General Sir] Henry J. Everett in China. 1912, 1913. 2 vols.

SOMERSET RECORD OFFICE

Obridge Road, Taunton, TA2 7PU

TROLLOPE–BELLEW PAPERS (DD/TB)

Volume entitled 'A Journall from Amoy up to Chusan . . . 1700', containing notes about various voyages, including:

1. 'A copy of a Journ[ll] from Emoy up along y[e] Shoar in a sm[ll] Junck to Chusan & from Chusan to Quemoy in a great Junck w[th]out all y[e] Islands October y[e] 6[th] 1699 kept by me William Hill.' 18 pp.

2. 'A Description of Places where hale Juncks a Shoar . . .' 1 p.

Log of the ship *Blessing* kept by George Smythes from

Bombay towards Amoy in China, 7–27 May 1702. (Sporadic and incomplete.) Also: 'Return from Amoy in China towards Malacca, 22 December 1702–14 January 1703. Loose sheets. 6, 13 pp.

Letters from William Martin and J. G. [Joseph Goodshaw] from Fort St. George, Amoy, and Bombay, to Sir Nicholas Waite, Consul-General for the affairs of the East India Company, about a dispute between Martin and Goodshaw on a trading voyage to China on the ship *Catherine*. 1704–5. 12 pp. A little worm-eaten.

Journals of the *Bombay Merchant*, May 1698–June 1699 on a voyage Bombay–Calcutta–Acheen, and April 1701–May 1702 for a voyage Bombay–Chusan. (Mathias and Pearsall, p. 137.)

TROWBRIDGE

WILTSHIRE RECORD OFFICE

County Hall, Trowbridge, BA14 8JG

PENRUDDOCKE PAPERS

Accounts of merchandise shipped to India and China, with memoranda relating to stores, dimensions of vessels, &c. 1747–51, 1751, 1755–6, 1755–7, 1758–9. 6 vols. (W.R.O. 332, no. 288.)

TRURO

ROYAL INSTITUTION OF CORNWALL

River Street, Truro

Letter of Dr. Robert Morrison (1782–1834), missionary, in China, to the Revd. Robert Ashton about his work, &c. 18 November 1828. 4 pp. (Enys Collection of Autographs, no. 986.)

WARRINGTON

PUBLIC LIBRARY

Museum Street, Warrington, Cheshire

PAPERS OF THE WARRINGTON CHAMBER OF COMMERCE

1. Minute books of the Warrington Chamber of Commerce containing references to foreign and colonial trade, including trade with China and the Far East: with inserted documents. 1876–1915. 5 vols. (MSS. 1014 and 1015.)

2. Annual reports and year-books of the Warrington Chamber of Commerce. 1895, 1897–date. Printed. (P.S. 5.)

WARWICK

WARWICKSHIRE COUNTY RECORD OFFICE

Priory Park, Cape Road, Warwick, CV34 4JS

SEYMOUR OF RAGLEY PAPERS (C R. 114 A. NRA 8482.)

Papers of Sir George Francis Seymour (1787–1870), Admiral of the Fleet, including:

1. Plan of the Canton River with entrances and islands. 1840. (465.)

2. Miscellaneous letters, including some from the Chinese campaign. 1844–61. (533/8.)

3. Miscellaneous correspondence, including letters of M. M. Ashby from the Chinese campaign. 1856–64. (533/15A.)

4. Miscellaneous correspondence, including letter from Mr. Jeans in China. 1858. (533/16.)

5. Miscellaneous correspondence, including letters from M. M. Ashby from the Chinese campaign. 1860–1. (533/18, 20.)

WIGAN

CENTRAL LIBRARY

Wigan, Lancs.

Diary of James S. Anderson, purser in the service of the East India Company, including accounts of voyages to China, 1819–21, 1822–3, 1824–5, 1826–7, and 1843–7. His first voyage to China was by way of Mauritius and India, where he joined the *Marquis of Huntly* in October 1820 arriving at Macao on 27 January 1821 and at Canton on 11 February: he stayed there until 20 March, and then left for Macao and home. The second voyage was in H.C.S. *Macqueen*, leaving England in January 1822 and arriving in China in September. He stayed in China three months and his diary gives some description on his life there, including accounts of dinners given by Chinese merchants, and a long description (1 November–11 November) of a fire at Canton which burnt down all the factories and thousands of houses. He again sailed to China in the *Macqueen* in 1824 and stayed there about four months from September. In 1843 he again visited China, arriving in June and staying there until January 1847, travelling between Macao, Canton, and Hong Kong. His diary gives some account of life in those places, including descriptions of anti-foreign riots in May, June, and July 1844, and in July and October 1846, accounts of dinners and entertainments given by Chinese merchants, and of other events. 12 August 1808–2 September 1865. 1 vol. (M 927/142.)

WORCESTER

WORCESTERSHIRE RECORD OFFICE

Shire Hall, Worcester, WR1 1TR

DAVIES PAPERS (705: 385. NRA 1308)
Papers of Major-General Henry Rudolph Davies (1865–1950), including:

1. Journal recounting his service in Shanghai at the time of the Boxer rising. 1900–10.

2. Diaries, China. 1906–9.

3. Map of Yunnan. 1906. Printed.

4. Field notes on birds in China. 1901. Printed.

Seven letters from Lieutenant John Huskisson, R.N., to his family, while serving in Hong Kong. 1840–56. (Huskisson–Turner papers.)

WALES

ABERYSTWYTH

NATIONAL LIBRARY OF WALES

Aberystwyth, SY23 3BU

The manuscripts in the National Library are described in *Handlist of manuscripts in the National Library of Wales*, Aberystwyth, 1943 seqq., and in the printed annual reports of the National Library. A typescript handlist of the latest accessions and typescript schedules of certain collections are available in the Library.

Log-book of the ship *York* under the command of William Huddart, 3 December 1785–29 March 1787, including an account of her voyage to St. Helena and China. (MS. 10833.)

Miscellanea from the Library of Benjamin Millingchamp (1756–1829), chaplain in the Navy and in India, &c., including some translations from Oriental texts, English–Chinese, English–Persian, and English–Arabic vocabularies, &c. Late 18th–early 19th century. (MS. 4409.)

Letters to Andrew C. Ramsay, geologist, Director-General of the Geological Survey, from various correspondents including John Milne, Tokio. 1852–81. (MS. 9641.)

Log-book of the ship *Viscount Sandon*, Enos Hughes, master, from Newcastle to Hong Kong, Singapore, Rangoon, and Liverpool. 1860–1. (MS. 615.)

Log-books of the *Celestial*, T. Jones, master, from Liverpool to Shanghai, Shanghai to London, and London to Shanghai. 1861–2. (Mathias and Pearsall, pp. 138–9.)

GLANSEVERN COLLECTION (MSS. 5021–55a)

A collection of letters to Mrs. Humphrey-Owen (*née* Russell) from Sir Daniel Brooke Robertson, British Consul in Canton, describing life and conditions in China, and giving local and general news. 1861–74.

A group of thirty letters addressed to Stuart, Baron Rendel (1834–1913), industrialist, Liberal M.P., and philanthropist. Five are from Sir Robert Hart, Inspector-General of Customs in China, seventeen from Granville George Leveson-Gore, 2nd Earl Granville, Minister for Foreign Affairs, and eight from J. D. Campbell, Commissioner of Chinese Imperial Maritime Customs. The letters are mainly concerned with Western relations with China and include references to relations between the Customs service and British Consuls in 1883, negotiations between France and China in 1884–5 leading to the settlement of the question of the frontier and of sovereignty over Annam, the reform decrees of 1898, the events of 1900, the Russo–Japanese conflict of 1904–5, &c. 1883–1910. (*Annual Report*, 1959–60, p. 64.)

Extracts from various printed sources on travel, ethnology &c. in various countries including China. 19th–20th centuries. (MSS. 6833–4. Hartland Papers.)

Letters and papers of and relating to the Revd. Timothy Richard (1845–1919), missionary to China. c. 1905–45. (*Annual Reports*, 1960–1, p. 23, and 1963–4, p. 31.)

1. Thirty letters from Richard to his mother. 1882–6.

2. Ten letters from Richard to his nephew [the Revd. T. R. Morgan]. 1905–19.

3. Two jotters belonging to Richard. 1917–18.

4. An envelope marked 'Peace Conditions', also containing photographs.

5. Letter from D. Pryse Williams, Swansea, to Richard. 1916. *Timothy Richard, D.D., Litt.D., LL.D.; an outline of his life and work in China*, by H. C. B. [Miss Hilda C. Bowser]. Printed.

7. Obituary notices. 1919.

8. Tributes by W. Hopkyn Rees and H. Cernyw Williams.

9. A chapter on 'Timothy Richard and the Christian Literature Society', by Evan Morgan, Shanghai, with a covering letter from the author to the Revd. Thomas Lewis, of the Baptist Missionary Society, and a letter from Thomas Lewis to the donor, the Revd. D. Wyre Lewis.

10. Notes by the donor [? in connection with an intended biography of Richard].

11. Script of a broadcast talk in Welsh by the donor on the occasion of the anniversary of Richard's birth. 1945.

'Letters descriptive of a visit to the Far East in the Service of the Salvation Army', November 1915–August 1916 (1 vol.); and 'Letters descriptive of a second visit to the Far East in the service of the Salvation Army', February 1917–March 1919 (2 vols.), by Brigadier (S.A.) William A. Salter. The first volume describes his journey out on the Trans-Siberian Railway, and his visits to China, Korea, and Japan; the second and third volumes cover his journey out via Canada, his stay in China and his return to England via the U.S.A. (MSS. 14455–7.)

A scrapbook entitled 'Characters and Principles of Chinese Life, 1921–28', consisting of press-cuttings and a few transcripts of weekly leading and 'star' articles contributed to the *Shanghai Times* by the Revd. Evan Morgan, afterwards of Bristol, some under the pen-name of 'Cymro'. The volume also contains a type-script index of articles and an annotated photograph of guests at a farewell dinner given by Mr. Wang I-ting, 'noted artist, calligraphist, philanthropist', to Evan Morgan in a Buddhist monastery. (MS. 10935.)

PAPERS RELATING TO THE ST. DAVID'S SOCIETY OF HONG KONG

1. Minutes, list of members, and autographed pro-gramme relating to a St. David's Day dinner held in Stanley Internment Camp, 1943. (MS. 11541.)

2. Rules and a brief history of the Society; also address of the President, H. G. Richards, at the annual dinner and dance, 1961. Typescript and print. (*Annual Report*, 1960–1, p. 36.)

Notes of Gwilym Hughes, journalist, for a lantern lecture on China. 20th century. (MS. 8462.)

Copy of correspondence relating to works in Chinese or on China by Griffith John, Evan Morgan, J. Lambert Rees, W. Hopkyn Rees, E. O. Davies, and Timothy Richard, together with lists of the works. 20th century. Typescript. (MS. 5792.)

BRECON

REGIMENTAL MUSEUM, SOUTH WALES BORDERERS

The Barracks, Brecon

Letter from W. Stanborough to Colour-Sergeant F. Price, from Tientsin. 24 January 1913. (Acc. no. L. 27. 55.)

CARDIFF

SOUTH GLAMORGAN COUNTY RECORD OFFICE

County Hall, Cathays Park, Cardiff, CF1 3NE

The letter-books of the Dowlais Iron Company, builders of rails, pipes, &c., may contain material relevant to the areas covered by this *Guide*. 1782–1900. *c.* 550 vols.

FONMAN COLLECTION (D/DF)

Papers of Captain, later Commodore, Oliver Jones of Fonman (1813–78), while stationed at Hong Kong in command of H.M.S. *Charlotte*, comprising Memo and Order books (2 vols.), Letter-books (4 vols.) and Enclosures (1 vol. D/DF/NLW/22). The Letter-books and Enclosures include detailed accounts of the China War, of fighting against Chinese pirates, capturing Chinese and sinking their junks, &c. 1866–70. 7 vols.

SCOTLAND

EDINBURGH

CHURCH OF SCOTLAND FOREIGN MISSION COMMITTEE

121 George Street, Edinburgh, 2

RECORDS AND PAPERS (Marchant, p. 47)

Foreign Mission Minutes, Pre-Union Church of Scotland. These include China. 1834–83. 8 vols.

Minute Books: Foreign Missions United Presbyterian Church. Includes China. September 1845–May 1878. 5 vols., with index.

Foreign Mission operations—a diary of events in four volumes. Vol. iii includes China and Japan.

Miscellaneous papers relating to the Manchuria Mission. (MS., typescript and print.) Comprising:

1. Presbytery Minutes. 1910–52.
Joint Home Board Minutes (Manchuria Christian College). 1912–34. 2 sets.

2. Council Executive Minutes. 1923–30.

3. Manchuria Minutes. November 1938–February 1949.

4. Medical College reports (incomplete). 1911–48.

5. Moukden Medical College. October 1938–February 1949.

6. Papers concerning proposed Juridical Person for Medical College. 2 envelopes.

7. Manchuria General Files. December 1942–July 1954.

8. Secretary, Manchuria Conference. August 1937–January 1951.

9. Manchuria Mission Conference. 1947– .

10. Conference Executive. 1947– .

11. Conference Minutes and lists of missionaries. 1 envelope.

12. Mission Council papers. 1 envelope.

13. Commission to Manchuria and Ichang. October 1945–May 1949.

14. Report of Dr. Kydd, 1937, and Commission, 1946.

15. Papers concerning Indemnity Fund, 1931. 1 envelope.

16. Letters about and to Missionaries. 1943– .

17. List of former Scottish Missionaries. 1 envelope.

18. List of former Irish Missionaries. 1 envelope.

19. Lists of Scottish and Irish Missionaries. 1 envelope.

20. File containing Manchukuo accounts of certain Missionaries.

21. C.C.C. papers. 1 envelope.

22. Papers concerning freezing order and inventory of land and property, 1940.

23. Property File (General Secretary's).

24. Papers concerning missionaries' land and houses. 1 envelope.

25. Miscellaneous papers from old file. 1 envelope.

26. Historical material, including Irish reports. 1 envelope.

27. Lectures by D. T. Robertson.

28. Miscellaneous material left by D. T. Robertson.

29. File relating to Tatyana Simenoff, deceased.

30. Envelope containing the following: articles on Manchuria by Peter Fleming for the *Glasgow Herald*, March 1935; report by Kenneth Maclennan to C.B.M.S. on 'Visit to Far East', 1934; papers from Mrs. Stewart.

31. Miscellaneous post-war material. 2 envelopes and file.

32. World Dominion Survey of Manchuria. 2 copies.

EDINBURGH MEDICAL MISSIONARY SOCIETY

56 George Square, Edinburgh, 8

Formerly known as the Edinburgh Association for Sending Medical Aid to Foreign Countries and founded in 1841, its interest in China began in 1841. (Marchant, p. 57.)

Records of former students. 1 vol. 1938.

Medical missionary addresses. 1 vol. 1850–81.

EDINBURGH UNIVERSITY LIBRARY DEPARTMENT OF MANUSCRIPTS

George Square, Edinburgh, EH8 9LJ

LAING MSS. (*See* H.M.C. 72. Laing. I–II)

Letter of Andrew Michael Ramsay, called the Chevalier Ramsay, to Dr. John Stevenson about the translation of certain Chinese letters and other literary matters. 24 August 1742. (La. II. 301. 3.)

Two letters of David Simpson, written in Canton. 1786. (La. II. 122/9, 10.)

Letter of B. Koto on Chinese and Japanese fossils, in connection with the publication of the fourth volume of Baron von Richthoven's *China*. [1870?] (In Geikie papers. Gen. 527.)

Records of Ben Line Steamers Ltd (formerly William Thomson & Co.), traders to the Far East. (Mathias and Pearsall, pp. 21–2.)

SAROLEA COLLECTION. Papers of Charles Sarolea (1870–1953), Professor of French at Edinburgh University, 1894–1931, Editor of Everyman, 1912–17, &c. Including:

Correspondence and papers relating to China. 1926–7. (Sar. Coll. 88.)

NATIONAL BIBLE SOCIETY OF SCOTLAND, EASTERN COMMITTEE, EDINBURGH

5 St. Andrew Square, Edinburgh 2

Founded in 1860, the Society opened its mission to China in 1863. (Marchant, 79.)

Society Minute Book. 1861–99.

Eastern Committee Minutes. 1861–1900. 6 vols.

Index to Minutes from 1893. 1 vol.

Finance Committee. Minutes. 1864–1913. 4 vols.

Correspondence Committee, Budget Committee and Joint Meeting of Subcommittees on Chinese Explanations (1892).
Minutes. 1898–1913. Vols. 3, 4.

Newington and Grange Auxiliary. Minute book. 1887–1920. 1 vol.

Newspapers and papers connected with the change of designation of the Society. *c.* 1895. 1 bundle.

Envelope, headed: Annotations for N.B.S.S. Chinese Bible.

National Bible Society of Scotland Ladies' Auxiliary. Minutes. 1863–80. 1 vol.

Edinburgh Bible Society.
Finance Committee Minutes. 1843–64. 2 vols.

Lists of subscribers, donors, and benefactors. 1809–22. 1 vol. Charter. 1821.

NATIONAL LIBRARY OF SCOTLAND

George IV Bridge, Edinburgh, EH1 1EW

The manuscripts in the National Library are described in 'Summary catalogue of the Advocates Manuscripts' (Edinburgh, 1971), and in *Catalogue of manuscripts acquired since 1925*, vol. i [Edinburgh, 1938], vol. iii, 1968. Accessions are briefly listed in *Accessions of manuscripts*, 1959–64 and 1965–70. There are inventories in the Library for some of the uncatalogued accessions.

MELVILLE PAPERS. Papers of Henry Dundas, 1st Viscount Melville (1742–1811), President of the Board of Control, 1793–1801, and of his son Robert Saunders Dundas, 2nd Viscount Melville (1771–1851), President of the Board of Control, 1807–9, 1809–12, and 1828. *c.* 1781–1825.

1. Letters of George Smith, Member of the Bengal Council, 1785–91, to [Henry] Dundas or his clerk, William Cabell, containing information and proposals regarding finance, trade, crops, China, and general matters. (MS. 1060, ff. 204–341.)

2. Eastern shipping, 1786–1817, 1825, n.d. The East India Company's shipping (ship-building, sailings, personnel, victualling, cargoes, harbours, the supply of timber in the East); also dealings of the Royal Navy with the Company, and other matters connected with Eastern waters. 263 ff. (MS. 1066.)

3. Papers relating to China, 1781–1823, n.d., including debts owed by the Chinese at Canton to George Smith, a merchant there, and other British subjects; the trade in tin and tea; affrays between British and Chinese, with accounts of places on the route from India to China; papers on the case of J. J. Voute & Sons and their purchase of tea, 1787–8. (MS. 1069.)

4. Russia and the Northern Confederation, 1789, 1800–1, n.d., with information supplied by Joseph Billings about his voyage to north-eastern Asia and the American coast. (MS. 1075, ii.)

5. Letter of John Milne to [Henry] Dundas, proposing a plan for securing Chinese trade. 1798. (MS. 3835, f. 188.)

Letter of Simon Phanoos Bagram, Calcutta, to the Government of India, regarding a remittance to China, 1792; with relevant modern correspondence. (MS. 3651, f. 51.)

PAPERS OF SIR GILBERT ELLIOT, 1ST EARL OF MINTO (1751–1814), President of the Board of Control, 1806, Governor-General of India, 1807–13. (Acc. 2794. Minto Papers.) Including:

Miscellaneous papers: Goa; misunderstanding in China; Buenos Aires. 1807. (M. 170.)

COCHRANE PAPERS

Correspondence and papers, private and official, of Admiral Sir Thomas John Cochrane, covering his service as second-in-command, 1842–5, and Commander-in-Chief, 1845–6, on the East India station [in China]. c. 1807–47. Including:

East India Station Papers

(a) Letters, chiefly semi-official, to Cochrane or to his Secretary, Edward Waller. 1842–6. Among the principal writers are James Brooke, Rajah of Sarawak, and Sir John Francis Davis, Governor of Hong Kong. 7 vols. (MSS. 2378–84.)

(b) Minutes of courts martial. 1843–7. (MS. 2385.)

(c) Miscellaneous papers. 1842–7. (MS. 2386.)

(d) Journal. 1842–4. 5 vols. (MSS. 2387–91.)

(e) 'Rough Journal.' 1844–7. 10 vols. (MSS. 2392–2401.)

(f) Letter-books, semi-official. 1842–6. 5 vols. (MSS. 2402–6.)

(g) Letter-books, semi-official. 1843–7. (MS. 2407.)

(h) 'Admiralty Letters', nos. 1–770. 1842–7. With index. 5 vols. (MSS. 2408–12.)

(i) 'Admiralty enclosures', including correspondence regarding Hong Kong. 1844–5. 2 vols. (MSS. 2413–14.)

(j) 'Admiralty letters sent.' 1842–7. With index. 3 vols. (MSS. 2415–17.)

(k) 'Admiralty Department letters.' 1842–7. With index. 2 vols. (MSS. 2418–19.)

(l) Notebook: purchases, &c. 1844–7. (MS. 2422.)

(m) Dinner-lists. 1845–7. 2 vols. (MSS. 2423–4.)

(n) Freight-list. 1844–7. (MS. 2425.)

(o) List of persons recommended to Cochrane, with remarks. (MS. 2426.)

(p) Reports of preparation for battle, on printed forms. 1842–7. 2 vols. (MSS. 2463–4.)

(q) 'General and Standing Orders.' 1842–7. (MS. 2465.)

(r) 'Squadron letters sent.' Letter-books with indexes. 1842–7. 6 vols. (MSS. 2466–71.)

(s) 'Register.' 1842–7. Being returns relating to stores and personnel. 2 vols. (MSS. 2472–3.)

(t) 'Arrivals and sailings.' 1842–7. (MS. 2474.)

(u) Orders and memoranda. 1842–7. 5 vols. (MSS. 2475–9.)

(v) Return, on a printed form, showing the number and disposition of ships under Cochrane's command. 1844–6. (MS. 2480.)

(w) 'Deck logs and Day's work.' 1842–7. 4 vols. (MSS. 2481–4.)

Account book: 'Value of articles bought before departure from England' for China. 1842. (MS. 2501.)

Private journal. 1807–13, 1815, 1821–33, 1835–49. 28 vols. (MSS. 2577–2604.) The volumes covering his service on the East India station, 1842–6 (MSS. 2599–2603), include descriptions of life in Hong Kong and of cruises to the Malay mainland, Borneo, Sarawak, the Ryukyu (Lu-chu Islands), &c.

Private letter-book. 1840–5. (MS. 2607.)

Report on relations between Russia and China. 1818. (MS. 6183, p. 861.)

Journal of a voyage from Scotland to China. 1839. *Xerox copy.* (*List of accessions to repositories in 1967,* p. 72.)

Letters to William Chalmers Burns, missionary in China. 1848, n.d. (MS. 980, ff. 81, 208. Lady Nairne Collection.)

Sketches of Chinese scenes, mainly in pencil, by Walter George Dickson (d. 1894), for many years a medical practitioner in Canton, author of *Japan* and *Gleanings from Japan. c.* 1850–60. A letter and a prefatory note by the Revd. John Stirton are inserted at the beginning of MS. 503. (MSS. 503–7.)

Volume of notes on the Chinese language, customs, &c., by Walter George Dickson. c. 1855. (Adv. MS. 51. 5. 19.)

Letters of Sir Colin Campbell concerning *i.a.,* the capture of Canton, 1857–8. (MS. 2257, ff. 312–21.)

FOREIGN MISSION RECORDS OF THE SCOTTISH CHURCHES which are now united to the Established Church. c. 1872–1933. (MSS. 7530–8020.) It should be noted that most letter-books in this series are not arranged topographically, so that letters to missionaries in many fields are found in the same volume.

I. *Church of Scotland.* Mission at I'chang, China, founded 1878

Letter-books of the Conveners of the Foreign Mission Committee. 1872–1907. (MSS. 7534–40.)

Letter-books of the Secretaries of the Foreign Mission Committee. 1875–95, 1911–29. (MSS. 7541–7605.)

Letter-books of the Treasurer of the Foreign Mission Committee. 1895–8. (MSS. 7622–3.)

Subcommittee minute book. 1918–22. (MS. 7619.)

Foreign Missions Ledger. (MS. 7621.)

Letter-book of the Conveners of the Women's Association for Foreign Missions. 1885–1915. (MS. 7624.)

Letter-book of the Women's Association for Foreign Missions: China. 1918, 1920, 1922–5. (MS. 7632.)

Letters from missionaries in China. 1923–5, 1927, 1933. (MS. 7611.)

Letters from women missionaries in China. 1927–9. (MS. 7633, ff. 112a–168.)

II. *United Presbyterian Church* (after 1900, *United Free Church of Scotland*). Missions in Manchuria and Japan from 1872.

Letter-books of the Secretaries and other officials of the Foreign Mission Committee. 1851–1931. (MSS. 7638–89.)

Letter-book of the Treasurers of the Foreign Mission Board. 1866–75. (MS. 7738.)

Letter-books of the Convener, Secretaries, and other officials of the Women's Foreign Mission Committee. 1899–1930. (MSS. 7923–81.)

Letters from missionaries in and about Manchuria. 1922–8. (MSS. 7850–3.)

Letters from women missionaries in Manchuria. 1900–1, 1921, 1925–9. (MSS. 7987, 7998–9.)

See also Marchant, pp. 81– .

Papers of General Sir J. Aylmer L. Haldane (1862–1950) who, after serving in India, 1894–8, and South Africa, 1899–1900, was military attaché with the Japanese Army in the Russo-Japanese War, 1904–5. His papers include: diaries, 1875–1946. (6 vols.); autobiography (2 vols.); letters, 1897–1922 (2 vols.). (Acc. 2070.)

Papers of Sir James Stewart Lockhart, K.C.M.G., Commissioner at Wei-hai-wei 1902– , including papers in Chinese. (Acc. 4138. Detailed list available, NRA 18511.)

PAPERS OF GILBERT JOHN MURRAY KYNYNMOND ELLIOT, 4TH EARL OF MINTO (1845–1914), Viceroy of India, 1905–10. (Acc. 2794. Minto papers.) Including:

Foreign Department. Vol. 1. Afghanistan, North-West frontier, Chinese Turkestan. Printed. 2 copies. (M. 841, M. 842.)

North-East frontier, Burma, Siam, and China. 1906. Printed. (M. 865.)

North-East frontier, Burma, Siam, and China. 1907. Printed. 2 copies. (M. 866, M. 867.)

North-East frontier, Burma, Siam, and China. 1908. Printed. 3 copies. (M. 868, M. 869, M. 878.)

Papers relating to orders and honours conferred on Admiral Sir Charles Hope Dundas of Dundas by various Governments including Japan. n.d. (Adv. MS. 80. 7. 14. Dundas of Dundas papers.)

Letters from members of the London Missionary Society in China (Alexander and John Stronach and G. O. Newport), to Mrs. Bowcher, London, with letters of a Chinese convert. 1864–75. (Acc. 4990.)

Letters of General C. G. Gordon. 1879–80, 1880–4. (Acc. 4083, 4031.)

Papers of W. A. L. Marr, M.B.E., relating to his military service, particularly on the Burma–Siam railway and in captivity in Changi jail, with explanatory notes, mostly 1941–50. (Acc. 4627.)

Journal of a voyage of Agnes Aird from Scotland to China. 1839. Xerox of a typescript. (MS. 8925.)

Diaries of Dr. Mary Cuthbert and two companions kept during travels in Tibet. 1932 and 1937. (Acc. 3514.)

REGISTRAR OF COMPANIES
FOR SCOTLAND

102 George Street, Edinburgh 2

The Registrar of Companies for Scotland has a complete record of all companies registered in Scotland from 1856, together with company documents, &c. There is an alphabetical index to the names of the companies, but no geographical or trade index. The records are likely, therefore, to contain further files relevant to east Asia than the single one noted below:

Hong Kong Navigation Co. Ltd.; incorporated 1906; dissolved 1916. (No. 6075.)

SCOTTISH CATHOLIC ARCHIVES

Columba House, 16 Drummond Place, Edinburgh, EH3 6PL

Three letters from François Pallu (1626–84), one of the three bishops consecrated for China in 1659. The letters are addressed to William Leslie, Archivist to Congregatio de Propaganda Fide in Rome. Two are dated 1662, the third 1671. [Probably seventeenth- or eighteenth-century copies. Photostat copies at School of Oriental and African Studies, London.]

SCOTTISH RECORD OFFICE

P.O. Box 36, H.M. General Register House, Edinburgh, EH1 3YY

The following records, all dating from the sixteenth century onwards, include occasional material concerning Scottish business relations with overseas territories:

1. Register of Deeds. [Books of Council and Session.] (Bound vols.)

2. Acts and Decrees of the Court of Session. (Bound vols.)

3. Processes of the Court of Session. (Loose papers.)

They are indexed up to 1688 and after 1770 under names of persons and companies.

CLERK OF PENICUIK PAPERS

Letters from Henry Clerk about his voyage to Java and the capture of three French China ships, 1744-5. (4180-1.)

Letter and memorandum from R. S. Dundas on the award of 'batta' to the crew of the *Melville* for their share in operations in China. 1843. (3554.)

Letters from Robert Philip, minister at Kingsland, on the opium war. 1843. (3562.)

Account of declared value of British produce and manufactures exported to China, 1843-6. (3804.)

KINROSS HOUSE PAPERS (GD. 29)

Correspondence of George Graham, of the East India Company Service, latterly of Kinross and an M.P

1. Business letters from Charles Crommelin in Canton, some in duplicate, with two accounts in duplicate covering 1773-6, and invoice of goods shipped on the *Principe de Beira* from Macao to Portugal in 1777. 1774-7. 13 papers. (No. 2058.)

2. Letters from David Killican in Calcutta, and others, referring mainly to business affairs in India and China. 1775-7, 1779-84. (No. 2061.)

Correspondence of John Graham, brother of George Graham

1. Personal letter from William Dalrymple at Canton. 25 November 1775. (No. 2127.)

2. Note of China silk sold at Amsterdam, and of account of Mayne & Co. 1779. (No. 1870.)

3. Bill of exchange from Canton for payment to David Killican. 1781. (No. 1871.)

HAMILTON BRUCE PAPERS

Translation of the manifesto of the Emperor of China on the occasion of electing a successor to the throne. 1795. (No. 48.)

Table reducing weights of English silver into Chinese weights according to the custom of the East India Company. NRA (Scot.) 0002 = NRA 9753. (Abercromby of Birkenbog, p. 8, no. 7.)

MELVILLE MUNIMENTS (GD/51)

This collection includes the papers of Henry Dundas, 1st Viscount Melville (1742-1811), President of the Board of Control, 1793-1801, Secretary of War, 1794-1801, 1st Lord of the Admiralty, 1804-5; Robert Saunders Dundas, 2nd Viscount Melville (1771-1851), President of the Board of Control, 1807 and 1809, 1st Lord of the Admiralty, 1812-27; General Henry Dundas, 3rd Viscount Melville (1801-76); and Vice-Admiral Sir Richard Saunders Dundas (1802-61).

Letter from Robert Thornton, chairman of the East India Company, to Lord Melville enclosing extract of letter, 31 July 1813, from Sir Evan Nepean, Governor of Bombay, regarding the internment of American trading ships at Canton, &c. 14 February 1814. (2/500/1-2.)

Letter from Chairman and Deputy Chairman of the East India Company, enclosing, for approval, draft of paragraph to be sent to the Select Committee of Supra Cargoes at Canton about their report of an affray between seamen from H.M.S. *Topaze* and the inhabitants of the island of Linting, 7 April 1823. (2/655/1-2.)

Letter, with enclosure, from Chairman of the East India Company about Eugene Maillefert, a Frenchman, who had proceeded as a passenger in the *Duchess of Atholl* from Calcutta to China in November 1822. 6 September, 1825. (2/695/1-2.)

Extract from the log of H.M.S. *Melville* on the Canton station. 26 February 1841. (2/736.)

Letters from Rear-Admiral James Hope in the Far East. 1859-60. (2/1088/3.)

Letters from Sir John Sinclair, 1784-5, subjects including China trade (3/192/3-4), and American trade with Canton (3/192/3).

Documents sent to Henry Dundas by an anonymous correspondent dealing with plan for regulating and extending the China trade of the East India Company and sale and smuggling of tea. 1784. (3/193/1-5.)

Notes on the East India Company's monopoly of saltpetre and opium [1786]. (3/197.)

Copy queries on saltpetre and opium trade with French and Dutch, with answers by William Wright, Auditor of Indian Accounts [16 July, 1790]. (3/206.)

Letters, with enclosures, from George Lockhart, dealing mainly with regulations governing private trade in China, and intention to establish a house of agency at Canton under firm of Baring, Money & Lockhart. 1795-9. (3/220/1-6.)

Letter from George Buchan Hepburn, Baron of Exchequer, regarding extent of American trade with the East Indies and China. 8 September 1807. (3/280.)

Letter from James Drummond stating injurious effects likely to result from a recent regulation relative to the opium trade. 26 February [1808]. (3/284.)

Letter from Henry Bonham giving information on location of first homeward bound fleet from China. 25 June 1808. (3/289.)

Letter from Mr. Innes enclosing extract from letter, 30 September 1809, from Canton, mainly on depredations of pirates and assistance afforded by the English against them. 10 March 1810. (3/292.)

Letter from James Drummond about state of affairs in China. 5 July 1799. (3/531.)

Letter from Alexander Dalrymple sending extract from letter, 20 November 1803, from David Lance, Canton, regarding a mission he had undertaken on instructions of the Secret Committee, damage to ships by gales on Chinese coast, and attempts to open trade between Japan and India. 23 June 1804. (3/532.)

Letter as above (3/532) enclosing extract from letter, 25 February 1805, from David Lance about Cochin China and depredations of pirates on China coast. 27 February 1805. (3/534.)

Letter from Thomas Reid enclosing extract of letter, 22 March 1807, from Alexander Shank, Canton, giving an account of dispute between the English factory and the Chinese government, occasioned by the death of a Chinese in an affray with seamen from the *Neptune*, 3 September 1807. (3/535.)

Copy letter from Lord Harrowby to George Canning, Foreign Secretary, about the Portuguese settlements in India and China. 25 August 1809. (3/543.)

Letter from William Groom to Robert Dundas sending Attorney-General's opinion on a case of affray at Canton. 28 August 1810. (3/545.)

Letter from Alexander Dalrymple, hydrographer to the Admiralty, giving extract from a letter on the accurate execution of a survey of the China Sea. 14 December 1807. (3/669.)

DALHOUSIE MUNIMENTS

A. *Section 5.* Papers of George, 9th Earl of Dalhousie (1770–1838), as Commander-in-Chief in India, 1829–32. Including:

34. Memorandum on a letter from Mr. Plowden concerning suspension of trade at Macao. 13 March 1830.

B. *Section 6.* Papers of James Andrew Ramsay, 10th Earl and 1st Marquis of Dalhousie (1812–60), as Governor-General of India, 1848–56. Including:

430. Copy of report by the Superintendent of Trade, Hong Kong, to the Earl of Clarendon concerning the opium trade. 1856.

518. Letter from Captain G. O'Callaghan to the Governor-General concerning Russian designs in the Sea of Japan. 1 February 1856.

235. Letter in Chinese characters, n.d.

C. *Section 8.* Papers of Fox Maule, 2nd Baron

Panmure and 11th Earl of Dalhousie (1801–74) as Secretary at War, 1846–52, Secretary for War, 1855–8, and a member of the Cabinet, 1849–52, and 1855–8. Including:

47. Letter from Lord Grey enclosing letter from Lord Fitzroy Somerset and memorandum by Major-General D'Aquilar about the garrison at Hong Kong. 1848.

138. Volume containing copies of letters from Lord Panmure to General Sir William Codrington, 22 October 1855–30 June 1856 (Crimea) and three letters to Lieutenant-General T. Ashburnham in China. 25 April–[—] 1857.

393. Printed copy of papers relating to proceedings of naval forces at Canton. October–December 1856.

418. Sixteen papers, including letters from Major-General T. Ashburnham, concerning the dispute with China and military expedition to Hong Kong. January–August 1857.

423. Letter from Colonel M. McMindo about the nature of the country and means of transport near Canton. 8 March 1857.

432. Printed copies of two draft dispatches from Lord Clarendon to Lord Elgin with instructions as High Commissioner and Plenipotentiary in China. April 1857.

SEAFORTH MUNIMENTS

Letter from John Mackay to J. A. Stewart Mackenzie, M.P., relating to trade with China, particularly the opium trade. 16 April 1833. (8/10.)

Bill for the regulation of trade with China and of trading in tea in contemplation of the ending, in April 1834, of the exclusive trading rights of the East India Company. May 1833. (8/11.)

Printed petition and resolutions on the China trade. 1833. (8/18.)

Journal by K. W. Stewart Mackenzie, Lieutenant 90th Light Infantry, including account of an attack on Canton. 14 October 1840–14 February 1842. (6/86–9.)

Copy letter by Keith Stewart Mackenzie to Sir F. Maitland asking to be employed as A.D.C. to Admiral Elliott on the Canton expedition. 11 January 1841. (6/87.)

Letters by Lieutenant-Colonel Ellis of the Royal Marines, Lord Fitzroy Somerset, Military Secretary at the Horse Guards, Sir Hugh Gough, Commander of the troops at Canton, Commodore Sir Gordon Bremer, and Sir John Wilson, commending the conduct of Lieutenant K. Stewart Mackenzie in the actions at Canton, and relating to his claim for a Canton medal. 12 January 1841–27 April 1844. (6/88.)

Medical certificates stating that Lieutenant K. Stewart Mackenzie, of the 90th Foot, was suffering from fever contracted in operations against the Chinese at Canton, and authorizing his immediate return to Europe. 18 June–3 August 1841. (11/89.)

Letter from E. Stewart serving on H.M.S. *Greyhound* on the China station. n.d. (17/vol. 82.)

MAPS AND PLANS

Charts of the harbour of Tinghai (Chusan), by A. Royer. 1840. (R.H. 2097.)

Views of elevations on coast lines in the Indian Ocean and China Sea. n.d. (R.H. 763.)

MURRAY OF LINTROSE PAPERS

Letters from M. Murray in India with news of the war in China. 1840. (2/142.)

DUNDAS OF OCHTERTYRE MUNIMENTS

Letter by J. K. Wedderburn in Chin-lai to David Dundas, describing conditions on the Chinese military expedition. 2 February 1842. (No. 214.)

CUNNINGHAME OF THORNTON PAPERS

Letter from William Macredie in Melbourne giving details of the wreck of the *Amelia* and of the rescue of the survivors, and of a talk with the Bishop of Hong Kong. 14 August 1859. (475.)

Bundle of letters from George Wrey to his aunt Mrs. C. E. Stuart in Reading, describing his travels in America, Canada, Japan, China, Australia, and New Zealand. 1876–9. (482/1.)

Diary of travels in Japan by George Wrey while on the above tour, with a list of curios bought there. 1877. (482/3.)

LOTHIAN MUNIMENTS (GD. 40)

Papers of Philip Henry Kerr, 11th Marquis of Lothian (1882–1940), Editor of *Round Table*, 1910–16, Secretary to the Prime Minister, 1916–21, Under-Secretary of State for India, 1931–2, Ambassador to Washington, 1939–40. *c.* 99 boxes, including:

Box containing miscellaneous papers, including notes on Japan. (GD. 40/17/5, pp. 178–212.)

Letters, memorandum, and other papers on Japanese policy in China 1919. (GD. 40/17/74.)

SCOTTISH UNITED SERVICES
MUSEUM

Crown Square, The Castle, Edinburgh

Documents relating to Admiral Sir Murray Anderson, including:

1. Translation of the Grant of the Order of the Rising Sun, 3rd Class (Japan), dated 9 May, 12th month of the 8th year of Taisho. Typescript. (No. 10.)

2. Letter of thanks from the Shanghai Municipal Council relating to the action of British Naval forces during the Civil War between the provinces of Kiangsu and Chekiang. 27 October 1924. (No. 13.)

3. Letter of thanks from the Shanghai Municipal Council relating to the action of British Naval forces during the general strike at Shanghai of June to August 1925. 1 September 1925. (No. 15.)

4. Letter from the Admiralty announcing his appointment as Temporary Commander-in-Chief on the China Station. 16 April 1925. (No. 17.)

5. Letter of thanks from the Admiralty on his relinquishing his appointment of Rear Admiral and Senior Naval Officer, Yangtse. 15 March 1926. Together with copies of correspondence, of various writers and dates, relating to his tenure of this appointment. (No. 18.)

Letter of Mr. McK.Annand relating to the uniform of the Tientsin Volunteer Corps, 1914–18. 12 March 1958. (Tientsin Volunteer Corps. 958. 1.)

Record of service of Captain Sutejiro Asami, whose sword is in the Museum (no. 1946–54). (Japanese Army 946. 1.)

'The Royal Hong Kong Defence Force', by Lieutenant-Colonel C. P. Vaughan. This mainly concerns questions of uniform, &c. Typescript. (Hong Kong Defence Force. U. 1.)

GLASGOW

NATIONAL BIBLE SOCIETY OF SCOTLAND WESTERN COMMITTEE, GLASGOW

224 West George Street, Glasgow, C. 2

The Society's mission in China began in 1863. (Marchant, p. 81.)
Some minute books.

REGIMENTAL HEADQUARTERS, THE ROYAL HIGHLAND FUSILIERS

518 Sauchiehall Street, Glasgow, C. 2

A volume of natural history notes on Perak, Singapore, Malacca, and China. 1877–80. (D. 255.)

UNIVERSITY LIBRARY

The University, Glasgow, G12 8QQ

The Hunterian Manuscripts are described by J. Young and P. Henderson Aitken in *A catalogue of the manuscripts in the Library of the Hunterian Museum in the University of Glasgow . . .*, Glasgow, 1908.

Abu al Shazi, Bahadur, Khan of Khuwarazm, Genealogical history of the Tartars. 18th century. *German.* (Hunterian MS. 308.)

Translation of embroidered characters on a Japanese panel belonging to Robert Wylie, and two related letters from Messrs. A. De Ath & Co., Kobe-Hiogo, Japan, to Messrs. Wylie & Lochhead Ltd., Glasgow. (Wylie Collection, 1921. Bh12–y15.)

PERTH

THE BLACK WATCH REGIMENTAL MUSEUM

Balhousie Castle, Perth

'Notes of a voyage round the Cape from Ireland to China via Java in the full rigged ship *Golden Fleece*.' Copy of letters from Colonel W. Gordon to his mother. 1886–7. (File H-7. Section G.)

'D' Company, 1st Battalion, War Log. Korea and Kenya. 1952–3. (Case 12, shelf 2.)

Folder containing typescript notes and maps relating to the participation of the 1st Battalion in the second and third battles of the Hook, Korea. 1952–3. (Case 12, shelf 2.)

Two envelopes containing typescript notes and aerial photographs relating to the participation of the 2nd Battalion in the same battles. 1952–3. (Case 12, shelf 2.)

File containing typescript list of casualties sustained by the 1st Battalion in Korea. 1952–3. (Case 12, shelf 4.)

Propaganda leaflets used by Communist forces in the Korean War. *c.* 1952. (Exhibition Room 4.)

ST. ANDREWS

UNIVERSITY LIBRARY

The University, St. Andrews, Fife

Correspondence of Sir D'Arcy Wentworth Thompson, Professor of Natural History at St. Andrews, 1917–48. (Not fully indexed.)

1. Twelve letters of Professor K. Mitsukuri, Science College, Tokyo University, about zoological specimens, &c. 1896–1901. (No. 899.)

2. Six letters to and from Sir Charles Norton Edgcumbe Eliot, Principal of Hong Kong University, about specimens of pteropods. 1906–7. (No. 524.)

3. Fifteen letters to and from Alan Owston, importer at Yokohama. 1910–14. (No. 796, MS. 25815–18.)

4. Two letters of Hiroshai Ohshima on zoological matters. 1921–9. (No. 879.)

5. Four letters of Dolly —, of the Church of England Mission in Peiping, giving local and personal news. [1939?] (No. 33.)

STIRLING

REGIMENTAL DEPOT THE ARGYLL AND SUTHERLAND HIGHLANDERS

The Castle, Stirling

Letter-book, 1st Battalion the Argyll and Sutherland Highlanders. The letters, which are mainly orders for goods for the Regiment, are written during the period February 1889–January 1892 from Hong Kong. August 1887–August 1911. (L. 18.)

Unofficial casualty list, 1st Battalion the Argyll and Sutherland Highlanders in Korea, 1950, together with a few related documents.

'Development of Tactics Frederick the Great to the Present Day', [by G. de B. Purves ?], giving an account of tactics, &c. in various wars including the Russo-Japanese War, 1904. n.d.

NORTHERN IRELAND

BELFAST

THE LIBRARY, QUEEN'S UNIVERSITY

Belfast

A collection of printed forms, completed in manuscript, relating to the career of David Taylor, including three certificates of discharge (nos. 5–7) in respect of his service as surgeon of the S.S. *Cyclops* on three voyages from Liverpool to China. 1 October 1880, 8 March 1881, 8 August 1881. (MS. 1/27.)

Papers of Professor C. MacDouall, Professor of Latin at Queen's University from 1849, including various lectures and other papers on Oriental religions, philosophical ideas, and philology. (MS. 6/1–42.)

Typescript of 'Kiangsi Native Trade and its Taxation' by Stanley Fowler Wright, Shanghai. 1919. (MS. 1/121.)

WRIGHT COLLECTION

Papers and books bequeathed to the University by Stanley Fowler Wright (1873–1953), Commissioner of Customs and Personal Secretary to the Inspector-General, the Chinese Maritime Customs. This collection fills fourteen shelves. In addition to manuscripts there are books in Chinese, books and pamphlets on China and on the Chinese Customs, many official printed papers, reports, &c., and copies of Customs publications, some with manuscript annotations by Wright. (See China. *The maritime Customs. IV Service series: No. 51. List of Customs publications with alphabetical index*, Shanghai, 1935. The copy in Queen's Library indicates which publications are in the Wright Collection.) Among the manuscripts in the collection are Wright's notes and papers for his various published works, including *Hart and the Chinese Customs*, Belfast, 1950; some letters of Sir Robert Hart; some of Wright's own official papers; and some of Wright's later correspondence, relating mainly to his published books. The manuscripts are listed and briefly described below.

A. *Notes for published works*

Notes on the China trade—list of books, extracts, and notes. 1 file.

Notes on State Papers relating to China. 1 file.

Notes on American State Papers relating to China. 1 file.

Notes based on Foreign Office archives relating to the Chinese Customs service, with extracts from correspondence. 1 file.

Notes from the Foreign Office archives relating to the Chinese Customs. 1 vol.

Hart-Campbell correspondence: extracts and notes. 1 file.

Notes from the Hart-Campbell correspondence, with newspaper cuttings, &c. 1 vol.

Notes and extracts from *The Times*. 1 file.

Notes on the Chinese Government Agency in London, later the London office of the Inspectorate-General of Chinese Maritime Customs (from 1874), with extracts from correspondence with Sir Robert Hart, &c. 1 file.

Telegrams to the Inspector-General from the Non-Resident Secretary, 1884–6. 1 file.

Eight notebooks of various sizes containing rough notes on the Chinese Customs, with extracts, summaries, &c.

B. *Sir Robert Hart's papers*

Private diary. 1854–1908. 77 vols. (2 missing).

Sir Robert Hart's letters to Paul King of the Chinese Customs. 11 August 1896–9 June 1907. 17 letters (originals and copies) in a large envelope.

Letter to Sir Robert Hart from Francis H. Carl, Customs House, Lappau. 27 June 1901. 3 pp.

Copies of S/O letters from Sir Robert Hart to Commissioners of Customs and others. January 1904–February 1908. 4 letter-books (192, 382, 377, and 378 pp.) with indexes, bound in 2 vols.

Letter from Sir Robert Hart to 'Sir Ernest'. n.d. 4 pp.

See E. LeFevour, 'A report on the Robert Hart papers at Queen's University, Belfast', *J. Asian Studies*, 33 (1974), pp. 437–9.

C. *Stanley F. Wright's private correspondence*

File of correspondence and papers relating to Wright's book *China's struggle for tariff autonomy, 1843–1938*, Shanghai, 1938.

File of correspondence containing letters to Wright

and copies of his replies, about the Chinese Customs Service, Sir Robert Hart, &c. 1939–44.

File of correspondence and other papers mainly concerning *Hart and the Chinese Customs*: most of the letters contain information about Hart, and some include copies of and extracts from his letters, &c. 1944.

File of correspondence containing letters to Wright and copies of his own letters relating to *Hart and the Chinese Customs*, &c. 1945–51.

Large envelope containing correspondence of Wright with Queen's University, many of the letters relating to the Chinese Customs, Wright's books, &c. 1932–44, with one or two earlier papers.

D. *Twelve folders of Wright's papers*

1. Notes from the Yule edition of Marco Polo's *Travels*.

2. Notes from the Secretary of State's archives, &c.

3. Rough calculations, &c., with some notes and letters.

4. Newspaper cuttings, 1927–8, being reviews of Wright's book *The collection and disposal of the maritime and native customs since the Revolution of 1911*, Shanghai, 1927.

5. Copy of a memorandum on statistics kept by the Customs, and on tariffs. November 1902.

6. Various papers dealing with Customs figures, &c.

7. Papers and tables on the collection and disposal of Customs revenues, 1912–24, with a copy of a dispatch from S. H. Li to Sir Richard Dane about the Hong Kong salt tax, September 1917.

8. Various papers, including a memorandum on financial reconstruction, 1920; a memorandum on Chinese finances by F. Aglen; Hart's statement of the extraordinary affairs transacted by him for China, &c.; and an account of the origin and growth of the Customs service.

9. Various papers on the Chinese Customs, trade, &c.

10. Copies of confidential papers, &c.—'Washington Treaty Surtaxes', &c.

11. Draft letters and papers from the Inspectorate-General of Customs, Peking, 1928, with some newspaper cuttings, 1928–37.

12. Copies of various official papers, including 'Report on the Organisation and Work of the Chinese Maritime Customs Preventive Fleet', Shanghai, 30 March 1938 (20 pp.); and a statement by Sir Frederick Maze about the seizure of the Manchurian Customs House, 21 July 1932.

E. *Official correspondence and papers of S. F. Wright* (in a large parcel)

1. Copies of two letters to Sir Robert Hart from Jules A. van Aalst, about telegraphy. 19 June and 5 August 1901.

2. 'Native and Alien Post Offices', Chinese dispatch to the Inspector-General from the Post Secretary. 18 July 1901.

3. Reviews of Wright's books *The Collection and disposal of . . . customs revenue since . . . 1911*, and *Kiangsi native trade and its taxation* (1920); with newspaper cuttings and the Edwardes/Maze controversy, 1928–9.

4. Various official memoranda, papers, and letters. Mainly 1920s and 1930s.

5. 'China and the Special Tariff Conference' by Sir Francis Aglen. 10 June 1924. 16 pp.

6. Memorandum on the treatment of Customs men to be compulsorily retired. 23 March 1928.

7. 'Chinese Maritime Customs (including Marine Department): nature of Chinese Government control explained. Confidential.' Incomplete.

8. Letter to Wright, in Belfast, from the Customs, Shanghai, 29 May 1939, with copies of correspondence about the balance of trade. Shanghai, July 1939.

9. Correspondence between Carl Neprud, Sir Frederick Maze and Wright. 1943 and 1944.

F. *Papers relating to the Chinese Customs*. 2 boxes

1. Letters and papers, originals and copies, relating to the work of the Chinese Customs.

2. Translations of extracts from *Tariff system in China* by Takayanagi; with copies of numerous other letters and papers on the same subject.

G. Translations of Chinese petitions, and of part of *Tariff problems* by Tang Meng Chen (95 pp.). In a large envelope.

H. A folder labelled 'Financial Secretary' containing letters and papers.

I. A folder containing notes on official correspondence from 1850 onwards; copies of official correspondence and papers, 1894 and 1896; copies of official Customs papers, 1935 and 1938.

J. Copies of dispatches, &c. from 1876 onwards. In a large envelope.

K. *Various loose papers*, including:

Draft statement about the proposed appointment of Von Gumpach to a post in China as Professor of Mathematics.

Memorandum concerning British commercial relations with China and the establishment of the Inspectorate-General of Chinese Imperial Maritime Customs, compiled chiefly from papers presented to Parliament. 17 pp.

Letter from the Chamber of Commerce of Shanghai [to the League of Nations representatives] about the Japanese attack on China. 18 May 1932. Typescript. 5 pp.

Report on the Whangpoo Conservancy Board. July 1938. 3 pp.

L. *Hong Kong and the Chinese Customs*, by Stanley F. Wright, Commissioner of Customs, Personal Secretary of the Inspector-General, Shanghai, 1930. Confidential. Author's copy with manuscript notes and with loose copies of correspondence, &c., at the back.

PRESBYTERIAN CHURCH IN IRELAND FOREIGN MISSION

Church House, Belfast, 1

The Presbyterian Church in Ireland Foreign Mission was founded in 1840 and the first missionaries were sent to India. Later missions were established in Manchuria, the first missionaries arriving there in 1869. Many of the printed records of the mission survive, but most of the nineteenth-century original letters have been destroyed, although many were printed in part or *in toto* in the *Annual Reports* and other publications. Field records were lost during the Japanese invasion. There is a complete set, 1840 to date, of the printed Minutes of Assembly of the Presbyterian Church in Ireland (51 vols.). See R. H. Boyd, *Waymakers in Manchuria. The story of the Irish Presbyterian pioneer missionaries to Manchuria*, 1940, and *The prevailing wind*, 1953. There are other papers relating to the Manchuria mission among the records of the Church of Scotland in Edinburgh. See also Marchant, p. 88.

Letters from China written by the Revd. Alexander R. Crawford. 1895–1908. 1 box.

The diary of the Revd. Alexander R. Crawford written in China. 1900–13. 13 vols.

Papers of missionary candidates. 2 parcels.

Findings of the Manchuria Conference (printed). 1901–41. Bound in 2 vols.

Letters and papers from and relating to the Manchuria Christian College. 1909–17, 1918, 1919–31. 3 files.

Manchuria reports (printed). 1911–50. Bound in 4 vols.

Minutes of the proceedings of the Joint Home Board of the Manchuria Christian College, 1912–34, with correspondence to 1938. 1 file.

Minutes of the Manchuria Mission Council. 1917–25, 1932–6. 1 file and 1 parcel.

Statistics of the mission staff, Manchuria mission, &c. 1918–40. 1 file.

Letters to mission agents. 1923–40. 1 parcel.

Circulars to the mission field. 1933–45. 1 parcel.

Manchuria correspondence, consisting of letters and papers from the Manchuria Mission Conference to the Convener in Belfast. 1937–41, 1941–2. 2 files.

Correspondence relating to the appointment of a 'juridical person' by the Manchuria Mission Conference of the Church of Scotland and Presbyterian Church in Ireland. 1938–9. 1 file.

Papers relating to the Manchuria mission. 20th century. 2 packets.

Letters from missionaries in Manchuria. 20th century. Numerous boxes.

Two large scrapbooks relating to all the missions. 20th century.

Papers of Dr. R. H. Boyd, missionary and author of *Waymakers in Manchuria*, 1940, and of other books concerning the work of the missions. Large collection, not yet sorted. 20th century.

A manuscript history of the development of Chinese picture writing (1 vol.), with an appendix entitled 'Chinese Pictograms' (1 vol.).

PUBLIC RECORD OFFICE OF NORTHERN IRELAND

66 Balmoral Avenue, Belfast, BT9 6NY

LONDONDERRY COLLECTION (D. 654)

Papers of Sir Robert Cowan, Governor of Bombay from 1728 to 1734, including papers relating to his private trade at Goa, Mocha, and Bombay. Cowan was chief of the Mocha factory from 1724 to 1728 and he engaged in trade with China. 1719–44. (D. 654/B1/1–18.) These papers are described in more detail in the *Guide to Western manuscripts . . . relating to South and South-East Asia*.

MACARTNEY PAPERS (D. 572 and 2225)

Correspondence of George, 1st Earl Macartney (1737–1806). These papers contain various scattered letters relating to Lord Macartney's embassy to China, 1792–4, but nothing of any great importance. There is a Calendar of the papers at the Public Record Office of Northern Ireland, a copy of which is deposited at the National Register of Archives, London (NRA 6465). 21 vols.

6/47. [? Sir Joseph] Banks to Lord Macartney concerning an essay by a Dr. Richardson and also maps of China, one made by Jesuits. 9 January 1805.

8/38. Dumazel, missionaire de St. Lazare, requesting an immediate reply to his inquiry whether the East India Company will be able to provide a passage to China. 6 March 1800.

8/64. Henry Dundas to Lord Macartney returning papers relating to some incident in China (?). 30 September 1800.

11/49. Memorandum for Mr. Staunton from Mr. Sinclair, with notes on the produce, trade, harbours of India and Ceylon and a proposal for trade with China and Japan. n.d. [1787–96.]

11/50. Thomas Cheap, London, to Lord Macartney, regretting the writer's inability to further Lord Macartney's wishes with regard to Sir George Staunton and the China mission. 26 October 1788.

11/49. Draft letter from Lord Macartney to William Pitt recommending Sir George Staunton in connection with the proposed China mission. 22 October 1788.

7/77. Letter from Jacobus Lysive Phim of Xansi province on Christian business rebellion in certain provinces. *Latin.*

7/78. Letter from N. J. Raux, Superior of French Mission at Peking. *French.*

China Papers (D. 2225/5)

1. Group of patents to Lord Macartney as Ambassador to China. 1792.

2. Letter from Duke of Clarence, recommending Mr. Fearson, fifth mate of the *Winchester*, which attended Lord Macartney on his embassy to China. 1792.

3. Account by Abdul Cawder Khan of the invasion of Lassa by the Rajah of Nepal's army and the subsequent invasion of Nepal by a Chinese army, in a translation signed by G. F. Cherry. 1792.

4. Letter from Sir George Staunton about an interpreter. 1793.

5. 'Camoens garden', a poem by Thomas Hickey. 1794.

6. Draft letter to Mr. Dundas, sending notes of his China expedition. 1794.

14/45. Sir George Staunton to Lord Macartney concerning a report of an embassy being sent to China, and detailing the writer's qualifications for the same, describing his services in China. 1 March 1800.

15/28. Cardinal Antonelei (?), Rome, to Lord Macartney thanking him for undertaking to bring

with him two Chinese Roman Catholic students returning to China. 6 April 1792.

15/29. Draft letter from Lord Macartney to Cardinal Antonelei (?) informing him of the safe arrival in China of the Roman Catholic students and thanking him for an introduction to Roman Catholic clergy at Macao and Peking. 12 December 1792.

15/64. Henry Baring, Canton, to Lord Macartney about the threatened failure of the principal Hong Kong merchant. 16 January 1795.

15/65 and 66. T. C. Bartholmey, Calcutta, to Lord Macartney about the China embassy. 5 and 31 December 1794.

17/85. Document in Italian endorsed 'Note from the Superior of the Chinese College at Naples enclosed in Sir William Hamilton's letter of 28 July 1795—sent to Sir G. Staunton.' n.d.

18/36. Note by Lord Macartney for the use of his wife, giving her instructions as to what should be done with his money and houses during his absence in China. 9 September 1792.

19/163–5. Letters concerning the China mission. 1793.

19/192. Sir George Staunton to Lord Macartney forwarding papers (not present) about the Dutch embassy to China. 16 December 1795.

20/33 and 35. Applications for employment on the China embassy. March and April 1792.

20/44–6. Letters concerning the China embassy. 1792.

20/53 and 54. Note of the dates of the various embassies to China; and note about the East India Company presents for the Emperor of China, 18 June 1795.

21/108. Maps and plates to illustrate the fine paper edition of Lord Macartney's Embassy to China, originally published at fifteen guineas.

MACARTNEY LETTER (D. 903)

Letter from Charles Mitchell to Lord Macartney, about Macartney's return from the Chinese Embassy. 1794.

Richard Bentley, R.N.: Log-books and sketches of Pacific voyages. 1824–6. (*List of accessions to repositories in 1967*, p. 84.)

JOHNSTON OF KILMORE PAPERS (D. 1728)

Three letters from the Revd. Robert Morrison, D.D., relating to his missionary activities in China. 1827–9.

WILKINSON PAPERS (D. 1292)

Papers of Hiram Shaw Wilkinson relating to his service in Japan and China. 1857–1924.

A. Correspondence. 2 boxes

1. Letters to and from Sir Harry Parkes. 1 envelope and a few loose letters

Copies of five letters from Wilkinson to Parkes. 1874–6 and 1878.

Twenty-one letters from Wilkinson to Parkes, written from Belfast, Hong Kong, and Shanghai. 1881–5.

Letters to Wilkinson from Parkes, including about 160 letters from Tokyo, 1875–9, and seventeen letters from Tokyo and Peking, 1883–5.

2. Drafts and copies of Wilkinson's out-letters, mainly relating to personal affairs. 1 envelope

Two letters written in Belfast. 29 August and 29 October 1870.

Two letters to S. MacGowan, from Hyogo and Yokohama. 2 December 1872 and 20 November 1873.

Two letters to his wife, from Hyogo and Yokohama, 5 March 1873 and 14 January 1878.

Draft concerning the supply of funds to consulates in Japan, from the British consulate, Kanagawa, 15 November 1875.

Letter from Shanghai, addressed to — Watters. 7 October 1891.

Two letters to his son 'Harrie' from Kobe and Yokohama. 16 and 18 July 1892.

Letter from Belfast, addressed to — Findlay. 18 August 1892.

Letter from Shanghai, addressed to — Fraser. 10 March 1894.

Letter from Yokohama, addressed to — Trench, about the detention of the *Gaelic*. 6 November 1894.

Letter from Shanghai, addressed to Sir Claude [MacDonald], Minister at Peking, on consular affairs. 16 February 1897.

Two letters about property in Ireland. 14 June and 30 July 1899.

Letter from Shanghai, addressed to F. H. Villiers at the Foreign Office, about leave. 25 October 1901.

Letter, addressed to — Cockerell, concerning his resignation. 18 April 1908.

Letter concerning a post in Shanghai for his son. 14 April 1908.

3. Loose letters, addressed to Wilkinson, mainly in Japan and China. *c.* 1864–1905.

Packet labelled 'Passage to Japan 1864 correspondence'.

Packet labelled 'Letters from Home' consisting of letters addressed to Wilkinson at Yedo (Tokyo). 1867–70.

Sealed packet labelled 'Letters from Home Jany to April 1873' containing letters addressed to Wilkinson at Yedo.

Bundle labelled 'Private letters & chits' containing letters and notes addressed to Wilkinson from Japan and Hong Kong, mainly dated 1895.

Various loose letters, telegram forms, &c., addressed to Wilkinson in Japan and Shanghai, from Japan, Shanghai, Belfast, London, and the U.S.A., relating mainly to personal matters but with some references to official duties. There are also some drafts of Wilkinson's letters, including a few to Sir Claude MacDonald.

4. Family and personal letters and papers. 1 box

Envelope labelled 'Family correspondence' including family letters to Wilkinson in Japan and Shanghai, and some to Wilkinson in Ireland from his son 'Harrie' in Shanghai, 1921–4.

Envelope labelled 'H. P. Wilkinson Shanghai to father Sir H. W —' containing one bundle of letters about official matters, 1892–3; loose letters mainly about business affairs, 1905–6; and letters mainly about business affairs, 1921.

Large envelope labelled 'H. S. W. Personal, references, certificates, commissions . . .'.

Envelope labelled 'H. S. W. Personal Ephemera', many items relating to Japan and China.

Envelope labelled 'Photographs of family in Far East'.

Envelope labelled 'Misc. unsorted' containing nothing of importance for Japan or China.

B. H. S. Wilkinson's official papers. 1 box

1. Copies of official letters and papers, from Hong Kong, Peking, and Shanghai, mainly to Sir Harry Parkes from Frederick W. A. Bruce, 1858–61; with a memorandum entitled 'Access to Peking how obtainable by H. M.'s Ambassador' signed H. S. P. 15 July 1857; a letter by Lieutenant-General Sir Hope Grant with a draft proclamation concerning the seizure of officials by the Chinese Government; and other letters and memoranda. 1860s.

2. Papers relating to the case of the Japanese Finance Department as owners of the S.S. *New York, v.* the Pacific Mail S.S. Company, heard in the U.S. Consular Court, 29 June 1874.

3. Bundle of draft letters, memoranda, and various loose papers. 1874–1905.

4. Memorandum by H. S. Wilkinson, British Consulate, Kanagawa, containing suggestions relating to the draft China and Japan Order in Council, 1876. 8 August 1876.

5. Papers relating to two cases heard in H.B.M.'s Court at Kanagawa before H. S. Wilkinson. 1877.

6. Papers in the case of the *Japan* (burnt at sea, 17 December 1874), heard in the Vice-Admiralty Court of Hong Kong: judgment was given on the 1 April 1878.

7. Memorandum on the judgment of the Supreme Court for China and Japan in the case of Clark *v.* Hall, on appeal. Kanagawa, September 1878.

8. Memorandum entitled 'Jurisdiction in Corea'. 23 November 1885.

9. Letters and papers concerning the smuggling activities of the S.S. *Esmeralda*, including a memorandum on the *Esmeralda*, 16 May 1887, and letters, 1893.

10. Letters and papers concerning the revision of the China and Japan Order in Council. 1891 and 1892.

11. Memoranda and notes by H. S. Wilkinson. 1894.

12. Shanghai papers of 'Mr. Justice Wilkinson', being official letters and papers, about half from his son. 1894–5.

13. Rough translation of an article about Wilkinson and his career which appeared in the Japanese papers Tin Wan Poo of 28 December 1895, with a copy of the original paper.

14. Diary containing memoranda and notes. 1896.

15. Official letters and papers relating to the administration of justice in the province of Yunan. 1902.

16. Correspondence and papers about the enforcement of the decrees of foreign courts; including a memorandum on enforcement by British courts in China of the judgments and orders of the courts of other nationalities, by Chief Justice Wilkinson. 1902.

17. Correspondence and papers relating to the China and Corea Order in Council of 1902. 1902–3.

18. Official letters and papers about consular fee tables in the Far East. 1903.

19. Official letters and papers relating to the judgeship at Weihaiwei. 1903–4.

20. A communication from the China Association and others relating to the riot at Shanghai. 1905. 5 pp. typescript.

21. Papers in the case of George William Lewis.

22. Incomplete draft paper on events in Japan.

23. Photographs of R. V. Carew's letters relating to the Far East.

C. Official reports (printed). 1 box

1. Printed memorandum on the draft China and Japan Order in Council of 1876. Cut up and bound in one volume. 80 pp.

2. Guide to the correction of Errors in Code (and other) telegrams. 4th edition. 1890. 1 vol.

3. International Telegraph Convention 1890: With Service Regulations and Tariffs. French, with English translation. 1 vol.

4. Documents de la Conférence Télégraphique inter-

nationale de Paris. Berne, 1891. 699 pp. and appendices.

5. List of the Higher Metropolitan and Provincial Authorities of China, compiled by J. N. Jordan, and corrected to 31 December 1890. Shanghai, 1891. 43 pp.

6. China: Imperial Maritime Customs. 1. Statistical Series: No. 6. Decennial Reports on the Trade, Navigation, Industries, &c. of the Ports open to Foreign Commerce in China and Corea, and on the condition and Development of the Treaty Port Provinces, 1882–91. First issue, Shanghai, 1893. 694 pp. and appendices.

7. Imperial Japanese Government *v.* the P. & O. S. N. Co.: report of the proceedings; case for the appellants; case for the respondents. In the Privy Council, No. 3 of 1894, on appeal from the Supreme Court for China and Japan. 48, 100, and 3 pp. bound in 1 vol.

8. The Corean Government: Constitutional Changes, July 1894 to October 1895. With an appendix on subsequent enactments to 30 June 1896. By W. H. Wilkinson, late H.B.M.'s Acting-Consul-General in Corea. Shanghai, 1897. 192 pp.

9. Envelope containing official printed papers relating to Japan and China.

D. Various books

1. The Treaty of Wanghia . . . Canton, 1856. 112 pp.

2. Treaties and Conventions between the Empire of Japan and other Powers. Compiled by Foreign Office Japan. Tokyo, 1899. 387 pp. and appendices.

3. The Bethell Trial. Full report of the Proceedings by the Special Correspondent of the Japan Chronicle. The trial of Ernest T. Bethell at Seoul, Korea, before the Supreme Court for China and Korea on a charge of sedition, 15–18 June 1908. 56 pp.

4. Report of Proceedings in Her Britannic Majesty's Court for Japan relating to the death of Walter Raymond Hallowell Carew. Reprinted from the *Japan Gazette*. Also, 'The Carew Case Miss Jacob arrested'. 342 and 23 pp.

MCKEAN PAPERS (D. 1164)
Papers of Edward J. McKean, Commissioner of Customs, China. 1871–91. 2 boxes

A. Letter-books

1. Letter-book containing copies of McKean's letters dealing with personal affairs and office finances, with, at the back, copies of letters to his family (1871) and a letter about opium smuggling (21 June 1879). June 1871–April 1878.

2. Letter-book containing copies of McKean's private letters, many relating to his financial affairs, written

from London (1878), Canton, Shanghai, and Peking. October 1878–December 1882. 494 ff.

3. Letter-book containing copies of McKean's private letters, many relating to his financial affairs, written from Peking, Shanghai, Ireland (1884–6), Swatow, and Shanghai. January 1883–December 1888. 500 ff.

4. Letter-book containing copies of letters from McKean to colleagues in the Customs service, on Customs affairs, written from Canton and Shanghai. June 1879–September 1881. 501 ff.

5. Letter-book containing copies of letters from McKean to colleagues in the Customs service, on Customs affairs, written from Shanghai, Peking, Swatow, and Shanghai. September 1881–March 1891. 566 ff.

B. Office diaries

1. Memorandum book, written in Letts Diary. 1873.

2. Rough note and memorandum book. 1874.

3. Diary describing Customs activities, and giving accounts of various tours of duty, including a visit to Japan and Formosa in 1874. 1874–8.

4. Office diary, written in Letts Rough Diary and Scribbling Journal, including summaries of letters to Sir Robert Hart and others, and of interviews with Chinese officials and others. 1876.

5. Office memorandum book, with entries similar to those described in No. 4 above. 1877.

6. Memorandum book, Canton, being a diary of Customs activities similar to Nos. 4 and 5 above. May 1879–January 1880. [In 1878 McKean visited Ireland and the U.S.A.]

7–19. Memorandum books, similar to those described above, but with fuller entries, and including copies of letters to Sir Robert Hart and others, accounts of interviews, &c. February 1880–March 1881 (4 vols.); March 1881–May 1882 and November 1883, with copies of letters, 1885–6 (1 vol.); April 1886–March 1891 (8 vols.).

C. Domestic accounts in English and Chinese.

ANNESLEY PAPERS (D. 1854/5/6)

Photographs, Bay of Nagasaki and British Consulate in Nagasaki, 1872.

Papers about Presbyterian missions in Manchuria. 1890–1910. (*List of accessions to repositories in 1965*, p. 60.)

CROOK LETTERS (D. 1727/2)

Two letters from Emma M. Crook referring to her activities as a Presbyterian missionary in Manchuria. 1904, 1907.

MCCAUL PAPERS (D. 1893)

Correspondence of the Revd. Matthew McCaul, Presbyterian Minister in India, his wife, Florence, and brother, George, 1914–34; with a memorandum on missionary work in Moukden, North China, 1921; and photographs of Tangi Gorge, Khyber Pass and Dakka, 1919. 1914–31.

Missionary and family letters from Elsie Hodgkin in China 1921–8. (*List of accessions to depositories in 1971*, p. 86.)

Missionary letters from China to Dr. Agatha Crawford. 1945–9. (*List of accessions to repositories in 1967*, p. 84.)

REPUBLIC OF IRELAND

DUBLIN

DUBLIN UNIVERSITY
FAR EASTERN MISSION

1 Trinity College, College Green, Dublin, Eire

The Mission was known as the Dublin University Church Missionary Association from 1885 to 1888, and as the Dublin University Fukien Mission 1888-1950. Available records are listed in Marchant, pp. 53-5.

HIBERNIAN CHURCH
MISSIONARY SOCIETY

35 Molesworth Street, Dublin, Eire

An auxiliary of the Church Missionary Society founded in 1814, it began its mission in China in 1844. In 1958 the Hibernian Auxiliary of the Church of England Zenana Missionary Society amalgamated with it. Few records as yet arranged and available. Marchant, pp. 61-2.

NATIONAL LIBRARY OF IRELAND

Kildare Street, Dublin

WINDER PAPERS (MS. 8799)

Letter from Charles (Agar) Archbishop of Cashel to Lord Macartney congratulating him on his embassy to China. 1792.

Diary of Thomas Winder, who accompanied Lord Macartney as his secretary. 1793. Only a portion of the diary has been preserved.

Commonplace book containing notes on Irish, Persian, and Far Eastern antiquities, with notes on Irish topography. *c.* 1800. (MS. 910.)

Copy of a resolution on the East India and China trade, dated Manchester, 21 January 1830. (Monteagle papers.)

Copies of dispatches from Sir Hugh Gough, 1st Viscount, to the Governor-General of India, Lord Auckland, during the Chinese campaign, 1841 to 1842 [with a letter-book of Sir Hugh Clough concerning army affairs in Ireland, 1854]. 1841-2. (MS. 638.)

History of the 5th Royal Irish Dragoons, 1689 to 1794, and of the 5th Royal Irish Lancers, 1858 to 1919, by Colonel J. R. Harvey. Typescript. (MS. 8000.)

TRINITY COLLEGE LIBRARY
DUBLIN

College Green, Dublin, Eire

Trinity College Association, Dublin, Auxiliary to the Church Missionary Association. Proceedings. 1839-43. 1 vol. (Marchant, p. 108.)

Collection of notices sent weekly to the *Guardian* by J. H. Bernard, with notices of Trinity College men.

Letters of George Salman, D.D., Provost of Trinity College, Dublin, to J. H. Bernard. 1891-1903.

PAPERS IN PRIVATE CUSTODY

PAPERS REPORTED BY THE HISTORICAL MANUSCRIPTS COMMISSION

Papers in private custody, described in the publications of the Royal Commission on Historical Manuscripts; arranged alphabetically by name of owner. Preliminary inquiries should be made to the Secretary, Historical Manuscripts Commission, Quality House, Quality Court, Chancery Lane, London, WC2A 1HP, unless otherwise stated.

COLONEL THE EARL CATHCART. H.M.C. 1. 2nd R.

Papers of Colonel Charles Cathcart, who was appointed ambassador to China in 1787, but died on the voyage to China in 1788. Including:

Extracts from early voyages to China, showing what presents were then taken.

Appointment of Charles Cathcart to be ambassador to China. 30 November 1787. Secret instructions, and other papers on the matter.

LORD DE L'ISLE AND DUDLEY. H.M.C. 77, II (1934)

Rowland Whyte to Sir Robert Sydney. 'Sir John Fortescu, understanding that two ships are come from China to Middleborough, is desirous to have 10 lb. of ginger.' 1600. (II, p. 455.)

MARQUIS OF SALISBURY. SALISBURY (CECIL) MSS. H.M.C. 9, I–XVIII, *and see also* H.M.C. 2–6: 3rd R.–7th R. (Inquiries to the Librarian, Hatfield House, Hatfield, Herts.)

Letter of Thomas Champneys in Naples to the Queen, recommending an acquaintance for an expedition of discovery to Cathaia. 3 November 1566. (H.M.C. vol. I.)

Receipt given by Michael Lok of London, mercer, to the Earl of Lincoln, Lord High Admiral of England, for the sum of £20, in full payment of £135, for his Honour's stock and venture in the third voyage outwards for the discovery of Cathay, &c. by 'the North-westwards'. 19 August 1578. (H.M.C. vol. II.)

Letter of Henry Cuffe in Paris to Henry Savile describing the recent hostility of the King of Giapone [Japan] against Christianity: his crucifixion of seven Spanish Jesuits and seizure of a Spanish ship. 4/14 June 1597. (H.M.C. vol. VII.)

PAPERS REPORTED BY THE ROYAL COMMISSION ON HISTORICAL MANUSCRIPTS (NATIONAL REGISTER OF ARCHIVES)

Papers in private custody described in the unpublished reports of the Royal Commission on Historical Manuscripts (National Register of Archives), arranged alphabetically by name of owner. Preliminary inquiries should be made to: The Assistant Secretary, Historical Manuscripts Commission, Quality House, Quality Court, Chancery Lane, London, WC2A 1HP, unless otherwise stated.

While every care has been taken to ensure that these lists are as accurate as possible, the Register accepts no responsibility for errors.

BROADLANDS ARCHIVES (NRA 12889)

PALMERSTON PAPERS

Correspondence and papers of Henry John Temple, 3rd Viscount Palmerston (1784–1865), Foreign Secretary 1830–4, 1835–41, Home Secretary 1852–5, Prime Minister 1855–8, 1859–65. Correspondents include:

Major-General Charles George D'Aguilar (1784–1855), Commander of British troops in China, 1843–8. (GC/DA.)

Sir G. T. Staunton on China Courts Bill and patronage and endowment of a China professorship. 1838–57. (GC/ST.)

John Abel Smith (1801–71). 1838–63.

Captain Charles Elliot, Chief Superintendent and Plenipotentiary on China Trade Commission. 1841. (GC/EL.)

Dr. John Bowring (1792–1872). 1849–60. (GC/BO.)

Hon. Frederick W. A. Bruce, Shanghai. 1860. (GC/BR.)

Sir John F. Davis. Hong Kong. 1847. (GC/DA.)

Rear-Admiral Sir George Elliot. 1840. (GC/EL.)

SIR CHARLES BUCHANAN (NRA 8677)

Letters to Sir Andrew Buchanan from Canton, giving details of political and social conditions. 1844–56. (5.)

W. G. DUNCAN THOMPSON (NRA 1030)

'China and what I saw there during a residence of five years'; a diary kept by Major-General Guy Rotton. 1850–5.

J. J. EDMUNDS (NRA 0341)

'A glimpse of the Past', by John Edmunds, gunner, H.M.S. *Pearl*, 10 June 1861–18 June 1864. This gives an account of his personal experiences in China against the Tai Ping rebels, 1862, against Japan in 1862 and 1863 in conjunction with France, Prussia, U.S.A., and Holland, and the voyage home from 3 February to 18 June 1864. (3 small notebooks. The first is missing.)

MAJOR-GENERAL J. B. FERMOR-HESKETH. FERMOR MSS. (NRA 7403)

Estate management, household management, and personal papers: including Yokohama. 19th–20th century. 1 sack. (Item 27.)

EARL FORTESCUE (NRA 6304)

Bundle of letters from and about Lord Ebrington, chiefly addressed to Lord Fortescue, from Harrow, Cambridge, U.S.A., India, and the Far East. 1896–1905.

COLONEL P. GELL (NRA 5438)

Papers concerning the Domains Company Limited (for mining in Siberia). 1902. (565.)

EARL OF HALIFAX. THE HICKLETON PAPERS.

The archives of the Wood family of Hickleton and Garrowby in Yorkshire. (NRA 8128. Inquiries to Major T. L. Ingram, 3 Darnley Terrace, London, W. 11.)

A. Official and professional papers

1. Papers concerning the business affairs of Sir Francis Wood, 1st Bart. (1728–96), East India Company merchant, resident in Canton, with other merchants of the Company in China. 1772–96. (A 4. 1.)

   1. Details of accounts with individual merchants, and a summary of accounts.

   2. Lists of bonds held.

   3. Correspondence with Messrs. Bradshaw, Pigou & Rogers of Canton.

   4. Probate of will of James Trudd (d. 1785).

   5. Letters of attorney, 1780.

2. Letters from James Brabazon Urmston, President of the Select Committee of the East India Company at Canton, to Vice-Admiral Sir Charles Richardson, R.N., about the Lintin affair, December 1821–March 1822. (A 4. 3.) (See H. B. Morse, *The chronicles of the East India Company trading to China, 1635–1834*, vol. 4, 1926, pp. 18–19.)

3. The correspondence of Sir Charles Wood, 1st Viscount Halifax (1800–85), President of the Board of Control 1852–5, First Lord of the Admiralty 1855–9, Secretary of State for India 1859–66, including some letters relating to East Asia, notably:

   1. Correspondence with 4th Earl of Clarendon on subjects including Lord Elgin and China. 1857–8. (In A 4. 57.)

   2. Letters from 3rd Viscount Palmerston on same. January–March 1857. (In A 4. 63.)

   3. Letters from 15th Earl of Derby on Russia, Far East. 1885. (In A 4. 87.)

   4. Letter from W. E. Gladstone about estimate for expenditure in China. May 1860. (In A 4. 88.)

   5. Letters from 1st Marquis of Ripon on (1) Military forces for China. September 1863. (2) Russia, Far East, Egypt. April–May 1885. (In A 4. 89.)

   6. Letter from 8th Earl of Elgin in Peking about his punitive expedition. October 1860. (In A 4. 119.)

   7. Letter from Admiral Sir R. S. Dundas about mishap to H.M.S. *Raleigh* in China. May 1857. (In A 4. 128.)

   8. Letter from Admiral William Loring on Far East Intelligence. September 1859. (In A 4. 146.)

B. Personal papers

1. Three letters of Sir Francis Wood, 1st Bart., to his brother Captain Charles Wood, R.N., about family news, business with China merchants, Prize money, &c. 29 December 1782 (20 pp.), January 1783, n.d. The last letter is incomplete. (A 2. 4/1.)

2. Letter of 1st Viscount Halifax to his son, Charles Wood, about India and China. 13 August 1857. (In A 2. 116.)

HARDWICKE COURT (NRA 1000)

Folder containing specimens of Chinese printing, with covering letter of David Hastings of Alnwick to Judith Sharp. 1757. (p. 8.)

EARL OF KIMBERLEY. KIMBERLEY MSS. (NRA 1274. No access at present)

Papers of John Wodehouse, 1st Earl of Kimberley (1826–1902), Colonial Secretary 1870–4, 1880–2, Secretary for India 1882–5, 1892–4, Foreign Secretary 1894–5, &c. Including:

Correspondence, Colonial Office. 1870–83. Large collection.

Journal of events during the Gladstone Ministry kept by Lord Kimberley. 1868–73.

Correspondence, Foreign Office, including:

1. Correspondence from China, Japan, Siam, &c. 1894–5. 1 vol. (bound).

2. Correspondence from St. Petersburg. 1894–5. 1 vol. (bound).

MRS. GEORGE LABOUCHERE. WOLRYCHE-WHITMORE MSS. (NRA 4482)

Book containing tables concerning imports from and exports to India and China, 1790–1828, &c. n.d. [Early 19th century.] (Item 211.)

L. COLLISON MORLEY (NRA 0798)

Diary of Lieutenant J. Lacy Morley, 2nd Battalion 20th Regiment, Hong Kong to England via South Africa. 26 February–22 September 1867. 223 pp.

THOROLD ROGERS CORRESPONDENCE (NRA 12396)

Letter from Michinori S. Nagasaki of Japanese legation, London, asking for details of lectures on international law for a diplomatic student. 31 October 1877. (500–1.)

EARL ST. ALDWYN. HICKS BEACH MSS. (NRA 3526)

1. Official papers of Sir Michael Edward Hicks Beach, 9th Bt. and 1st Earl St. Aldwyn (1837–1916), Colonial Secretary 1878–80, Chancellor of the Exchequer 1885, 1895–1902, &c. Including:

Correspondence &c. concerning a loan to China, Chinese customs, Talienwan and Wei-hai Wei, railway concessions in China, U.S. interests in China. 1896–9. (PCC/72/3.)

Correspondence concerning the withdrawal of troops from China. 1900–2. (PCC/72/1.)

Correspondence concerning a loan to the Viceroy of Wuchang. 1900. (PCC/72/2.)

Copies of telegrams concerning the threatening situation in China and action to be taken. 1900. (PCC/72/4.)

Letters from Lord Lansdowne on various subjects including Chinese affairs, 1900; Chinese loans, 1902. (PCC/84.)

2. Papers of Michael Hugh Hicks Beach

Letters from M. H. Hicks Beach to his mother during his travels in India, China, Japan, and Canada. 1903. (PPC/22.)

Certificate of identity of M. H. Hicks Beach issued by the British Consul at Chefoo. 10 July 1903. (PPD/1/5.)

Diary of a trip in Mongolia by M. H. Hicks Beach. 1903. (PPD/5/1.)

Map of Mongolia, &c., showing route followed by Messrs. Russell and Hicks Beach. 1903. (PPD/5/2.)

Two letters from Sir J. N. Jordan, of the British Legation, Seoul, to M. H. Hicks Beach. 1904. (PPC/23.)

Journal of a journey by M. H. Hicks Beach via America, Japan, and Singapore. 1905. (FGH/10.)

H. DE S. SHORTT (NRA 4791)

Correspondence and papers of Vice-Admiral Francis Henry Shortt, including letters written to his wife, Emily, when serving as Commodore at Hong Kong. The letters deal with life and social engagements at Hong Kong as well as with personal and domestic affairs. [c. 1870–3.] (Bundles 37–42.)

MRS. V. TOLLEMACHE (NRA 6957)

Letter of Hon. A. Lyttelton to Sir Joseph West Ridgeway about Rand Lords, Chinese labour, and the exclusion of Asiatics from the colonies. 13 September 1904. (211.)

CORBETT PAPERS. (NRA 7518) Papers of Sir Julian Stafford Corbett (1854–1922), Director of the Historical Section of the Committee of Imperial Defence, Official Naval Historian of the Great War, &c. (See Brian Tunstall, *Catalogue of the Corbett Papers*, Bedford, 1958.)

1. Letters from Lieutenant-Colonel E. Y. Daniel, R.M., Secretary of the Historical Section of the Committee of Imperial Defence, to Corbett, and other letters, mainly about the C.I.D. History of the Russo-Japanese War. (Box 6 h.)

2. Official memoranda written during the war, include: 'Nanshan and Bulair: 1st March 1915: for Fisher; comparison between Nanshan in Russo-Japanese War and Gallipoli.' (Box 7 d.)

3. Papers relating to the C.I.D. History of the Russo-Japanese War: (Deed Box e):

(a) Manuscript of chapters III–VI.

(b) Miscellaneous notes and correspondence.

(c) Nanshan: notes.

(d) Lecture notes.

4. 'Lectures on naval strategy by Sir Julian Corbett.' This includes, 'The Russo-Japanese War'.

SIR RICHARD WHITE, BT. WHITE (BOULGE) MSS. (NRA 7051)

Letter of J. G. Frith in Calcutta to his mother describing his escape from shipwreck in the *Countess of London* in the China Sea and his journey to China, Penang, and Calcutta. 16 February 1817. (G/2/2.)

Letter of J. G. Frith in Calcutta to John Bott in

London, describing the shipwreck of the *Countess of London*. 17 February 1817 (G/2/3.)

Letter of J. G. Frith in Macao to Mrs. John Bott in London. 31 October 1825. (G/2/7.)

WOMBOURNE WODEHOUSE MSS. (NRA 6393)

Papers on expedition of William Gyfford to China, Ship *George*. 1687–8. (p. 33: 46/2.)

PAPERS REPORTED BY THE NATIONAL REGISTER OF ARCHIVES (SCOTLAND)

Papers in private custody, described in the unpublished reports of the National Register of Archives (Scotland), arranged alphabetically by name of owner. Preliminary inquiries should be made to: The Secretary, National Register of Archives (Scotland), Record Office, H.M. General Register House, Edinburgh 2.

CAPTAIN C. K. ADAM OF BLAIR-ADAM, D.S.O., R.N. (RETD.)

Letter by J. Elphinstone, Canton, about Lord Macartney's embassy. 1795.

Another letter by Elphinstone giving account of the landing of troops at Macao, to which action the Court of Directors [of The East India Company] took great exception. 6 February 1811.

Returns of ships in China Seas and Far East generally. 1833–9. [Admiral Sir Charles Adam, Miscellaneous papers, Box T.]

MAJOR J. M. E. ASKEW

Bundle of letters and other papers relating to the East India company's trade with China. 1787–1831. Including:

1. Copy instructions by Lord Sydney to Colonel Cathcart on his embassy to China. 30 November 1787.

2. Duplicate letter from the Chairman to Lord Macartney, Ambassador to the Emperor of China. 8 September 1792.

3. Copy letter from the Prince Regent to the Emperor. 19 January 1816.

4. Translation of letter from the Emperor to the King. September 1816.

5. Accounts of imports and consumption of opium in China. 1816–29.

6. Letters from the Board of the Finance Committee to the Resident and Select Committee of Supercargoes at Canton. 26 May 1830–28 April 1831.

7. Address to the Governor of Canton by Lord William Bentinck, Governor-General of India, protesting against measures taken against British merchants. 27 August 1831.

8. Letter from Lord W. Bentinck in Simla to Charles Marjoribanks in Canton assuring him of the support of the whole of 'our Bengal resources'. 28 August 1831.

9. Copy letter to Lord W. Bentinck from British Factory, Canton. 25 October 1831.

10. Copy private letter to same from [Charles Marjoribanks (?) in Macao]. 3 November 1831.

Volumes, 1802–31

1. Journal of the fourth voyage of the ship *Arniston* to St. Helena, Bencoolen, and China, by Hugh B. Askew, 1802–3.

2. Journal of the seventh voyage of the ship *Exeter* to China, 1808–9.

3. Journal of the seventh voyage of the ship *Ceres* to the Cape of Good Hope and China, 1811–12.

4. Journal of the second voyage of the *Thomas Coutts* to China, 1819–21.

5. Report on conditions in China and trade there. 1831.

J. C. BALFOUR OF BALBIRNIE

Letters concerning the military expedition to China. 1926.

DR. C. C. BURT (NRA Scot. 891)

Papers of Andrew Burt, mining engineer with the Chinese Engineering and Mining Company. 1898–1902.

Photographs of Hong Kong, China, and Japan, including military activities during the Boxer Rebellion.

MICHAEL CAMPBELL OF DUNSTAFFNAGE

Letters, accounts, and other papers concerning the mercantile activities of Peter Cameron, second officer and later captain in the East India Company service, on voyages to India, Malaya, and China. 1806–27. (Box 5.)

Account book containing accounts of goods bought in London by Peter Cameron, Captain of the East India Company ship *Balcarras*, for shipment to the East, and of tea, silk, and cloth bought by him at Canton, China. 1826. (Box 7.)

P. R. CHALMERS OF ALDBAR

Letter by Robert Inglis, Canton, regarding trade conditions there. 1835.

Letters by John Inglis and others relating to mercantile affairs in India and Canton. 1826–41.

N. A. COCHRAN-PATRICK OF LADYLAND

Letters from J. G. Cochran-Wilson in India, Singapore, Hong Kong, and China. 1849.

BRIGADIER H. N. CRAWFORD

Letters from J. Duncan Crawford of the consular service in China, 1870–8. NRA (Scot)/0413 = NRA 12609, p. 4.

MESSRS. DAVIDSON AND GARDEN, ADVOCATES, ABERDEEN

1. MAJOR-GENERAL D. FORBES (Decd.)

Papers of Captain D. Forbes, consisting of accounts and letters concerning trading voyages to the East, including letters from Alexander Matheson and Matheson & Company, Hong Kong. 1865–70.

2. MISCELLANEOUS PAPERS

Log-book of ship *Woodford*, Charles Lennox, commander, on a voyage from England to Bencoolen in China, with list of passengers and crew. 1791–2.

Diary of a journey to China and trading there, with sketches of scenery. 1832–3.

MAJOR T. C. J. DICKSON OF MONYBUIE

Printed form of visa issued at the British Consulate, Canton, in favour of Dr. W. A. Dickson, to travel to Hankow, 30 March 1861.

CAPTAIN J. BRANDER DUNBAR. DUNBAR OF PITGAVENY PAPERS

Letters from Charles Gordon in Canton, mainly on financial and commercial matters. 1773–6.

DRUMMOND OF CADLAND.

Two letters from Admiral Sir Thomas Cochrane, Penang and Hong Kong, about the situation in China, prospects for trade, &c. 1845. (B 5/16/41–2.)

EARL OF DUNDONALD. DUNDONALD MSS.

Dundonald Family Papers. Box IV

Letters between the 10th Earl of Dundonald and his son Thomas, Lord Cochrane, concerning the latter's career in the army, including service in Canada and China. Other correspondents are General Lord Hill and General Seaton. 1830–59. 4 bundles.

Letter to the 10th Earl from Lord Cochrane concerning his departure for China. 1841.

Pocketbook of Lord Cochrane while at Hong Kong. 1845.

Doctor's reports on the ill health of Lord Cochrane at Hong Kong, and papers concerning the regiment. 1847.

Box XII

Naval papers and letters, 1810–48, including letter to 10th Earl from Lord Napier asking for information concerning the expense of a steamer between Macao and Canton, 1834. (7a.)

Box XIII

Volume containing Lord Cochrane's official correspondence while at Hong Kong as Assistant Quarter-Master-General, China, 1842–9. (6.) Shows signs of damp.

EARL OF HADDINGTON (NRA (Scot.) 0104 = NRA 10114)

Narrative by a British resident at Macao of Lord Napier's proceedings at Macao and Canton. n.d. (1840s).

Papers as First Lord of the Admiralty, including China War. 1840s.

EARL OF HADDO. HADDO HOUSE MSS. (NRA (Scot.) 0055 = NRA 9758)

Letters to and from Dr. Ahmed Fahmy, missionary at Changchow, Amoy, South China. 1879–1933.

HOPE OF LUFFNESS (NRA (Scot.) 0117 = NRA 10172)

Correspondence of G. W. Hope on use of Chinese labour in West Indies 1841–5. (p. 19.)

MELROSES LTD. (NRA (Scot.) 0352 = NRA 11635

'Papers connected with district shipments [of tea] from China, 1835–6.' (p. 2.)

Letters from William Melrose in Hong Kong, Macao, Canton. 1845–53. (16.)

LIEUTENANT-COLONEL J. W. NICOL OF BALLOGIE, D.S.O.

Copy of correspondence between the Viceroy of Canton and the Captains and officers of East India Company ships—the former protesting against the Company's landing soldiers in Macao. Reply explains that troops were landed at request of Portuguese to defend it against the French, and a further reply from Canton insists that the troops be removed or trade will be stopped. 1808.

W. H. ROBERTSON-AIKMAN OF THE ROSS

India and East India Company Papers, including:

1. Manuscript chart of 'the island to the eastward of New Guinea showing what appears to be the best route from Botany Bay to China', by George Robertson. 1792.

2. Two charts of eastern passages to China and of the China Sea. 1824. Printed.

3. Log, by Henry Aikman, of the East India Company ship *Orwell* commanded by J. Lancaster from London to Madras, Singapore, China, and return. 1836–7.

STEWART OF SHAMBELLIE. (NRA (Scot.) 0272 = NRA 11018)

Letters and papers relating to property in Shanghai owned by Alexander McCulloch of Ardwall, incl. comments on political developments in China, trade prospects, &c. 2 bundles. 1857–63, 1889–96. (Third row, 5.)

MAJOR A. B. WARDLAW RAMSAY

Correspondence from Calcutta and Canton with Captain Wardlaw of the *Asia*, including accounts for a voyage of the *Asia*, 1807. (Sec. Ib, bundle 3.)

EARL OF WEMYSS

Portfolio of letters, including some from China, 1860. (Drawer 48.)

IRISH MANUSCRIPTS COMMISSION
AND
NATIONAL LIBRARY OF IRELAND

Reports on private collections of papers have been compiled for the Irish Manuscripts Commission and the National Library of Ireland. The inspectors' reports are kept in the manuscript department of the National Library of Ireland, where they are known as 'National Library Reports on Private Collections', and some have been printed in *Analecta Hibernica*, no. 15, 1944; 'Survey of Documents in Private Keeping: First Series', and in *Analecta Hibernica*, no. 20, 1958, 'Survey of Documents in Private Keeping; Second Series' which includes (pp. 311–18) a list of reports at the National Library up to 1957. As a rule the reports do not catalogue in any detail collections of private correspondence. The National Library acquires collections of private papers when possible, and some of the papers described in the reports are now deposited in the Library. Persons interested in private collections of papers in Ireland should therefore first apply to the National Library of Ireland, Kildare Street, Dublin.

PAPERS NOT YET REPORTED

Papers in private custody, not as yet reported by the National Register of Archives or the Royal Commission on Historical Manuscripts, arranged alphabetically by name of owner.

REUBEN V. ROBERTS, Rectory Cottage, Depden, Bury St. Edmonds, Suffolk

File of correspondence of Frederick Owen Roberts, Minister of Pensions 1924 and 1929–31 on conditions in China in 1928. (C. Hazlehurst and C. Woodland, *A guide to the papers of British Cabinet ministers 1900–1951* (Royal Historical Society guides and handbooks, Supplementary series, 1), London, 1974, p. 122.

JOHN CHARLES SHARP, 64 Poplar Avenue, Birmingham, 17

Diary of a prisoner of war [of the Japanese] in Singapore and Siam, 1942–5, by John Charles Sharp. Original and indexed transcript. *c.* 1000 pp. in transcript.

THE REVD. R. D. M. SHAW, Steeple Langford Rectory, Nr. Salisbury, Wilts.

Extracts from the diaries of the Revd. R. D. M. and E. May Shaw relating to mission work in Japan from 1909 to 1919. 1 vol. 118 pp., with 5 pp. of explanatory notes. Typescript.

'Inside semi-feudal Japan'; an account by R. D. M. Shaw of the daily life of the common people of Japan in city town and village during the late nineteenth and early twentieth centuries. 1 vol. 225 pp. Typescript.

Notebook of R. D. M. Shaw containing jottings about Shinto Gates (Torii), stone images, shrines, rosaries, &c., and of a Dutch grave in Kakegawa.

A collection of press-cuttings relating to Japan immediately after the surrender in 1945.

INDEX

Note: Chinese and Japanese names are given in the index in the same form as they appear in the text.